Helen Zimmern

## Gotthold Ephraim Lessing

His Life and His Works

Helen Zimmern

**Gotthold Ephraim Lessing**
*His Life and His Works*

ISBN/EAN: 9783743373525

Manufactured in Europe, USA, Canada, Australia, Japa

Cover: Foto ©Thomas Meinert / pixelio.de

Manufactured and distributed by brebook publishing software (www.brebook.com)

Helen Zimmern

**Gotthold Ephraim Lessing**

# GOTTHOLD EPHRAIM LESSING

## *HIS LIFE AND HIS WORKS*

BY

## HELEN ZIMMERN

AUTHOR OF

ARTHUR SCHOPENHAUER HIS LIFE AND HIS PHILOSOPHY

---

. . . . . der Mann
Steht seinen Ruhm. Sein Ruhm ist bloß sein Schatten

---

LONDON
LONGMANS, GREEN, AND CO.
1878

# PREFACE.

AN English 'Life of Lessing' requires little in the way of preface or apology. It is only astonishing that the task of preparing such a work has not been undertaken long ere this, and that this peculiar good fortune should have been reserved to me. My main purpose has been to exhibit Lessing as the intellectual pioneer of our present culture, no less in this country than in his own; to show how few are the departments into which he did not penetrate, or in which his influence is not felt. I have tried to depict him as a centre of these manifold intellectual interests; a pathfinder in aesthetics, religion, and poetry; to paint his revolt against authority as such; and to exhibit his death-dealing onslaught on the Gallic and pseudo-classical tradition. Furthermore, I have wished to draw attention to his prophetic comprehension of modern liberal theology, expressed in his 'Education of the Human Race,' which, translated by the late Rev. F. W. Robertson, of Brighton, has exercised a great and avowed influence on the Broad Church

school of this country. Thus, to a large number of
English readers, Lessing is familiar only as a theologian ; whilst to others, artists especially, he is, through
his 'Laokoon,' known simply as an aesthetic writer.
Hence Lessing, the whole man, with his extensive,
varied, and catholic interests, is still unfamiliar to the
English reader.

There are several German biographies of Lessing,
but none of these would be well adapted to English
requirements, and lend themselves to translation.
Chief among these is the work of Messrs. Danzel and
Guhrauer, which singularly illustrates the justice of the
strictures recently passed on German literature by Mr.
Mark Pattison. These volumes are a perfect mine of
valuable materials, but offered in a cumbrous, undi-
gested form, that makes it almost impossible to read
them, and renders them available only as a quarry for
the special student. Out of this quarry has been con-
structed the more popular life of A. Stahr, that finds
a favour in Germany which its redundant style and
excessive panegyric would scarcely attract to it in
this country. Besides this truly encyclopaedic work of
Messrs. Danzel and Guhrauer, there exist innumerable
smaller works, dealing either with Lessing or with his
writings. Indeed, it would take half a lifetime to
read the Lessing literature of Germany, and at the
end, would it not have been better to read the man
himself? Should we not resemble the wooers of
Penelope who made love to the waiting-women ? I
would not be understood to imply by this that these

works are of no value. On the contrary, I have availed myself of many of them with profit and pleasure. But it will be readily conceded that all cannot be of weight and value, when I add, that the catalogue alone of works written upon 'Nathan the Wise' forms a goodly octavo volume. The ingenuity of some of these critics at expounding and elucidating is prodigious. Lessing fares with too many of them as Baron Münchausen's horse fared with the wolf, who began at his tail and ate into him, until finally the Baron drove the wolf home enclosed in the skin of the horse. But Lessing is not the only classical author doomed to illustrate the proverb, ' *Wenn Könige bauen, bekommen die Kärrner zu schaffen.*' Now, my object in this work is not to expound Lessing, but solely to introduce him to the English reader. I have endeavoured to do this as briefly as was consistent with interest and colour, avoiding prolixity, the fault of most modern biographies. The biography of a man of letters should be no more than an ante-room, giving admission into the sanctuary of his works. Of these works I have endeavoured to give an abstract, refraining from over-minute analysis of those which may be assumed to be more familiarly known, such as the 'Nathan' and the 'Laokoon,' and reserving a fuller treatment for the 'Dramaturgie' and other works, at present accessible only to the German scholar. Since writing my book, however, I have been entrusted with the agreeable task of preparing for 'Bohn's Library' an

English version of the chief portion of the ' Drama-
turgic.' This valuable work will therefore soon be
accessible to the English student. While treating of
Lessing's writings, I have kept in memory his own
caution, that one must not exhaust one's author ;
and while treating of his life, I have endeavoured to
remember that I am not writing for a German public,
and have consequently omitted or touched lightly
upon various minute matters unlikely to interest
English readers.

I have yet another word to add before concluding
this preface, for the involuntary egotism of which
I must apologize. This is to justify my claim to be
Lessing's first English biographer. It so happens,
that after my book was entirely completed and out
of my hands, a work dealing with the same theme
made its appearance unannounced, and thus gained
the priority of issue. In the face of this fact, I must
still insist on my claim, and in justification refer to
the advertisements of my book constantly issued by
Messrs. Longmans since July 1876. This other
work I have not yet read, and my own book, as I have
said, has been out of my hands some time. As,
however, its information cannot be derived from
other sources than mine, Lessing having been
thoroughly exhausted by the industrious writers of
Germany, resemblances cannot fail to exist between
the two books. At the same time, the wonderful
many-sidedness of Lessing's mind would alone be a
sufficient justification for putting before the world the

views of two independent biographers, even if the very great difference of scale between the two works were not such as to bring mine within reach of that larger portion of the reading public for which it is especially intended.

H. Z.

LONDON: *November* 1877.

# CONTENTS.

# GOTTHOLD EPHRAIM LESSING.

## CHAPTER I.

### CHILDHOOD.

(1729-1741. AGED 1-12.)

*' What is the use of a child ?*
*It may become a man.'*—B. FRANKLIN.

NORSE legends tell how Thor, with a mighty flourish of his hammer, cleared the murky sky of clouds and made the daylight shine upon the world.   There are men who perform this part for their age, and though we must beware of over-rating the immediate influence of individuals on events, instances arise when it is impossible to emphasize it too strongly.   Such an influence was born to Germany in the person of Gotthold Ephraim Lessing.   Between Luther and Lessing lies a barren tract of centuries ; it was reserved to this powerful mind to bridge the gulf between the mediæval and the modern spirit.

Gotthold Ephraim Lessing was born at Camenz in Upper Lusatia, a province of Saxony, on January 22, 1729.   The Lessings, though of burgher extraction, were able to trace their ancestors back to the six-teenth century, and it is interesting to observe that all Gotthold's forefathers were men of marked power,

B

rectitude, and enlightenment. They filled public
offices either as Lutheran pastors or magistrates ; the
clerical element predominated. Theophilus Lessing,
the grandfather of Gotthold, was burgomaster of
Camenz, and died there in his eightieth year, shortly
before the birth of his distinguished grandson. He
was a man of great ability. Born at the end of the
terrible Thirty Years' War, as he grew up his impoverished parents found themselves unable to afford
him a larger sum than two thalers wherewith to enter
the University of Leipzig. Nothing daunted, he
fought a sturdy fight against obstacles and privations,
and took his doctor's degree with honours. The
theme which he chose for his inaugural dissertation
was characteristic of the Lessings : from the earliest
known ancestor who signed the *Formula Concordiæ*
that reunited the Protestant Church, left without a
helmsman at Luther's death, to the author of
'Nathan' and the editor of the 'Wolfenbüttel Fragments.' *De religionum tolerantia* was its theme, its
matter an earnest plea for universal toleration, not
only of the Christian, but of all religions.

Johann Gottfried, the son of Theophilus, was
educated in this atmosphere of enlightenment, reverent in its breadth, and by no means estranged
from the ancient faith. At the University he chiefly
studied philosophy and theology, besides Latin,
Greek, French, and English (the latter a rare ac-
complishment in those days), and finally turned to
oriental studies for a more critical investigation of
biblical literature. He was aspiring to a professorial
chair, when, at the age of twenty-five, he was invited
to fill the post of catechist and afternoon preacher to
his native town, and seeing a higher dispensation in

this call, held it his duty to accept the offer. Henceforward he was unwearied in the fulfilment of his pastoral duties ; but notwithstanding these claims, and later, those of a rapidly increasing family, he found time to correspond with the most eminent theologians of his time, to keep himself up to their standard of knowledge, to compose numerous polemical pamphlets and religious works, and to translate sundry of Archbishop Tillotson's writings. Throughout all these labours ran a definite thread of purpose. Gottfried Lessing was an orthodox Lutheran, but no zealot ; he condemned the narrow strife of factions and desired to see the reformed community united on the broad basis of Protestantism as opposed to Papacy. He hated indifference, he condemned the personally abusive form of conducting arguments customary among his countrymen ; moreover he feared excess of zeal, and in this respect he held that English theologians had found the middle way. Even freethinkers, he contended, should be treated with respect : an opinion foreign to the prevalent ideas, and proving how far he was in advance of his times. It was on this account he translated Tillotson, intending his version as a preface to a collection of similar polemical writings in exposition of Protestantism. His son was justly proud of this. He wrote to a friend in after years : ' What praises would I not bestow on him if he were not my father ; he was the first translator of Tillotson.' Theophan, the hero of Lessing's youthful drama, ' *Der Freigeist* ' (The Freethinker), the worthy pastor whose excellence and worth disarm the *odium anti-theologicum* of the freethinker Adrast, the dramatic representative of Bishop Hall's axiom that ' temper is nine-tenths of Christianity,' is a portrait of his father. Charity, right-mindedness, pride of family, love of earnest study, contempt of money and the luxuries which wealth can buy, hatred of injustice, a hasty temper and a consequent inclination to act upon impulse : all these characterised the father. His irascibility was inherited by his son. Whenever he was annoyed, he found himself involuntarily biting his under lip, exactly as his father had done. The father saw this inherited trait with sorrow, and often with tears in his eyes lamented his own quickness of temper. ‘I entreat of you, Gotthold,’ he would say, ‘take example by me, and be on your guard. For I fear—I fear—and I should like to think I had improved in you.’ His writings were distinguished by their excellent style, free from all gallicisms and other adulterations of language too common in the early part of last century. He insisted on historical accuracy and critical research as the touchstones of true scholarship. All this was impressed on his son, whose early education he conducted ; and beholding·what manner of man the father was, it is not difficult to conclude what was the mental atmosphere of the home.

It was the paternal rather than the maternal influence that told on the child Lessing, contrary to the popular creed that remarkable men spring from remarkable mothers. Lessing's mother was a good, honest, amiable woman, in no wise above the average, and narrow in her views of life, as was inevitable to the daughter and wife of a country clergyman, who had never been beyond the precincts of Camenz. Justine Salome Feller was the daughter of the chief pastor of the town, whom Gottfried Lessing eventually succeeded. They were married in 1725, a year after his appointment as deacon, and in due course their quiver was filled after the manner usual to the poorer clergy. Frau Lessing worshipped her husband as a superior being, and made him an excellent and devoted wife, but she lacked the intellectual gifts that could have influenced her son's development. The cares inevitable to a large family with small means also did their part to hinder any mental growth; her influence on Lessing's development was consequently insignificant. But as she held the reins of government in her hands, she was able at times to put disturbing obstacles in his path, although even these were founded in deep love for the son whose character was one wholly foreign to her comprehension.

Gotthold was the eldest son of his parents, and though all too quickly the pastoral home was filled by eleven other children, in his early youth means were not so restricted, his father's time not so absorbed, his cares not so deadening as they became afterwards, and he could devote himself to the boy's training. It was from his studious father therefore that Gotthold imbibed his first knowledge of and love for all humanistic studies, establishing that mutual attachment which survived all later divergencies. An earnest religious element was the ground tone of the home. Little Gotthold could hardly babble when he was taught to pray; he learnt reading out of the Bible and his father's catechism, and at the age of five he knew what, why, and how we should believe. At morning and evening prayers he learnt many hymns, and as these are among the richest and pithiest utterances of the German language, he early imbibed a taste for good national poetry. The parents often told their other children how easily and gladly Gotthold learnt, and how, even for amusement, he would delight in turning the leaves of a book before he could read them. Here again may no doubt be traced the example set by his diligent father. When he was five years old, the pastor engaged a cousin, Christlieb Mylius, as his private tutor. This circumstance alone proves that money troubles had not begun to burden the family beyond measure. Both father and mother wished their son to repair to the University in due course ; indeed here their views were in accord. As a pastor's wife and daughter, Frau Lessing thought it a moral duty that at least her eldest son should follow in the traditional footsteps and take orders. The parents held no sacrifice too great that would ensure this result.

Gotthold's evident capacity and love of learning were a source of real pleasure to them, and when, in 1737, Mylius was removed from Camenz, the boy was sent at the tender age of eight to the public grammar-school. Here he continued to distinguish himself, and enlarged his views of life beyond the intentions of his father.

The rector, a certain Heinitz, had been appointed shortly before Lessing's entrance. He was a young man of open mind, taking keen interest in all scientific and literary studies, and was connected with the young Germany of the day, whose head-quarters were at Leipzig. To the horror of Camenz, he defended the abhorred stage as an educator and a school of declamation. The town was scandalized, the magistrates reprimanded, Pastor Lessing denounced the rector from the pulpit as a dangerous tutor of youth. The consequences were inevitable. Having taken this step, Pastor Lessing was forced to remove his son from the school ; but not before the boy had eagerly imbibed some of his master's extended ideas.

It seems almost ludicrous that the future champion and reformer of the stage should have been taken from school lest he should contract these very notions, which subsequently bore fruit a hundredfold.

Meanwhile another event had helped to bend the twig into its destined shape. In 1739 an artist, and by Lessing's testimony no mean one, strayed into the remote town of Camenz, and was commissioned to paint the pastor's eldest sons, Gotthold and Theophilus. The artist proposed to represent Gotthold with a bird-cage. This proposal roused all his youthful ire. ' You must paint me with a big, big heap of books,' he exclaimed, ' but I would rather not be painted at all.' He was so determined that his wishes were respected, and the future librarian was portrayed holding an open book on his knee, while his right hand points to a pile lying at his feet. Theophilus, the future preacher, is dressed in black, and feeds a lamb. Gotthold, modishly dressed in red, is a child of open countenance, high, wide forehead, honest mouth and broad energetic nose, who cannot be called beautiful, but in whose face and bearing there is something vivacious, speaking, firm, and unaffected. The artist was engaged as drawing-master to the boy, and from him Gotthold derived his earliest knowledge of art and its principles.

Thus, even in the small town of Camenz, with its circumscribed interests and arid mental atmosphere, could be laid the foundation-stones of the future polemical, æsthetic, and dramatic writings, that were destined to work mighty reforms in their several departments of thought.

# CHAPTER II.

## BOYHOOD.

*' Character is nature in the highest form. . . . . Care is taken that the greatly destined shall slip up into life in the shade, with no thousand-eyed Athens to watch and blazon every new thought, every blushing emotion of young genius.'* — EMERSON.

ON thus finding himself, as he deemed, under a moral compulsion to withdraw his boy from the grammar school of his native town, Pastor Lessing obtained for him a nomination to the *Fürstenschule* of St. Afra, at Meissen. While waiting admission, Gotthold was sent to study with a relative, Pastor Lindner, of Putzkau, a former scholar of the institution. Lessing matriculated as *alumnus* on June 21, 1741 : a day which St. Afra celebrated one hundred years after with great honours.

Meissen is best known for the porcelain factory that produces the valued Dresden ware. A hundred years ago it was also celebrated as the site of one of the three great Saxon schools, founded by the Protestant hero, Elector Maurice, with the property of suppressed convents. The institution preserved some monastic characteristics ; its regulations savoured of the cloister, food and clothing were gratuitous, and though some pupils paid small entrance fees, a large

number were received free of expense on the nomination of patrons. The original design of the founder
had been to train efficient champions of the Reformation, and when the Evangelical cause had triumphed,
and such were no longer needed, the school developed
into a nursery for theologians and Lutheran pastors.
The curriculum naturally tended to this end, in accordance with the expressed wish of Luther, who
desired that language and knowledge should serve as
bulwarks of the faith. 'Through orthodox learning,
to the glory of God and the spread of His Gospel,'
was the motto of the institution.

In Lessing's case, the mental atmosphere of St.
Afra was but a continuation of that of home. It
instilled the doctrinal spirit of Pastor Lessing, and
would therefore, he hoped, further his intention that
Gotthold should be a theologian. The boy himself
does not appear to have thought about this ultimate
career. In his studies he merely followed his bent,
and though these by and by led him to ignore his destination, he did so quite unconsciously. This apparent
carelessness of and for the future is most characteristic of the man. In thought, as in deeds, he
suffered matters to take their course and pursue their
natural development, unthwarted by the fear of consequences. His nature was independent and self
reliant ; he held by the good and acted up to it for its
own sake. It is this strongly marked individualism
that constitutes the nobility of his character : he trusted
himself with childlike confidence to the leadings of
his inner bias, which prevented any discord between
his life and deeds.

At St. Afra he was removed from all material
anxieties, such as were beginning to press in the over-

filled parsonage : the plan of the institution annulled distinctions between rich and poor. A hundred and twenty boys lived together on terms of perfect equality. It was a small republic in its best form. Opinion was circumscribed by the school walls ; the everyday world and its interests unknown or ignored ; the social conditions of Greece and Rome more eagerly discussed than those of Saxony ; dead languages more cultivated than living; and religious observances placed above all else. Latin was the cherished study ; Greek only so far as it elucidated the New Testament. Modern languages and mathematics were included in the programme, but so much time was absorbed by Latin, chapels, and biblical expositions, that very little was left for other things. The German language and literature were entirely disregarded.

'You would not count knowing German as one of your acquirements?' Lessing asks satirically in the '*Junge Gelehrte*,' indicating how early he recognized the absurdity of discarding the mother tongue.

But for all this rigid curriculum, it was possible here, as at all public schools, for an industrious lad to strike out a path for himself. The first two years Lessing scrupulously followed the prescribed course, taking high places in his form, and rising with unexampled rapidity. 'A good boy, but somewhat satirical,' was the note appended to his name by a school inspector, and the Conrector remarked to Theophilus on his entry, ' Be as industrious as your brother, but not so pert.' Both remarks prove that Lessing exhibited all the faults as well as the virtues of cleverness. The growth of mental power is of its very nature aggressive, though in Lessing's case it was free from the too common accompaniment of arrogance. The conrector, however, had a petty spite against Lessing. It was the rule that every master should live a week in the house, to superintend in person and to conduct the morning, afternoon and evening prayers. A general meeting of masters was held every Saturday, and was attended by the class monitors. The rector asked one day why during that whole week the pupils had all been late for prayers. No one replied. Lessing, one of the monitors on that occasion, had the indiscretion to whisper to his neighbour, ' I know why.' The rector overheard ; he had perhaps counted on Gotthold's candour, and bade him speak. 'The conrector is not punctual,' was his straightforward reply, ' so everyone thinks that prayers will not begin when the clock strikes.' 'Admirable Lessing !' ex-claimed the conrector, who could not deny the charge ; and from that day Lessing retained this name among his comrades, and was put down in the black books of his master, who until then had rather favoured him, because of his diligence in classical studies, the department in which he taught.

The autumn examinations of 1743 show how far Lessing had advanced beyond his comrades, and it was then that he began to strike out an independent course of studies.

' My industry kept me from boyish misdemeanours,' he wrote ; and this industry was indeed prodigious. One of the masters, J. A. Klemm, exercised great in-fluence over him. He was an indifferent pedagogue, whose shy, awkward manner failed to command respect, but he was an accomplished scholar, kind and generous-hearted, free from pedantry and class preju-dice, and delighted to aid any boy who cared for him and his favourite pursuits. It was not long before Lessing recognized his worth. Midnight often found them together in the master's study, exchanging thoughts about classical authors and the means and ends of learning. This intercourse revealed to Lessing how little real knowledge he possessed, how much he had still to acquire, that Latin, Greek, French, English, and Italian were but the tools of learning, not the thing itself; ideas rankly heterodox at St. Afra, where the letter was held supreme. Klemm often said, 'A scholar who does not know philosophy and mathematics is not worth much.' Forthwith Lessing plunged into Euclid, and with such zeal that he even translated the second, third, and fourth books. Its appeal to reason fascinated him and saved him from stranding on the quicksands of quibbling scholasticism towards which he had shown danger of drifting. He also began to write a poem, 'On the Plurality of Worlds.' A few fragments and a criticism by himself have been preserved.

' The new theories of Whiston and Huygens' " Cosmotheoros " had filled my imagination with conceptions and pictures that seemed the more enchanting that they were wholly new to me. I saw they were more capable of poetical dress than any other philosophical matter. But the art of working my material was lacking. I rhymed my thoughts together in a somewhat mathematical manner; here and there a metaphor, here and there a digression.' Then Fontenelle's dialogues on the same theme fell in his way, and he was ashamed of his audacious attempt. The fragment however contains some noble words that do honour to his mental development. The last stanza of the poem, and especially the last line, is worthy to rank beside his later saying.

*Beherzter als Colomb, trat ich den Luftweg an,*
*Wo leichter als zur See die Kühnheit scheitern kann,*
*Mag doch die Sinnlichkeit des frommen Frevels fluchen!*
*Genug, die scheitern schön, die scheiternd Welten suchen.*

Klemm's intelligent study of the Greek and Latin writers, inciting to an understanding of their hidden soul, taught Lessing to enter into their spirit, besides following their grammatical structure of phrase, and gave him his peculiar insight into the life of the ancients. He read authors not usually perused at St. Afra. ' Theophrastus, Plautus, and Terence were my world, which I studied leisurely within the narrow confines of a monastic school . . . . and I must confess, at the risk of being ridiculed, that of all forms of literature, comedy was the one I attempted first. In those years, when I only knew men from books, I busied myself in picturing foolish beings, whose existence was indifferent to me.' The ' *Junge Gelehrte* (Young Scholar) is the only one of these dramas that has survived, and this was merely sketched at Meissen.

The scanty German literature of the period was also put into his way by Klemm, and he appears to have read the current journals that recorded the squabbles of the antagonistic *literati.* The time of Lessing's youth coincided with a blind groping for the literary daylight which was to be shed abroad by the clearsighted boy now studying the attempts of his elders. To try his hand at the fashionable imitations, he wrote some clever Anacreontic odes. Neither then nor later did he produce for production's sake. It was to clear

his own mind of doubts, to put difficulties visibly
before himself, that he gives them written shape. He
hesitates, he reproaches himself, makes suggestions
and arrives at a result. Of this character was a 'New
Year's Address,' written in 1743 to his father; the
theme, 'That one year resembles another,' was
to prove to his parents the fallacy of their now too
constantly recurring complaints of the increasing
hardness of the times. The boy defends his theories
in a scholastic manner, adduces biblical proofs, refers
to Solomon and his vanity of vanities, contends that
human nature is the same throughout all time, and
that therefore neither a golden nor a leaden age is
possible. All these remarks might be held mere
truisms, only they were in opposition to current ideas
which considered happiness in the light of an external
gift and not as an often painfully acquired possession.
Therefore, for all its formal precocity, the essay is
remarkable as a revelation of the severe inner accord
which Lessing had so early attained, not by any means
a mere resigned submission, but a contented acquiescence in the things that be. By thus working out his
perplexities he extended his mental vision beyond the
confines of the school, and saw that the narrow limits
of St. Afra had engendered a bias towards pedantry.
To recognize a fault was to amend it ; and to bring
about this result he sketched the '*Junge Gelehrte*,'
a play wherein he relentlessly lashed his own tendencies, even to the congratulatory address sent to his
father.

'I think,' he writes, 'that it was thanks to my
choice of subject that I did not quite fail with this
play. A young pedant was the only kind of simpleton
("*Narr*") that was not at that time utterly unknown

to me. Reared among this vermin, was it astonishing that my first satirical weapons were turned against them ?'

A letter to his sister, also of 1743, contains the last trace of a didactic spirit, and is a comical mixture of old-fashioned sophistry and healthy gravity.

' Dearest Sister,

' Though I have written to you, you have not answered me. I am therefore obliged to think that either you cannot write or you will not, and I am inclined to believe the former ; however, I will also believe the other—you will not write. Both are culpable. Still, I cannot understand how two such things should be compatible : to be a reasonable being, to be able to speak sensibly, and at the same time not to know how to compose a letter. Write as you speak, then you will write well. Yet, even if the contrary were the case, and it were possible to speak sensibly without being able to write sensibly, the shame would be still greater, that you had not even learnt as much as that. It is true you ran away very early from your schoolmaster, and in your twelfth year you held it a disgrace to learn any more ; but who knows which is the greater disgrace—to learn still in your twelfth year, or to be unable to write a letter in your eighteenth or nineteenth ? Pray write and rid me of this mistaken opinion about you. I must just allude to the New Year, of which I am reminded. Almost everyone speaks good wishes at this season. But what shall I wish you ? It must be something special. I wish that your whole mammon may be stolen. It might be a better service to you than if

some one were to add one hundred ducats to your
purse at New Year.[1]

'Your faithful brother,
'G. E. LESSING. '
'*Meissen: Dec.* 30, 1743.'


The examinations of 1744 again showed Lessing
far advanced beyond the average, so that in 1745 he
was already in the first form, where, according to the
rules of the institution, he must remain another fifteen
months. He felt he had outgrown the school. It
fretted him to stay in a sphere which he had exhausted,
and he therefore implored his father to obtain his
dismissal. The Rector's report confirmed his judgment: 'He is a horse that needs double rations.
The lessons which others find too hard are child's
play to him : we can scarcely do with him any more.'
Pastor Lessing unwillingly acceded to his son's
repeated requests, and craved permission to remove
him. The governors refused. Pastor Lessing was
not the man to interfere with established rules.
Gotthold was told he must bide out his term.

The second Silesian war, conducted by Frederick
the Great against Maria Theresa, was then agitating
Saxony. In December 1745, Meissen was aroused
out of its calm existence by thundering cannons, and
the lurid light of burning villages. Old Dessauer, as
the Prussians fondly named their general, had forced
Meissen to surrender, defiling his troops through the
town. Hussars and infantry filled its streets ; flying
parties scoured backwards and forwards on the Dres-

---

[1] The sister had already shown the miserly disposition that distinguished her in after years.

den road. The young king remained in the place, awaiting news with feverish anxiety. Late at night on the 15th, an officer brought tidings that the allied Saxons and Austrians had been routed on the field of Kesseldorf. Whereupon the disturbers marched to the deserted capital to conclude the Peace of Dresden, by which Silesia was ceded to Frederick.

Lessing took a lively interest in all this military hubbub that had suddenly broken into his tranquillity. It was his first peep into active life, and could not be hidden even from sequestered St. Afra, whose monotonous course the turmoil of war had subverted. Three-fourths of the scholars were sent home and did not return for fear of infection. Provisions had also run scarce. Lessing received a commission from his father to celebrate in verse the bravery of the defeated Saxons, as a compliment to Lieutenant Carlowitz, his nominator at St. Afra. He obeyed, but the poem was not to the pastor's satisfaction, whereupon he was told to write another. He replies to this, February 1, 1746 :

'Most Honoured Father,

'The undeserved praise which you have given me for the poetical missive to the Lieutenant-Colonel von Carlowitz incites me to take the subject in hand again, though against my inclination, to make, as you desire, a shorter and, if I can, a better one ; though, to be frank with you, when I consider the time I have already spent and must now still spend on the poem, I am forced to reproach myself with having frittered it away unprofitably. My best consolation is that it is done at your desire.

'You do right to pity poor Meissen, which resembles

C

a grave more than its former self. Everything is full
of stench and filth, and those who need not enter it
remain as far away from it as they possibly can. In
most of the houses there still lie from thirty to forty
wounded men, and no one dare go very near them,
because all who are at all seriously hurt have raging
fevers. It is providential that these fatal circumstances have occurred during the winter, because, if it
were summer, the plague would certainly rage ; and
who knows what may still happen ? We will trust in
God and hope the best. But in all the town I do not
think a place looks more miserable than our school,
when its former aspect is remembered. Formerly all
was life here ; now it is inanimate. Formerly it was
an unusual thing to see one healthy soldier inside the
walls ; now there are heaps of wounded, who cause no
little discomfort. The Cœnaculum is transformed into
shambles, we are forced to dine in the little Audit-
orium. The scholars who are gone away are as little
inclined to return for fear of falling ill, as the rector
is inclined to reinstate the tables that have been given
up. As far as I am concerned, it is the more annoy-
ing to me to have to remain here, that you even seem
determined to leave me here during the summer,
when things will probably be ten times worse. I do
think the reasons that urge you could be easily
removed. Yet I do not like to waste any more
words over a matter I have so often pressed upon you,
and which, in short, you do not wish. I assure myself,
meanwhile, that you understand my welfare better
than I do. And in this assurance, even if you adhere
to your refusal, I shall continue always, as is my duty,
to love and honour you as my father. The ear-ache
that has distressed me some little time so confuses

my head, that I am unable to write more. I therefore conclude, once more assuring you that during my whole life I shall always remain

'Your most obedient son,

'G. E. LESSING.'[1]

Not even the dangers to which his son was exposed by remaining at Meissen could shake the pastor's submission to rules. Still, he appears to have made another application, for Lessing's dismissal was at last granted in June 1746, when he left the school, reading as his farewell dissertation, an essay *de Mathematica Barbarorum.*

[1] This letter in the original is more formal, as Lessing employs the deferential ' Sie,' and not the familiar ' Du:' a fine distinction lost in the English ' You.'

# CHAPTER III.

## THE UNIVERSITY.

### (1746-48. AGED 17-19.)

*' Sein persönliches Wohl opfert er dem objektivem Zweck ; er kann eben nicht anders, weil dort sein Ernst liegt. Dass er nicht sich und seine Sache sucht, dies macht ihn, unter allen Umständen, gross.'*—SCHOPENHAUER.

LESSING entered the University of Leipzig (September 1746) by the help of one of the hundred stipends annexed to the *Fürstenschule.* His parents still expected him to study theology, though he had very decidedly told them, during his short residence at home, that neither his talents nor his inclinations lay in that direction.

A new world was opened to the youth. Reared in the seclusion of a monastic school, he was by an abrupt transition plunged into the stirring and many-sided life of a city ; for Leipzig, though small in area, possessed all the characteristics of a capital. Its University took a foremost rank. A mediæval corporation, the established dogmas only were taught, and new lights were forced to penetrate obliquely. But the town had been for a quarter of a century the scene of Gottsched's literary activity. It was also a busy commercial centre. Moreover, it was the scene of the annual book fair (*Jubilate-Messe*), that patriarchal form of literary intercourse which railroads and telegraphs have not superseded in our day, and which in Lessing's made it a unique intellectual centre.

No wonder it somewhat bewildered Lessing, accustomed to the jog-trot of Meissen and the Little Pedlingtonianisms of Camenz. At St. Afra there had been no distinctions between rich and poor, neither privation nor luxury were known in its cloisters; here both presented themselves with their attendant hardships and temptations, and the youth who had only known the world through books, who had left school in the firm conviction that happiness consisted in books alone, found himself plunged into a miniature world. He was young and strong, full of vigorous animal spirits, his powers of enjoyment unimpaired, his receptive capacities enormous; he had dabbled in many studies, he was possessed with an ardent desire to know everything; moreover, his filial duties were at conflict with his desires. Is it astonishing he had to look about him first and understand his surroundings before he could bring himself to submit to the restriction of a definite Faculty?

Imbued by Klemm with a love for genuine learning, he beheld with scorn the perfunctoriness of University training tolerated at Leipzig. Scholarship was degraded to a trade. The subjects treated by the respective professors were not defined; they lectured first on one theme, then on another, reading up for the purpose, and the inevitable result was superficiality. In those days there was no generally cultured, as opposed to a professional, class. National education had still to develop out of school learning. The resulting narrow and heavy pedantry, united to ludicrously pompous observances, roused all Lessing's innate spirit of sarcasm. Theology was represented by a humdrum unattractive orthodoxy, and there were few men of real power to give distinction to the University. Foremost among these were J. A. Ernesti and J. F. Christ. Ernesti was the pioneer who brought philological research to bear upon Scripture and paved the way to a sound critical knowledge of the Bible. An elegant Latin and Greek scholar, he enforced the proposition which Lessing had already heard from Klemm, that the ancients must be regarded from the standpoint of their age : a truism now-a-days, but not then. He changed a study of language into a study of thoughts. Christ was the founder of artistic archæology, the forerunner of Winckelmann. He possessed all the needful accomplishments for this study, being himself an artist, a critic, an erudite scholar, and a man of independent thought. The classes of these men alone attracted Lessing, but even they failed to make him a regular attendant at lectures.

It was not youthful conceit on Lessing's part that made him unable to settle upon any faculty, still less was it indolence. Work was life and nourishment to him. Only he could never work according to rule, or at what he did not himself approve. A youth like Lessing, qualified for independent study and competent to seize rapidly the gist of a subject, finds the small doses of knowledge doled out at lectures highly distasteful. This is often the case with men of unusual powers. Their minds are singularly antipathetic to a systematic college course, such as must exist in any institution adapted to the average capacity. To such men even an indifferent book is of more use than lectures, because affording exercise for the faculty of selection. Lectures irked Lessing's impatient spirit, so he amassed books and read eagerly. The writings of Wolf specially interested him. This learned scholar was decried for metaphysical heresies ; but Lessing, ever unawed by popular outcries, knew how to value the courageous independent spirit who became a connecting link between Leibnitz and Kant. Moreover, Wolf wrote German. He was the first professor who ventured to discuss literary and philosophic topics in his mother tongue, an innovation which Leibnitz had advocated in polished Latin. The masculine national speech was relegated ' to the horses' quite in accordance with the ideas of Charles V.

Thus, buried in his books, following no definite study, Lessing lived for a few months in greater retirement than at Meissen. But this isolation did not last. The scales fell from his eyes : he perceived that books might make him learned, but would never make him a man. He therefore ventured out of his study among his fellows, and instantly saw his unlikeness to them. His manners were boorishly timid, his movements uncouth, he even feared that his bashfulness gave him an air of misanthropy. A feeling of shame hitherto unknown stole over him, and with the perception of his failings, the stern resolve to be rid of them at any cost. To the perplexity of his father, to the horror of his mother, he learnt to dance, ride, fence and leap, and soon distanced his companions in agility. This encouraged him ; no longer awkward, he could now seek society to acquire *tournure*. Books were laid aside for a time, while he plunged into the distractions offered by a city, and all too soon found himself involved in debt, for his slender theological stipend would not permit the amusements of a cavalier. But economy was impossible to Lessing,

who regarded money with his father's indifference.
He did not let the need of it deter him now, and undaunted by the price of admission, he soon made the
theatre his chief resort.   The world he had hitherto
found in Plautus and Terence was now presented by
the living drama.   His love for the stage once
awakened, soon acquired such complete possession
of him that every idea that came into his head took
dramatic shape.

His study was now real life.   He thirsted to
enlarge and correct his knowledge by actual experience.   He had the gift of extracting the essential out
of every new situation.   It is a mistake to examine
too minutely the educational influences brought to
bear on a great mind, for a great mind contains its
own centre of gravity.   Such constant oscillation
between secluded study and a many-coloured worldly
life was a distinctive peculiarity of Lessing's.   It was
a part of the inner unrest that impelled him to
investigate all phases of life.   His very studies were
alive to him ; he took hold of them for themselves, not
for what they could do for him.   He felt the craving
to impart his reading, to jostle with his fellow men
and sharpen his faculties by reciprocal incitement.
A student who shared his lodging had been a congenial comrade so long as Lessing was buried in his
books, but drew back from him when he began to
haunt the theatre, that resort of vice and depravity.
About this time Lessing became acquainted with
J. C. Weisse, who was also stage-struck.   Hardly a
day passed that they did not meet.   In summer they
took long walks together, and their evenings were
chiefly passed in the theatre.

Weisse and Lessing at first attended the same

lectures ; but very soon Lessing began to shift from
one class into another, dissatisfied with all, and he
often persuaded Weisse to play truant with him.
Professor Kästner's classes became the only ones he
eventually attended with regularity. Kästner's friendship and teaching took the place of Klemm's. Like
Klemm, he was a man of many-sided culture, and
possessed the art of attracting clever youths. For
these he arranged a debating club, of which J. K.
and J. A. Schlegel, Zacharia, and other men afterwards well known, were members. Lessing was the
most ardent and constant speaker. The exercise
evoked his polemical vigour, aided him to shake off
the trammels of tradition, and called his logical
faculties into exercise. Christlob Mylius, a brother
of his early tutor, also belonged to this circle. He
was seven years Lessing's senior, a man of keen
though ill-regulated talents, who was held in bad
repute at the University on account of his doubtful
moral character, his bearish manners, and slovenly
person. It was a disdain of all conventional fitness,
as well as poverty, that made him constantly appear
with shoes trodden down at heel and ragged coats.
He had no settled lodging, and, pariah himself, associated with pariahs in the shape of actors and
actresses. Moreover, his want of resources and his
facility of pen had led him to start a periodical,
‘the Freethinker,’ which increased his bad repute by
the advanced opinions it expressed. Lessing contended that this paper was wholly guiltless of offence
towards morality and religion, but he was already
beginning to regard the exercise of Christian virtues
as antagonistic to, rather than harmonious with, rigorous formalism. Such, however, were not the views

of the period, and it was a bold step for a youth to put himself under the patronage of Mylius, who already, two years before the publication of the 'Freethinker,' had scandalized Leipzig by an explanation of the retrogression of the shadow on the dial of Ahaz, deduced from natural causes. But Lessing was indifferent to any prejudices. In his social intercourse, as in all else, he rebelled against conventional trammels. He was not slow to recognise the real worth concealed under Mylius' unattractive exterior, and soon found his acquaintance to act like a mental tonic. In his companionship he read the English liberal theologians, studied natural history and physics, and became acquainted with Frau Neuber.

This woman 'of manly intellect,' as Lessing afterwards called her, was really the founder of the German theatre, which she raised from a state of veritable barbarism. She was the first actress who had any idea of poetry and tragic action. As a girl she had joined a company of strolling players, and upon its dissolution reorganized them under her own management and went to Leipzig, where she conducted a theatre with brilliant success. Gottsched and his school brought out their plays on her boards, and in concert with the dictator she banished the harlequinades, which till then had proved the chief attraction of the stage. Lessing was soon a favourite in her green-room, and learnt from the actors the stage business and the stage routine which no books can teach. Yet, though so young and wholly inexperienced, he took the players' verdict not as final, but as a starting point for independent investigation, and so intuitively did he recognise the first principles of histrionic art, that very soon actors came to him for instruction and advice. It was quite understood at the theatre that young Lessing should be appealed to in difficult matters, and one of the troupe afterwards acknowledged that he owed much of his success to this assistance. Many a time Lessing would declaim and gesticulate his characters, teaching him to see their varied capacities of treatment. At last these theatrical connections began to tax Lessing's slender purse too heavily ; still he and Weisse would rather eat dry bread than be absent a single evening from the play. But even this did not avail, so to procure themselves a free pass they translated several French dramas, and among them Marivaux's 'Hannibal,' a pattern of the fashionable Alexandrines and artificial treatment of the period. Weisse next attempted an original play founded on Petronius' 'Matron of Ephesus,' and Lessing, who loved contests, and was stimulated by them, also tried his hand on this subject. This frivolous and licentious drollery evidently possessed a certain attraction for Lessing, for he made three different sketches of the theme, but they none of them approached the original, because they attempted to import a moral lesson into what was avowedly only a libertine *jeu d'esprit.*

These sketches, together with a large number of other plays projected by him, are still extant. He used to plan the acts and scenes of his dramas with great care, and only fill in the framework when required for press ; for though he conceived with ease, he elaborated with effort. Of these fragments more than fifty are extant, and many date from this period. He turned to the English playwriters for models, and contemplated a comedy founded on Wycherly's

'Country Life.' But these were not the only literary ventures made by Lessing. He also wrote for two periodicals edited by Mylius. One of these was devoted to natural history, a department of science Mylius thoroughly understood. Lessing's contributions were Anacreontic Odes, in parody of Mylius' essays. He pretended to prove that Anacreon was a great naturalist, and had disguised his discoveries under the names of love and wine. These witty and vivacious verses excited and deserved attention. For the other paper he wrote various lyrical poems ; versified theories of pleasure after the pattern of Catullus and Martial ; and all these, though imitations, bore an individual stamp which lifted them above the contemporary dead level. By these poems he appeared to range himself among the Anacreontic poets of his day, who were opposed to the ecstatic mysteries of Klopstock and his friends. But notwithstanding their innocence, and the very distinctly visible effort of these imitators of Anacreon, who employed his form and lacked his grace and burning passion, their productions were in bad repute. Gleim's Pastorals had even been publicly burnt in Hamburg in 1740. To declare himself a poet of this school, was therefore to fly in the face of opinion, and young Lessing entered his literary career by a derided road. He was however minded to try his hand at every form of poetical composition, that he might learn its nature.

It further occurred to him to bring forward his school production, '*Der Junge Gelehrte.*' The slight plot was founded on fact. A young scholar, Damis, sunk in learned trifling, had submitted an essay on Monads, to the Berlin Academy, and confidently expected to receive the prize. But the friend entrusted

with the precious treatise had not even sent it in,
finding that Damis had wholly misunderstood the
theme. Damis' dismay on learning this news is
comically depicted, and a little love intrigue into
which he is dragged against his will, enlivens and
complicates the action. The piece was necessarily
crude. Lessing's experience was narrow, his personages were stock comedy characters, his world a
comedy world, where chance reigned supreme, his
complications were clumsily hewn through, not cunningly unravelled, the servants were the traditional
French factotums, the scenes dragged. Though the
dialogue was sparkling, there was a marked tendency
to caricature. With all these defects the play showed
merit. It was written in prose, in place of the stilted
Alexandrines introduced by Frau Neuber. Damis,
the pedant, is drawn with spirit. Excrescence though
he appears to us, he was a typical character, such as
walked the streets of Leipzig daily, and such as Lessing had once feared to become. This stamped the
play a mirror of the actual world. The dramas of
Gottsched's period were works of the pen, not products
of the intellect ; it was impossible to move freely in the
fetters imposed by convention. Nevertheless Lessing's
play showed marked symptoms of independence. With
all diffidence he submitted his attempt to Frau
Neuber's criticism. To his surprise, she not only
praised the play, but put it into rehearsal, called him
a theatrical genius, and encouraged him to proceed.

Who was happier than Lessing ? He never
stopped to think what his good parents would say.
He had made out a philosophy of his own, according
to which theatrical labours might be made just as
useful and more entertaining than sermons. But his

father knew nothing of this philosophy, and his
mother condemned it outright. Lessing may have
flattered himself that they heard nothing of his theatrical life, when he was suddenly made aware of his
mistake. There came a letter from the father to
whom some kind friend had sent a caricatured account
of his son's mode of life in Leipzig. It contained a
paternal lecture on the neglect of his academic purpose, on the degrading intercourse with comedians,
on the godless friendship with the freethinker Mylius,
and concluded with an earnest appeal not to sacrifice
the *dic cur hic* to his favourite occupations. His father
may also have represented to him that the magistrates
of Camenz would probably deprive him of his stipend,
destined for a student in divinity, if he persisted in his
present courses.

The letter disturbed Lessing greatly. He rushed
off to his friend Weisse ; threw the paper down on
the table before him and cried, 'There, read that
—letter which I have just received from my father.'
In the heat of his anger he wanted to send each of
the magistracy of Camenz a copy of the playbill just
issued, announcing the ' *Junge Gelehrte*' with the full
name of its author, G. E. Lessing, from Camenz.
Weisse pacified him as well as he could, and urged
him strongly not to take such a step, and for once he
followed advice. It does not appear how he replied
to his father, but the ' *Junge Gelehrte*' was performed
early in January 1748, and met with great applause.
This would no doubt have afforded him much com-
pensation for the grief it gave him to displease his
father, had not another vexatious matter occurred.

It was the custom in Saxony for parents to give a
certain kind of cake called *Butterstritzel* to their

children at Christmas. Frau Lessing sent such a cake to her son by a friend who was going to Leipzig for the New Year's fair, and begged him to find out all about Gotthold's doings. This friend was much too pious to have anything to say to actors and authors, who would certainly not have suppressed Lessing's praises. He listened to the town's talk, and learnt that the pastor's son had become a playwriter, and associated only with doubtful characters ; and not only this, but he was able to impart the tragical news that such was Lessing's depravity, he had even shared his Christmas cake over a bottle of wine with a party of actors. On hearing this his mother wept bitterly and gave up her son as lost for time and eternity. Even his more enlightened father considered him to be on the brink of destruction, and held it best to snatch him suddenly from the burning. He at once wrote to the erring youth : ' The moment you receive this, take your place in the coach and come home. Your mother is at the point of death and wishes to see you again before her end.' On receipt of the letter, without an instant's delay, Lessing departed, not even stopping to take a change of clothes with him. The weather had been mild, but suddenly a severe frost set in. This revived his mother's tenderness, and much as she had urged his recall, she fondly hoped that this time he would not obey ; for now she was anxious about him, she remembered his good kind heart, his filial obedience, and the utter disregard of self with which he would undertake the journey. She reproached herself, she even thought it might have been better for him to continue his association with freethinkers and comedians, than to be frozen in the coach. She could scarcely await the hour when he

was expected, and allayed her terrors by exclaim-
ing, 'He will not come, disobedience is learnt in bad
company.' But at the time expected, he entered the
room half frozen. He had come, and the rejoicing
over the safety of this beloved son, twice given up as
lost, mitigated the anger that had prompted this recall. The mother even reproached him with his
obedience. 'But why did you come in this terrible
weather?' 'Dearest mother, you desired it,' he
replied calmly, while his whole body shook with cold;
' I suspected at once that you were not ill, and I am
heartily glad I was right.' In short, the scolding in
store for him gave place to a hearty welcome, and
when by and by the parents' cause for disapproval
found words, they induced only such friendly alter-
cation as was inevitable from the different points of
view from which each regarded the theatre. The
father looked at the real theatre of the time, the son
upheld the possibility of improvement. Pastor Lessing recognised that Gotthold's mind had ripened to
independence, and wisely discussed their differences'
in lieu of imposing paternal authority. · Every day
the father brought forward all that could be said
against poetry and the stage, the son defending his
opinions. That they did not jar seriously was owing
to the humour with which Lessing often dispelled his
father's gravity, who, though he entirely differed from
his son's reasoning, had too much good sense to condemn it as utterly foolish. He also saw with pleasure
that Gotthold's moral character was uncorrupted, and
that he had made great advances in all branches of
learning. It was however not so easy to mollify the
mother, whose mind was not so broad as her husband's,
and to whom friends expressed, in words and gesture,

their sincere sympathy with her trial in having such a freethinking son. At last he composed a sermon, to prove to her that he could become a clergyman any day if he only liked.

Lessing remained at Camenz until Easter, using his enforced leisure to the uttermost. He ransacked the library, which was not inconsiderable for a country parsonage, reading theological authorities and discussing them with his father, who noticed with satisfaction his intelligent interest in all departments of learning ; unlike the poets of the pastor's fancy, who despised study and could only converse on trivial themes. That he had not forgotten his Leipzig interests is evident, for he sketched his ' Old Maid ' during this visit, and wrote some Anacreontics. One day when he was out, his sister saw these poems, read them, and was so scandalized that she threw them into the fire. On Lessing's missing them among his papers, one of the little brothers betrayed the occurrence, and few people would have met it with Lessing's good-nature. The first outburst of his indignation over, he contented himself with throwing a handful of snow into Justine's bosom, to cool her pious ardour, as he said, was immediately reconciled, nor did he ever bear her the least ill-will.

Before returning to Leipzig, Lessing once more decidedly expressed his disinclination towards theology, but promised to devote himself more assiduously to school studies, so that he might at least become a professor. With this the father had to rest satisfied. He paid his son's debts, and sent him back to the University armed with good advice.

Lessing did indeed attend lectures more regularly, but he did not give up his literary and dramatic

interests.  He had wholly refused to give the promise,
his parents had tried to exact, that he should break
off all connection with the theatre, and his long
absence had only intensified his love for the drama.
Morning found him at rehearsal, evening at the performances.  He studied the dramatic art with eager
assiduity, as if a chair of histrionics were to be founded
for him at Leipzig.  The fragments the ' Woman Hater,'
suggested by a comedy of Menander, and ' Jehanghir,'
his first attempt at tragedy, were commenced, and would
have been completed had not a change occurred at
the theatre.  Frau Neuber lost some of her best actors,
her prestige began to wane, and shortly after, she saw
herself obliged to disband her company.  This was a
serious blow to Lessing in more ways than one.  He
had stood security for several of the actors, who left
Leipzig with their debts unpaid.  The creditors
applied to Lessing, who was unable to meet their
demands.  The remittances promised by the actors
did not arrive, and Lessing had no alternative but to
leave Leipzig in secret.  Mylius had quitted the
University a short time previously for Berlin, and had
already urged Lessing to join him in time to see an
eclipse of the sun in July.  These two circumstances,
combined with a tender interest he had felt in the
actress, Fräulein Lorenz, made Leipzig distasteful to
him.  He did not impart his intentions to anyone.
One day, when Weisse called on him, he was told that
Lessing had gone away for a few days.  He had left
Leipzig for Wittenberg with a cousin who had been
visiting him.

It was Lessing's intention to stay only a few days
at Wittenberg, and to be at Berlin in time for the
eclipse.  But anxiety and vexation brought on illness:

an untoward event which complicated his difficulties, and made life a burden to him. Fortunately he found a home with his cousin and designed to prosecute his studies in Wittenberg. He soon saw that he could not afford to remain. His illness and his debts had drained his resources, and determined him to carry out·his former project of going to Berlin.

With Lessing's departure from Wittenberg his student life may be regarded as virtually ended. He was firmly resolved henceforward to fight his own way in the world, and trust to his own exertions for support.

# CHAPTER IV.

*' He hated to excess,*
*With an unquiet and intolerant scorn,*
*The hollow puppets of a hollow age.'*

BERLIN was in many respects distinguished from other German cities. After the Revocation of the Edict of Nantes, the Great Elector had offered to the Huguenot refugees special inducements to settle in his territories. His discerning eye had recognized their worth as industrial colonists, and he hoped their sober intelligence would prove of educational value to his somewhat barbarian subjects. Though Frederick William of Prussia (his grandson), by his true German feeling, differed honourably from his brother sovereigns with their admiration of French usages, he was unable to grapple with these exaggerated notions of foreign superiority, induced by the meteoric splendour of the 'siècle de Louis XIV.,' that developed the Gallomania, even now a fatal obstacle to a genuine Teutonic spirit. How much more so then! In vain did the bigoted national feeling of Frederick William I. contend against the tyranny of French fashions and language. It manifested itself strongly in his own son, Frederick the Great, who, for all his father's imperative demands that his children should be Germans, not Frenchmen, that they should drive these intruding foreigners out of the land, proved himself the aptest pupil of the French philosophic school of the period, and not only encouraged, but invited the visits of its foremost disciples to his capital. The prestige given to Frederick by the treaty of Aix-la-Chapelle, and the eight years of peace that followed, gave him an opportunity of indulging his literary fancies. He instituted an academy of sciences consisting entirely of foreigners, and chiefly of Frenchmen, who enjoyed his special favours. By permitting unbounded freedom of discussion, he imparted to Berlin a character hitherto unknown. 'Let my people write, talk, think and speculate as much as they please,' he would say, 'what care I, provided they obey?' 'Let everyone go to heaven in his own way,' was another of his favourite dicta.

The capital of such a ruler promised a congenial mental atmosphere; and this, united to Mylius' invitations, decided Lessing to try his fortunes there. He arrived in December 1748, a youth barely twenty, with no friend save the decried Mylius, and no resources but his undiminished stock of hope and youthful powers of endurance. When his parents learned his whereabout, they were even more horror-struck than they had been on hearing that he wrote comedies and associated with actors. What could he want in this hotbed of irreligion, where he would be subjected to every godless distraction and temptation, while a veritable Mephistopheles was his friend and guardian? They made various underhand inquiries as to his conduct, and the answers received seemed to them far from reassuring. Then they demanded his return home.

Lessing replied (January 1749) to this summons by a long letter addressed to his mother, in whom he rightly recognised the prime instigator of these reproaches. He reviews his University career, and explains his reasons for his removal to Berlin. His long silence he excuses on the ground that he had nothing pleasant to impart, and did not like to appear constantly before his parents with petitions and complaints, which they no doubt were as tired of reading, as he was of writing them. ' I could have been provided for long ago, if I could have presented a better appearance in the matter of dress. This is so very needful in a town where a man is almost entirely judged by his appearance. Now it is almost a year ago that you were good enough to promise me a new suit of clothes : you can judge from this whether my last demand was too presumptuous. You refuse it me.' This refusal he is convinced is based on her unjust dislike to Mylius. Will she never abandon her prejudice against this man ? He endeavours to convince her again that he is not bound to him in any way ; not entirely under his influence, as she supposes. At the present moment, it is true, he owes him gratitude for providing food and lodging in his bitter poverty, and it is a pleasure to him to find that this unjustly depreciated friend has warm adherents in Berlin, among respected and aristocratic personages. He repeats his readiness to leave the city as an assurance of his filial obedience, if his parents continue to desire it, and will send him some money. ' Return home, however, I will not,' he adds ; ' neither will I go any more to universities, because my stipends would not suffice to cover my debts, and because I will not ask you to meet this expense. I shall certainly go to

Vienna, Hamburg, or Hanover. In all three places I
shall find good friends and acquaintances. Even if I
do not learn anything in my wanderings, I shall learn
how to behave in the world. Gain enough. I shall
no doubt come to a place where they can use such a
bungler ('*Flickstein*') as I am.'

The worthy parents must not be judged severely.
It was impossible for them to take a comprehensive
view of things outside the narrow range of Camenz ;
nor could they know that the ugly duckling who
caused them so much trouble was in truth a swan.
He awaited their reply, and busied himself with Mylius'
help in gaining a livelihood.

Rüdiger, the proprietor of the 'Berlin Gazette,' of
which Mylius was the editor, commissioned Lessing
to arrange his library, offering him, in return, free
board and moderate remuneration. The library was
valuable and enriched Lessing's book knowledge considerably. He further translated the 4th, 5th, and
6th volumes of Rollin's 'History of Rome,' and
learnt Spanish and Italian for the same end. He
put the finishing touches to his poems, and began
several plays. He also sketched a critical essay, 'On
the employment of pantomime in the ancient drama,'
incited by the appearance of a ballet company, whose
performances were erroneously criticized as identical
with the classical pantomimes.

Meanwhile his proposal to visit Catholic Vienna
had redoubled his parents' uneasiness. They feared
it would prove but the first step to a change of religion. Once more he was desired to come home,
until a post as tutor should be found for him in the
University of Göttingen, where Mosheim, a friend
of Pastor Lessing's, was rector. This letter was

accompanied by nine thalers. Lessing replies under
date April 11, 1749:

'Honoured Father,
        'You still insist I should return home. You
are afraid that I might go to Vienna with the intent
of becoming a writer of comedies. You profess to
know that I drudge for Herr Rüdiger and suffer
hunger and want. You even write to me quite openly
that I have written you a collection of lies about
opportunities of work. I beg of you for one moment
to put yourself in my place, and to consider how you
would be pained by such unfounded reproaches,
whose falsehood, if you only knew me a little, would
at once become apparent. But I am most surprised
that you could revive the old reproach about the
comedies. I have never promised that I would
neither write nor read any more, and you have always
acted much too sensibly towards me, seriously to
make such a demand. How can you write that I
bought nothing but plays in Wittenberg, since among
the books there probably only two could be found?
        'My correspondence with actors is quite different
from what you imagine. I have written to Baron
Seiller at Vienna, who directs all the Austrian theatres,
a man whose acquaintance does me no discredit, and
who may yet be of use to me. I have written to
similar persons at Danzig and Hanover, and I do not
think it is any reproach to me to be known elsewhere than in Camenz. Do not reply to this that I
am only known by comedians. If these know me,
of necessity all must who see my work rendered by
them. I could also show you letters, for instance
from Copenhagen, not written by comedians, as a

proof that my correspondence does not deal merely
with the drama. And it is a pleasure to me to
extend this correspondence daily. I shall shortly
write to M. Crebillon at Paris, as soon as I have completed the translation of his " Catilina." You say my
manuscripts prove to you I have begun much and
completed little. Is that so great a wonder?

*Musae secessum scribentis et otia quaerunt ;*

but "*Nondum Deus nobis hæc otia fecit.*" And yet
if I were to name all that is scattered here and there
(I will not count my plays, since most people imagine
they cost as little effort as they bring honour) it would
still amount to something. I shall take good care
not to name the least of them, since they might
please you even less than my plays. I wish for my
part I had only written plays ; I should be in different
circumstances now. I have been well paid for those
that have reached Vienna and Hanover. But if you
will have the goodness to be patient a few months,
you shall see I am not idle in Berlin, nor work for
others. Do you fancy I do not know from whom
you receive such intelligence? that I do not know to
whom and how often you write about me to persons
who must necessarily derive a very bad opinion of me
from your letters? But I will believe that you have
done it for my good, and not blame you for the
inconvenience and vexation it has caused me. With
regard to the post in the Seminarium Philologicum at
Göttingen, I pray you to take all possible pains in
the matter. I promise you solemnly that as soon as
it is certain, I will at once come home, or go thither
from here. But if you know of nothing certain for
me, it is better I should stay here, in a place where I

can make my fortune, even if I should have to wait.
What should I do at home? I have therefore used
the money you were good enough to send, together
with some I earned myself, in purchasing a new suit of
clothes, and I am now in condition to show myself,
and to apply personally to those whose services I
seek. This was more needful than for me to trouble
you with my useless presence at home. At present I
have everything I want except linen and my books.
I have written a list of them and expect them eagerly.
You may well imagine how troublesome it is to make
use of borrowed books; I therefore beg this one
favour of you. Good clothes without sufficient linen
are as good as none. I beg of you, give me time till
Midsummer, and if by then nothing has been settled
in my affairs here, I will do all you desire. Permit
me to quote the speech Plautus puts into the mouth
of a father who was also somewhat dissatisfied with
his son:

> Non optuma haec sunt neque ego ut aequum censeo,
> Verum meliora sunt, quam quae deterrima.
> Sed hoc unum consolatur me atque animum meum
> Quia, *qui nihil aliud, nisi quod sibi soli placet*
> *Consulit adversum filium, nugas agit :*
> Miser ex animo fit : secius nihilo facit.
> Suae senectuti in acriorem hyemem parat, &c.

The ideas are so sensible, that you must agree to
them. Why should my mother make herself so
unhappy over me? It must be the same to her
whether I make my fortune here or there, if she
really wishes me well, as I certainly think. And
how could you imagine that even if I had gone to
Vienna I should change my religion? From this I
infer how prejudiced you are against me. But God

will yet, I trust, give me an opportunity of evincing my
love for my religion as well as for my parents.

'I remain your most obedient son,

'L.'

Notwithstanding the upright tone that pervades
this letter, the parents continued to attach more
credence to their secret informants than to their son's
avowals. Pastor Lessing wrote an instant reply full
of reproaches, intimating his doubts as to Gotthold's
orthodoxy and morality, and ending with the ironical
taunt that no doubt he desired to become a German
Molière ; evidently the *non plus ultra* of reproach
with the worthy pastor.

Lessing replied, April 28, 1749 :

'Honoured Father,
    '. . . I await my trunk impatiently, and I once
more entreat you to put in the books I mentioned in
a former letter. I also request the bulk of my manuscripts ; also the sheets "Wine and Love." They are
free imitations of Anacreon, some of which were
made already at Meissen. I do not think the severest
moralist would censure them.

Vita verecunda est, Musa jocosa mihi.

Thus Martial excuses himself in a similar case, and
anyone who knows me at all, knows that my feelings
do not at all harmonize with them. Nor do they
deserve the epithet you bestow on them in your
character of stern theologian. Else the odes and songs
of the greatest of our poets, Hagedorn, would deserve
a much worse designation. In point of fact, only my
fancy to try my hand at all forms of poetry, has given

them being.   If we do not try which is our real sphere,
we may often venture into a false one, where we can
scarcely rise above mediocrity, while in another we
might have soared to a wondrous height.   Perhaps
you may have observed that I broke off the work,
and grew tired of practising such trifles.

'If I could be called a German Molière with truth,
I should be assured of an eternal name.   Truth to
speak, I have the greatest desire to earn it, but its vast-
ness and my impotence are two matters that would
stifle the greatest desires.   Seneca counsels : " Omnem
operam impende, ut te aliqua dote notabilem facias."
But it is difficult to become notable in a branch in
which but too many have excelled.   Have I done so
very ill if I have chosen for my juvenile works a
branch wherein so few of my countrymen have tried
their powers?   And would it not be foolish to desist
before I have produced masterpieces?   I cannot
understand your demonstration that a playwriter
cannot be a good Christian.   A playwriter is a man
who depicts vice from its comic side.   Is a Christian
not allowed to laugh at vice?   Does vice deserve so
much reverence?   And if I were to promise to write
a comedy which the theologians would not only read,
but even praise?   Do you hold my promise impossible?
How if I were to write one about the freethinkers and
the scoffers at your cloth?   I know for certain you
would relax much of your severity.

'With respects to my mother,
            'Your most obedient son,
                        'LESSING.'

Still Lessing has to defend himself.   He writes,
May 30, 1749 :

'Honoured Father,
'The trunk with the specified contents has come safely to hand. I thank you for this great proof of your goodness, and I should be more profuse in my thanks if I did not unfortunately see too plainly from all your letters that you have for some time been in the habit of thinking meanly of me. Therefore of necessity the thanks of a person whom you regard so unfavourably can only be suspicious to you. What am I to do? Shall I excuse myself elaborately? Shall I abuse my calumniators, and expose their weaknesses in revenge? Shall I call God and my conscience to witness? If I were to demean myself so far I should be employing less principle in my actions than I in fact do. Time shall decide. Time shall teach whether I have reverence for my parents, religious convictions and virtue in my morals. Time shall teach which is the better Christian, he who holds the doctrines of Christianity in his memory, has them often on his lips without comprehending them, who goes to church and conforms to all usages because they are customary; or he who has once wisely doubted and attained conviction by the path of inquiry, or who at least still strives to attain it. Christianity is not a matter to be accepted in faith from one's parents. It is true most persons inherit it as they do their fortune, but they show by their actions what manner of Christians they are. So long as I do not see one of the foremost commands of the Christian religion, to love our enemies, better observed, so long I shall doubt whether those are Christians who profess themselves such. . . . . . . . . . . .
'Shall I never be rid of the reproaches you make

me concerning Mylius : " Sed facile ex tuis querelis
querelas matris agnosco, quae, licet alias pia et integra,
in hunc nimio flagrat odio. Nostra amicitia nihil
unquam aliud fuit, adhuc est et in omne tempus erit
quam communicatio studiorum. Illane culpari
potest ? Rarus imo nullus mihi cum ipso sermo inter-
cedit, de parentibus meis, de officiis quae ipsis vel
praestanda vel deneganda sint, de cultu Dei, de pietate, de fortuna hac vel illa via amplificanda, ut habeas
quem in illo seductorem et ad minus justa instigatorem
meum timeas. Cave, ne de muliebri odio nimium par-
ticipes. Sed virum te sapientem scio, justum aequum-
que : et satis mihi constat te illud, quod scripsisti,
amori in uxorem amore tuo dignissimam, dedisse.
Veniam dabis me haec paucula latino sermone literis
mandasse, sunt enim quae matrem ad suspicionem
nimis proclivem offendere possint. Deum tamen
obtestor me illam maxumi facere, amare et omni
pietate colere." ' [1]

The want of a theatre in Berlin discouraged Lessing's dramatic productiveness, and his accurate per-

---

[1] ' But in your complaints I can easily recognise those of my mother,
who, though kind and just in all other matters, is unreasonably prejudiced here. Our friendship never was, is, or will be other than an
intellectual intercourse. Is this blameworthy? Rarely, I may say
never, do we exchange a word about my parents, about the duties
which are owing or which may be refused to them, about the worship
of God, or piety, or this or that way of making our fortune, as you
seem to think when you fear that he is my seducer and my tempter to
unrighteous actions. Take care lest you participate too much in your
wife's prejudices. But I know you are a wise, just, and equitable man, and
I am quite sure that you wrote what you did out of love for a wife most
worthy of your affection. You will forgive me for writing these few
things in Latin, but they might offend my mother with her too ready
suspicion. But I call God to witness that I most exceedingly regard,
love, and honour her.'

ception of the requirements of his environment showed
him that Berlin was not the soil for poetry. Learned
and critical productions were more in harmony with
its spirit. What if he brought these to bear upon the
despised drama, and by historical analysis awakened
a public interest in the living stage? Nothing, he
contended, was more characteristic of the genius of a
nation than its drama. Now whoever would judge
the German genius by its stage, would find it displayed
a special facility in appropriating the productions of
other nations. 'We have,' he said, 'few pieces really
our own, and even in these a foreign element is nearly
always present.' His own plays had been praised by
Frau Neuber. He had confessed that it was only
needful to praise him on any point to ensure his pursuing the subject with increased ardour. He pondered
day and night how he could manifest power in a
department in which as yet no German had distinguished himself. He aspired to endow Germany with
an original drama, but he saw it would be needful
first to initiate the people and instruct them to understand the nature of the drama in its highest form.

In concert with Mylius, he commenced a quarterly
journal (*Beiträge zur Historie und Aufnahme des
Theaters*), to be devoted to reviews, historical sketches,
treatises on the arts of the poet and player; in short,
every ramification of the drama was to be treated and
elucidated by translations of the best foreign dramatists. The Greek and Roman, and after them the
English and Spanish, were to be principally considered. 'Shakespeare, Dryden, Wycherly, Van-
brugh, Cibber, Congreve, are poets known to us almost
only by name, and yet they deserve our admiration
quite as much as the vaunted French poets.' A

remark thrown out, that if the Germans followed their natural bent in dramatic poetry, their stage would resemble the English more than the French, is the first indication of Lessing's defection from the law of the three unities, hitherto deemed inviolable.

The first number appeared in October 1749, and was provided with a preface setting forth its purpose. The audacity of this juvenile enterprise reveals the penetrating instinct with which Lessing worked, apparently at random, and time alone taught him as well as others the full significance of his energetic gladiatorship. This encyclopædic plan bore in itself the seeds of destruction, but this was hastened by a disagreement between Mylius and Lessing. The former had declared that there was no good Italian drama. Lessing considered their whole undertaking disgraced by this ignorant assertion. Would not everyone who knew anything of Italian literature exclaim : 'If you know the dramas of other countries no better than you do the Italian stage, we may look for nice things from you.' He therefore withdrew from the journal after its fourth issue, and his secession proved fatal to the undertaking of which he had been life and soul ; but its purpose remained in his mind, and he continued to prosecute researches in this direction.

His contributions had however gained him a certain notoriety, on account of the independent spirit which they displayed. This tentative effort was prompted by a positive aim. Lessing found art adrift, without social or æsthetic purpose, idly copying lifeless works, and sublimely ignorant of the possibility of a nobler goal. The German theatre had been considerably influenced by the English drama of the seventeenth century, introduced by bands of strolling players. But the German genius took to itself only the lawlessness and grossness of the contemporary comedy, and this degenerated into the harlequinades and Shrove-tide plays that disgraced the boards and justified the animosity of theologians. This animosity had been retained by clerical zealots after Gottsched had removed the cause. For if he had purified the stage till it presented nothing but the conventional character borne by the masks of antiquity and the Italian comedy, he had at least made it harmless. Lessing, who had personal experience of such opposition, ardently advocated the cause of the theatre, and put forth the bold declaration that the highest philosophical and religious truths were capable of impressive representation ; nay, more, that the vocation of comedy was to become a school of culture for the people. On this account he insisted on a healthy conception of real life in place of the empty abstractions of the later dramatists, and therefore refers to the Roman playwriters as deriving their materials from familiar surroundings.

Whether from having imbibed the French atmosphere about him, or merely as a linguistic exercise, Lessing began to write two comedies in that language, 'Jadis' and 'Palaion,' and he projected various others in German. 'But,' as he himself wrote later, 'I no longer know what I intended with these scribbles ; I always wrote very briefly, relying on my memory, by which I now see myself betrayed.' Throughout the year 1750 Lessing held a temporary engagement under a certain Baron Golz ; indeed he seemed to take such root in Berlin that his father reproached him with losing sight of the Göttingen plan.

'You wrong me,' he replies, 'if you think I have

E

changed my mind about Göttingen. I assure you once more that I would go there to-morrow if it were possible, not because I am now badly off in Berlin, but because I have promised you to do so. For indeed I have good hopes my fortunes will soon change. The acquaintance of Baron von der Golz has been of no little use to me in helping me to gain a firmer footing, for not only have I earned about thirty thalers, but he has also introduced me to several of his friends, who at any rate have given me a heap of promises. These are not to be despised, provided they do not always remain promises. I do not count upon them, and have arranged my affairs so that I can live comfortably in Berlin this winter without their help. What I call comfortable, another might call miserable ; but what care I whether I live in plenty or no, provided I live ?....Whoever wrote to you that I was badly off because I no longer board at Herr Rüdiger's, wrote you a great untruth. I never wanted to have anything more to do with this old man after I had made myself fully acquainted with his large library. This I have done, and so we parted. My living troubles me least of all here in Berlin : I can get a good meal for one groschen, six pfennige (1½d.). La Mettrie, whom I have several times named in my letters to you, is physician in ordinary to the King. His work, '*L'homme machine*,' has created a great sensation here. I have read one of his writings, '*Anti-Sénèque, ou le souverain bien*,' which has been printed not less than twelve times, but you may judge its immorality by the fact that the King himself threw ten copies of it into the fire.'

This same year (1750) brought Lessing into personal contact with Voltaire, then at the height of royal favour. He had made the acquaintance of Richier de Louvain, Voltaire's secretary, an amiable young man of his own age, with whom he often disputed on the respective merits of German and French literature. Voltaire was then involved in his notorious lawsuit with Abraham Hirsch,[1] brought about by his attempt to speculate in illegal stock-jobbing, on which occasion the famous advocate of enlightenment and truth was guilty of perjury and falsification. His opponent was a notorious rogue: the whole matter turned on the question which rogue would outwit the other. Voltaire, who did not care to have his cards exposed, pleaded his own cause, and for this purpose he employed Lessing, at Richier's recommendation, as translator. This necessitated much personal intercourse between Voltaire and Lessing, and laid the foundation for Lessing's low opinion of this philosopher. The suit was decided, or rather compromised, in February 1751. 'Voltaire picks the pockets of the Jews,' Frederick wrote to his sister, 'but will get out of it by some summersault;' and this truly expressed the case. The King was seriously annoyed, however; and while congratulating Voltaire satirically on the conclusion of this 'scurvy affair,' enjoins him to have no further quarrels either with the Old or New Testament, as unworthy the finest genius in France. Berlin scoffed at the man whom the King delighted to honour. Lessing held his peace at the time, but one of his later epigrams, and a paper found after his death, reveal his opinion. Apropos of one of Phædrus' fables, he remarks: 'The moral is, it is a difficult matter to decide a quarrel when both parties

---

[1] For detailed account of this discreditable affair see Carlyle: 'Life of Frederick the Great,' vol. vi.; and D. Strauss: 'Voltaire.'

are rogues　For instance, on occasion of the lawsuit between Voltaire and the Jew Hirsch, people might have said to the Jew:

*Tu non videris perdidisse quod petis !*

and to Voltaire:

*Te credo surripuisse, quod pulchre negas !*

Lessing is significantly reticent of his personal estimate of the little-great man, with whom during this time he dined almost daily.

Various projects were now crowding upon him. His journalistic attempts had obtained him a certain standing. Mylius having quarrelled with the 'Berlin Gazette,' its editorship was offered to Lessing. He refused, on the plea that he did not care to waste his time on political trifles ; for the news of those days was submitted to severe censorship, and amounted to the trivial gossip-mongering familiar in French newspapers under the head of '*faits divers.*' Rüdiger died shortly after, and the paper passed into the hands of his son-in-law, who called it the '*Vossische Zeitung,*' after his own name. The journal lives to this day, and is the organ of the party of progress. Lessing undertook the conduct of its literary department, and thus found himself called upon to give an opinion on all the questions that agitated Germany. These critiques, being little more than short announcements, had no chance of distinguishing themselves from the ordinary run, but the same procedure evinced itself as in his poetical attempts. He infused his own spirit into extant forms, and created something really original.

His minor poems, published anonymously in a collected form (Easter 1751) as '*Kleinigkeiten*' (Trifles), passed under his own review. He treats of them without false modesty, and with a conscious knowledge of their merits and faults. 'Is the author to be blamed,' he asks, 'if his taste was less pure three years ago than it perhaps is at present ?' But these meagre announcements hardly sufficed for the needs of the reading public, who began to feel the impulse of new life communicated to the habitual stagnation by the famous quarrel between the Swiss and Leipzig schools, begun in 1740 and still raging in all its intensity ; as well as the forced intellectual life which Frederick endeavoured to graft upon his capital. Frederick the Great indirectly aided the growth of a national literature by infusing his own energy into the character of his people, and giving them something of which they could be proud. The result was a general quickening, which gave birth in this instance to a monthly supplement of the 'Voss Gazette,' entitled : 'The newest out of the Kingdom of Wit.' It was edited and almost entirely written by Lessing. Here he had free scope, and first exhibited the full powers of a genius which won for him afterwards the proud title bestowed by Macaulay, of being 'beyond all dispute the first critic in Europe.'

The essays are remarkable on various accounts. They first showed Lessing's symmetrical intellect, his miscellaneous acquirements, the pregnant conciseness of style and breadth of treatment that sprang from his penetrative sympathy. They are more remarkable than his later productions· in so far that they are not the expressions of ripened manhood, but of an enthusiastic youth, whose affluence of juvenile thought was given forth with a sobriety most commendable in an age of rhetoric. By one bold stroke

he raised himself above the strife of parties, asserting
his independence of either coterie, and displaying
himself, in Homeric phrase, a head and shoulders
higher than his contemporaries. Even these early
efforts testify that Lessing's sole fixed literary principle was to have none. He was free from prejudice,
from *la morgue littéraire;* he neither followed nor led
any literary clique. He abhorred the spirit of *cama-
raderie*, and taught that real genius must find and
follow its own path.

'When a bold intellect, confident in its own
strength, penetrates into the temple of taste by a new
entrance, a hundred imitators follow it, hoping to
steal in through this opening. But in vain. The
same strength that has forced the door flings it back
in their faces. The astonished followers see themselves shut out, and the eternity of which they dreamt
is suddenly changed into mocking laughter.'

On the strength of this, the Swiss thought they
might claim Lessing as one of themselves, but they
were soon to see that he looked at matters from a
broader platform.

'Alas, poor poetry!' he exclaims; 'to-day,
instead of enthusiasm and gods in the heart, rules
suffice you. One Bodmer more, and the young
poet's brain will be filled with fine fooleries, instead
of inspiration and poetic fire.'

And he proceeds to define genius in pregnant
verse :

> *Ein Geist, den die Natur zum Mustergeist beschloss,*
> *Ist, was er ist, durch sich, wird ohne Regel gross ;*
> *Er geht, so kühn er geht, auch ohne Weiser sicher ;*
> *Er schöpfet aus sich selbst. Er ist sich Schul und Bücher.*
> *Was ihn bewegt, bewegt ; was ihm gefällt, gefällt :*
> *Sein glücklicher Geschmack ist der Geschmack der Welt.*

To understand Lessing's position then and later, a rapid review of German literature is requisite.

German literature is one of the youngest of the European family. After the political anarchy of the fourteenth century, when poetry fell from the lyrical elegances of the Minne-, into the burgher hands of the Meister-singers, Pegasus was first put to harness and his flights reduced to the paces of the riding-school. But these worthy burghers kept guard of the despised mother tongue, for the learned could condescend only to Latin, and even national poems had to be translated into a dead language before German professors, who Latinized their very names, could condescend to read them. Then came Luther and gave to it a national glory, and it is small wonder that in his all-cleansing fury he should for a time have swept away good and bad together and stifled the Renaissance spirit which, with its love of beauty and humanity for their own sakes, was beginning to influence and civiliz anew the higher minds. Luther was not only the founder of a new Church, but the consolidator of a true German language. He 'overturned the tables of the money-changers and the seats of them that sold doves.' He reinstated a higher tone of thought, freed from scholasticism and rhapsody. He left to his people in his Table Talk and his hymns, veritable models of nervous language ; and well might Heine name his magnificent psalm, '*Ein' feste Burg ist unser Gott*,' the Marseillaise of the Reformation. It subverted more, it exalted more, than ever did that vindictive strain. Nor is it grand old brother Martin, but the times that came after him that must be blamed, if on his death literature grew barren, stale, and unprofitable.

The seventeenth century displayed a sad picture

of literary degradation. It is strange that at a time when England was already highly civilized, Germany was still half barbaric, torn and shattered by internal wars, over or under educated, bearing a French polish on its native boorishness, with no folk-life or national integrity to give it dignity. The Thirty Years' War and the subsequent ambitious conquests of Louis XIV. had ravaged and impoverished the country, forcing the people to consider only material interests, while the Courts, sunk in servile imitation of the French, relegated the German language to the lower orders, who soon learned to ape the Gallicisms of their betters and spoke a barbarous jargon. The condition of Germany at the close of the Thirty Years' War needs to be constantly kept in view, in order rightly to estimate the difficulties with which the Germans have had to contend in their national development, though at the same time they are too prone to lay their political nonage wholly to its account. It is the fault of a people, as it is that of an individual, if it remain eternally a minor. But in those days, lacerated, trampled down by the foreigner, degraded to be the battle-field of Europe, its provinces annexed or split into petty states, the naturally weak national spirit was lost in apathetic phlegm. Its slender popular liberties disappeared ; and whatever did not from sheer exhaustion resolve itself into atoms, the people helped to kill, suicidally destroying all that could make it a nation, by their obsequiousness to the fashions of other countries. Excepting in the department of hymn-writing, all feeling was overlaid by far-fetched conceits, and the spurious classicism of the French was regarded as the touchstone of excellence.

At length a few princes and scholars rebelled

against this foreign bondage, and formed themselves
into an academy after the Della Crusca type, with the
object of cultivating the vernacular. This society,
'the Palm-tree,' of necessity engendered affectation
and literary trifling ; its purisms bordered on the
absurd, but it broke the ice and produced a Martin
Opitz, rightly held as the precursor of a new epoch.
He was the founder of the first Silesian school, whose
works, lacking pith and purpose, flourished and de-
cayed like weeds, but at least instilled the sentiment
of form and correctness of diction. They were superseded by the second Silesian school, or ' Shepherds of
the Pegnitz,' as they preferred to be called : an affected
title, characteristic of their triviality and mannerism.

When the eighteenth century dawned, it found
Germany very sick, politically and intellectually.
Kant tells us that the importance of this century cannot be overrated, since it witnessed man's issue from
the intellectual nonage which he had brought upon
himself. In literature it saw its blooming period, and
culminated like the aloe in one grand effort, producing the great artistic trio, Lessing, Schiller, and
Goethe. In philosophy it saw the rise of faith in
humanity, and preached the gospel of progress that
had been crushed by the misery entailed by the religious wars, and the disconsolate fatalism thus inevit-
ably engendered. But many quagmires had to be
traversed first. The early years of the century saw
the Silesian schools trebly divided : one faction upheld natural style and natural sentiment ; another
defended the artificial elegances of Boileau and Horace
as the highest types of style ; while the third lauded
descriptive verse, and pointed to the English authors,
and especially to Thomson's ' Seasons,' as their ex-

amples. For all their lofty talk, the results were mere fustian. Then uprose Gottsched, a vain pedant of mediocre ability, who assumed to himself a literary dictatorship which his brother authors were too feeble to dispute. His criticism was hard and cold, his productions and those of his friends jejune imitations of the French, lacking every spark of inspiration. He denied the rights of imagination ; his narrow reason condemned Milton, Shakespeare, and Tasso ; he advocated laws of rhyme that presupposed poetical genius on the one hand and clipped the poet's wings on the other.

This imperious sway aroused Breitinger and Bodmer, two Zurich professors. They incited an Anglomania in antagonism to Gottsched's Gallomania, asserted the independence of genius, and reduced poetry to expressions of the marvellous or picturesque. Journals after the fashion of the *Spectator* were the organs of this warfare of naturalism in polarity to mannerism, of an exaggerated regard and absurd disregard of established rules. This strife was at its height when young Lessing came to Berlin and wrote independently of either party. A mind whose moral and intellectual faculties were less finely balanced might have been lost for a while in this conflicting sea, and have asked itself in hopeless despair whether a standard of good taste could really exist. Lessing was undisturbed by this perplexity. In his unconsciousness that his lines were cast in a reaction, his loyalty to æsthetic truth and his simple force of conviction helped him over all swamps which his ardour prevented him from even perceiving. He petrified Berlin by the audacity with which he denounced the dictators of taste, so that even the vain Gottsched

trembled. He attacked him with all the acerbity excited in his nature by Gottsched's meretricious poetical
attempts, acknowledging his merits in other departments of literature, and wishing he would remain
within the limits of what he could achieve. Reviewing a volume of his cold versifications, Lessing writes :

'The exterior is so excellent, that we hope it will
do the bookseller's shop great credit, and we wish it
may long do so. To give an adequate idea of the
interior exceeds our powers. These poems cost 2
thalers, 4 groschen. Two thalers pay for the absurd,
and four groschen about cover the useful.'

He laughs at the passion for the new at all costs,
which the Swiss faction displayed, at their love of the
mystic and obscure ; but he laughs equally at the
platitudes, the poor pretentiousness, the servile imitations of Gottsched's followers. He upholds the claims
of reason and lucidity against the one, the claims of
free imagination against the other coterie ; defends
the future against the Leipzigers who hold by
nothing that is not of the past ; and the past against
the Zurichers who esteem nothing but the future.
Thus he judged, calm and firm between the two
parties blinded by passion, with the alert intelligence
that made him regard the struggle as though he were
removed from it by half a century, instead of being
its contemporary.

These *feuilleton* essays, though apparently fragmentary, are strung upon a definite thread of connecting thought. After referring to the title, and
remarking that many readers will scarcely find this
kingdom in their atlases, he proceeds to speak of J. J.
Rousseau, who would erase it thence. Rousseau had
just startled the world by his brilliant paradox of the

immoral tendency of the arts and sciences. Lessing
confessed that he could not resist a secret reverence
for the man who defended virtue against all established
prejudices, even if he went too far. 'Happy would
France be if she had many such preachers!' he
exclaims, and then proceeds to give an abstract of
Rousseau's view that the arts and sciences bring
about the destruction of states. Then with true
insight he destroys the whole paradoxical house of
cards, by showing that the rise of the sciences and
the decay of morals and states are two separate
matters, which may co-exist without being related as
cause and effect. Everything tends to a culminating
point; a state will grow till this is attained, and so
long as it grows the arts and sciences will grow beside
it; but its decline is not owing to its having been
undermined by art and science, but because nothing
in the world is capable of indefinite and perpetual
growth. 'True, brilliant Athens lies in the dust; but
did virtuous Sparta flourish longer? Art is what we
choose to make it; it is our fault if it becomes hurtful.
In one word, Rousseau is in the wrong, but I know
of no one who is in the wrong with more show of
right.'

He then proceeds to speak of Klopstock's
'Messiah,' that had just taken the literary world by
storm. The Swiss hailed him as their spokesman,
the offspring of their doctrines, and claimed a place
for his crude juvenile effort beside the ripe product of
Milton's maturity. The Leipzigers saw all their rules
violated in this epic, and were as violent in their abuse
as the Swiss in their admiration. Lessing went to
the heart of the matter with a certainty bordering on
genius. He rejoices that Germany has at last pro-

duced a creative genius whose work is the result of
pure enthusiasm kindled by a worthy theme.   He
sees that here at last is a true national poet with faith
in his native tongue.   But he sees also that the genius
of this writer is lyrical rather than epic, that the
'Messiah' wants artistic form.   Its glaring faults :
mysticism, inflated inanity, high-flown language and
commonplace thoughts, called forth his censure.   He
predicted that the 'Messiah' would be more vaunted
than read by future ages, while insisting on its value as
a contemporary production, and contrasting it favourably with French efforts in the same direction.   Here
was a real German poet, and Lessing alone perceived
the national shame that Klopstock must be indebted
to a Danish King for the pension that gave him leisure
to finish his work.   To the tedious imitators of Klopstock who instantly arose, Lessing rightly showed no
mercy.   They well deserved the derisive epithet of
'Seraphic school.'

Lessing is as impartial to the faults of the French
as to the Germans ; the latter he might hear dis-
paraged any day in Berlin, but only to the glorifica-
tion of the former.   This did not daunt the buoyant
vigour of his criticism.   He pronounces Fénélon's
rules of government the maxims of a schoolmaster.
His classical standpoint led him to insist that politics
should only be treated by politicians and the arts of
government only by practical statesmen and rulers.
He condemns Diderot on the occasion of his letter to
Batteux on the deaf and dumb, calling him 'a short-
sighted theorist, and one of those philosophers who
are at more pains to collect clouds than to dissipate
them.'

In this wise, by outwardly disconnected, inwardly

harmonious reviews, Lessing surveyed the entire field of current æsthetic interests. He then perceived that for the past year he had been expending ideas without absorbing fresh ones in their place. The scholar in his nature once more asserted his rights and demanded a spell of sequestered study. Berlin was a somewhat distracting residence, owing to the various connexions into which his position as a helpless youth, living by his wits, had forced him on his arrival. He wished to shake these off and retreat awhile into seclusion.

Before his departure, a vexatious matter took place that gained him more notoriety than his writings had done. Voltaire, quit of his lawsuit, had retired to Potsdam to complete his 'Age of Louis XIV.' Lessing happened to be with his friend Richier when he was selecting the first complete copies intended for the King, before the work should become public. He began to read, and was so enthralled that he implored permission to take home the sheets he had not finished, promising solemnly to return them in three days and show them to no one. Richier consented without Voltaire's knowledge. A friend of Lessing's saw the sheets in his lodgings and wished to borrow them. Lessing, loth to refuse what had been granted to himself, unwarrantably consented. This friend was a tutor at Count Schulenbourg's, and a Countess Bentinx, Voltaire's intimate friend, espied the book when visiting at the house. Full of wrath that Voltaire should have accorded to a stranger what he had refused to herself, she hurried off to the philosopher and demanded an explanation. Voltaire was furious, and sent for Richier, who confessed the whole business, and hurried to fetch the sheets from Lessing. To his dismay, he found Lessing had suddenly departed for Wittenberg, taking the sheets with him. Voltaire, beside himself, dictated a letter which Richier was to send in his own name, accusing Lessing of fraudulent designs upon the work, such as reprinting or translating it without leave. Lessing's answer not arriving at the very moment when Voltaire had expected it, he wrote an autograph letter, so injurious in its implications, under a polite disguise, that it aroused all Lessing's irascibility, and he replied by a letter which, as he said later, Voltaire no doubt did not exhibit. The sheets had accompanied his answer to Richier, in whose strange missive Lessing had plainly recognised the hand of Voltaire.

All sorts of versions of this story were circulated in Berlin, and it was for some time the theme of the town's talk. Lessing meantime, quite unconscious, had settled himself anew in Wittenberg (December 1751) after an absence of two years, exceedingly momentous for his mental growth.

# CHAPTER V.

*'Say then that he was wise as brave;*
*As wise in thought, as bold in deed ;*
*For in the principles of things*
*He sought their moral creed.'*—WORDSWORTH.

TWO men were always at war in Lessing : the erudite scholar who seeks seclusion for undisturbed study,
and the man of the world who seeks active experiences
and human contact. The strife between these two
natures often came to an abrupt crisis, and induced
a sudden flight, such as his departure from gay Berlin
to peaceful Wittenberg. His brother Theophilus was
studying theology at the University. Lessing joined
him, and the two boarded and often fasted together ;
for if the younger brother had little to spend, the
elder had still less. He resumed a life of study
without attending classes, and spent his days in his
own modest apartment, or in the University library,
opened to him by his friend F. J. Schwarz, a young
theologian who held the post of under-librarian. This
privilege was of inestimable value to Lessing, and he
studied there with such zeal that he could boast with
truth that there was no book on the shelves which he
had not held in his hands.

After the mentally exhausting process of literary journalism, he enjoyed yet more keenly the luxury of scholarly research, carried on in his own peculiar spirit, equally remote from the narrow interests of the bookworm and the abstruse speculations of specialist professors. His busy restless brain would never permit him to spend his life wholly on one pursuit, while his idiosyncrasy led him always to connect his studies with the place or the circumstances in which he found himself. It followed naturally that in an exclusively theological University, and the cradle of the Reformation, his universal curiosity penetrated into the 'sanctuary of bookworm scholarship,' whence this movement had taken birth. The contrast between the general tone of thought in Wittenberg and Berlin would alone have afforded Lessing food for reflection. Here he found the sectarian spirit of Lutheranism rampant to intolerance, a dogmatic system of ecclesiastical belief ignoring the very existence of pure moral religion apart from creeds and formulas. At Berlin philosophical scepticism reigned under royal patronage. The character of scoffing levity imparted to it by Voltaire, embodying questions of moment to humanity in *persiflage*, was revolting to the innate seriousness of the Teutonic mind, which cannot dismiss with contemptuous raillery the sacred objects of yesterday's reverence. Granting the whole edifice of the Christian faith is founded on superstition, it has too long formed the bulwark of many peoples, and must not and cannot be rudely sneered away. Lessing, whose independent views of theology were yet in process of formation, stood rooted himself in Christianity, and was therefore able to understand and aid the process of mental evolution out of an old faith into a newer

F

and larger one, unconsciously craved by his times. He was a freethinker in the true sense of that much-abused term,—one who refuses to think as a slave ; and his views, like those of every true thinker, changed and enlarged with time. But it was at Wittenberg that he first gave a critical shape to what had already begun to form in his mind. The general tendency of the age was to effect a compromise between revelation and reason, presenting, by its ingenious theological sophisms, some curious analogies with the England of our own time. But Lessing loved truth for its own sake with passionate ardour ; and, loving it, he could not sink into a state of contented credulity. He must investigate.

' Not error,' he said, ' makes the misfortune of men, but sectarian error, or sectarian truth, could truth be sectarian.'

His enemies were dogmatism and intolerance, whether under the disguise of rationalism or orthodoxy. He regarded every sect that would not listen to tolerance as a popery, and in the Wittenberg of his day he found the Lutheran popery of intolerance strongly represented. He wished to see not only Lutheranism, but Christianity, subjected to an impartial examination.

' What is more needful than to obtain conviction concerning our faith, and what more impossible than conviction without previous examination ? We should not say that the examination of our faith is sufficient, and that it is needless, when we have once found in it the divine impression, to seek for this in others also. Nor should we use the simile, that when we once know a right way we need not concern ourselves about by-paths. We do not learn to know the one by the other, but rather the former by the latter.'

With a certain filial piety towards the faith in which he had been nurtured, and with a naturally reverent religious spirit, he brought his youthful vigour and precocious penetration to the task of theological inquiry. In critical analysis he did not despise the day of small things.

'To pronounce a matter trivial,' he explained, 'is more often a confession of one's own weakness of vision, than a just estimate of its worth. Nay, it often happens that the scholar who is rude enough to tax another with trifling, is himself a wretched trifler in his own particular department. Everything outside of this is small to him, not because it really looks small to him, but that he does not see it at all, because it lies entirely outside his vision. His eyes may be as sharp as they please ; one quality is wanting to make them really good eyes. They are as immovable in his head, as his head is immovably fixed on his body. Therefore he can only see those objects before which his whole body is planted. He knows nothing of the rapid side-glances so necessary to the survey of a great whole. It would need a machine to turn the ponderous man in another direction ; and, when he has at length been turned, the other point of view has passed from his memory.'

Out of stagnation nothing results. At the same time Lessing never allowed minute examination to blind him to the larger meaning of the whole. While thus instructing himself, he produced ; for to write and think, to conceive and undertake, to acquire knowledge and engage in a polemic, were with him processes almost identical. Hence he has left more fragment than complete works; his thoughts moved faster than his pen could follow ; sometimes in the act of thinking

out a subject by aid of the pen he outstripped his
own preliminary views, or changed them entirely.
But wherever he touched he woke ideas, sowed truths,
redressed wrongs, destroyed usurped reputations; into
whatever domain he entered, he infused life. His
purpose was not satirical and destructive; he built
anew while he pulled down; while denouncing slavish
imitation, he demanded a profound respect for the
great works of antiquity. He found theology a petrifaction. Now it was one of his marked characteristics
that his theological and æsthetic interests always ran
parallel. It was therefore inevitable that in this crisis
he should turn to Pierre Bayle as his master.

The influence of Bayle upon the eighteenth century was immense; indeed its distinctive character, as
the epoch of protest against the traditional, may
be said to have been impressed on it by him  The
'Critical Dictionary,' designed 'not to inculcate scepticism, but to suggest doubts,' this ample and tolerant
monument of erudite acumen, thoroughly commended
itself to Lessing's temper. He determined to work
on this model, and, as Bayle had taken his starting
point from the dictionary of Moréri, 'to compile the
largest possible collection of mistakes found in dic-
tionaries, and also to make digressions concerning
all manner of authors,' so Lessing took up a
similar, and with all its shortcomings a very useful,
work by Dr. Jöcher. He criticised its faults and
began to supply its numerous omissions, publishing
three sheets. The matter reached the ears of Jöcher,
who applied to the rector of the University for information regarding this presumptuous young man
who had publicly undertaken to rectify his mistakes. The rector's statement must have been satis-

factory, for Jöcher wrote a polite letter to Lessing, regretting he had not communicated with him, with a view to the production of a supplementary volume, and hinted his willingness to buy up Lessing's materials. At the same time, he remarks, Lessing might have been a little less biting in his criticisms. The result was that Lessing desisted from the project, but not before a scandalous rumour had spread of his having tried to extort a large sum from Jöcher under a threat of making him ridiculous in the eyes of the whole learned world. Coming so soon after the Voltaire matter, and a second time impugning his probity, this mischievous gossip greatly annoyed Lessing.

Nevertheless he continued to work in the manner of Bayle, writing brief erudite articles in which, like Bayle, he only occasionally assumed the tone of philosopher, while it gave him play to ventilate his opinions. Like Bayle and Voltaire he would put himself in the position of an antagonist, and could make a true analysis of a contrary opinion serve as a development of his own. His criticism, though bolder than Voltaire's, was less subversive, for, as with Bayle, his scepticism was rather a suspension of belief and a desire, if possible, to find a common ground of re-conciliation. *Ecraser l'infâme* by the weapons of ridicule was in his eyes a confession of weakness. He desired to see bold discussion, free from flippant irreligion. He held with Bayle that philosophy could render no aid to religion, but differed in his inferences. The aims of philosophy and religion are diverse. Truth is the object of reason ; conduct, of religion. Bayle held that philosophy has no concern with the demonstration of religious truths, because if the historical foundations of Christianity are once established, all the rest is matter of faith beyond the cognisance of philosophy. Not so Lessing, who, while admitting that the intrusion of metaphysics into the domain of Christianity had corrupted its primitive simplicity, still contended that, even if it were deprived of its supernatural character, its continued existence would be justified through its teaching and practice of universal charity, in which lies its true essence.

Lessing's own opinions were so entirely at variance with those of any of the schools, that no party quite knew where to place him, nor can they classify him to this day. His pure reverent spirit transcended the limitation of creeds: he was opposed to the Apologists who desired to prove the truth of the Christian faith against the freethinkers; to the freethinkers who thought they could substitute their own reason in place of a creed; to the Wolffian school who wished to demonstrate dogma by mathematics; to the Lutheran theologians who knew no higher source of religion than the letter of the Bible; and finally to the Neologians and Semi-naturalists. Of all this, however, Lessing was wholly unconscious. He worked and thought in his characteristic manner, heedless of the goal.

An interesting fragment dealing with the newly founded sect of Moravian brethren dates from this time. In Lessing's eyes the grand merit of its founder, Count Zinzendorf, was to have separated religion from theology. 'Man was created for action rather than speculation,' and religion's place is to aid him herein. Rapidly surveying the histories of philosophy and faiths, he shows how Christianity, when no longer oppressed, busied herself in embellishing her creed and supporting divine truths with human reasons. The Reformation had amended this condition, but not radically ; and the present times show so strange a mixture of worldly and theological wisdom, that it is as difficult to discover a true Christian as in the dark ages. Count Zinzendorf merits praise because he has gone farther than the reformers towards rendering religion simple and inward ; to preach love and charity is to aid the cause of progress, for creeds and dogmas are but the forms of religion. Lessing had already attained to the clearer perception that all faiths are equally good, because they are merely the national and general expressions of the one true religion.

The influence of Bayle is more immediately to be traced in some short essays written, though not published, at Wittenberg. Lessing calls them ' Rehabilitations' (*Rettungen*), for in each case he has a reputation to defend. The one dealing with Jerome Cardan is the most remarkable. This eccentric thinker had been popularly branded as an Atheist on account of a passage in his '*De Subtilitate*,' which had on its publication drawn down upon him the wrath of a J. C. Scaliger. The obnoxious matter was a comparison which Cardan had instituted between the Heathen, Jewish, Mahommedan, and Christian faiths, without pronouncing in favour of any. This was considered equivalent to a declaration of indifference. Lessing, on the contrary, held that Cardan had decidedly leant towards Christianity, and that he had not given Islamism its due. After therefore vindicating Cardan from the stigma of Atheism, he enters into an apology of Islam.

Cochlaeus, the Romish divine who published a blustering pamphlet against the marriage of Henry VIII., was in Lessing's eyes another unfairly abused personage. He was generally credited with having spread the defamatory remark that Luther's work had sprung from no higher motive than the mutual jealousy of the Augustinian and Dominican monks.

Why quarrel about this? asks Lessing. Granted it be true, which he doubts, the work done by the Reformation does not on that account lose in value, as even Catholics would admit.

Simon Lemnius and the anonymous author known as *Ineptus religiosus* next engaged his attention. He thought that they had been handled with undue severity by the fanatic adherents of the Reformation, in Lemnius' case by Luther himself. Lemnius was a writer of coarse Latin epigrams, in which he attacked all the chiefs of the new movement. Luther and he were vehemently opposed. Lessing saw in Lemnius the victim of Luther's violent temper, and held that historians had perverted the facts in order to preserve Luther's glory unblemished. Reason enough for Lessing to take Lemnius under his protection, asserting that it was Luther's unjust persecution that drove Lemnius to his most outspoken work. Lessing's purpose is rather to take from Luther the character of infallibility claimed by Protestant zeal, than to absolve Lemnius. Even if Luther did not act worthily in this particular, what matter? Does he not remain, for all that, one of the greatest men the world has seen? 'I reverence Luther so highly, that on consideration I am heartily glad to have discovered a few little failings in him, inasmuch as I should otherwise have actually been in danger of

deifying him. The traces of humanity I find in him
are as precious to me as his most dazzling perfections;
they are even more instructive than all these taken
together. God! What a terrible lesson for our pride!
How deeply anger and revenge may degrade the
holiest! But would a less vehement spirit have been
capable of Luther's achievements? Certainly not!
Let us therefore admire the wise Providence that can
use even imperfections for its instruments. . . . In
fact, what does it matter what instruments God has
employed? He does not always choose the most
blameless, but rather the most convenient. If envy
was the source of the Reformation, would to God
that all envy might have such fortunate consequences!
The Exodus of the children of Israel was brought
about by a murder, and, say what one will, by a
culpable murder; but was it any the less God's work
and a miracle?' He then treats of the scoffers who
wish lightly to laugh away the earnestness of history.
'A modern writer lately hit on a witty conceit: he
said the Reformation was in Germany a work of
selfishness; in England the work of love; and in
singing France the work of a street ballad. Much
pains have been taken to refute this conceit, as though
a conceit could be refuted. The only way to refute
it is to take away its sting; and where that is impossible, it remains witty whether it is true or false.
But to deprive it of its sting, if it has one, it might be
expressed thus: Eternal Wisdom, which knows how
to use all things to its ends, has brought about the
Reformation in Germany by selfishness, in England
by love, and in France by a song. Thus the censure
of man would be changed into the praise of the
Highest.' And he concludes with the significant

remark that, since Luther was but a man, there is no reason why Protestantism should remain for ever at the point of enlightenment where he had left it.

Another fragment dates from this time. Although it is but a fragment, and although Lessing soon after pronounced the attempt a fancy which he had far outstripped, yet the fact that he should have undertaken it at all proves how he was at the time engrossed with theological interests. Indeed, he writes himself: 'The best part of my life—happily or unhappily?—fell in a time when writings in defence of Christian truths were, so to speak, the fashion. What wonder, then, that my reading was also directed to them, and that I soon could not rest until I had got hold of and devoured every new production in this department!' This essay, the 'Christianity of Reason' ('*Das Christenthum der Vernunft*'), attempts to prove the Trinitarian doctrine philosophically, after the manner of the speculative theologians whose paths had been prepared by Leibnitz in his attempts to justify belief by raising it to a science. The fragment was never published—a circumstance which shows that Lessing attached no value to it ; but it deserves mention on account of the attempt that has been made upon the strength of it, to prove him an orthodox thinker. Far more likely does it appear that the paper was written as a polemical exercise, such as Lessing loved, and that he tried to rehabilitate Christianity as he had rehabilitated Cardan, &c. Throughout life he regarded himself as the defender of the persecuted, and Christianity was then suffering much from friends and foes ; and that he abandoned the attempt is equally in keeping with his intellectual character, for his theological reading soon showed him the weakness of the defenders of the faith,

and how such defences betray the cause they would
serve.   He saw that religion was a matter of feeling,
not of reason, and this gave him an isolated position
with respect to his contemporaries.   He continued to
consider himself a Christian, but his Christianity was so
large that it could include Deism, if Deism were only
tolerant.   Fearless investigation, historical and logical
criticism without limit and without end, was his theological faith.  When, having explored the most abstruse
corners of theology, he found that they only stored
mildew and dust, he turned away to more living fields
of interest, until late in life, with matured judgment
and increased erudition, he once more resumed the
study, and proved himself the most ardent polemic
that ever raised the standard of enlightenment.

These religious studies did not, however, absorb
all his time at Wittenberg.   His favourite Roman
poets again engaged his attention, and more particularly Martial, whose epigrams incited him to independent endeavours in this field.  The faculty of expressing
ideas with condensed brilliancy and unexpected turns
of phrase was natural to Lessing, and shows that his
mind was most un-German ; for this concise form of
expression is almost foreign to his countrymen.
Lessing loved it and cultivated it with great care.
His prose as well as his verse bears this stamp.   He
was singularly happy in his steely brevity, and the
vistas of ideas which he could open out in a few
words.   His brother relates that at Wittenberg his
thoughts were so occupied with this graceful structure
of speech, that he would express himself in epigrams.
He made a thorough study of the subject and read all
the ancient and modern epigrammatists, besides translating, adapting, and originating.   His epigrams are

of various merit ; they handle the unexpected with
vivacity, vigour, and delicacy, but their aim is rarely
loftier than *persiflage*, and their salt not always Attic.
Horace was another writer whom he studied with care,
in concert with Theophilus, whose interests lay in this
direction, and who afterwards became known as a re-
spectable Latin poet. Together they began a Latin
rendering of Klopstock's ' Messiah,' intended as a
vindication of Klopstock, who had been severely
attacked by some critics for obscurity of thought.
Lessing wished to show by a Latin version that this
was not so absolutely the case. The ungrateful task
was fortunately abandoned before they had advanced
far, on hearing that it had already been undertaken
by a Dane.

Lessing's study of Horace, on the other hand, involved him in a quarrel that extended over two years,
gave birth to one of his bitterest polemics, and made
his name feared far and wide. This refined, graceful
lyrist, with his loose loves, his liking for quiet country
life, is, says Goethe, as modern as any modern. Lessing recognised this quality and was attracted by it.
When, therefore, while at Wittenberg, he saw a long
promised translation of the Odes announced as published, he devoured it eagerly, having been led to
expect much from the translator, a clergyman of the
name of Lange, who was cried up as the German
Horace, and to whose poems Lessing had given some
attention at Leipzig. Knowing that the author had
laboured nine years at his translation, Lessing was
justified in expecting good work, and great was his
amazement to find his anticipations of pleasure changed
to intense astonishment at the incredible schoolboy
faults which disfigured it.

Lessing mentioned this in a letter to Professor Nicolai, of Halle, whose acquaintance he had made that March, and added that he was not ill-disposed to warn the public against this translation. Nicolai, who was a friend of Lange's, and who was sufficiently acquainted with Lessing's critical prowess, was alarmed for the pastor's reputation, and wrote to Lessing warning him to desist from his project on the score that Lange had court interest. He advised him to write privately to Lange, offering to point out the faults in consideration of payment. Lessing wrote an ironical acquiescence in this proposal, which he never regarded as serious ; Nicolai took it in earnest, and it resulted in a mischievous report, credited and published by Lange, that Lessing was willing to suppress his criticisms for a pecuniary consideration. This exasperated him beyond measure. His good name had now been twice attacked. It was high time he should free himself from the unenviable character of a literary freebooter who only lived on quarrels and defamations. After a protest in the ' Voss Gazette ' against the coarse personal attack of Lange, he published (1754) his ' *Vademecum for Pastor S. G. Lange*,' in which he bestowed on his adversary a certainly well-deserved but somewhat rude lesson in Latinity, annihilating him in an insulting manner which the provocation alone can excuse. He concludes with an account of his correspondence with Professor Nicolai, expressing his disgust at having been thought capable of levying black mail. Sorely though he needed money, the manner of gaining it, he said, was not indifferent to him. As an example of the personal manner in which literary differences were, and occasionally still are, conducted in Germany, the ' *Vademecum*' is curious, and also as a proof of Lessing's philological attainments. His panegyrists see in it a masterpiece of negative criticism ; his friends regret that he should have degraded himself to use the most vulgar weapons of satire ; and it is just to his memory to add that if he employed the heavy artillery of abuse against his adversary, he himself desired that his criticism should only live as long as the translation that had evoked it, for he acknowledged that it did him no great honour. It was his ' English Bards and Scotch Reviewers,' and it is to be regretted in each case that both amber and fly have survived.

But matters had not yet reached this point when Lessing quitted Wittenberg, in December 1752, having taken his degree as Doctor in Philosophy. He had worked all this year in industrious seclusion ; his natural liveliness and liking for a wider sphere made him again crave for his Berlin life. He therefore returned thither, once more without the consent or knowledge of his parents.

# CHAPTER VI.

'Εξίει δ' ὥσπερ κυβερνάτας ἀνὴρ"Ιστιον ἀνεμόεν.

*'Loose free ; like a mariner, thy sail unto the wind.'*—PINDAR.

ON Lessing's return to Berlin, he at once resumed
his position on the ' Voss Gazette,' to the dismay of
his father, who as usual laid the blame on Mylius.
Lessing vainly protested that, as he would have returned to Berlin in any case, his literary endeavours
and those of Mylius should in no way be confounded.
It took some time to convince Pastor Lessing, who
held journalists, playwriters, and comedians in the
same abhorrence, though personally he liked above
all things to read the newspapers. But gradually
and imperceptibly Lessing's reputation increased ; his
quarrel with Pastor Lange drew upon him the attention of learned Germany ; truth and talent were declared on his side, and the accomplished Michaelis of
Göttingen publicly complimented the young controversialist. Lessing was much gratified by praise from
such a quarter. His letter in reply to Michaelis' personal inquiries regarding him is highly characteristic.
After briefly narrating the main incidents of his life,
he adds :

' I have studied in the *Fürstenschule* at Meissen
and afterwards at Leipzig and Wittenberg. I should

be greatly perplexed if I were asked what. I have
been in Berlin since 1748, during which time I only for
half a year resided elsewhere. I seek no promotion
here ; I only live here because I cannot live in any
other large place. If I add my age, which amounts
to twenty-five years, my biography is ended. What
will come yet, I leave to Providence. I scarcely think
anyone could be more indifferent to the future than
I am.'

It is natural that his father should not share this
indifference, and could not see whither his son's erratic
plans of life were to lead ; but he grew mollified when
he read the praises of erudite professors, and heard
that his poems were found on the tables of ladies ;
and his satisfaction increased when, shortly after Gotthold's return to Berlin, he received the first volume
of the Wittenberg writings, and a republication of his
' Trifles.'

' Thus are authors,' says Lessing in the preface.
' The public gives them an inch and they take an ell.'
His first efforts having met with success, he again
submits to the final and most decisive test of print,
and concludes with the remark that if these volumes
meet with encouragement, he reserves other and more
important matters for publication.

The volumes contained the fragment, ' Samuel
Henzi,' a bold attempt to treat dramatically a contemporary historical incident. Its worth was hailed
by the critics. The execution by the Bernese oli-
garchy of the patriot Henzi, the hero of the Berne
insurrection in 1749, had awakened Lessing's deep
interest, and revealed to him the discrepancies that
exist between burgher freedom and privileged despotism. He admits that he might have retained the

incidents and changed the names and times ; the fact
that he did not, shows that he was beginning to
assert his independence.  The fragment, modelled on
Otway's ' Venice Preserved,' also betrays the influence
of Shakespeare's ' Julius Cæsar ; ' and though the
cumbersome Alexandrines and the almost violent
preservation of the Unities show him still held in
traditional bondage, the audacity of the theme, and
the significant preface that though great spirits may
disregard established rules, it is not well for beginners
to be too hasty in subverting them, affords an augury
of speedy enfranchisement.

These three years at Berlin are among the happiest in Lessing's life.  Plunging with joyous ardour
into the most varied branches of literary creation, he
had the satisfaction of obtaining not only the recognition, but in most cases the friendship, of the best
minds of his country.  True, his resources were of the
meagrest, and he was compelled to have recourse to
much literary hack-work to eke out his means and to
give himself due leisure for original production ; but
he always endeavoured that these labours should
enlarge his knowledge, or in some indirect manner
touch his deepest interests.  Among them are a translation of the Spaniard Huarte's striking but wildly
hypothetical work, the ' Trial of Wits.'  Its flashes
of penetration, that anticipate some of Gall's discoveries, its striking and suggestive paradoxes, fascinated Lessing, and he issued it with critical notes.
His ever living interest in all champions of mental
freedom made him continue his studies of Cardan,
and project works on Giordano Bruno and Campa-
nella, and the translation from the Dutchman Bekker's
' *De Betooverde Weereld*,'—the famous work that

G

drew odium on its author for daring to combat the
prevalent notions respecting the influence of evil
spirits, and the unjust theological and juridical persecution of witches and magicians. For this work Lessing had amassed a number of additional materials.

Indeed the list of all these hack labours, projected,
executed, or commenced, speak of his stupendous
industry. He was beginning to feel himself easier
both in a pecuniary and social position, and could
offer to relieve his parents by taking charge of a
younger brother. The consent accorded proves that
Pastor Lessing had at last regained confidence in
Gotthold. That the arrangement had speedily to be
abandoned because the little brother, fresh from
Camenz, would never have done gaping with wonder
at the sights of Berlin, was not Lessing's fault. He
had hoped time would blunt the edge of novelty ;
but the boy was too well off in his brother's company,
and had to be consigned to stricter hands.

Three months after Lessing's return to Berlin,
Mylius had been entrusted with a scientific mission to
America, which was frustrated by his death in London. Lessing was asked to edit his fugitive writings.
His criticisms of Mylius' literary worth, wherein
he assigned a low place to productions that had
sprung from no higher principle or motive than that
of securing daily bread, occasioned some surprise
among those who had known him as Mylius' friend,
and provoked Schönaich's epigram, that such treatment from friends he wished to his enemies. Professor
Kästner taunted Lessing with the remark that such a
memoir from anyone else would have brought him
into the field with a rehabilitation. Lessing felt the
justice of the criticism ; but he esteemed exact truth,

even if not palatable, above all else ; he should feel it
against his conscience, he explains, to flatter in death
one who had always heard the truth from him.  He
replied to Kästner, October 16, 1754 :

'Etrange monument, disez-vous, peut-être, et j'en
conviens.  Pourquoi me l'a-t-on extorqué ?  On voulut
absolument un recueil de ses pièces fugitives et sur-
tout de ses poésies, et le voilà donc.  Sans ma préface
il ne manquerait pas de charmer M. Gottsched.  Mais
jugez vous-même, si je n'ai pas bien fait de sauver les
mânes de Mylius de la honte d'être loué par cet op-
probre des gens d'esprit.'

Lessing had now a congenial circle of acquaintances about him, and he formed some of the firmest
friendships of his life.  With all his industry he found
ample time for the social and human intercourse which
his restless spirit needed.  In his very small lodging,
hard by St. Nicholas' churchyard, would be found
assembled many a merry little party, persons of the
most varied occupations as well as all manner of
opinions, which they freely ventilated.  There was Professor Kies, the astronomer, a lively witty little man ;
Brückner, an apprentice at the 'Voss Gazette' office,
who evinced marked histrionic talent ; Kirnberger, the
erudite musical theorist and violin player to the King ;
Meil, the engraver ; Sulzer, the eclectic philosopher and
professor of mathematics, the first critical writer on
art who aimed at popularity ; Ramler, the correct
lyrist, then professor of *belles-lettres* ; Prémontval,
the French thinker, an opponent to the Wolffian philosophy generally professed in this society.  A truly
eclectic gathering and after Lessing's own heart.

But these were only acquaintances ; there were also
closer ties.  In Nicolai and Moses Mendelssohn he

found two growing minds which he might have moulded into disciples had he desired, and one of whom, Mendelssohn, unquestionably owed his public distinction to Lessing. The acquaintanceship deepened into a life-long intimacy ; and though in the course of years their mental paths diverged somewhat, this remained practically unbroken until the death of Lessing, whom Mendelssohn speedily followed, dying of over excitement in excess of zeal for his friend's memory.

After Frederick the Great's accession the Berlin Jews began to evince the capacity and zeal for culture that made them a little later the focus of the city's intellectual life ; but even this most tolerant of monarchs could not learn to regard them as equal to his other subjects. The laws were no less hostile to them than were the conventional traditions. Among the few who had emancipated themselves was Dr. Gumpertz, a physician, and successively secretary to d'Argens and Maupertius. He knew Lessing, they often played chess together, and he one day introduced to him a little nervous deformed Jew as an excellent player. It is doubtful whether there was much chess-playing after that : Lessing at once recognised the spirit that was here struggling for liberation ; each found in the other complementary qualities ; Lessing's strong clear nature, sanguine temperament and inquisitiveness, imparted self-reliant strength to the timid, meditative Oriental dreamer, while the latter's just sense and modest wisdom often moderated Lessing's propensity to paradox. His life-history was further calculated to rouse the interest of one who loved the outcast and persecuted.

Moses Mendelssohn was the son of a Hebrew

schoolmaster, who, notwithstanding his poverty, gave his boy a good elementary training, especially in Rabbinical and Hebrew lore. A treatise of Maimonides first awoke independent thoughts in the boy, and led him to study so strenuously, that it induced the nervous spinal disease, the consequences of which he never overcame. The extreme indigence of his parents forced him to wander away from Dessau at the tender age of thirteen, a homeless beggar, heavily weighted by the Jewish stigma in the struggle for existence. Notwithstanding all disadvantages he fought a brave fight with the world, educated himself in Latin, mathematics, and German (a study forbidden by the Hebrew congregation), and pondered the systems of Wolff and Leibnitz. He earned a trifle by copying for Rabbis; but when they found him one day carrying a German book across the street, they expelled him from the community. He nevertheless continued to **learn** German, and remained a scrupulously ceremonious Jew. A Jewish family engaged him as tutor, and he afterwards became a clerk, and later a partner in their silk manufactory.

When Lessing first knew him he was just twenty-four years old, and still a busy clerk, only able to devote his early mornings or late evenings to study. Lessing initiated him into Greek, lent him books, and soon it was an established thing that Mendelssohn should come to Lessing's lodging every morning between seven and nine, when they discussed all manner of philosophical and literary subjects. Their very differences were matters of delight to Lessing's disputatious spirit, that always learnt most from friendly opposition. Mendelssohn became in after years the emancipator of his people from prejudiced opprobrium;

they prize him so greatly that it is a current saying among them that 'from Moses to Moses there was none like Moses;' and, even allowing for the pardonable partiality of race, his mental development and achievements are sufficiently remarkable. Lessing's clear insight foresaw his worth. He wrote at this time:

' I regard him in advance as an honour to his nation. His probity and his philosophical spirit make me consider him in advance as a second Spinoza, who wants nothing save his errors for perfect equality.'

Lessing's faith in his powers gave Mendelssohn the confidence he had hitherto lacked, and spurred him to independent action. Upon Lessing's lending him an essay of Shaftesbury's, and asking him how he liked it, Mendelssohn ventured to reply, ' Well enough, but I could do such a thing too.' ' Indeed,' said Lessing, ' then do write something of the kind.' In due course Mendelssohn brought his MS., but never dared ask Lessing's opinion, which was not vouchsafed, until a few weeks later Lessing gave it him back in print: the most practical answer conceivable.

Shortly after the formation of this friendship, the Academy of Berlin propounded as its prize essay the theme 'Whether Pope's maxim, "Whatever is, is right," was designed to convey the same philosophical meaning as Leibnitz's "Best of all possible worlds."' Lessing perceived the absurdity of such a proposition; was this projected comparison to prove Pope's saying the more philosophical, or Leibnitz's the more poetical ? He persuaded Mendelssohn to help him to write a refutation ; the essay, with its ironical title, ' Pope a Metaphysician !' was the result. The main idea was the establishment of a fundamental difference between philosophy and poetry. Lucretius was a versifier, not a poet ; no doubt a philosophy can be rhymed, but such rhymes will not be a poem. Pope himself could not have claimed to be a philosopher on the strength of the ' Essay on Man ;' he only versified borrowed ideas, as he expresses in his letter to Swift, who had not recognised his hand in the work : ' I have only one piece of mercy to beg of you : do not laugh at my gravity, but permit me to wear the beard of a philosopher, till I pull it off and make a jest of it myself.' ' What,' ask the essayists, ' would Pope have said when he found that a learned Academy mistook his false beard for a real one ? '

The condemnation of didactic poetry, the accurate erudition displayed, are clearly Lessing's, while the philosophical dress must be ascribed to Mendelssohn. This satirical production, that made the Academy ridiculous, could not be submitted for a prize ; but it is recorded that its publication called forth some Academical blushes. Lessing was far from undervaluing Pope. He saw that he must be judged as an artificial poet living in an artificial period, which it was his great merit to reproduce ; and though this is not the highest form of genius, still it is one of its manifestations. Poetry is speech appealing to the senses ; therefore to claim from a poet a metaphysical system is absurd.

' His great, I will not say greatest, merit lay in what we call the mechanism of poetry.' Consequently, when he found a subject like the ' Rape of the Lock ' level with his genius he could make of it one of the most perfect poems of his language.

The interest which both Mendelssohn and Lessing showed in English literature was shared by Christian F. Nicolai. He was the son of a Berlin bookseller, and trained for the trade ; but his refined tastes and

extensive reading made him aspire to authorship.
He was brother to Professor Nicolai, from whom he had
received some classical teaching, and his father's shop
enabled him to muster all the products of contemporary literature. Lessing's daily contributions to the
' Voss Gazette ' were eagerly perused by him, and inspired his first attempt, a review of current *belles-
lettres*, a creditable work for a youth of twenty.
Lessing saw the proof sheets and desired to make his
personal acquaintance. Nicolai was at that time the
only man in Germany with whom Lessing could har-
monise with regard to German literature. Both of
them owed their cultured basis to English influences.

English literature had been the support round
which German ideas had twined for the last half
century ; the fresh breezy instincts of individuality pervaded it ; every Englishman, according to Goethe,
dared to have a heart of his own in his breast. The
Germans were anxious to be on the right side, but
hampered by self-consciousness and over-sensitive-
ness of opinion. This made them pull up their productions by the roots to see if they were growing, and
produced a code of rules collected from masterpieces,
with which rules they demanded masterpieces should
be made. It was the cart put before the horse.

Lessing had always protested against the reigning
French taste, but until now he had been influenced by
it in spite of himself ; he had always pointed to English models, but he had not yet shown wherein they
excelled. His intercourse with Nicolai gave his views
greater precision, and conjointly they gave them
written expression as far as the drama was concerned
in the ' *Theatralische Bibliothek*,' a kind of combination
of the earlier undertaking with Mylius.

The Horatian-Lange dispute was waging in full fury in 1754, and aroused Lessing to write a more direct vindication of his favourite poet than the '*Vade-mecum.*' 'The Rehabilitation of Horace' resulted, a short essay that contains, *more suo*, far more food for reflexion than appears at first sight.

'For the credit of the ancient writers I am a veritable knight-errant ; my gall'rises instantly when I see them so miserably ill-used.' What he principally attempted was the moral justification of Horace, who had been accused of immorality, cowardice, and irreligion. Lessing refutes these accusations with philological penetration and acute criticism, without wielding the heavy controversial weapons of his earlier work. The chief point of his argument is, that we should not accept everything that the poet says as plain, blunt truth. 'The greater the poet, the farther removed from strict veracity will be the casual mention he makes of himself. . . . . The true poet knows that he must adorn everything in its own fashion, and accordingly himself also, and sometimes he does this so cunningly that dull eyes see a confession of his faults where the connoisseur discerns a touch of his flattering pencil.' Thus Horace's self-accusation of irreligion and immorality is no more to be taken literally than the 'miserable sinners' of the theologians.

A farce that appeared in Leipzig about this time, called '*Gnissel,*' Lessing's name spelt backwards, shows how universally he was known and feared. The play is the miserable revenge of a Gottschedian on one of Lessing's reviews, and Lessing thought it sufficient to reprint it and distribute it gratis in Berlin.

In 1754 Lessing issued his seven juvenile dramas

in a reprint.   Of these only the ' Jews ' and the ' Freethinker ' can now attract attention ; and this more for
their tendency than as works of art.   The ' Jews ' has
too much the character of a thesis put into action ; as
a play it is weak, but its composition was a great
moral achievement.   The hero has accidentally
benefited a family, who are anxious to show him
some marks of gratitude.   He repels all their advances and desires to quit their domains, while they
attempt to retain him.   He will not give his name,
the real fact being that he is a Jew, a fact Lessing
cleverly manages  to hold back until the hero's
generous character has won public sympathy.   The
culminating point is the terrible avowal of his religion :
he is a social outcast whom no Christian will receive,
though he be their benefactor.   ' The Jews would be
estimable if they all resembled you !' exclaims the
Baron, abashed at the lesson he has received.   The
critics justly objected to this play on its appearance,
that its hero was the Jew of a poet's phantasy ; the
picture would have been truer, the lesson more instructive, if, instead of making his Jew a perfect character,
Lessing had shown how the treatment of Christians
tends to embitter and vitiate the Jewish character, and
that the Christians are thus really answerable for the
vices they condemn.

The ' Freethinker ' (' *Der Freigeist* ') was no doubt
the play which should redeem Lessing's promise to his
father that he would write a comedy which ' the theologians would not only read, but even praise.'   The
hero is a shallow young man who refuses to believe
that any good can exist in the ancient theological
forms, because he has himself recently stripped off
their bondage.   This prejudice is overcome by a worthy

pastor, whose disinterested kindness and personal rectitude convince the bigoted freethinker, much against his will, that a clergyman is not necessarily a Pharisee.

The studies of English drama Lessing conducted together with Nicolai, and the republication of his early plays again stimulated the theatrical interests that had lain dormant awhile. But the social and literary distractions of Berlin did not allow him sufficient concentration for creation. He therefore retreated to Potsdam for eight weeks in the early winter of 1755, and brought back with him the finished play, 'Miss Sara Sampson,' a work that marks a period, not only in his writings, but in the development of the national literature. The title, the names of the personages, as well as the place of action, sufficiently announce its source of inspiration. It was in truth a domestic drama after the English pattern. The immediate materials were clearly derived from 'Clarissa Harlowe' and Lillo's 'London Merchant.'

Lillo's dramas consist of a peculiar species of what may be called tragedies of domestic life, an innovation admitted by Lillo when he wrote that the aim and object of tragedy is 'the exciting of the passions in order to the correcting of such of them as are criminal, either in their nature, or through their excess. If princes, &c., were alone liable to misfortunes arising from vice or weakness in themselves or others, there would be good reason for confining the characters in tragedy to those of superior rank' Lillo's plays, like the imitations which they evoked, excited much admiration on the Continent, where class distinctions were more sharply defined. They prompted Lessing to consider whether Aristotle's definition of

the design of tragedy, that it is intended to purge our
passions by means of pity and terror, was of inherent
necessity confined to royalty—whether our interests
can only be roused on behalf of those who stand above
the laws. The conditions of ancient life had limited
tragedy to heroes, as figures who were existent to do
and suffer great things. Tragedy *per se* is dependent
on the exhibition of violent passions producing deep
disasters. Now those actions which move us when
applied to kings, if applied to those who are subject
to the law, are in danger of becoming criminal ; judicial punishment takes the place of grand remorse and
gigantic struggles with inexorable fate ; the mental
conflicts become actual conflicts with the police, and
therefore such burgher tragedies dangerously approach
the verge of bathos. To avoid this, a domestic
tragedy must be based on purely human passions,
and treat conditions peculiar to the class with which
it deals and amid which scope for destructive action
can also be found. Even though these conditions of
force do not produce the very finest tragic cata-
strophes, they as adequately fulfil Aristotle's demand
that tragedy should stimulate pity and fear, while they
are at the same time more natural, and bring home
their effects to the hearths of each spectator.

'The names of princes and heroes may give a piece
pomp and majesty ; but they contribute nothing to
its pathos. The misery of those nearest to us must
naturally affect us most powerfully ; and if we feel
compassion for kings, we feel for them as men and
not as kings. If their rank often makes their misfortunes more important, it does not make them more
interesting. Whole peoples may possibly be involved
in the disaster, and yet our sympathy demands a

single object, and a State is far too abstruse an idea for our feelings.'

The story of ' George Barnwell' is that of a London apprentice who is lured by the artifices of an abandoned woman, and the force of his own passion, into embezzlement, and then into murder, crimes which he expiates on the gallows, that actually appear on the stage. Lessing improved upon his model in avoiding this Newgate element, and treating of the tragedies of domestic life that do not fall within the province of criminal jurisprudence. His hero is an irresolute and dissolute man, Mellefont, whose name is derived from Congreve's 'Double-dealer.' Like his prototype Lovelace, he feels a great aversion to the binding tie of matrimony, but has nevertheless conceived a real affection for the heroine, Sara Sampson, a hyper-romantic and self-torturing Clarissa. She quits home with her lover, believing his protestations that he merely defers his marriage on account of an inheritance. His whereabout is discovered by his old mistress, Marwood, the copy of Lillo's feminine demon, who, after endeavouring to regain her empire over him, and only partially succeeding while in his presence, revenges herself by poisoning her rival at the moment when Sara's father arrives on the scene, intending to forgive his daughter and her lover and bring about a happy solution. Mellefont kills himself over the corpse of Sara, who dying, forgives Marwood for her treachery. The play, which is only read now-a-days for its literary interest, sins by excessive length and tedium, as well as by weak construction. Its catastrophe is not just, in that the impersonation of evil is made to execute the poetic justice, and herself escapes punishment. Nevertheless, it electrified Lessing's contemporaries, and, besides the revolution which its general purpose induced, the fact that it was written in prose opened a new and more natural dramatic vehicle than the long French Alexandrines.

The value which Lessing himself attached to 'Miss Sara Sampson' may be judged by the fact that he undertook what was then a considerable and costly journey to Frankfort-on-the-Oder, to conduct its first scenic representation, which took place in July 1755. Ramler writes to Gleim : 'Lessing's tragedy has been played in Frankfort, and the spectators listened for three and a half hours, sat still like statues and wept.' A young Englishman who heard it, made a bet of 50*l*. that the play was only a translation, and that he would prove it by sending to England for the original. Its democratic tendency did not escape Goethe, who reckoned it among those dramas that increase the moral self-respect of the third estate. He held that its literary revolt against the princes of the stage heralded the political revolution that soon after subverted the thrones of monarchs, and made liberty and equality no longer empty words.

The success of his play, the renewed immediate contact it had afforded him with actors, the circumstance that Brückner had joined a company in Leipzig, combined with his desire to associate again with friends who loved the real stage, led Lessing once again abruptly to quit Berlin. He disappeared suddenly, without a word of farewell, and in October (1755) the 'Voss Gazette' announces that he has removed to Leipzig.

# CHAPTER VII.

## LEIPZIG.

### (1755-1758. AGED 26-29.)

*' To push on is the law of Nature ; and you can no more say to men and to nations, than to children, " Sit still, and don't wear out your shoes.'"*
BULWER, *The Caxtons.*

LEIPZIG was at that period the only town that boasted an established theatre, and a public capable of an intelligent interest in a national drama. Lessing at once fraternized with the comedians, some of whom were old acquaintances, and lived and moved in their sphere as in his student years. Mendelssohn, with whom he kept up a brisk correspondence, twitted him with the partiality for actors into which he himself could not enter, though he would theorize with Lessing on the emotions excited by the drama. He consoled himself with the reflexion that this fancy would not last long. Mendelssohn's letters are touchingly tender and affectionate. He missed his robust friend sorely. Never, he tells him, has he made so many acquaintances as since Lessing left Berlin, and yet never before has he felt such difficulty in occupying his leisure hours. Lessing recommends him to visit Nicolai.

' Do you often see him ?' he asks. ' When I hear that two such dear friends whom I have left in Berlin, are friends also, and intimate friends, I shall hear that which I desire for the good of both.'

Sometimes he writes them letters in common, but to their entreaties that he should return to Berlin he turns a deaf ear. Contact with the stage was once more a necessity. He resumed his friendly relations with Weisse, who had just brought out a new play, also derived from English sources, and who adapted ' Miss Sara Sampson ' for the Leipzig stage.

Lessing had not been long in this dramatic circle before Goldoni's comedies fell into his hands, and interested him deeply, from the fact that their pictures of manners were drawn from the range of everyday life. He studied them exhaustively for treatment in his ' Theatrical Library,' proposed to rewrite ' *L'Ercle Fortunata*,' and produce five new plays by next Easter, promising Mendelssohn that these should for a time be the last. This became yet another of his abandoned projects ; he acknowledges that he must use the first white heat of inspiration, or fresh ideas efface older ones.

An impatient longing for a wider sphere had been gaining ground in Lessing's mind. It was discouraged by Mendelssohn, whose tranquil nature did not need the immediate contact with life. But his remonstrances could not appease Lessing's craving to travel, a craving that must be felt to be understood in all its imperiousness. Lessing held no position to restrain him. He was free, young, strong, and when he heard that a rich merchant of Leipzig had been inquiring of Weisse for a travelling companion, he accepted the post without hesitation. Informing Mendelssohn, he writes, December 8, 1755 :

' I must have left Berlin in a lucky hour. I shall travel, not as a tutor with the burden of a boy entrusted to my care, not according to the directions of an opinionated family, but as the mere companion of one person, who is wanting neither in will nor in means to make the journey as useful and pleasant to me as I could wish to make it for myself. His name is Winkler, his age about the same as mine, his character very good ; and he has neither relations nor friends whose fancies he must consult. He is inclined to leave all arrangements to me ; and thus, really, he will rather travel with me than I with him.'

He was not blind to the fact that his companion was only making the conventional grand tour, and would probably care more to go over much ground and make acquaintance with the kitchens and cellars of foreign countries than with their inhabitants and remarkable objects. But Lessing felt assured that he himself could extract real value out of these wanderings, beside the advantage of a compulsory cessation from his assiduous literary labours. The journey was to commence Easter 1756 ; and Lessing agreed so eagerly that, but for the circumspect care of a friend, he would not even have made a written contract. Winkler was to pay Lessing three hundred thalers a year and all his expenses.

Pending their departure, Lessing prepared himself for his journey by a visit to the art treasures of Dresden, where he unexpectedly met his parents, after a separation of eight years. Their mutual pleasure was so great that they carried him home to Camenz, that brothers and sisters might share the joy of beholding what a stately polished gentleman Gotthold had grown. He remained with them a few weeks, and then resumed his preparatory studies at Dresden. Here he became acquainted with C. G. Heyne, his contemporary in age ; also a pupil of Professors Christ

and Ernesti, then amanuensis to Count Brühl, in whose
library he had become acquainted with Winckelmann.
Heyne was already favourably known to the learned
world by his editions of Tibullus and Epictetus, and
his comprehensive knowledge of antiquity must have
been of scarcely less value to Lessing than the artistic
advice he received from his old master, Christ.

On May 10, 1756, Lessing and Winkler started
on their journey. Their first goal was Holland, regarded at that time as a wonderland of culture and
wealth, that must not be left unvisited in a European
tour. It took the travellers two months to reach
Amsterdam, for travelling was then more deliberate
and thorough than now-a-days. Unfortunately Lessing's journal has been lost. His brother records
that he diligently visited all the art galleries he could,
and even induced his companion to buy a rich collection of engravings. Neither did he lose sight of
his dramatic interests. He tells Nicolai that he has
made some notes on the domestic drama, which he
purposes to send him, and at Hamburg he learned
to know and admire the greatest living German actor,
Conrad Eckhof. Lessing writes to his father that
after they have exhausted the Netherlands they will
cross to England, probably early in October. This
plan was frustrated, because, says Lessing, the King
of Prussia was too great a warrior.

The peace of 1748 had been little better than an
armistice. In August 1756 the Seven Years' War
broke out, and in an instant Saxony was overrun by
the well-exercised Prussians. Troops were levied
and contributions exacted. Leipzig was garrisoned
by Brandenburgers, and the commander billeted on
Winkler. The news filled him with dismay, and they
posted back to Leipzig. Still the idea of the journey

was not at once abandoned. Lessing therefore remained in Winkler's house, waiting for a resumption of the interrupted project : an interruption that grieved him the more, as, from the turn which political affairs were taking, he greatly feared that the hopes he had built on a long absence would be eventually defeated.

The winter passed in an uncertainty peculiarly trying to Lessing. He complains to Mendelssohn that if it did not cost him money, it cost him time, his only and most precious possession. Intercourse with Winkler, which had sustained some rude shocks during their travels, grew more and more precarious as the rich merchant saw the disturbed state of the country ; and when Lessing demanded his salary, or the sum stipulated if the journey were abandoned, Winkler affirmed that war had dissolved their contract, that his unbidden guests cost him enough already, and bade Lessing be satisfied with the free board and lodging enjoyed in his house. An opportunity for an open rupture soon after occurred. The tavern where they dined was frequented by merchants, who freely ventilated their complaints of the Prussian extortions in a tone of bitterness most natural to innocent sufferers. Lessing, who had no contributions to pay, could afford to be unbiassed. He took the part of the King, when he was too unjustly abused, and even lauded some of his acts that could scarcely find favour in Saxon eyes. The ironical wit with which he defended Frederick, and with which the stolid burghers could not cope, enhanced the annoyance which he caused them, and to this he heedlessly put the crowning touch by inviting Major Kleist and some other Prussian officers to join the common dinner-table. The merchants, who regarded the presence of these officers as a restraint on their freedom of conversation, stayed away, and the hostess complained to Winkler that through his fault she was deprived of her best customers. Winkler, instead of pointing out to Lessing that this want of tact had placed him in a dilemma, wrote a note saying that they must part company, and that Lessing must quit the house that day. This forced Lessing to insist on the fulfilment of their contract. Winkler refused to comply with its terms. The matter gave rise to a lawsuit, decided seven years later in Lessing's favour; but meanwhile he found himself suddenly houseless and penniless, chased from his employment as a partisan of the King of Prussia, and doubly suspected as the author of pamphlets on the Prussian and the Saxon sides : 'An absurd accusation, which either proves me the most unbiassed man in the world, or the most abominable sophist.' The name of patriot was the last he affected : of the patriot, that is to say, who forgets that he is a citizen of the whole world as well as of his native land.

But such imputations increased his difficulties. Whither should he turn for resources? The theatre had succumbed under the ills of war; there only remained his untiring pen and invincible courage, for he was completely thrown back into his former position. Mendelssohn implored him to cease his restless cravings for variety of scene, and settle down contentedly in his garden-house, where he could work undisturbed amid loving friends. In vain; Lessing could not tamely settle down.

The year that ensued (from May 1757 to May 1758) was one of dire need, and a hand-to-hand ‑

struggle with poverty, little removed from his first
Berlin experiences, and, for all Lessing's brave heart,
there were times when dejection mastered him. Recourse was yet again had to literary hack work.
'What would you?' he replies to remonstrances on
this point. 'They are the productions of a man who
is an author partly by inclination, partly by force.
What can I do? I cannot study at my own expense,
so I try to do so at the expense of the public.' He
translated Richardson's 'Familiar Letters for the Use
of Young People.' To please his sister, who was a
sworn enemy of all worldly levities, and who had
often begged him to do 'some really serious work.'
he also began a translation of William Law's 'Serious
Call to a Devout Life,' but his leaving Weisse to
finish it looks as if it had not exercised over him
the charm it had for Dr. Johnson, who held this book
'the first occasion of his thinking in earnest of religion
after he became capable of rational inquiry.' More
to Lessing's taste was Hutcheson's 'System of Moral
Philosophy.' While rejecting its fundamental doctrines as undefined and vacillating, he and Mendelssohn both admired some detached portions. Lessing
still inclined with his friend to the emotional theories
of the English, but his practical common sense applied them to everyday use.

Nicolai had started a literary journal, whose publication was removed from Berlin to Leipzig, owing
to the war disturbances. It was edited by Nicolai;
Lessing attended to press details. The opening paper
was an essay on Tragedy. This became a starting-
point for an important correspondence between the
three friends, Lessing, Mendelssohn, and Nicolai on
dramatic poetry. Lessing based his inquiries on the

emotional theory ; and as his thoughts, as he himself
tells, ripened under his pen, this correspondence, which
contains the germ of his ' *Dramaturgie*,' first made
clear to himself the essence and purpose of the
drama.

He considers that Nicolai has rather strained Aristotle's axiom that the moral end of tragedy is to
excite the pity of the spectators. Not only their pity,
contends Lessing, but their sympathy. He blames
the indiscriminate rendering of the Aristotelian φόβος
now by terror, now by fear. No one who has not
read the second book of the Rhetoric and the Nico-
machean Ethics can understand Aristotle's Poetics.
According to Aristotle's interpretation φόβος is simply fear, and he says that those things cause fear in
us, which, if we saw them in others, would awaken
sympathy, and those things awaken sympathy, which,
if they were impending over ourselves, would provoke
fear. Therefore, Aristotle's fear is not an immediate
effect of tragedy, but a reflected idea, inasmuch as a
tragedy does not represent evils impending over ourselves.

'Aristotle would only have said, tragedy is to
purify our passions by sympathy, if he had not intended at the same time to point out the means
which make this purification by sympathy possible, and
he therefore adds fear, which he regards as this means.
The former proposition is correct, the latter false.
Sympathy undoubtedly purifies our passions, but not
by means of fear.' It does so by enlarging man's
narrow individuality into the wider self of all mankind. Lessing adduces an example from physics.

' It is well known that if two strings have an equal
tension, and the one is sounded by touch, the other

sounds also without being touched. Let us imagine the strings to have feeling, and assume that every vibration would be agreeable to them, but not every touch. Thus the first string which vibrates at the touch may have a painful sensation, while the other, in spite of similar vibration, may experience a pleasant sensation, because it is not touched, at least not so immediately. Thus also in tragedy. The personage represented experiences an unpleasant emotion, and I with him. But why is the emotion in me a pleasant one? Because I am not the immediate sufferer of the unpleasant emotion; I experience the emotion merely as emotion, without at the same time thinking of any particular unpleasant matter. Such secondary emotions caused by seeing these emotions in others, hardly deserve the name of emotions, therefore I have already said in one of my first letters that tragedy does not really call forth any emotion but sympathy.'

' The representation of unpleasant emotions pleases for the reason that they awaken in us similar emotions, not directed to any definite object. The musician makes me sad ; and this sadness is agreeable to me, because I experience it merely as an emotion, and every emotion is agreeable.'

Referring to the stilted plays founded on super-lative perfections, he says: 'A rope-dancer is ad-mired but not pitied. In proportion as our aston-ishment increases, our sympathy diminishes. . . . If the whole art of the poet tends to the deeper excitement and duration of individual sympathy, I say the object of tragedy is this : to enlarge our capa-bility of sympathizing. The sympathetic man is the best man, the most inclined to all forms of generosity and to all social virtues.'

Of Comedy he writes : 'It is to help us to a readiness in perceiving the ridiculous in all its manifestations. Whoever possesses this readiness will seek to avoid the ridiculous in his behaviour, and thus he will acquire polish and refinement. Thus we may establish the use of comedy.'

Nicolai, who could afford to play Mæcenas, an attitude of which· he grew dangerously enamoured, announced a competitive prize for the best modern tragedy. Lessing was chosen arbiter. A tragedy by von Cronegh obtained the first prize, and one by von Brawe the second. Lessing had taken great interest in both productions, and had indeed given substantial assistance to von Brawe. When, by a singular coincidence, both these young poets died, the one before, the other shortly after the adjudication, Lessing begged Nicolai to repeat his offer, intending to enter the list himself, but secretly.

'A young man is working here at a tragedy,' he writes to Nicolai, 'which might perhaps prove the best of all if he could devote a few months' time to it. Its theme is burgher tragedy, and its title "Emilia Galotti." '

But this play, then first contemplated, was not finished till fifteen years later. Lessing's Leipzig life was too distracting for original production. For with all its hardships, it had some pleasant social compensations. Among the Prussian officers whom Lessing had indiscreetly introduced as bombshells among the Saxon merchants, was Ewald Christian von Kleist, whose enthusiastic admiration for Frederick the Great had induced him to abandon poetry, in which he had acquitted himself respectably, and adopt a profession otherwise uncongenial to him.

Shortly after his arrival at Leipzig he was taken ill. His indisposition was chiefly mental. He was hypochondriacal, and his having been placed at Leipzig in charge of the hospital, instead of going into active service, preyed on his mind. Lessing, who knew him to be a friend of Nicolai's, visited him. Very soon the tenderest friendship sprang up between them. Kleist wrote to Gleim that he owed his recovery to Lessing's cheerful intercourse. He would comfort him with a quotation from the 'Cyropaedia,' that the bravest men are also the most compassionate ; and certainly if his axioms did not reconcile Kleist to Leipzig, his society did. After Kleist's recovery, the two rode out together. Then Weisse was also introduced, and von Brawe, and soon a merry little party was assembled every evening in Kleist's rooms, who talked of German literary interests in midst of the din of a war that first created a German national spirit.

Kleist, who was fourteen years Lessing's senior, was anxious to help him to a secured means of support; for he not only saw the straits to which his friend was reduced, but gave him actual assistance. Indeed, but for his help and Mendelssohn's, Lessing would have had a yet harder struggle during this disturbed time, when literary interests naturally paled before political. Kleist tried to obtain for Lessing some state appointment, some librarianship ; he thought the King of Prussia ought to have shown himself grateful to such a zealous ally. But Frederick, though he made war on the King of France, was not the less French in spirit, and it was no passport to his favour for a young man to have attacked his favourite literature. Nor did he believe in German literature.

He judged the German genius by Gottsched, whom he had, when at Leipzig, admitted to an interview, wherein he challenged him to defend the roughness of German speech, and vindicate it by translating a French stanza into moderately soft language. The result was that the royal poet shrugged his shoulders disdainfully. But by presenting Gottsched with a golden snuff-box the King so gratified his inordinate vanity, that he did not perceive his ill success. This snuff-box provoked a poem from Lessing. 'What can it mean?' he asks in Gottsched's person, 'that the golden box King Frederick gave me is full of hellebore instead of ducats?' It was therefore vain to expect aid from such a King, even had Lessing not offended both Voltaire and the Berlin Academy.

'You see what harm this war has done me,' writes Lessing to Ramler. 'I and the King of Prussia will have a big account to settle. I am only waiting for peace. Since he, and he alone, is to blame that I have not seen the world, would it not be fair for him to give me a pension to help me forget the world? You think he will take care not to do so. I think so too ; but, in return, my wish for him shall be that none but bad verses may be made on his victories.'

Lessing was better than his wishes. He was the first to give publicity to the only really good verses which this war had inspired. On his own responsibility he inserted in Nicolai's Journal the 'War Songs of a Prussian Grenadier.' Lessing suspected that Gleim was their author, though the poems had not come to him direct. Gleim, as secretary to the Chapter of Halberstadt, was able to devote much time to poetry. His generous hospitality, together with his

patronage of young literary aspirants, earned him
the surname of Father Gleim. He and Lessing had
already met at Berlin, but their acquaintanceship had
improved during some flying visits which Gleim had
paid to Kleist, and was strengthened by their common admiration for the King. Gleim had many
sympathies which Lessing could not share, and he
had not up to that time admired his somewhat lachry-
mose writings, but the war had roused his muse to a
manlier tone, which Lessing instantly appreciated. He
saw that these lyrics possessed the essential attributes
for war songs, that the very march of the numbers
suggested their martial origin. Without actually
saying so, he lets Gleim infer that he has penetrated
his *incognito*.

'Just imagine the impudence of your King's
soldiers ; they will soon want to write the best verses
because they know best how to conquer. What unbounded ambition ! A few days ago I received from
Berlin a war song, with the comment that it was composed by a common soldier, who was going to make
one for every regiment. To think that a man, a common soldier, who doubtless never learnt poetry as a
trade, nor has served his time to it, should dare to
make such excellent verses!'

These poems made a great impression on Lessing.
A year after he published them in a collected form,
and prefaced them with an essay on the nature of
war songs in general, for which purpose he had read
up much early lore. The poems had indubitably
made clear to him that lyrics, and indeed all poetry,
must be inspired by real life, must deal with feelings
as manifested in actions, and have individual and
national truth ; and he recognized a modern Tyrtaeus

in Gleim, whom he compared favourably with the
Norse skalds and the true Germanic bards.

Meanwhile Lessing's political leanings, and the
vicinity of Leipzig to the scene of action, made the
city more and more intolerable to him. He began to
long for Berlin, 'where I shall no longer need to
whisper to my acquaintances that, for all that and all
that, the King of Prussia is a great King.' To this
was added the dissolution of the pleasant coterie.
Brawe died, Weisse could not in the long run compen-
sate for his two Berlin friends, and when at length
Kleist was called into the field, the last link that held
him to Leipzig snapped. Both deeply felt the parting which was to prove eternal.

'I have grown so used to Lessing,' writes Kleist,
'and love him so, that I feel as if he were dead, or
rather as if I were half dead without him.'

The Berlin friends, on their part, as warmly welcomed him back, when in May 1758 he again took up
his abode among them.

# CHAPTER VIII.

## THIRD BERLIN RESIDENCE.

### (1758-1760. AGED 29-31.)

*'Weite Welt und breites Leben,*
*Langer Jahre redlich Streben,*
*Stets geforscht und stets gegründet,*
*Nie geschlossen, nie geründet,*
*Aeltestes bewahrt mit Treue,*
*Freundlich aufgefasstes Neue,*
*Heitern Sinn und reine Zwecke,*
*Nun! man kommt wohl eine Strecke.'*—GOETHE.

THOUGH Lessing hated war, and his development was to all appearance independent of the political conditions of his time, this state of military ferment was destined to become an active agent in his history. He found a very different Berlin from the one he had quitted. 'The upstart of Brandenburg,' as his enemies called him, by his military exploits was raising his sandy kingdom to the dignity of a European power. The Prussian capital felt itself the focus of a novel movement. The glory of its army was reflected upon it, and demanded that the people should do honour to the prestige which it was earning for Prussia. Lessing had imbibed some of this elevated atmosphere in the society of the enthusiastic soldier-poet, Kleist. At Berlin he found his friends ardent adherents of the King, and, with his ever living sympathy, he also was

infected by this universal agitation. But more
guardedly, and with a different end in view. He saw
that this awakening to the sense of collective national
life might beget an understanding for national literature, but he recognised that such demands at such a
time should be as concrete, terse, and emphatic as the
military energy that had kindled them. Journals like
Nicolai's, filled with long-winded philosophical disquisitions, might suit 'the piping times of peace,' but
this rapid, anxious, bellicose season needed something
bolder and more resolute.

The result was the 'Letters concerning Contemporary Literature' (*Briefe die neueste Literatur betreffend*)
that became a literary war manifesto, and brought
about nothing less than a revolution in criticism.
Lessing wished to strengthen the nascent self-reliance
of his nation, to clear out the Augean stable of German literature, and he felt in himself the Herculean
strength necessary to the task. The Letters staggered
his contemporaries, but they finally compelled their
respectful, then their admiring attention. They were
written for ordinary readers, not for a narrow, learned
coterie, nor did they claim to be regular reviews.
They were simply excursions into the literary realm,
and their pre-eminent merit was, that they were productive, not destructive, criticism.

The very name of these Literary Letters has become
so identified with that of Lessing, that it must be
enforced that not until after his death was his real connexion with them ascertained, though people soon
began to suspect that in such incisive reviews the critic
militant Lessing must have a hand. But the full extent of his share in them, and the certain knowledge
what letters really issued from his pen, or from his co-

labourers Nicolai and Mendelssohn, has only been recently established. Anonymity was then in great favour, and Lessing in this instance had an additional motive for adopting it, in his unwillingness that the influence of his periodical should be impaired by even the suspicion of party spirit. He had for some time desired an organ wherein he could express his own views. The actual opportunity came from Nicolai, who, by the death of his father and brother, had become the head of his firm, and could therefore publish at his own discretion. Abandoning the Leipzig paper to Weisse's editorship, he desired to found another in Berlin.

One day in November (1758) he was in Lessing's room, discussing contemporary journalism and condemning it for its partisanship and insipidity. 'We have so often said we should write as we speak,' said Nicolai. The idea pleased Lessing. He pursued it farther, and finally the plan was started of founding a periodical that should abandon all abstract theoretical criticisms, examine new works with all the frankness of conversation, and only demand from the works what they would express or had actually accomplished. To make this the easier, the epistolary form was chosen. . The letters were to appear irregularly, according to the needs of the subject ; and, in order to connect them with the war that was exciting all minds, they were to be written for the diversion of a fictitious wounded officer, who desired to be kept *au fait* of current literature. Kleist was in Lessing's thoughts. All the first letters are from his pen. It was only later, when his ardour cooled and other circumstances interposed, that Mendelssohn and Nicolai took up the thread, but it was Lessing who gave the publication

the prestige it maintained long after his connexion
with it had ceased.

'You will not have much to retrieve with regard to
literature since the opening of the campaign,' he tells
his officer. 'I seek in vain for a single new genius
evoked by this war, else so rich in marvels, to counterpoise the hundred hero names that are making it
illustrious. What are the new books that come into
my way? Translations, nothing but translations: and
what sort of translations? Linguistic exercises that
should be banished into the domain of private study
to which they belong, but for which these men manage
to get pay into the bargain. Ignorant of their authors'
language, they venture to translate writers whose chief
merit perhaps is their style.' He then proceeds
to give examples. One miserable scribbler has rendered Pope into prose, another has entirely overlooked
the fine satire of Gay. Oh! very likely these men
had good intentions, but they have not hindered them
from spoiling two English poets. And he uses the
word 'spoiling' advisedly. Unsparing severity must
be dealt out to such mutilators. Here is another who
has attacked Bolingbroke, and so many words so many
faults.

Such intrepid remarks fell into the literary world
like thunderbolts. Writers had hitherto been used to
abuse from certain papers, to praise from others, because they happened to represent or oppose their
especial faction. But criticism such as this—an objective analysis of merit or demerit, an application of the
only true critical solvents, expressed in dignified tones
of assured superiority, free from arrogance and enlivened by *naïve* wit, extensive reading, and apt quotation—was a wholly new phenomenon. Demurs made

themselves heard, but these only provoked yet sharper attacks. Lessing is willing to admit, for instance, that the neighbourhood of war scares the Muses ; but had there been any to scare ? However, he will not dwell on this sad theme, but try and search for the faintest trace yet lingering of their divine footsteps. For surely the Muses have not all departed ? Civilized war is the bloody lawsuit carried on by absolute rulers only, leaving the republic of letters unruffled, save to arouse another Xenophon or Polybius.

'You are right,' he says in Letter 7, in reply to a pretended objection from his correspondent ; 'such miserable translators as those to whom I have introduced you are beneath criticism. But it is well that criticism should now and then descend to them, for the mischief they do is incredible. Suppose that through some great and wonderful catastrophe, all books, except those written in German, should perish ; what a miserable figure our Virgils and Horaces, Shaftesburys and Bolingbrokes, would cut before posterity ! '

Ah, but, he continues ironically, he had forgotten that Germany did not lack men who could take the place of the great foreigners, and the yet greater ancients. Klopstock would become Homer ; Cramer, Pindar ; Gleim, Anacreon ; Wieland, Lucretius. This name checks him, and he speaks at length concerning Wieland, whom he calls beyond question one of the finest living spirits ; for his quick eye had penetrated the great natural gifts of this eclectic genius, even at a time when he was lost in some of his strangest aberrations. In seven consecutive letters, Lessing takes this young idealist through an educational process, in a tone of righteous acerbity. Wieland, then twenty-three, was passing through his pietistic stage. The guest

I

and disciple of Bodmer, he wrote under his eye an epic
on the 'Temptation of Abraham;' piously denounced
Utz, the lighthearted writer of erotic odes, as unchristian and immoral; and tried to forget the fact that
while in his teens he had himself penned a didactic
poem 'On the Nature of Things,' that had earned him,
in those days of classic comparisons, the surname of
the German Lucretius. But Lessing had not forgotten.
He demonstrates that it by no means becomes Wieland
to play the defender of Christianity, for he has not
always been such a specifically Christian writer.

He will not dwell on some doubtful anecdotes of
his school-life, for what does the private life of an
author concern us? but he wishes to recall what Wieland forgets, that epithet Lucretius, and contrast it
with the 'Moral Letters,' neither of which contain
Christian matter.

'The Christian religion,' he goes on to say, 'is
always Wieland's third word. We often boast of
that which we have not, that we may at least appear
to have it.'

With his power of reducing to simple proportions
whatever came within his vision, where puerilities
died a natural death, Lessing further demonstrates
that Wieland's religion is really nothing but an
æsthetic dallying with religious emotions, and that
his austerity is but affectation.

Wieland throughout life remained in terror of
Lessing. Nevertheless he pondered his remarks, and,
*mirabile dictu*, they influenced him. How adequately
Lessing had gauged this volatile author, Wieland's after
career proved. After his removal from the evangelical influence of Bodmer, his highly receptive and
purely imitative nature, swayed by the popular philo-

sophy of enjoyment rampant under Louis XV., assumed a Gallo-Hellenic dress made by a German tailor. He became the favourite author of the Frenchified portion of society, to whom his uncouth levity was more acceptable than the more gracefully polished productions of the French. He had the merit, at Lessing's instigation, to be the first to translate Shakespeare into German, for which he earned the redoubtable critic's praise, but at the time of the 'Literary Letters' Wieland was still cutting his teeth on the English drama.

Lessing bids his officer (in the 36th Letter) 'rejoice with him, for Wieland had quitted the ethereal spheres and again wanders among mortal men; he has written a drama, "Lady Jane Grey." But, alas! stern truth obliges the writer to proclaim that this first sign of mortality in the Seraphim is a plagiarism from Nicholas Rowe's tragedy of that name, and an awkward plagiarism, in which he has inadvertently left a personage belonging to an episode which he has omitted. He has torn down the stately temple of his author, to build a tiny hut out of the materials, and passes over this obligation in dead silence. But no doubt Wieland has wandered too long among Cherubim and Seraphim to get quickly used to the ways of common men.'

Amid all these humorous sallies, Lessing does not lose sight of his serious aims. This historical tragedy affords him an opportunity to speak of the poetic treatment of such themes.

'The poet,' he says, 'is master over history;' and he makes his first bold reference to Shakespeare, who, though he had not written *secundum artem*, and was ignorant of Aristotle and the classical drama, had better

I 2

observed the rules and approached more nearly to the
ancients than the rigidly correct Corneille. This
affords him an opportunity, which he never neglects,
for springing into the arena and breaking a lance with
Gottsched. It had been written, ' Nobody will deny
that the German stage owes a large portion of its im-
provements to Professor Gottsched.'

' I am that Nobody,' says Lessing, ' I deny it
entirely.'

He then gives his reasons for this statement, which
he finds in the French taste foisted by Gottsched on
the nation, while he (Lessing) insists, very properly,
that the German mode of thought is more in harmony
with the English. Lessing overlooks that a somewhat
artificial atmosphere was needed at first to take the
place of the gross excesses that had held possession
of the stage, and thus rouse the national taste to a
spirit of opposition that would prepare it to receive
the more congenial English drama. That Lessing could
overlook this patent truth, explains his fierce attacks
on Gottsched, and shows how even the most clear-
sighted intellect is yet so far immeshed in the trammels of his age, as to be unable to render full justice
to the endeavours of his immediate predecessors.

' That our old dramas had much of the English
element I could prove to you at length with little
trouble. Only to mention the best known, Dr. Faust
has a number of scenes that only a Shakespearean
genius could have thought out. And how enamoured
Germany was and still is of its Dr. Faust ! '

' One of his friends,' he goes on, ' has lying by
him an old draft of this tragedy ; he will insert a specimen act.' Then follows an act of his own projected
play ; for Lessing, like Goethe, from the commence-

ment of his career, was occupied with this theme.
The Faust legend has always attracted the Germans,
and in Lessing's time a perfect Faust epidemic raged,
that found its final apotheosis in Goethe's splendid
poem. Was it for the reason given by Heine, that
the German nation suspects that it is itself this learned
Dr. Faust, this spiritualist who, having at last understood with the spirit the insufficiency of mere spirit,
desires material enjoyments and restores its rights to
the flesh?

However this be, the theme attracted Lessing also,
and he twice composed a drama on the subject. The
sketch of the one is preserved, that of the other lost;
and though recently its recovery has been asserted,
internal evidence, in the opinion of those best capable
of judging, is adverse to its authenticity.

In his Letters, Lessing continues his patronage to
the Grenadier's muse: he praises the poems of his friend
Kleist; he announces the publication of a poor tragedy by Weisse; and as he skimmed each field, he
scattered important truths.

'Tragedy should be the work of matured manhood,
not of youth.'

'The merit of a work does not depend on individual beauties; these must constitute a beautiful whole,
or the connoisseur cannot read it without displeasure.
Only when the whole is found irreproachable, the
judge must desist from a censorious dissection, and
regard the work as a philosopher does the world.'

Because he had found in the early cantos of Klopstock's 'Messiah' the true national ring that proved
its inspiration to have sprung from the innermost life
of the nation, he had welcomed it and dealt gently
with its failings; but the Odes which Klopstock was

now giving to the world, with their perverted religious transcendentalism, their false pathos, their painted fire, aroused his disdain. Their inspiration was rather theological than poetical. He demands the rigid demarcation of the domains of poetry and religion.

'What do you say to Klopstock's Sacred Odes?' he writes to Gleim. 'If you condemn them, I shall doubt your orthodoxy; if you acquit them, your taste.'

He explains himself more fully to his officer, to the effect that Klopstock's gorgeous tirades are so full of the poet's emotions, that the reader has nothing left to feel. An admirer of Klopstock had called these songs rich in thought. If this be so, Lessing only wonders that this wealthy poet has not long since become the favourite of all old women. He is quite willing to believe that Klopstock may have been in a state of lively emotion when he composed these lyrics, ' but because he sought merely to express these emotions, and concealed the depth of clear thoughts and conceptions by means of which he has kindled in himself the pious flame, it is impossible for his readers to raise themselves to his level.'

There was no department of current literature into which Lessing did not make an inroad. His censure of commonplace superficiality and verbiage reveals to what a degree mediocrity had pervaded German literature, while some of his criticisms remain pertinent to this day, as when he shows why Germany boasts no good historians.

' Our wits are seldom scholars, or our scholars wits. The former are wholly unwilling to read, investigate, collect, in short, to work; the latter are unwilling to do anything else. The former lack material, and the latter lack skill to give form to their material.'

At the same time he is indignant at Leibnitz, who had said that the French were superior to the Germans in intellect, the only national pre-eminence of the Germans being their industry.

'Now let no one wonder again how it is that Frenchmen are apt to depreciate German scholars, when the best German intellects abase their country-men below the French, merely to gain a reputation for politeness and good breeding.'

Lessing regards the French as too truly polite to be gratified by compliments paid at the expense of their neighbours. He admits that German literature was only in course of development, that it would be long ere it could boast of really good works, especially in the higher branches ; but for this very reason it must be encouraged. He therefore hails talent wherever it shows itself, and strives to aid its progress, but at the same time to correct its aberrations.

But Lessing's sharpest feud was waged against the distorted supersensuous piety and spiritual pride of Klopstock and his followers, and more especially against the journal edited under their supervision, in which they constituted themselves the moral censors of the nation.

'You shall be satisfied,' he writes to his officer. 'The praises bestowed by so many papers on the "Northern Guardian" have excited my curiosity also. I have read it, although I generally make it almost a rule to leave our weekly moralists unread.' This 'Northern Guardian' tries to be something quite above the average, and is something below it. Its intention was to infuse a specifically Christian sentiment into

the people, and it was pervaded by a devout zealotry
that knew no bounds.    It pretended to be a literary
journal, but all criticism was made subservient to religion.    Poetry, in the eyes of its pious conductors,
must needs be the handmaid of the flesh, and they
therefore turned criticism into inquisition.    They
laid down as an incontrovertible proposition, that
morality without religion is a contradiction in terms,
and proved it by—nothing more—than their positive
tone.

This is too much for Lessing.    He exposes the
confusion of ideas and the sophistry underlying this
dictum, and holds that the poetical religious extravagance of this set has made them sin against sense
and humanity.    Even from a theological point of
view, their arguments will not bear examination ; they
are endeavouring to combine orthodoxy and heterodoxy into a mild *tertium quid*, and the results are
insipid metaphysics.    This pretentious new-fangled
theology deviates from the old dogmas, while retain-
ing the old dogmatism.

No wonder the Northern Guardians ascribed the
Literary Letters to a Freethinker and a Jew, and they
again asserted that integrity is impossible without
religion.

Presumptuous assertion, Lessing tells them, for by
religion they mean only their own way of thinking.

The rage with which the assailed turned against
Lessing only increased the vigour of his attack.    Polemics were his very life-blood.    Opposition stirred
him into action.    An almost joyous atmosphere pervades the Letters.    Their strong consciousness is ex-
hilarating, and they are masterpieces of unexpected
dramatic thrusts and caustic wit.    The defence of the

adversaries was lamentably weak. They complained
that the accusations made by the Literary Letters
were 'strange,' 'cruel.' Lessing gives his officer a
few extracts :

'My criticism is hard, bitter, loveless, heedless ;
indeed, so loveless and heedless that it is impossible
to reflect on its existence in these days without sadness. It is a phenomenon whose reality will not be
believed by mere hearsay : I possess a shameless
audacity. I calumniate. I have an unfortunate character. I deserve the abhorrence of the world,' and so
on ; and he ends with the quiet remark, ' Well now,
such is your friend.'

Though most of the writers with whom the Literary Letters deal are long forgotten, or merely remembered through these pages, the Letters themselves are enjoyable for their inherent youth and
freshness, and will be always perused for their own
sake. But they have a yet prouder claim ; they became the founders of modern criticism. Criticism up
to this time had been the application of general rules
derived from ancient standards ; Lessing raised it
to a science. He had studied literature in all its
branches, not only theoretically but productively, and
could bring practice to bear on precept. He aimed
at the presentation of the peculiar laws and processes
of production, as manifested through the medium of
consciousness. Moreover, in these Letters he first
evinced himself a consummate master of German
prose, raising it to a height that has rarely been approached, never surpassed. He not only used fewer
foreign words than his contemporaries, he coined new
ones to take their place, or revived old German
words that had fallen into disuse. Lessing's language

differed from that of his contemporaries in its trans-
parency, vigour, and compactness.   His sentences
were short ; he avoided, as far as he could, the auxiliary verbs that render the German language so cumbersome ; he preferred the present tense to the future ;
the active voice to the passive ; and made use of many
of the pregnant Lutheran phrases.   Some of his in-
flexions are now out of date, but they strike us as
idiosyncratic rather than antiquated.   He employed
metaphors freely ; these are always correct and to the
point, and often of startling originality, enthralling
attention.   Every sentence, says a German writer, is
like a phalanx in which no word is superfluous or out
of place.

These Letters, however, did not fill up the whole
of Lessing's time at Berlin.   According to Ramler,
he had ten different matters on hand at once, and he
himself writes to Gleim : ' Ramler and I make plan
upon plan.   Wait another quarter of a century, and
you will marvel at all we have written, especially I.
I write day and night, and it is the least part of my
ambition to write three times as many plays as Lope
de Vega.'   The studies incidental to Gleim's war-
songs had referred Lessing back to genuine national
poetry.   The fruit of these studies was an interest in
a Silesian poet of the seventeenth century, Frederick
von Logau, whose epigrams he edited in concert with
Ramler, who modernised their language, while Lessing compiled a glossary.   The epigrams lost much
of their quaint originality, through Ramler's correct
transformation.   The glossary it was hoped would
incite others to catalogue the words used by old
German writers.   This was a creditable innovation,
and the first systematic attempt of its kind.

Never losing sight of his dramatic interests, Lessing translated Diderot's domestic dramas, '*Le père de famille*,' and '*Le fils naturel*,' and his essay on this new genus. Diderot and Lessing had independently arrived at the same conclusions concerning the subjects and the social classes that may be treated dramatically; they both insisted that in all civilized countries the middle class best represent the world, because, while their duties are sharply defined, they escape the harshest strokes as well as the over-pampering of fortune. Lessing prized Diderot as the most philosophical mind that had occupied itself with the theatre since the days of Aristotle. It is a satisfaction to him to think that perhaps Diderot will earn more favour in Germany than in France, and that for once the Germans will escape from the ridicule of only appreciating French authors when they are already passing out of fashion in their own country.

Pastor Lessing once more urged his son to seek a settled subsistence. The latter again protested his unwillingness to be an official slave, adding, at the same time, that should any permanent appointment be offered to him he will not refuse it, but to make any efforts in this direction he is either too conscientious or too lazy. Socially, Berlin was pleasanter to him than ever. The Monday Club, to which all the literary men of the time belonged, counted him a member; then there was the Friday Club, a more select gathering, that consisted of his closest friends. The most cultured society opened its doors to him, not to mention the renewed daily intercourse which he enjoyed with Nicolai and his dear Mendelssohn. Healthy delight in his work and the success which it brought told on his spirits. Mendelssohn always recalled these years with tender regret, when Lessing was the life and soul of a happy circle, and his ' flashes of merriment were wont to set the table in a roar.'

Lessing now considered himself called upon thoroughly to revise his earlier writings, and began upon his fables, rejecting those written in verse, or changing them into prose. This led him to write an essay on this mode of composition in general. Fables had enjoyed great popularity in Germany during the eighteenth century, owing to the national taste for symbolism and allegory. The Swiss contended that fable united both the essential conditions of poetry, the moral and the marvellous. Fables in their eyes were epics in miniature. Not so in Lessing's. He beheld in this definition one of those confusions of æsthetic boundaries which he felt called upon everywhere to rectify. A true poem is complete in itself, and therefore didactics should be limited to the sphere of fable. Utility is their *raison d'être.* He then proceeds to show that action in fable and action in epics and drama are essentially different. Action is not merely a movement of body and change in space ; every inner conflict of passion is an action. Action in drama, besides the poet's design, must have a purpose pertaining to itself ; action in fable does not need this inner aim, it is sufficient if it enforces its moral. He carefully distinguishes between an allegorical action and a fable. De la Motte's definition, that ' la fable est une instruction déguisée sous l'allégorie d'une action,' he rejects. When Tarquinius Superbus cut off the poppy-heads, he instructed his son by an allegorical action ; but this was no fable. Nor is a fable necessarily an allegory at all. It only becomes an allegory when to the fictitious individual case a similar real one is added. The fable is not in itself an allegory, since the moral precept contained in it is a general one. A fable must deal with an individual case, and deal with it in such a manner that its application shall be obvious. The more determinate the individual case, the more forcible the intuitive application. The merely possible case is a species of general one, for everything which is possible is possible in several ways. An individual case, considered as merely possible, is still in some degree general, and therefore weakens the effect of the intuitive application. The fable requires the assumption of a positive fact, because a positive fact suggests more motives than a merely possible one, and carries a much stronger conviction.

After confuting the definitions of fable given by Richier, Batteux, le Bossu, and Breitinger, Lessing passes on to his own theory. When we deduce a general moral principle from a particular case, give reality to this particular case, and invent a story from it in which the general moral principle is intuitively perceptible, such invention is called a fable. The advantage of introducing animals he holds to be our knowledge of their salient characteristics. There is no objection to the introduction of human actors if their peculiar characteristics are sufficiently defined. Thus, it would be a great loss in the fable of the sour grapes if, in place of a fox, a man were substituted, for we should not know what kind of man might be meant, while the fox naturally suggests the idea of shrewdness and vanity. But if, instead of fox, the word Gascon were substituted, the fable would lose less, because these qualities are the recognized characteristics of a Gascon.

Again, the object of fable is the clear and graphic perception of a moral truth; and as nothing obscures our perceptions more than our passions and sympathies, the fabulist must avoid their interference as much as possible, and this cannot be done when the actors are human beings.

Lessing then passes in review the various manners of Æsop, Phædrus, and La Fontaine. He praises the clearness and brevity of Æsop's Fables, and the finished precision of his narrative. Phædrus, who aspired to improve Æsop's invention by the adoption of verse, paid the strictest attention to his model's concise treatment; but, where he deviated for the sake of metre, he sometimes fell into absurdities. La Fontaine, though recognising the inappropriateness of ornament in fable, felt the difficulty of imitating the terse precision of Æsop and Phædrus; he therefore attempted to atone for this defect by some attempts at ornament. Lessing greatly admires La Fontaine, but censures his imitators, who carried his innovations to excess. La Fontaine turned fable into a pleasant poetical pastime, and attracted a great number of followers. Lessing's own juvenile attempts had included many rhymed fables; his more mature judgment condemns such embellishment of Æsop. La Fontaine's treatment of the Phrygian fabulist suggests to Lessing one of his own fables.

'A man had a beautiful ebony bow, with which he shot very far and sure, and which he valued highly. Once, while inspecting it carefully, he said, "You are really a little too uncouth, you have no ornament save your polish; that is a pity." But that can be remedied, he thought. "I will go to the best artist and get him to carve devices on my bow." He went, and the artist carved a whole hunt on the bow, and what could be more appropriate to a bow than a hunt! The man was delighted. "You deserve these ornaments, my good bow."

'He wishes to try it, bends it, and the bow snaps asunder.'

Plato, who banished all poets from his commonwealth but allowed Æsop to remain, would now bid him depart too, since he is ornamented by La Fontaine.

Finally, as examples of his proposed reforms, Lessing appends his own fables, which he modestly says are no masterpieces, for criticism, not genius, is their source of inspiration. Nevertheless they are models of graceful brevity, distinguished by fine observation and pregnant truths, though at times perhaps they are a little too subtle and too paradoxical, and a too conscious effort after novelty at all hazards is visible, which detracts from the simplicity requisite in fable.

If the object of his essay was to quench the rage for this form of writing, which was really assuming giant proportions, one single Leipzig fair having given more fables to Germany than all that France had ever produced, it certainly accomplished his purpose. Fable fell down from the high place which it had usurped, and, losing its poetic adornment, lost its importance. A few fabulists who had fancy enough to clothe an ethical axiom in action, while lacking phantasy to create a poem, continued to cultivate it for a while; but even these soon abandoned the attempt. Bodmer attacked Lessing in the coarsest manner for his fable theory, and Lessing details all these insults in his 'Literary Letters;' but he makes no attempt to defend the theory he had established, as indeed it was a characteristic of Lessing's willingly to let his adversary have the last word.

The philological studies necessitated by the essay on fable revived his interest in the Greek poets, and he writes to his father that he is busy with a large work on the subject. Of this the only direct result was an unfinished life of Sophocles, intended as a supplement to Bayle, who had passed over Sophocles in his dictionary. Why Lessing abandoned this work is not recorded. It is of strictly erudite character, ascertained facts are recorded in short sentences, followed by the reasons for receiving these and accompanied by notes. Though superseded by more copious works grounded on modern extended knowledge, scholars can still turn to Lessing's 'Sophocles' with advantage.

These Sophoclean studies, however, were not a mere philological pastime ; they were in Lessing's eyes a proper accompaniment to the study of Shakespeare. He aimed at effectually exposing the pretensions of French tragedy to be an imitation and continuation of the ancients. He wished to oppose the caricature with the prototype, to place Sophocles in lieu of Corneille, genuine in place of spurious nature. And since critical perception and practical creation ever went hand in hand with Lessing, he wrote his drama 'Philotas,' intimately connected with these Sophoclean studies and with the definition of action which he had given in his essay on fable. He was just now enamoured of brevity, which may be accounted for partly by the quicker life struck into the universal lethargy by the war, and partly by his close association with Kleist, whose manly earnestness,

antique rectitude and reserve, afforded a sharp contrast to the current effeminate tone. If 'Spring'
betrayed a weak imitation of Thomsonian sentimentalism, not so his 'Seneca,' written at Lessing's instigation, and praised by him as approaching Sophocles
in colouring and pithy conciseness. Kleist exercised
more influence over Lessing than any of his other
friends, by his noble disinterested nature. It was
finally in emulation of his tragedy, that Lessing
wrote 'Philotas,' a one-act play, devoid of episode,
love or adventure, whose action wholly turns on the
headstrong obstinacy of the hero. The motive of
the play is the same as that of Plautus' 'Captives,'
only that here the issue is tragic. Prince Philotas has
been permitted at his earnest desire to go into active
service, notwithstanding his extreme youth. To his
despair he is taken prisoner in his first engagement.
Tormented by fear lest his father should sacrifice
throne, country, and the advantages gained in the
war, to the temptation to rescue his only son, he
determines to prevent this by a voluntary death. He
obtains a sword by stratagem and kills himself upon
it. Military honour is the dramatic mainspring of
' Philotas,' which embodied the heroic sentiments of the
period. Frederick himself was known to carry poison
about him to use in the event of captivity. The play
in its tragic simplicity is strictly in accordance with
antique art, and so is the circumstance that the tragic
action is not evolved in the course of the drama, but
is primarily existent in the conditions, and necessitated
from the very beginning. The unbending defiance
of the youthful hero recalls 'Ajax,' while the admix-
ture of humorous tones, that disturb the majestic
tragic style, shows Lessing's familiarity with Shake-

K

speare. Every sentence is an epigram; a protest
against the declamatory verbosity of French tragedy.
At the same time Lessing knew that mere imitation
would never rejuvenate German poetry, if the poets
lacked power to find their subjects in national history
and tradition, as the Greeks had done; and this was
another reason why he held Shakespeare as the model
to be followed, because of his thoroughly modern and
patriotic character, while on the other hand he also
knew, as Goethe says, ' that the first step to rescue the
Germans out of this watery, verbose, arid epoch could
only be attained by firmness, precision, and brevity.'

' Philotas' was issued anonymously. Lessing sent
a copy to Gleim as the work of an unknown author.
Gleim praised its bearing, but disapproving its prose
dress, had the ludicrous arrogance to put it into
iambics, and naïvely sent it back to Lessing as
'improved.' Lessing's comments, full of satirical
*persiflage*, caused Gleim to suspect the true authorship of the drama. In dismay at this, he knew no
better way out of his dilemma than in true old
bachelor fashion to send Lessing a cask of the best
Rhine wine out of the canonical cellar. Lessing was
good-humoured enough not to enter into further
details about the matter. He caused this enlarged
' Philotas' to be printed, and his only piece of malice
was that he substituted the word 'verified' instead of
'versified,' by the Prussian Grenadier, on the copy
intended for Gleim. Meantime he enjoyed the good
wine in a summer lodging he had rented outside
Berlin. While returning thanks for it, he begs his
generous friend not to imagine he is working. No,
he is buried among books, and his desire for study
increases in the same ratio as his desire to write

declines. He had never been lazier than in this hermitage. If he did much, he made projects for tragedies and comedies ; but they were only acted in his head, and he laughed and wept over them himself, or imagined that the friends whose approval he most coveted did so with him. He had nominally come here to revise the new edition of his writings ; but he could not quell his keen anxiety concerning Kleist, whom he knew to be in the field.

Early in August (1759) successive couriers brought conflicting news to Berlin, throwing the town into alternate paroxysms of joy and sadness, until the crushing news of the defeat of Kunersdorf was undeniably attested. The rumour also spread that the valiant soldier-poet Kleist was wounded, and a prisoner. The news stabbed Lessing to the heart, as a realization of his worst fears, and the details, as they slowly reached him, were calculated only to inflame his anxiety. Kleist, regardless of two wounds and several contusions, seeing his Colonel fall, had taken his place, and boldly led the regiment forward. A case-shot threw him from his horse and shattered his leg ; falling, he exclaimed, ' Children, don't forsake your King ;' then fainted, and was carried from the field. His bearers were shot away from his side, the ground on which he lay passed over to the Russians, and late at night Cossacks found and stript him, throwing him naked into a swamp. Rescued and covered by some humane Russians, he again fell into Cossack hands, and it was not till the next day that some Russian cavalry officers mercifully moved him to Frankfurt on the Oder, and into the house of Professor Nicolai. Lessing instantly took measures that the friend who had so generously aided him should be

supplied with the money he now needed himself ; he
wrote to his Frankfurt acquaintances, imploring them
to look after the wounded man.   He then heard of his
whereabout, and that there was still hope ; the next
news was that Kleist had died of his wounds. Lessing
could not, would not believe this.   There must be an
error of persons ; he knows there is another Major
Kleist, who has also been wounded and is captive,
and it must be he that is dead, and not 'our Kleist,' he
writes to Gleim.   'Our Kleist is not dead, it cannot
be, he still lives.   I will not grieve beforehand, nor
will I grieve you.'   He proposes to venture among
the enemy to seek his friend.   'If he still lives, I will
seek him out. That I should not see him again, never
see him again in all my life, speak to him, embrace
him.'   He cannot pursue the thought ; and yet the
terrible news is but too true : Kleist has died from his
neglected wounds.

'Alas, dear friend!' he writes to Gleim a few days
later, 'it is too true. He is dead. We have lost him. He
died in the arms of Professor Nicolai, and in his house.
He remained calm and cheerful under the greatest
suffering.   He desired to see his friends once again.
If it had but been possible!   My grief at this loss is a
wild grief.   I do not demand that the balls should
take another direction because an honest man stands
in their way.   But I demand that the honest man——
There you see, sometimes my sorrow leads me astray
to be angry with the man whom it concerns.   He had
three, four wounds already ; why did he not retire?
Generals with fewer and slighter wounds have retired
honourably.   He wanted to die.   Forgive me if I am
hard on him.   He would not have died, even of the
last wound, it is said, if he had not been neglected.

Been neglected! I do not know against whom to rave. The miserable wretches who could neglect him! I must break off. No doubt the Professor has written to you. He made a funeral oration over him. Some one else, I do not know who, has written an elegy on him. They cannot have lost much in Kleist, who are able to do this just now. The Professor means to print his speech, and it is so poor. I know for certain Kleist would rather have borne yet another wound into his grave, than that such stuff should be chattered after him. But has a Professor a heart? He demands verses from me and from Ramler, to append to his speech. If he should also demand them from you, and you yield to his wish—— Dear Gleim, you must not do that! You will not do that! You feel more just now than you could express. It is not the same to you as it is to a Professor, what you say and how you say it.

'Farewell. I will write more when I am calmer.

'Yours faithfully,

'LESSING.'

The wild grief was calmed, but a void had entered into Lessing's life which no other friend could fill. He strove to drown his sorrow in work, and bring the revision of his 'Trifles' to a conclusion. Throughout the winter he toiled hard; then he was taken ill. Berlin was growing distasteful to him. The exaggerated patriotism that was rampant was too contrary to his nature not to provoke his opposition. He was ready enough to hail the aggrandizement of Prussia as an awakening to German national life, but he could not echo the narrow and extravagant sentiments that pervaded the air. He was put down as

'too Saxon,' while at Leipzig he had been condemned
as 'too Prussian.' He tells Gleim that in the Grenadier's latest war songs the patriot outvoices the poet.
If these poems are to have permanent value, they
must raise themselves above the level of over-excited
momentary feelings.  Slowly the conviction was
forced upon Lessing that a mental gulf had opened
between his friends and himself.  He was weary of
Berlin, and believed his friends were also weary of
him.  He stood alone in their midst; they had not
grown with his mental growth, while he had risen out
of their standpoint into a higher one.  He saw that
his friends felt uneasy at working with him.  His
superiority weighed on them, an unspoken estrange-
ment made itself felt ; they could not reconcile the gay
boon comrade Lessing, who in social intercourse lived
and let live, with the ardent writer who in the mental
domain would concede no hairsbreadth to defaulters
from the cause of truth.  Moreover, he was one of
those natures that quickly exhaust the medium in
which they move, who make time more comprehensive,
and realize George Sand's saying : ' Il y a des gens
qui vivent beaucoup à la fois, et dont les ans comptent
double.'  He could save himself from lassitude only
by variety.  Then, too, for the past years he had
again led a purely literary life, confined to books and
writing.  He felt the need to pause, that it was
time to look about him among men.  He wanted
money to purchase a library, and to live and work in
peace.  What if he attained this end by the sacrifice
of a few years of life ?  He fully understood how
Plautus gave up writing for some years, and followed
a trade.  Here he was, over thirty years of age, and
still nothing more than 'the old bird on the roof.' For

all his love of independence, he began to crave for an office. Even if he worked day and night and produced incessantly, he still foresaw that he could not shake off the yoke of poverty, aggravated by the exorbitant claims of his family.

In August his brother Gottlob paid him a visit. Lessing tells his father he is glad the visit did not last longer, for events might easily have occurred that would agitate Berlin and force him to leave it. His anticipations were not groundless. In October General Tottleben, with a vanguard of three thousand men, encircled, bombarded, and finally entered Berlin, and Lessing witnessed the public flogging of two journalists, one his successor on the 'Voss Gazette,' on account of some expressions in their papers deemed offensive to the enemy. This finally overcame Lessing's hesitation ; a deep melancholy mastered him, he looked around him for a settled post that might assure his existence amid these military vicissitudes. Chance came to his aid. General Tauentzien, the heroic defender of Breslau, had just been appointed governor of that city and director-general of the Silesian mint. He needed a secretary to aid him in his intricate labours, and remembering Kleist's friend, Lessing, whom he had known at Leipzig, offered him the post under the most advantageous certain conditions, and the additional prospect that he would be able to enrich himself in a very short time. This bait mastered Lessing, weary of

> the toil
> Of dropping buckets into empty wells,
> And growing old in drawing nothing up.

Without giving warning to his housekeeper, without a word of farewell to his friends, he stole away from Berlin (Nov. 1760).

# CHAPTER IX.

## BRESLAU.

### (1760–1765. AGED 31–36.)

*' Die eigentliche Epoche der Bestimmung und Befestigung seines Geistes scheint in seinen Aufenthalt in Breslau zu fallen, während dessen disser Geist, ohne literarische Richtung nach aussen, unter durchaus heterogenen Amtsgeschäften, die bei ihm nur auf der Oberfläche hingleiteten, sich auf sich selbst besann und in sich selbst Wurzel schlug. Von da an wurde ein rastloses Hinstreben nach der Tiefe und dem Bleibenden in allem menschlichen Wissen an ihm sichtbar.'*—FICHTE.

LESSING had not long left Berlin ere the Academy elected him an honorary member. Mendelssohn wrote to inform him, adding reproaches for his abrupt departure. He entirely disapproved of Lessing's step, though as a rule he was far from considering that scholars should live merely by their learning. But he feared that Lessing's easy goodnature and ignorance of business details might involve him in unlooked-for complications, and moreover, Moses understood, what Lessing had as yet failed to comprehend, that the minting business in which he would be engaged was of a more than questionable character.

Certainly, Lessing had not considered these details. He ardently desired to live for a while independent of pecuniary care, and seeing a chance open had eagerly seized it. When he was brought face to face with the conditions of fortune, his upright-

ness revolted. The finances of the King had been
utterly exhausted by the war ; he needed money at
any price, and had recourse to a continuous debase-
ment of the currency, that was, in truth, but a form of
progressive bankruptcy. Lessing was given to understand that, as the right hand of Tauentzien, the first
knowledge of new minting operations would reach
him, and it would therefore be an easy matter to gain
thousands by speculation exempt from all manner of
risk. He had only to imitate his chief, who, according
to Frederick's own testimony, acquired 150,000 thalers
in this manner. This way of getting rich was not
regarded as by any means reprehensible. Tauentzien
was a really honourable man, whose sincere disposition won Lessing's regard. He was an ardent lover
of his King, and would have held even more ambiguous actions as not only justifiable, but praise-
worthy, if commanded by his beloved sovereign. ' If
the King's misfortunes had reduced him to assemble
his whole army under one tree, General Tauentzien
would have stood among them,' was Lessing's characterization of his loyalty. Lessing, fully alive to
Frederick's claims to admiration, did not carry them
to the extent of deadening his own conscience. At
first he really did not understand the nature of the offers
made to him from various quarters, especially from
the Jews, who hoped to win his protection by holding
out baits of fortune for Mendelssohn as well as himself. Lessing laid these proposals before his friend,
who speedily enlightened him as to their real nature,
and sternly warned him against the snares laid for
him. Thus he saw his hopes of opulence vanish.

He had maintained in his Letters that after thirty
a man must fill his purse as well as his head, and

as soon as that was done he should return to Berlin and resume his studies. 'Oh, if this·"as soon" were but to-morrow!' At first his good spirits kept up, the ever welcome change of scene diverted him, but gradually disappointment at the failure of this step mastered him, and found vent in his Letters.

'Dearest friend,' he writes to Moses Mendelssohn, two months after his departure, in answer to reproaches, 'I deliberately quitted Berlin without bidding you farewell, because I did not wish to expose myself to the risk of suddenly seeing the folly of my resolve put in full light before me. Remorse will nevertheless not be absent at having undertaken so radical a change in my method of life for the mere purpose of making my so-called fortune. How near I am to this remorse, I hardly know, for as yet I have not come to myself in Breslau. Your news out of the Berlin paper (his election) is real news to me. I need not stop to assure you that this honour leaves me perfectly indifferent, particularly in my present circumstances.' He then begs Mendelssohn to write to him often and in detail about all his occupations; it will be the only way to save him from sinking into frivolity. He further promises to send copy without fail for the 'Literary Letters.'

Lessing's friends knew better than to reckon on such promises. His 'copy' was at all times an extremely uncertain ware. His restless activity caused him always to have more matter on hand than he could possibly compass, and, removed from the influences of any interest, his assistance could not be depended on. Indeed he had already begun to flag with his contributions before leaving Berlin, and Nicolai, who recognized that the success of the Letters mainly depended on Lessing, had contemplated winding up the periodical. This was not however done till some years later, and Lessing sent a few contributions from Breslau.

The fatiguing routine of business duties weighed like lead on Lessing's intellect, and the remorse which he had foreseen too soon set in. But since he held remorse to be 'the most useless of all unpleasant emotions,' he determined to avoid it, and threw himself heart and soul into such distractions as Breslau afforded. He had always found pleasure in the society of officers. Here he became intimately acquainted with the chiefs of the Prussian army, and was able to observe garrison life, and military and financial administration. The man of action was once more uppermost, and Lessing threw himself into the tumult that surged about him, learnt to know the various and bizarre life of war, and could satisfy to the full his craving for acquaintance with the most varied conditions of society. He had feared to grow too exclusively literary at Berlin ; here he could gaze as in a peepshow upon a whole moving and diversified panorama. He had never been choice or exclusive in his associates ; he was not so here. He knew that a student of life must regard it in all its aspects.

Lessing's official capacity demanded his presence with his general until after dinner, which was usually at four ; after this he went to a bookshop or auction. The purchase of books was his one extravagance at Breslau. Books were to be bought more cheaply with bad money than with good ; besides Lessing knew that he could keep books more securely than cash, which the first applicant could draw from his purse. Giving was his delight. He was enjoying what was for him opulence, and with his natural carelessness he threw his money away recklessly, not to name the perpetual claims made upon him by his family, so that he often saw himself forced to be generous before he was just, and had to borrow in order to satisfy his parents, who vastly over-estimated his income. If there were no books to be bought, he went home and attended to personal concerns, applicants for aid, or business details. Or the few literary students of Breslau would step in, and Lessing would interchange thoughts with them concerning art and science. Rector Arletius and Rector Klose were chief among these, both profoundly learned men ; the former indeed was in Frederick the Great's estimation the typical German scholar, i.e. a straight-forward, unpolished worthy, who could account for every Greek and Latin word, and was the more ignorant of the concerns of every day. Klose was rather more a man of the world. In company with him, Lessing diligently searched the monasteries and libraries around Breslau, for rare editions and obsolete books. His Berlin friends warned him against his reckless expenditure on books ; indeed his heedlessness often involved him and them in expensive and vexatious difficulties, as when, for instance, he commissioned two friends to buy the same book, and they dutifully bid against each other. But he drew upon himself yet graver remonstrances by his love of play, that first showed itself in Breslau. He played so high that it reached the ears of his chief, who reproached him in a friendly manner. Lessing replied that it was of no consequence whether he played high or low, for in the average he lost little or nothing, but that high stakes fixed his attention, and complete distraction from thought was all he sought in cards. Faro was his favourite game. A friend relates that he often observed him at the gaming-table so intensely interested that the perspiration would run down his face with excitement, nor was this by any means the case only when he lost. His friend reproached him, saying he would not only ruin his purse, but, what was worse, his health. 'On the contrary,' replied Lessing. 'If I played in cold blood I could not play at all.' And he proceeded to explain that hygienic reasons were hidden under this strange disguise, that he regarded the excitement as a healthy counteraction to his sedentary life.

The early part of his evenings was spent in the theatre. A harlequinade company was playing popular burlesques ; notwithstanding his raid against this species, he gave the countenance of his presence to their performances. At least these outrageous farces were, in spite of all their grossness, national, which was more than could be said of the tame Gottschedian tragedies. Here he could laugh, the others made him yawn. He saw that the people were diverted, and confessed that 'even the severest connoisseur is not so severe in a crowd as he is when alone. For when he sees that this or that makes an impression, he forgets that it ought not to do so. And if the piece does not please him, it pleases him to see that so many can be pleased so easily.' He at once made acquaintance with the actors, and took great pains to educate one of them to be a competent player. It did not disturb him that some of them were of the very lowest class of comedians. Irreproachable everyday folk were never to Lessing's mind ; he demanded that a man should be something besides an eating, drinking, and sleeping animal. He esteemed such people as useful burghers, but he did not love their society. It was after the theatre that he went to the gaming-table, and early morning saw him home, so that nine and even ten o'clock found him still in bed. His late hours angered his landlord, a gingerbread maker by trade. To revenge himself upon his dissipated lodger he sold gingerbread caricatures of Lessing disguised as a night watchman, with his full name, Gotthold Ephraim Lessing, embossed underneath. The stamp became traditional, and long after Lessing's death he was eaten in gingerbread at Breslau.

But there were periods when Lessing bitterly cursed this distracting life. He did not write to his friends, he was too much out of humour to do so. Moses wrote repeatedly and urged him to reply. Why did he not answer? Was he serving a Pythagorean apprenticeship? If so he hoped it would soon be over. Then he again writes to tell Lessing that he has heard from a Jew, Joel, that Lessing is well content and working hard. Is this so?

At last Lessing breaks silence :

'Breslau : March 30, 1761.

' Ah! dearest friend, Joel is a liar. To you least of all do I like to confess that I have hitherto been nothing less than content. But confess it to you I must, since it is the only reason why I have not written to you for so long. I have only written to you once from here, is it not so? You may therefore safely infer that I have only once been truly myself.

' No! I could never have imagined this! this is the tone in which all fools complain. I could and should have imagined that trifling occupation must fatigue more than the severest study ; that in the circle into

which I have allowed myself to be conjured, false pleasures and distractions upon distractions would ruin a
blunted soul, that——

'Ah! my best friend, your Lessing is lost! In a
year and a day you will not know him again. Nor
will he know himself. Oh, my time, my time, my
all that I have—to sacrifice it thus to I know not what
objects! A hundred times I have already thought of
forcibly tearing myself away from this connexion.
Yet can one thoughtless act be repaired by another?

'But perhaps this is only a dark day on which I see
nothing in its true light. To-morrow I may write you
a more cheerful letter. Oh, do write to me very often;
but more than mere reproaches for my silence! Your
letters are true alms to me. And would you give alms
merely for the sake of the requital?

'Farewell, my dearest friend. The first good hour
that my discontent allows me shall certainly be yours.
I am looking forward to it with all the restless longing of a fanatic awaiting heavenly visions.

'LESSING.'

Yet in spite of all this worldly and military tumult
Lessing found time for serious study, and results show
that he must have been right when he affirmed that,
for all appearances to the contrary, he surpassed himself in industry during the four-and-a-half years of
his Breslau sojourn. Relieved from the anxiety of
daily bread and the consequent obligation to make
the results of his studies immediately marketable,
Lessing saw himself, almost for the first time in his
life, able to study purely for study's sake. Critical,
antiquarian, dramatic interests all had full play. He
immersed himself in the Fathers to obtain a better un-

derstanding of the early history of the Christian faith, and planned an essay on heathen persecutions and on the heterodoxy he discovered in Justin Martyr. Instigated by Mendelssohn, he took up Spinoza and read him exhaustively. He planned various plays and wrote rhymed facetiæ for the amusement of his officer comrades. The letters to his friends grew rarer, they only looked at his outer life, and could not follow that he was observing keenly, and laying up stores for future use. He wearied of their counsels not to waste so much money over books ; of their grave disapproval of his gaming. He wrote oftenest to Mendelssohn, but rather to keep himself in his memory than to carry on a critical correspondence. Practical active life was claiming his attention. Mendelssohn grieved greatly over what he held a total relapse. To a volume of his philosophical writings he prefixed a preface only printed in the copy intended for Lessing, and a few intimate friends. It was headed :

‘ Dedication to a singular Mortal.

‘ The authors who worship the public, complain that their deity is deaf. They may adore it, pray to it, call on it from morn to noon, without voice or answer. I lay my pages at the feet of an idol who is obstinate enough to be equally hard of hearing. I have called and he does not answer. I now accuse him before the deaf judge, the public, who often pronounces just sentence without hearing.

‘ Mockers say: Call aloud. He is rhyming, is busy, has gone into the fields, or peradventure he sleepeth ; call louder, that he may wake. Oh no, rhyme he can, but alas ! he will not : roam he would gladly, but he cannot. His spirit is too lively for sleep, too idle for business. Formerly his seriousness was the oracle of the wise, and his irony a rod on the back of the fool, but now the oracle is dumb, and the fools exult with impunity. He has resigned his scourge to others, but they smite too gently, for they fear to draw blood. And he—

> If he neither hears, nor speaks, nor feels,
> Nor sees, what does he then? He plays!'

In his official capacity Lessing seems to have given complete satisfaction. During the summer of 1762 Tauentzien was named Siege Captain of Schweidnitz, and Lessing accompanied him into the field. For two weary months they lay before the fortress until it capitulated. Lessing wrote a merry letter to Nicolai from a little village outside, enjoining him to buy some English books at a Berlin auction. 'I will send you the money at once; you can count on it more securely than if I promised you contributions to your periodical. Do you know where this place (Peile) is? Wish I didn't.' Five months later the Peace of Hubertsburg brought the Seven Years' War to a close, and it was Lessing's duty to proclaim it solemnly to the good citizens of Breslau. The peace was no sooner signed than Frederick's restless energy set about the repair of his ruined finances. The debased currency came first under consideration. Tauentzien was summoned to Potsdam, and Lessing accompanied him, obtaining a few days' leave of absence to visit his Berlin friends. Frederick named Tauentzien Governor of the whole province of Silesia, but the work proved lighter for Lessing and he found more time for study.

L

It was in this summer (1763) that one bright morning, while enjoying the sunshine in a public garden of Breslau, he sketched and partly wrote 'Minna von Barnhelm.' The play, though not finished for press until a couple of years later, entirely belongs to this period of his life.

The inexorable pressure of exhausted finances had obliged Frederick ruthlessly to disband a considerable portion of the motley army that had served under his banners. Though these free corps had been largely recruited by adventurers, some gentlemen had joined from enthusiasm for the cause, and now saw themselves cashiered without even a partial repayment for the money they had spent in enlistments; destitute, and forced to earn their living by menial labour. Frederick was certainly placed in a most difficult position. His lands lay waste for lack of labour, his coffers were empty. His impetuous nature wished to put all straight in a twinkling by arbitrary expedients. Let these men till the fields, he would provide corn, flour, and cattle. Besides, plenty of them had stolen like ravens during the campaign; they must now shift for themselves. And wheat and tares were remorselessly uprooted together. The strangest stories were afloat concerning such dismissed soldiers. Thus, that one, a miller by trade, returned to the King his order *pour le mérite*, lest it should get dusty in the mill to which he, a late major, saw himself forced to return. The fate of these worthies aroused Lessing's interest. He saw in their unmerited ill fortune material for an original drama, in which he could embody the observations he had made on military life. The play based upon it became an appeal to public sympathy on their behalf; and, conveying thus an indirect censure upon the Government, it is scarcely astonishing that, for all the liberty of the press accorded in Prussia, its performance was at first forbidden. 'It is permitted to argue about God, but not about government and the police,' was the sententious verdict of the authorities. No doubt their characterization in the play as a body who 'want to pry into everything and above all to get at secrets,' must have offended the august police. Whether their scruples were overcome by a direct appeal to the King is not recorded, but overcome they were in due course, after four weeks' deliberation.

The military as a class had, even in Latin plays where the profession was highly honoured, been always brought upon the boards in caricature. They were used by the Spaniards, French, English, and Italians, as the grotesque element. Lessing desired to paint their best side, in a totally modern spirit, far removed from the chivalrous dramas with their artificial sentimentalism. The fable of 'Minna von Barnhelm,' is briefly that of Lovelace's touching ballad :

> I could not love thee, Dear, so much,
> Loved I not honour more.

The hero, Major Tellheim, a man of indubitable honesty, unflinching sense of honour, and almost impracticable virtue ; indeed, a modern embodiment of the best form of knighthood, sees himself at the conclusion of peace among the cashiered officers. This does not offend him ; he acknowledges the King cannot be expected to know all the worthy men who have served under him. Besides, the peace has rendered many such as he superfluous. Indeed, no one is indispensable to the great. But that the motives

of an action of his during the campaign should be
misconstrued, this hurts him beyond measure ; he
sees himself disgraced, degraded, his honour wounded,
his good name blasted. Sent by the King to levy a
heavy war contribution on the Saxon States, he found
the oppressed people unable to meet his demands.
His generous nature revolted against employing coer-
cion, and prompted him to advance them the needful
sum for eventual repayment. But at the conclusion
of peace, the Prussian Government disputed the validity of his loan, and accused him of low motives in
making this advance. The matter was under investigation, and meanwhile he was on parole not to quit
the city. During his sojourn in Saxony he had become acquainted with and engaged to Minna von
Barnhelm, an heiress who had attached herself to
him, ere ever she saw him, for his generous conduct
towards her States, for she is a Saxon. Finding on
the conclusion of peace that he does not seek her,
and suspecting some Quixotic scruples on his part, she
goes in search of him, and chances to light on the very
hotel from which the landlord has just expelled him on
account of impecuniosity, which has even forced him to
pawn his betrothal ring. Chance throws this into
Minna's hands. They meet, and Tellheim at once
releases her from her engagement on account of the
stigma that rests on his name. In vain she protests,
and proves to him with clear-sighted logic that he
overstrains the duties which honour demands, that it
does not require of him to make one who loves him
unhappy, and blight his own life because the Government has failed to recognize his claims. It is fruitless :
her happy thrusts of sound sense fail to confound
his stilted views of honour. Women cannot compre-

hend such things. 'Honour is not the voice of our conscience, nor the testimony of some righteous——'

'No, no; I know well,' she interrupts him; 'Honour is just—honour.'

He further affirms that that man is a villain who can consent to owe his good fortune to the tender love of a woman. Minna sees that only stratagem will avail her. She instructs her maid to represent her as disinherited because of her persistent determination to be the wife of a Prussian soldier, and now that she seeks out her protector he too forsakes her, while she has only kept silent on this point not to add more sorrows to his own. In an instant Tellheim's decision is revoked. Minna penniless, unhappy, shall soon see that he is no traitor. He permits his old sergeant to lend him the money, which he had till then persistently refused. He makes all arrangements for their union, but now his entreaties are refused.

At this juncture a letter from Frederick arrives, fully exonerating the Major, showing that the investigation had proved the justice of his claims, which the Treasury has instructions to honour, and further adding that the King hopes his health will permit him again to take service, as he can ill spare such brave and highminded men from his army.

'What justice! what clemency!' exclaims Tellheim joyfully, and claims Minna's hand, which she again refuses him, on the plea that she is now unfortunate, and cannot drag him into her misery. For surely, she adds, turning his own words against him, the woman is contemptible who is not ashamed to owe her good fortune to the tender love of a man.

Some further complications arise, owing to an

exchange of rings, Tellheim not having perceived that Minna had returned to him not the one he had given her, but the one he had pawned. At last, seeing she has carried her stratagem almost too far, and that she is in danger of seriously wounding his pride, she confesses all, and the piece concludes to the foreshadowing tune of marriage bells.

This play is in every respect the best written by Lessing, and its claim to be not only a national comedy, but the only German one, has not yet been disputed. The circumstances of its inspiration were singularly happy. Interest in the characters had not to be artificially evoked in the course of the play, but were pre-existent and inherent in its conditions; it did not speak to the sympathies of only one class, but to the community at large. The self-respect of the Germans had just been awakened by their victories, here was a play derived from their national life and contemporary conditions, German in names and thoughts, no imitation of French or English models. They felt proud to see in Tellheim such a representative of their uprightness.     ..

But 'Minna von Barnhelm' has higher claims to admiration than the narrow limits of nationality. It is a really noteworthy production, and justly deserves esteem. It is a genuine character comedy, a healthy delineation of real life, not a one-sided impersonation of human vices or foibles. The actions arise gradually out of the situation, hence the solution is natural and easy, while its purpose is at bottom a serious one. 'Genuine humour and true wit,' says Landor, 'require a sound and capacious mind, which is always a grave one.' 'Minna von Barnhelm' is the reflexion of Lessing's healthy and unaffected intellect.

It was the first play of his that did not attempt to translate theory into practice, in which the author rather than the critic is ascendant ; hence it is endowed with the lifelike reality his plays too often lacked, and though the form in which it was cast showed the influence of Diderot, nature in this instance entirely subjugated art. And since a good comedy is of all times, so these characters will always interest for their native poetic truth ; and that its *dénouement* results from justice pleases equally. The principal personages are ably drawn, and form a proper contrast. Minna is a really lovable heroine, unsophisticated, ingenuous, sincerely affectionate, but free from even a suspicion of sentimentalism, determined amid her impulsiveness, outspoken and just, a trifle obstinate, of a merry disposition that can treat even serious questions cheerfully. And why not ?

' Is it not possible to be very serious while laug. ing ? What objections have you to mirth ?' she asks Tellheim. ' Dear Major, laughter keeps us more reasonable than vexation.'

She knows life is not all laughter, but a strangely mixed affair, yet to look at life in a happy spirit surely cannot offend the Creator, who must prefer to behold cheerful mortals. Tellheim's melancholy tone is infectious, she tells him, she prefers her own.

Tellheim is devoid of all sense of humour, he can only see misfortunes of the deepest dye in his destiny ; his immaculate honour slurred, it is difficult to convince him that the world is wide, that his griefs are not the cynosure of all eyes, that injustice does not deserve to be met by the wreck of a life. His noble generosity, hard indifference to his own fate, sincere desire to make others happy, by main force, if need be, fail to comprehend that Minna's happiness is too entwined with his for the forcible separation which he would compel.

The minor figures are as ably depicted : the prying rapacious landlord, the devoted and the indifferent domestics, the soldiers of various types. Tellheim's sergeant is a military man from love of the profession, and will serve under any leader, provided war is his watchword ; mere errant butcher-boys, as Tellheim contemptuously calls such soldiers ; one must be a soldier for sake of cause or country. All Lessing speaks out of the explanation which Tellheim gives why he himself wears a uniform.

' I became a soldier from the fancy that it is good for every honest man to look about him for a time in this profession, to become intimate with all forms of danger, and to learn coolness and resolution.'

'Minna von Barnhelm,' with its racy point of dialogue, hits the mean of good style, in that, though polished, it is natural, and in accordance with the individualities of the characters, while it avoids Lessing's over elaborated epigrammatic manner, terse to a fault. The joyous vitality which breathes through the play may be accounted for by the prosperous circumstances under which it was composed.

This easy leisure, however, soon made Lessing restless. With the peace all the varied excitement of military life had gradually subsided into the monotonous routine of military discipline, and Lessing experienced the insipidity of this profession. He wearied of following his general from one review to another. He further declined a call to a Professorship at Königsberg, because one of the conditions attached to the post required that a yearly panegyric should be pronounced on the reigning sovereign, a condition against which Lessing's independence revolted : for though we have a good King now, he says in a letter, who will answer for his successor ? Moreover, mere outer case never held Lessing in bonds. He began to think it was high time he should return into his own grooves, and informs his parents to this effect, in reply to one of their numerous demands for money.

'Breslau : Nov. 30, 1763.

'My dear parents look on me as though I were already established here at Breslau, while this is really so little the case that it is quite possible that the larger half of my stay here is already over. I am only awaiting one more event, and if this does not turn out as I wish, I shall return to my former mode of life. I hope that you do not in any case believe that I have abandoned my studies, and mean only to devote myself to wretched occupations *de pane lucrando.* I have already wasted more than three years over these trivialities. It is time I returned to my groove. I have already attained all that I intended from my present mode of life ; my health is pretty well re-established. I have rested, and with the little that I have been able to save I have bought an excellent library, which I do not mean to have bought for nothing. Whether some few hundred thalers will remain to me, I do not know myself. At any rate, they and the money accruing to me from my lawsuit (with Winkler) will be of very good service to permit me to study for a few years in comfort. However, this shall not prevent me from doing my utmost for my brothers.'

This was a subtle intimation that Lessing would

like to keep a little of his hardly earned money for
his own use : an intimation that was most unwelcome
to the Camenz family, who had grown more and more
used to apply to him in all financial needs, and had
hoped Gotthold was at last well provided.   They
remonstrated with him on the idea of throwing up so
lucrative a post ; and he was forced to explain in all
good nature that, after all, he saw a higher object in
life than grubbing like a day labourer in order that
all his brothers might study and become pastors, and
that he was of age, and able to dispose of his life
according to his own ideas.   He even hinted that the
brothers might also do something for themselves,
neither must they be always appealing to him for
advice.   He hates giving advice, and those that ask it
can have no established character, they only want to
gain time.   He would rather give his last penny than
advice.   Everyone must know best what he can or
cannot do, if he be fit for anything.

'Breslau : June 13, 1764.

'I should be sorry if my dear parents have formed
a false idea of my present circumstances from incor-
rectly retailed intelligence.   For my part, I have certainly given no occasion for it.   Indeed I have more
than once stated that my present engagement could
be of no duration ; that I have not renounced my old
plan of life ; and that I am more than ever resolved to
avoid all permanent employment that is not entirely to
my inclination.   I am more than half through my life,
and I do not know what should oblige me to make myself a slave for the shorter part that remains to me.   I
write this to you, dearest father, and must write it to
you, so that you may not be surprised if you should

shortly see me far removed from hopes and desires of
what is termed a settled position. I only need a
little more time to extricate myself from all the debts
and complications in which I am involved, and then
I shall certainly leave Breslau. What will happen to
me then is the smallest of my anxieties. Whoever is
healthy and willing to work, need fear nothing in this
world. To anticipate long illnesses, or I know not
what events, that may incapacitate from work, shows
but a poor trust in Providence. I have a better, and
I have friends.'

The latter remark about Providence is a delicate
irony, that can scarcely have escaped the Pastor's
notice.

While thus revolving his future plans, Lessing
employed the leisure which peace had brought into
his official duties in such strenuous study, that the
close application, united to his wild tavern life and
over-excitement at cards, brought on a fever in the
summer of 1764. For some time his life was in
danger. On the day of the crisis his doctor found
him lying quite quietly, with so strange an expression
that he could not resist asking him of what he was
thinking. 'I was anxious to watch what was going
on in my soul while dying,' replied Lessing. The
doctor tried to represent to him that this was impossible. 'You annoy me,' said Lessing curtly, and
turned away. The trait is curious, as proving that,
even face to face with death, his passion for investigation of psychological processes was not quelled. By
a comical irony of fate, this doctor was an admirer of
Gottsched's, and persisted in entertaining Lessing's
convalescence with laudations of his literary merits;

discourses that teazed Lessing more than the fever.
The recovery left his nerves in a state of unwonted
tension and irritability. Till then his strong frame
had endured unharmed all fatigues and excesses ; he
perceived that with this illness had come a turning
point in his life.

During his convalescence he wrote to Ramler :

'Breslau : August 5, 1764.
'My dear Friend,
        'A thousand thanks for your anxious friend-
ship. I may be ill once, but for all that I do not
mean to die. I am pretty well recovered, except that
I am still troubled by frequent giddiness. I hope that
I may soon lose that also, and then I shall be as though
new-born. For I believe that all our changes of temperament are connected with the action of our animal
economy. The serious epoch of my life is approaching ; I am beginning to be a man, and I flatter myself
that in this hot fever I have raved away the last remainder of my youthful follies. Fortunate illness !
Your love may wish me to be well, but ought poets to
wish for the health of athletes ? Does not a certain
amount of indisposition seem far more conducive to
phantasy and feeling ? Horaces and Ramlers live in
weakly bodies. The healthy Theophiluses[1] and
Lessings become tipplers and gamblers. Therefore,
wish me health, dear friend, but with a little token of
remembrance, a little thorn in the flesh, that from time
to time will cause the poet to remember his perishable
humanity, and call to mind that not all tragedians live
to ninety, like Sophocles ; or even if they did, that

---

[1] Lessing refers to Theophilus Doebbelin, a broad-shouldered actor.

Sophocles also composed about ninety tragedies, and I have as yet only made one. Ninety tragedies ! I am suddenly seized with giddiness ! Oh let me leave the subject, dear friend !

Farewell, dear friend, farewell. I am yours ever,

LESSING.'

Though physically exhausted, his brain soon began to regain power, and curiously enough took a totally new direction. He began to write comic verses, and take an interest in fiction, particularly in long forgotten romances. The 'Gesta Romanorum' were eagerly perused, and he often wished that some scholar would critically examine their origin and diffusion. He looked over a number of learned and antiquarian essays that had accumulated in his desk, and doubting whether he could combine them into an harmonious whole, proposed to issue them under the title 'Hermaca,' whereby the Greeks define things accidentally found by the wayside. The publication of Winckelmann's 'History of Art,' inciting him to make further researches in this department, checked him awhile, and he began to bestow especial attention on the Laokoon group, and the limits of painting and poetry generally. He expressed his fears to Rector Klose lest he should be unequal to the composition of a good connected work, after pausing for so many years; he was more particularly uneasy lest his style should have suffered.

This semi-invalid state was a painful trial to Lessing's activity.

'Do not become ailing,' he writes to Ramler. 'I say ailing, because for some time past I have come to regard ailing as worse than illness. It is a vexatious

life to be up and vegetating, and to be regarded as
well, without being so really.    Before my illness I was
in such a mood for work as I have seldom known.
Now, try as I may, I am unable to find it again.    I
burn with desire to put the last touches to my 'Minna
von Barnhelm,' and yet I should not like to work at
it with half a head.    I have not been able to tell you
anything about this comedy, because it is really one of
my latest projects.    If it is not better than all my previous dramatic pieces, I am firmly resolved to have
nothing more to do with the theatre.    It is possible
that I may have paused too long.    You shall be the
first whose opinion I shall ask.'

Lessing's accurate self-criticism told him that he
was far removed from having as yet produced dramatic masterpieces, although contemporary critics
counted his among the best German originals.    He
also knew where lay their main fault ; that they smelt
too much of the lamp.

Once more he fell to making projects ; one among
these was to translate and annotate Burke 'On the
Sublime and Beautiful.'    He again thought of Vienna
as a residence, for he wished to use the Imperial Library.    Then arose the wish to visit the classic ground
of Greece, and become better acquainted with its
monuments and people.    These daydreams enlivened
many a weary hour in his sick room.    One thing he
was determined upon, and that was not to remain in his
present situation.    It was not discontent with his post
or his chief, that caused him to demand his leave, but
that he rated learned labours too highly to exchange
them permanently for administrative ones.    Besides,
though he was no hater of work, he hated prescribed
work, and chose rather to be dependent on inexorable

necessity than on the arbitrary will of men. He announces his resolve to leave Breslau in a letter to his father (January, 1765), begging that his brother Karl may not count on him to pay his University fees and debts, though he will do what he can to help him, and is willing to sell part of his library when he is again in Berlin. The Winkler lawsuit is at length decided, but the costs have left him a scanty residue, and he has some little claims of his own that require settlement. Still he again protests that his parents shall find him willing to help as far as he can.

A few months after, and Lessing was once more 'the old bird on the roof,' without fixed home or occupation. Whither should he wing his flight? His art studies attracted him powerfully to the South; he longed to see the Apollo Belvedere and the Laokoon group, with his own eyes. The news that his Berlin friends fancied they at last saw an opening for him there quite to his taste, and the desire to see them once again, determined him to return thither; but his resolution was only to do so provisionally, if the prospective inducements seemed unlikely to be realized. Taking Camenz and Leipzig on his way, he once again returned to Berlin in May 1765, no richer, thanks to the incessant claims of his family, than he had left it five years ago, except for a splendid library of over six thousand volumes.

# CHAPTER X.

## BERLIN AGAIN.

(1765-1767.  AGED 36-38.)

' *Quod non dant proceres, dabit histrio.*'   JUVENAL.

THE post which Lessing's friends had in prospect for
him, was that of Royal Librarian and Custos of the
Gem Collection ; but on the appointment being proposed to Frederick, he at once rejected it. The King's
memory was better than his acquaintance with German
literature.  He was ignorant of Lessing's solid claims,
while he remembered the Voltaire matter, and associated the name with that of a doubtful character.

Winckelmann was next suggested, and to this the
King assented.  To be set aside for Winckelmann could
be no discredit.  Lessing felt this, and abandoning all
idea of the post, began to resume his plan-making.

Again his family begged for money, and he was
forced to ask them to have some patience.  He had
a few necessary expenses of his own, and his slender
capital had long ago gone to Camenz.  He had, moreover, been robbed to a serious extent by a man-servant,
whom he had sent direct to Berlin from Breslau with
his books and clothes, and who, pretending to landlord
and friends that he was Lessing's brother, had obtained
money and credit, and, in short, had acted so very

much too 'brotherly,' that Lessing was forced to dismiss him on his return, but not before his stock of
clothes was considerably diminished and his debts
increased. Impecuniosity made travelling out of all
question for a time.

To aid his parents, Lessing therefore undertook
the charge of his younger brother Karl, and resumed
his former life of literary drudgery.

His first labour was to write the closing Letters of
the '*Literatur Briefe*,' that had dragged on a miserable
life without his co-operation, and were now about to be
supplanted by a new periodical of Nicolai's, '*Allgemeine deutsche Bibliothek*,' which, set up as a critical
tribunal, exercised a monstrous intellectual tyranny,
that gradually made the name 'Nicolaite' a by-word
of narrow-mindedness and arrogance. From the beginning Lessing declined all participation in this
journal, foreseeing it was intended as the organ of a
coterie. But he had started the Letters, and was
willing to fulfil the obligations of paternity. This
contribution also closed an epoch in his literary life.
He never again wrote for a periodical.

The subject which he chose was a review of
Meinhard's Essays 'On the Character and the Works of
the best Italian Poets.' Lessing, so sparing in praise,
calls these Essays excellent. They give him occasion
to speak at some length concerning the peculiarities
and charms of Italian poets ; nor does he neglect the
opportunity of holding up a mirror to his compatriots,
who 'give but a dubious reflexion.'

A remark of Meinhard's on the paucity of good
poets produced by the cultured Mæcenasship of the
Medici, and explained by the fact that Mæcenases

M

cannot make geniuses, but can spoil them by injudicious patronage, was spoken out of Lessing's very soul. ' A remark as acute as it is true,' says Lessing, 'very applicable to the external condition of contemporary German literature, one that should silence for ever those scribblers who are loud in their complaints of want of patronage, and overrate the influence of the great in tones of fawning flattery.' These words sharply defined Lessing's own position in the world of literature, and were probably written not without design at this moment.

Finding the expenses for two persons press inconveniently, Lessing was forced to be yet more industrious, and especially to direct his industry to the completion of some of his Breslau projects. It then became clear to him that he had despised unduly the benefits that accrued to him from his monotonous occupation at Breslau. He also found it difficult to accustom himself again to an unhealthy sedentary life, though at Breslau he had looked back upon it as pleasant and easy. It was evident to his friends and to himself that it did not suit him mentally or physically. If he had not been his own master at Breslau, the occupation had generally been mechanical and did not so strain his mental powers as to incapacitate him for his own work. Now he was working for himself, but it was as great a slavery, for he could not work for his own ideas and those of humanity, but he had to work for mere subsistence. Less inclined to such toil than before, he was more sensitive to interruptions, and these came to him not from outside but within his own study.

As he walked up and down thinking out his work, the title of a book would catch his eye; he would look into it, and there perhaps find an idea that had no bearing whatever on his present subject of meditation, and yet started so excellent a train of thought that he must at least note it down, lest it should escape him for ever. This would lead to another thought, that again must be examined, and thus an hour would pass, he knew not how. The printer's boy would knock and ask for copy. Copy, oh yes, that was ready, only it must be revised once more, and that was why he had set to work early to-day, but walking across the room had distracted him. The boy was to come again, which he duly did, only to find Lessing started off on another track, and the required copy for the half-printed work not forthcoming. He himself recognized the difficulty of all this, and would determine not to set foot out of his room until the MS. was complete. But the day would wane; he felt all his senses oppressed by the close air; he told Karl he must breathe some fresh air, or he could not think at all. So he would start forth, and generally his way led him to a friend's door. What more natural than to go in? The friend and he would chat on some interesting theme; they would get hot in discussion; Lessing made a point of breaking off early, but when he got home the MS. was forgotten. He had to pursue his friend's train of thought, analyze or adopt it. He went to bed with good resolves for the coming day; he got up feeling dull, and saying he would rather do anything than sit and read through his own writings, which did not please him at all.

'Brother,' he would say at last, 'authorship is the dreariest and most disagreeable of occupations. Take warning by me.'

Sometimes he did get into a good vein, but if he

looked up at his books it was fatal. Those books were always playing him some new trick, said Karl ; if only he had had no books !

But inner unrest and discontent had as much to answer for as the books. Meanwhile all chance of the librarianship was not over. Frederick was haggling with Winckelmann about 500 thalers, and Lessing's friends urged him to write some complete work that should worthily represent him in the eyes of the King. It was now five years since he had printed anything. Thus urged, Lessing applied himself to the completion of his antiquarian essays. He submitted the fragments to Mendelssohn, and they verbally discussed the philosophical portion, besides which Moses annotated the MS. and Lessing made use of many of his suggestions. On purely artistic questions he consulted Nicolai, who, besides a fine feeling for art, had studied it critically.

Rumour spread abroad that Lessing was writing against Winckelmann, and a book of ordinary polemics was anticipated, written with perhaps extraordinary erudition, but still a book that merely borrows its glory from the work which it endeavours to controvert. Early in 1766 the first volume of the ' Laokoon ' was issued, ' carelessly flung upon the world,' as Lewes well remarks ; for so doubtful was Lessing of its success, that he begged the publisher only to print a small edition, as no one would read it. The world was surprised to receive an independent work that only made Winckelmann a starting point, and was complete in itself. Lessing modestly defined his book as a series of remarks which had casually grown to their present dimensions rather in consequence of the course of his reading, than through any methodical development of general principles. His notes were rather unarranged memoranda for a book, than a book. 'Yet I flatter myself that, even as such, they will not be wholly despised. We Germans have no lack of systematic treatises. We know, in spite of one nation in the world, how to deduce what we desire out of some established definitions.'

The 'Laokoon' was a pioneer. It had to create itself a public; but critical voices soon made themselves heard, and its fame reached the Villa Albani. The rumour that had preceded the work had also reached Winckelmann. He had lived so long in Rome, that he was ignorant of Lessing's very name, and it angered him to think that some pedant, devoid of any understanding for aesthetics, should attack him. But when the work appeared, with its respectful admiration for his ability, its courteous and profoundly learned criticism of his faults, he changed his opinion and honourably retracted the remarks which he had written on mere hearsay. He regrets that he had never yet seen any of Lessing's writings, or even heard of him, and adds, 'Lessing writes as oneself would wish to have written.' He proposes to address him direct, 'for he deserves a dignified reply to the points wherein I can defend myself. As it is glorious to be praised by competent persons, so also it may be glorious to be held worthy of their criticism.'

Meanwhile Winckelmann had sent a definite refusal to King Frederick's proposals. He was disgusted by the petty meanness of the Prussian monarch, and preferred the patronage of a cardinal and the delights of Roman life to immurement in bureaucratic Berlin. Lessing was again proposed to Frederick. The King was seriously annoyed at the persistency with which

this name was thrust upon him, and passionately exclaimed that he would not have any German pedants.
When told that Lessing was one of the most learned
men in Europe, and that if he did not take a German he
would have no really learned librarian, he forbade all
further mention of the subject, and said he would
write to Paris and obtain a learned librarian for himself without help of the Germans. His failure in this,
and the manner in which he was duped into appointing
an ignorant superstitious monk, is matter of history.
Frederick's want of appreciation for his greatest contemporary must be sought in his entirely French education and in the fact that his prejudice against German
scholars was not wholly without ground, for, excepting
Lessing, who was a polished man of the world both in
bearing and culture, the representatives of literature
were apt to be slovenly dreamers or pedantic bookworms. That he was not blind to the abilities of his
own people, and that he even occasionally despised
French literature, is notorious, and he had the keen
insight to write that 'the German nation is not
wanting in genius and intellect (*Geist*), but it has been
retarded by circumstances which prevented it from
soaring aloft at the same time as its neighbours. Some
day we shall have our classical writers ; everyone
will read them to aid them in their culture ; our neighbours will learn German ; it will be spoken with
appreciation at courts, and it may happen that when
our language is perfected it will extend from one end
of Europe to the other.'

On learning the King's final decision, Lessing's
one desire was to get away from Berlin, no matter
whither ; the city and the Prussians had grown hateful.
A young nobleman begged for his company in an

excursion to Pyrmont. They left Berlin in June, taking Halberstadt on their way, to visit Gleim, who supplied Lessing with money and books, and could not believe but that his adored King would yet alter his decision and not let go the services of the most competent man in his dominions. On the return journey Lessing stopped at Göttingen to visit his old master, Kästner, and his first patron, Professor Michaelis, whom on this occasion he instigated to one of his most important labours, the addition of critical notes for lay readers to his translation of the Bible. Lessing had remarked sarcastically, ' that Christians heard so little and could use so little of that which bookworms invented in their studies, delivered in their lecture-rooms, or published in their learned and usually Latin works.'

After Lessing's return in August, plans and counterplans and annoyances of various kinds pressed upon him. In October he wrote a despondent letter to Gleim, returning the money he had borrowed, and begging indulgence for his negligence and ill-humour. One evening, in company with Ramler and other intimate friends, conversation turned on the themes best suited to comedy. Lessing, in one of his wayward moods, chose to maintain that all subjects could be adopted for comedies and tragedies, for the essential was the elaboration of the subject, not the subject itself : a proposition exactly opposed to the spirit of the ' Laokoon ' and the letter of Lessing's theatrical writings. His friends exclaimed, ' Prove it by example.'

' Why not ? ' said Lessing.

' Well then, write a comedy of which a sleeping draught is the catastrophe.'

Lessing assented, and set to work at once. The

play was sketched, and, to judge from the draft, would have been no important contribution to the drama. As in 'Minna,' the scene is laid in the upper middle class, but the tone is lower, and the sketch exhibits no signs that it would have approached that play. An unexpected application from Hamburg hindered its completion and changed all Lessing's plans and ideas.

A miserable stage cabal, occasioned by the jealousy and vanity of a prima donna, had caused the break-up of the theatrical troupe then playing in that city. An association of wealthy merchants, actors and writers, had started the project of founding a permanent theatre which should aspire to the dignity of a national stage, and should be a school for the cultivation of healthier taste and a higher style of drama. It was proposed that Lessing should aid the undertaking as dramaturgist (dramatic critic), with a salary of 800 thalers. The committee requested Nicolai to sound Lessing on the subject. The plan of the enterprise was after Lessing's own heart, even if he had not been 'standing idle at the market-place waiting for hire.' He determined to go to Hamburg and see after matters with his own eyes. His love for the theatre was in danger of extinction, but this proposal instantly rekindled it into flame. A national permanent theatre, that was indeed a sweet dream. His dramatic zeal had been wrecked so often from this need. With no established stage, no organized troupe, all had hitherto been tentative. Progress could not be hoped for, and it was no wonder that both actors and public were mistrustful and indifferent. Here was a real chance for amelioration, and the source whence it was offered was peculiarly favourable to the hope of success. Hamburg, an independent Hanseatic city, opulent, commercial, could not be narrow and pedantic in ideas like Leipzig, or repressed with servile court adulation like Berlin. Moreover the republican burghers were too independent to be infected with the national taint of French imitation. Eckhof had been drawing good audiences when Lessing passed through the city with Winkler, and consequently he retained pleasant memories of its theatrical taste. The design of the new undertaking could not but gain Lessing's approval ; his optimistic temperament made him sanguine as to its success, while his ingenuous trusting nature made him neglect to look behind the scenes and discover the mines and countermines that were at work.

On its surface the project was briefly this. In order that Art need not abase itself to pecuniary needs and thus pander to the low taste of the vulgar, a certain capital had been advanced by the rich merchants, and over this capital, from which the promoters were not hopeless of ultimate dividends, a financial committee was appointed. The dramatic management was to be quite apart from the pecuniary, and it was anticipated that thus relieved of any money anxiety, it would apply itself solely to high artistic ends. They were to found a histrionic academy, producing first-class artists, and a man of letters and aesthetic taste was to assist in the formation of a *répertoire* and in the choice of plays. No other than Lessing could fill such a post, and the directors showed their penetration in enlisting his services.

'All goes well in the matter concerning which I have come to Hamburg,' Lessing writes to Karl in December 1766 ; 'it only rests with me to conclude the most advantageous terms. But you know me, and

that chinking advantages are not the chief things in
my eyes, and accordingly some considerations have
arisen concerning which I must be satisfied before I
quite decide.'

These considerations referred to the demands of
the directors that he should engage to produce a prescribed number of original pieces for the new stage.
This he declined decisively; production was no easy
process with him.

'What Goldoni did for the Italian theatre, when he
enriched it with thirteen new plays in one year, that I
must leave undone for the German stage. Nay, I
would not attempt it even if I could. I do not feel
in me that living spring which works its way upwards·
by its own power, and by its own power bursts forth
into rich, fresh, pure streams. I must work everything out of myself by high pressure. I should be
poor, cold, and shortsighted, had I not in some degree
learnt how modestly to borrow foreign treasures, how
to warm myself at alien fires, and to strengthen my
sight by the glasses of Art.'

In any case, however, he tells his brother to give
notice to his landlord, because, come what may, he
will not stay in Berlin after Easter. The directors,
who desired at all costs to have Lessing's name associated with their scheme, acceded to his proposal and
appointed him theatrical critic only.

Lessing could not wholly blind himself to the fact
that this appointment did not rest on an absolutely
sure basis. He cast about him for other means of
revenue, and concluded an arrangement with a jour-
nalist of the name of Bode, who had just made a rich
marriage and desired to found a printing press with
his wife's money. The press was to be connected

with the new theatre and print all its requirements, and the plan was to start a publishing business in combination. Of this Lessing was to have the management; his own works and those of his friends were to form a starting point. Another project after his own heart.

Lessing returned to Berlin full of sanguine joy at the unexpected future that had opened before him. His first step was to reissue his plays and put the finishing touches to 'Minna von Barnhelm,' that it might be published among them. As he had promised, he showed it first to Ramler, bringing it to him act by act. Ramler read them, and appended to each a criticism or a suggestion; these were all accepted with two or three exceptions. The pecuniary profits being microscopical, Lessing saw himself forced to part with his library, only reserving such books as he needed in his new enterprise. He hoped to pay his Berlin debts with the result, and to have a good surplus left for investment in Bode's scheme. It grieved him sorely to part with these books, and especially to have to part with them in Berlin, where their rare value was not in the least appreciated. The proceeds fell short of his expectations; moreover he had at the same time the mortification of being robbed by another servant, who had not only helped himself to money and clothes, but to what Lessing valued far more, some of his rarest books. At this very moment a professorship of archaeology was offered to him at Cassel. He refused it. He was bound, and moreover he preferred the Hamburg post, free from bureaucratic slavery. Inclined to illusions, he thought it promised him a freer and more independent position; and though a cynic would have predicted that this project would go to wreck on national indifference, that it would do so with extraordinary speed was not to be foreseen.

' Berlin : February 1, 1767.

'Dear Friend,

'Your letter of the 6th ult. was searching for me at Hamburg when I had already left. I did not receive it back again till yesterday, and there-fore hope forgiveness for my tardy reply.

'I do not know where to begin, I have so much to tell you. Yes, I have been to Hamburg, and in 9—10 weeks I think of going there again, probably to remain there for ever. I hope I shall not find it difficult to forget Berlin. My friends there will al-ways remain dear to me ; but all else, from the greatest to the least ——— but I remember, you do not like to hear disapprobation expressed of this queen of cities. And *que diable allais-je faire dans cette galère ?*

'Do not ask on what I am going to Hamburg. Really on nothing. So long as they do not take anything from me at Hamburg, they will give me just as much as they have given me here. But I need not hide anything from you. I have certainly made a sort of arrangement with the new theatre there and with its *entrepreneurs*, which promises me a calm, pleasant life for some years. As I concluded with them, these words of Juvenal occurred to me :

Quod non dant proceres, dabit histrio.

'I intend finishing my theatrical works, which have long waited for the last touches, and represent-ing them there. Such events were needed to rekindle my almost extinct love for the theatre. I was just

beginning to lose myself in other studies, which
would soon have made me quite incapable of any
work of imagination. My "Laokoon" is now again
a secondary interest. It appears to me that I shall
be early enough with its continuation for the great
mass of readers. The few who do read me at
present understand as much of the matter as I do,
and more . . . . . . Yet one word. When your
pastoral is finished, Schuck is not to have it, but I will
have it, and get it represented in Hamburg. Send
it me ; the sooner the better.

     'I am always your sincere friend,

               ' LESSING.'

    Early in April Lessing left Berlin, as usual with-
out warning. Taking leave of friends gave him a
keen pain which he gladly spared himself. Chance
even brought about that he did not bid good-bye to
his brother. He disliked all sentimentality in feeling
and words, and it was characteristic of him to write
to Karl on his arrival at Hamburg : 'You will have
heard from Herr Ramler how it came that I had to
go away without speaking to you again. All that
brothers have to say to each other at parting is a
matter of course between us both.'

    'I have quitted Berlin,' he writes to his father,
'because the only thing I hoped for, and which was
so long held out to me, has come to nothing.'

    He was bitter on this score, and yet he had pro-
claimed in his closing Literary Letter that princely
protection is more hurtful than useful ; that royal
patrons of literature substitute their personal taste
for good taste ; that genius left to itself forces its
way like to a torrent that makes its own bed, not-

withstanding obstacles.    Conformably to his theory, he was about to force obstacles like the torrent, but, unlike the torrent, he was not to find a peaceful bed. But happily for man, the future is hidden from his gaze, and Lessing arrived at Hamburg full of youthful faith and enthusiasm, believing that he had at last secured a permanent resting-place.

# CHAPTER XI.

## 'LAOKOON.'

*' J'écrirai ici mes pensées sans ordre, et non pas peut-être dans une con-fusion sans dessein : c'est le véritable ordre, et qui marquera toujours mon objet par le désordre même.'—*PASCAL.

WHILE at Breslau Lessing had occupied himself greatly with archaeological studies, and had come to take a keen interest in the fine arts, though he had seen few classical works, and his knowledge was principally derived from engravings and from the writings of Spence, Webb, Richardson, Hogarth, and Caylus. The publication of Winckelmann's early Essays 'On the Imitation of the Ancients in Painting and Statuary' had led him to go more deeply into the subject. In this first work Winckelmann had declared war against the aberrations of the Rococo taste, and proclaimed that the only way to become great was to follow the road trodden by Michael Angelo, Rafael, and Poussin ; but here he stopped short. He had spoken against the unnatural, against outrageous passion, and referred to the noble sim-plicity and placidity of Greek art ; but he had not objected to the current rage for allegory : nay, indeed he had spoken warmly in its favour. He thought it possible for the painter to follow the poet. This afforded another instance to Lessing how prone were even the best minds of the day to confuse two sister but distinctive arts.

These Essays were followed by the publication of Winckelmann's more important work, the 'History of Art.' Lessing read it at once. He found that its antiquarian, portion rested on an unstable foundation, and that whatever advantage Winckelmann might possess in actual acquaintance with the works of art, he compensated by more accurate scholarship, the want of which had betrayed Winckelmann into some errors. It was with the purpose of rectifying these errors, still more of assigning to poetry and painting their respective boundaries, that Lessing wrote his 'Laokoon.' His motive was no spirit of critical asperity, but a sincere desire to amend a valuable work. He had also a deeper motive. He feared that Winckelmann's authority would contribute yet further to confound the provinces of the arts. It was his aim to establish their boundaries once and for ever, and his success is attested by the unanimous verdict of criticism, that Lessing has effected for Art and Criticism what Adam Smith did for Political Economy.

In order to understand this marvellous effect, it is needful to carry back memory to the days before the 'Laokoon' was written ; for the principles which it inculcates have now become such common property, are so merely the alphabet of culture, that we might be tempted occasionally to rebel at this minute analysis of the obvious. But such matters were by no means the obvious a hundred years ago, when the greatest confusion of ideas existed concerning the capabilities of the various arts. The endeavour to fix general principles for the regulation of opinion

was the characteristic of the eighteenth century.
Everything was to be defined by and subject to laws.
That this love of classification should lead to errors,
and restrict ideas within too narrow principles, was
an inevitable result, but one that sprang from a noble
wish for enlightenment at all risks, and is therefore
entitled to respect. Taste, as a matter of positive
law and not of individual fancy, was unknown. The
first who tried to formulate a theory of the Fine Arts
was A. G. Baumgarten, a follower of Wolff, who
hazarded the term Aesthetics to denote the theory of
emotional perception. His labours, however, extended
no further than to trace broad outlines, the contrast
between the hideous and the beautiful. Learned
men took up the work and dogmatized with painful
pedantry. They failed to see that the Fine Arts,
rooted in psychology and sensuous perception, could
only furnish *axiomata media* and could not be formu-
lated too sharply, and they ran themselves hopelessly
aground in their acceptance as an indisputable dictum
of the antithesis of Simonides, that ' Painting is silent
poetry, and poetry eloquent painting.'

It was this problem which had given birth to
Baumgarten's Aesthetics, and whose solution was
reserved for the ' Laokoon.' This axiom had been
propounded and accepted by the first writers who
had attempted to define art. It was enunciated by
Dryden in his ' Parallel of Poetry and Painting,'
insisted on by Du Fresnoy, who cites Horace's
' *Ut pictura poesis* ' and interprets it abusively in its
support, by Fénélon, the Abbé du Bos, and others.
More especially was it held by the English. Spence
and Addison could see no independent virtue in
works of art except in so far as they illustrated pas-

N

sages in the Roman poets. The similarity and harmony of Poetry and Painting were held as incontrovertibly fixed. It was the great idea of the period that
the painters should poetize, the poets paint. Thomson's 'Seasons,' with their imitation of pictorial effects,
had led the way as far as poetry was concerned, and
Lessing himself in his youth had acknowledged
Thomson as the greatest descriptive poet. While
everyone exaggerated the resemblance of the pictorial and poetic genuses, they determined their
relative claims according to their own respective
idiosyncrasies and inclinations; the one faction demanding that the painters should imitate the poets,
the other that the poets should imitate the painters.
The seventeenth century had loved mythology in
its poetry and arts; the eighteenth substituted
allegory. This allegory, a cold and conventional
masquerading of contemporary ideas and personages,
appealed to an age enamoured of the spirit of abstraction. Everything was to rest on a philosophical
basis. Hence poetry was reduced to express ideas
rather than emotions, and the arts of design were to
reason with the brush. In Italy the confusion of
styles may be traced to the revival of Platonic studies;
in England, to Bacon's division of man's understanding into three parts : Memory, Imagination, and
Reason ; whereby Fancy was made a common factor of
poetry and painting, and hence the true principle of
ancient art, objective imitation, became confounded
with the subjective principle of fiction, and false
idealism took the place of nature and truth.

Certain critics had already endeavoured to establish some distinctions essential to the two *genres*.
Thus Winckelmann in his early Essays had remarked

that the essential condition of Greek sculpture was simplicity and quiet grandeur, while Hagedorn defined
the distinguishing feature of representative art as the
elimination of the uncomely.  This was the state of
the question when Lessing attempted to solve it in a
definite manner.  He perceived that a great number
of ingenious observations and just ideas had been
expressed by these various critics, but no actual principle had been demonstratively established.  A
variety of circumstances had given him the needful
preparation for entering the lists.  To begin, he was
ignorant of nothing that had been written on the
subject.  Already at Leipzig he had learnt from
Christ the use that could be made of ancient texts in
the study of the arts, and scarcely had he been
appointed critic on the ' Voss Gazette ' than it devolved
on him to review his friend Mylius' translation of
Hogarth's ' Analysis of Beauty.'  He hailed a work
that endeavoured to fix the fluctuating ideas of taste,
and, free from metaphysics, reduced beauty to the
firm and sure conception of form : form reduced to
its elements the curved line, the source of beauty ; the
sinuous, the line of grace.  Here at last was a book
that opposed something definite to the vague sensations of those who satisfied themselves with the adage,
' *De gustibus non est disputandum.*'

'Here is a book,' writes the youthful Lessing,
'which we must thank if in future, when we apply the
word " beautiful " to a thousand things, we shall think
as much as until now we have felt.'

The practical bearing of any mental department,
never left out of regard by the thinker Lessing, for all
his purely theoretical interests, speaks out of this
passage.  To give to each department its due, to

introduce order into the reigning confusion, was the mission which Lessing had unconsciously taken upon himself. In ' Pope a Metaphysician ' he had demonstrated the distinction between a poet and a philosopher ; in his Essay on Fables he had enfranchised poetry from the yoke of ethics ; in his correspondence with Nicolai and Mendelssohn concerning Tragedy, he had had the same end in view, the separation of different departments ; and now in the ' Laokoon ' he proposed to divorce the arts of design and poetry from the union in which they had hitherto been held, to the detriment of both. He felt convinced that every *genre* contained an expression of beauty proper to itself alone, that the effort to engraft it with alien qualities is to mar its very *raison d'être.* The ' Laokoon ' was to establish this, to clear the ground that others might follow in the wake. It was a peculiarity of Lessing's thus to put forth problems ; his modesty never let him venture beyond La Fontaine's ' *On le peut, je l'essaie, un plus savant le fasse.*'

It would have been out of keeping with Lessing's mental peculiarity if he had set out to write a philosophical treatise *modo et formâ* on Art. All theory was to him a polemic ; he needed an adversary and he found him in Winckelmann. The fable of the Laokoon was merely to furnish him with an occasion to express certain principles ; yet in choosing it he by no means pretended to limit himself to the study of this plastic group. But his spirit was pre-eminently synthetical. He loved to argue from the particular to the general ; he had therefore to choose an example and the Laokoon was peculiarly happy. Sculpture and poetry had both worked masterpieces from this theme. It would thus be easier to judge the differ-

ences and resemblances of these arts. Winckelmann
had already instituted a comparison between the work
of the painter and the sculptor, giving the preference
to the latter in virtue of his aesthetic dogma that the
expression of noble grandeur of soul is more beautiful
than the expression of passion. He had then proceeded to compare Virgil and the sculptor. This comparison furnishes a starting point for Lessing, who
undertakes to prove by the same examples that the
two artists were obliged to seek totally divergent
beauties by reason of the difference of their art. He
applied himself to elucidate this.

The similarity of Poetry and Painting had been
amply discussed. It seemed to him worth while to
reverse the medal, and investigate their inherent dis-
similarity, to ascertain whether such divergence did
not follow from some law, peculiar to each, which often
compelled the one to tread a different path from her
sister. The second title he bestowed on the treatise,
' Laokoon, or the Boundaries of Poetry and Painting,'
marked his starting point and the object of the book,
as well as the motto prefixed, "Ὕλῃ καὶ τρόποις
μιμήσεως (as well in the object as in the manner
of their imitations). He begs the reader to note that
under the name of Painting he includes the Plastic
Arts generally ; nor will he deny that under the name
of Poetry he has also some regard to the other arts
that possess the characteristic of progressive imitation. This is a reference to the drama, regarded by
Lessing, like his master Aristotle, as the acme of all art.

Lessing held that the first person who compared
Painting and Poetry was a man of fine feeling, who
perceived that both these arts produced a like
effect, by placing absent things before him as pre-

sent. The second person sought to penetrate into
the nature of this pleasure, and discovered that it
flowed from the same source, the love of the beautiful;
the third reflected upon the value and distribution of
these general rules. The first was an amateur, the
second a philosopher, the third an art-critic. The
first two could not easily make a wrong use of their
feeling or their reasoning. Not so the critic. The
principal force of his remarks depend on their correct
application to the particular case; and since few
critics are really acute, the application has not always
been made with the caution requisite to hold the
scales equal. We may feel assured that in the lost
writings on Painting of Apelles and Protogenes,
the same moderation and accuracy prevailed that
is illustrated in the works of Aristotle, Cicero and
Horace, when they apply the principles and experiences of Painting to Eloquence and Poetry. The
dazzling antithesis of the Greek Voltaire, that
Painting is dumb poetry, Poetry eloquent painting,
was a smart saying, like many another spoken by
Simonides. Its brilliancy had dazzled the moderns
and caused them to overlook its want of precision.
The ancients did not overlook this, and the author
of the dictum was well aware that it would receive
due modification in practice from the right feeling of
the artist, since it is the privilege of the ancients in
no one thing to do too much or too little. Not so
with the moderns, who believe that in many things
they have surpassed them. The ancients perfectly
understood that for all their similarity of effect, the
arts differed, while the moderns have promulgated the
crudest notions concerning their harmony. At one
time they compress poetry within the narrow limits of

painting, at another painting is desired to fill the wide
sphere of poetry. And why? Because they choose
to hold that whatever is right in the one must be permitted to the other. This false taste has infected the
creators themselves, generating a mania for description
in poetry, and allegory in painting, until they no
longer know what ideas can or ought to be painted,
what expressed in writing. The deductions to be
drawn from these trenchant comparisons determine
the degree of pictorial imitation permissible to a poet.
He must not enumerate details as though the listener
had an actual picture before his eyes, he must present
the visible with a few bold traits capable of stimulating
phantasy. The mission of poetry is through outward
forms to represent the inner life of action, hence this
art must only represent forms suggestively through
the medium of actions.

Lessing then proceeds to give an elaborate definition of the principles of formative art, side by side
with a definition of the principles of poetry, not for the
sake of contrast, but because the imperfect apprehen-
sion of this contrast had led critics and artists into
error, and even so consummate a judge as Winckelmann
had gone astray. Winckelmann censures Virgil for
the horrible shriek he makes his Laokoon utter, and
praises the sculptor for having expressed the sufferer's
agony in his body alone, without displaying anguish
in his face, that remains great and calm for all his
intense suffering. The reason Winckelmann finds in
the fact that Laokoon's greatness of soul had overcome all expression of pain. The marble Laokoon
suffers, but he suffers like the Philoctetes of Sophocles ;
he does not shriek like the Roman's hero. Such an
observation put Lessing on his mettle. Nourished on

Homer and Sophocles, he is able to confute Winckelmann with chapter and verse. If the unfavourable
side-glance at Virgil had startled him, how much more
the comparison with the Philoctetes of Sophocles.
Does not Philoctetes exclaim piteously throughout the
whole third act? how could he lament more audibly
than by his long-sustained *αἲ, αἲ πάπαι, πάπαι* ? A
scream is the natural expression of bodily pain.
Homer's wounded heroes scream, so does Aphrodite ;
not that she may thus appear soft and womanish, but
to prove her nature capable of suffering. Even the
brazen Ares, when struck by the lance of Diomedes,
shrieks so dreadfully that he terrifies both armies.
However Homer may exalt his heroes, they are true
to human nature whenever there is a question of
anguish. In their deeds they are higher creatures, in
their feelings true men. We refined Europeans of a
wiser posterity, it is true, know better how to command our voices ; high breeding forbids screams. Not
so with the Greek, he had no false shame for his
mortal weakness ; with him the scream of bodily pain
was quite compatible with greatness of soul. Homer
hides a deep meaning when he relates how the Greeks
wept hot tears while burning their dead, but Priam
forbids his Trojans to weep. The cause is this. The
civilized Greek can at the same time weep and be
bold, not so the uncivilized Trojan. And hence, the
conclusion established that a cry of suffering may
according to Greek thought consist with greatness of
soul, Winckelmann must be wrong when he adduces
this as the reason why the artist has not imitated the
cry in marble. There must be another cause why in
this respect he differs from his rival the poet, who lays
especial stress on this cry.

Lessing then pronounces beauty to be the essence and soul of Greek art. Legend tells how the daughter of Dibutades, a potter of Corinth, outlined the shadow of her lover on the wall the day before his departure, and how her father, to assuage her longing for the one, copied the outline in clay.

It is to this fable that Lessing refers, when, presuming his readers to be as well versed as himself in Hellenic lore, he proceeds to say: 'Be it fable or history that Love caused the first attempt in plastic art, so much is certain, it was never weary in guiding the hand of the great old masters.' The wise Greek confined himself to the imitation of beautiful bodies: the perfection of the object itself was the thing that enraptured him. Nothing was dearer to him in his art, nothing nobler, than the aim and end of Art itself. After some digressions on Caricature and realistic Art, he returns to his primary proposition, that with the ancients beauty was the highest law of the imitative Arts, and this principle established, it follows that everything that did not harmonize with beauty must give way to it, and therefore such passions as distort the countenance were either avoided altogether or used in a subordinate degree, in which they were susceptible of some measure of beauty. Hence the reason why the sculptor would not permit his Laokoon to utter a cry of anguish. The master strove to attain the highest beauty under the given circumstances of bodily agony. He could not combine the disfiguring vehemence of the latter with the former, he must therefore diminish it, soften shrieks to sighs, not because the shriek degrades, but because it disfigures. An instant's thought will show how the wide open mouth, a blot in painting, a cavity in sculpture, would change a creation

that inspired sympathy by its union of beauty and
suffering, into a hideous figure from which we should
instinctively turn away.

A counterpart from the best period of Greek Art
occurs to him in Timanthe's picture of the Sacrifice of
Iphigenia, in which the artist distributed to all the by-
standers their proper share of grief, but veiled the
countenance of the father.   This veiling is a sacrifice
which the artist has made to beauty : he knew that
Agamemnon's grief was of the deepest kind that can
only find expression in distortion.   This is another
example of the need of subjecting expression to the
first law of art, the law of beauty.   From this consideration Lessing deduces an important rule, namely,
that as the painter can only represent a single
moment of an event, that moment must be chosen
which is most fruitful of effect.   For since a work of
art is intended to be considered long and repeatedly,
that point of view is most fruitful of effect which leaves
most scope to the imagination.   Therefore the ex-
tremest point of passion must not be chosen, because
that binds the wings of Fancy and compels her, since
she cannot go beyond the impression made on the
senses, to busy herself with feeble and subordinate
images.   When Laokoon sighs the imagination may
hear him scream, but if he screamed imagination could
go no further, but must descend to behold him in a
more tolerable and therefore less interesting condition.
The observer must not see but surmise the crisis.   The
eternal Now of the painter and sculptor, that freezes
a transitory moment into motionless immortality, must
express no phenomena that are essentially evanescent,
such as a smile, a cry.   The grievous pain that extorts
the cry must cease or destroy the sufferer.   The most

enduring man may cry out, but not incessantly, and this apparent perpetuity in the material imitation of art must be borne in view. This the artist of the Laokoon must have regarded, even if the outcry had been compatible with beauty.

Having thus established the reasons why the artist must observe moderation in the expression of bodily emotions, i.e. that they are altogether derived from and necessary to the peculiar nature, limits and requirements of his art, Lessing proceeds to examine whether these same reasons apply to poetry. By no means ; nothing constrains the poet to concentrate his picture upon a single moment. He can pursue the train of thoughts and actions that would cost the painter a multiplicity of works, and therefore he may touch on such traits, as, considered by themselves, would jar on the imagination, because immediate reparation is made by what follows after. Virgil's Laokoon shrieks, and shrieking is repulsive ; but this screaming Laokoon is the same whom we have already learnt to know and love as a wise patriot and kind father. We attribute his outcry to his intolerable suffering, not to his character ; and it is not by it alone that the poet can make us sensible of his sufferings. Hence the great divergence between painting and poetry. The painter, limited to a single moment in which to tell his tale, not able like the poet to prepare his audience for an effect by previous recital, unable to soften immediate impressions by subsequent narration, must choose the most pregnant moment, i.e. that in which the mind of the spectator best perceives the preceding and what is to come.

Aristotle had defined both poetry and painting as imitations of Nature. Lessing does not discuss this

point, which he holds incontestable. He only wishes
to show how these arts ought to differ in the means
which they employ. Painting employs figures and
colours in space : the artist articulates sounds in time ;
and this eminently philosophical distinction of time
and space constitutes the great originality of Lessing's
theory. The objects of painting are bodies, bodies
with their visible qualities. The objects of poetry are
actions. Painting also imitates actions, but she
imitates them in representing the disposition of the
body in which they take place. Poetry on the other
hand may also be said to imitate bodies, but she
imitates them in elucidating by successive traits the
actions that take place. The law regarding time does
not apply to the poet : hence his scope of representation is wider, and this brings Lessing to his culminating
point, the supremacy of the poetical over the plastic
arts. Homer creates two classes of beings and of
actions, visible and invisible. Painting is incompetent
to represent this difference. With it everything is
visible, and visible after one fashion only. It was the
folly of the age to believe it possible to reproduce in
painting or sculpture every striking scene in a poet.
Caylus advocated the illustration of Homer, and it
was just Homer, on whom Caylus built his theory,
who was its most striking negation. What idea should
we have of Homer, asks Lessing, if, nothing remained
of the 'Iliad' or 'Odyssey' but such pictures, though
they be from the hand of the most perfect master, and
though Homer is the most picturesque of poets?
But a poetical picture is not necessarily capable of
transmutation into a material picture, while on the
other hand some circumstances are picturesque and
others not. The historian, the prose writer, can

.arrate in a very unpicturesque manner those that are most picturesque, while the poet by virtue of his imagination can clothe in a picturesque manner those that are most unpicturesque. When Homer paints, he paints nothing but progressive actions, and hence produces no picture which the painter can imitate with his pencil. He places his single object in a successive series of movements, for the last of which the painter is obliged to wait in order that he may show us that object completely formed, whose gradual for-- mation we have followed with the poet. Thus when Homer shows us the chariot of Hêrê, Hebe puts it together before our eyes, and the picture is made up of movement. Poetry must be sparing in the descrip- tion of bodily objects, and should confine itself to one trait in the use of picturesque epithets. Homer does not even describe the shield of Achilles when made, but paints the action of the divine maker. Lessing wishes it to be distinctly understood that he does not deny to language the power of painting a corporeal whole in its parts, he only denies that such a use of language should be regarded as poetry. He thus closes to poetry the domain of pure description.

He distinguishes between the poet and the pro- saist. The prose writer may be content with per- spicuity, but the poet must awaken in us ideas, illusions, and we must be unconscious of the means, i.e. of the words, he employs for his purpose. Virgil in his ' Georgics ' may describe a cow which is a good breeder, but he is only dogmatizing on her good points, and in so far as he dogmatizes he is no poet. No description of a flower, however detailed, can approach the vivid- ness of a flower painted by Van Huysum. Descriptive poetry is thus entirely condemned, on the high ground

that, vying with an alien art, Poetry compromises her
power.   Let her renounce a useless and unequal
struggle, and throw her whole energy into the far
wider field which lies outside painting, for to her it is
given to attain the sublime beyond the reach of
painting.   He makes an exception in the case of
didactic poetry, because, as he hastens to add, it is not
poetry at all.   Every attempt of a poet to describe
corporeal beauty, be he even an Ariosto, seems to
Lessing as if he saw stones rolled up a mountain out
of which, on the top, a superb building is meant to be
erected, but all of which of their own accord roll down
again upon the other side.   When Anacreon analyzes
the beauty of his maiden, he treats of it in a manner that
exempts him from this error, for he imagines he has
a painter before him, and causes him to work under
his eyes.

'But,' objects Lessing, 'does not Poetry suffer too
great a loss if we take away from her all images of
corporeal beauty?   Who wishes to take them away?'
he replies.   If we seek to prevent her pursuing a
particular path, following in the footsteps of a sister
art without ever reaching the same goal, is every other
path therefore closed to her?   By no means.   Poets
can work by effect, they must paint for us the pleasure,
inclination, love, rapture, that beauty causes, and by so
doing they paint beauty itself.   And since movement
is at the root of all poetic pleasure, it follows that the
drama is its highest expression, while the epic takes
the second place, because it is a dramatic poem.

It was this idea of the high calling of the drama,
an idea conformable to Lessing's views from boyhood,
that was to have been worked out in the concluding
portion of the 'Laokoon.'   But the fine work remained

a Torso. After his death there were found among his papers notes for a second and third part, and though these are in a rough state, they are full of pregnant suggestions. From them we see that Lessing intended to treat of music in its union with poetry. In speaking of opera, he observes that poetry is always the auxiliary art, the union n which music is the auxiliary art has yet to be invented : a remark that goes to prove how cordially he would have welcomed the reforms inaugurated by Gluck very shortly after.

Still, fragment as the ' Laokoon ' is, its influence was enormous, both for its luminous discrimination of distinct styles of art as for its occasional discussion of side issues, such as the nature of the ugly and the ridiculous. The mass of combative criticism that has arisen regarding the work, all the modification and correction which it has undergone, have left its fundamental axioms untouched. The condition of archaeology as a science in Lessing's day made it impossible for him always to penetrate to the truth ; but he has often skirted it where he has not defined it. He certainly contributed largely to the advancement of this science, if only by clearing the ground from the mass of obstacles that had hitherto impeded its progress. The ' Laokoon ' has sometimes been censured as having only a negative tendency ; but, as Kant well observes, ' merely to ascertain the boundaries of the different species, which might seem a negative science, is of the greatest positive use for the development of each species in its whole individuality.' Together with Winckelmann, Lessing evoked beauty as the watchword of the new movement ; he differed from him in that Winckelmann was content with a vague fantastic expression of beauty only, as the grand purpose of art, while Lessing insisted on beauty of form. But while his ideal of beauty consisted in beauty of lines, he would never have contemplated the exaggerated materialistic conception of art into which this view has of late degenerated. A voluptuous school of art, that rates sensuous perception, colours and accessories, above true artistic thought and feeling, would never have been in accordance with Lessing's views. With all his fine feeling for artistic beauty, he was above all the philosophic critic, resting his conclusions on a sound learned basis. How could such a one have applauded an art void of intellect and mind?

Winckelmann, on the other hand, was an enthusiastic votary of art, who, brought face to face with the glorious results, deduced from them his theories, that were calculated dangerously to shackle the artist, tempt him to substitute the means for the end, and to lose, in a hopeless chase after beauty in the abstract, all that can alone make beauty interesting—expression and mind. Lessing's standpoint was as narrow in its way, but its results were calculated to be healthier. He was before all else a thinker ; therefore, in treating of a work of art, he started from the thoughts and concrete perceptions which it awoke in him, and thus abstracted his conclusions logically from sensation. Thence he deduced beauty of form, and such beauty of form is attained artistically by idealization. This is but faintly possible with regard to animals, not at all with inanimate nature. Hence his slight esteem for landscape painting, since landscape has no settled beauty of form, and owes its attractiveness to colour and transitory effects. With this same principle of idealization, it naturally follows that he condemns the

Dutch painters of vulgar interiors, common-place, and still-life, as well as portraiture, since the end of this is likeness, and likeness is not compatible with idealization. His want of appreciation of landscape painting must be partially sought in his own indifference to scenery. Neither in his Diary nor Letters does any reference to scenery occur. It is indeed recorded of him that once when a friend was expatiating enthusiastically about the approaching spring, Lessing said ' Oh, it has been green so often, I wish it would be red for a change.' But here some allowance must be made for his love of paradox and hatred of the tedious sentimentality rampant in his day. He was free from any trace of German ' *Schwärmerei*,' a state of feeling for which the healthier English mind has not even a corresponding word. Pressed hard, he once owned he preferred a landscape in the Harz to a flat waste, but he added that he would rather live in view of the latter than in a crooked room. In this he showed once more how pre-eminently Hellenic was his tone of mind.

Lessing did not recognize sufficiently the effect which the modern Christian spirit exercised over the plastic arts. This is the more remarkable, as with respect to poetry, he was fully aware of the merits of romanticism in contrast to classicism, as evinced by Shakespeare and Milton. He overlooked the fact that there is no abrupt line of severance between the old world and the new, and to this is traceable a certain hardness of tone in his aesthetics, as though the standard of ancient art were the only standard; a hardness that was overcome by later writers, notably by Schiller, Herder, and Kant. Thus ignoring the period of the Middle Ages, he omitted to remark that

O

pictures were for a long time the books of the people, and that the mediaeval painter, with this knowledge in view, strove to clothe expression of sentiment in his figures, and hence leant to allegorical representation.

Wherever Lessing's theory is narrow, it is so from the excessive rigour of his deductions. It is difficult to bend the works of the intellect to the details of rigorous classification. But this fault, which is a fault to-day, was a virtue at the time when some clear division was absolutely needful, and by the influence which the ' Laokoon ' exerted on the young minds of the generation, the fermentation for action which it called forth, a fermentation that culminated in the ' *Sturm und Drang* ' period of German literature, the decisive sway which it exerted can best be judged. Goethe at eighty cannot speak of it without enthusiasm. Its perusal must ever be a pleasure, for its charm of style, its easy sequence of ideas, that seem visibly thought out before us like the successive stages of the·shield of Achilles, its close reasoning and the terseness of its precepts. The fault is with the reader, if he does not after perusal find his mind strengthened and enlarged, if every subsequent perusal does not open new pathways of thought. It is a pre-eminently suggestive, rather than an exhaustive work, and will ever remain the finest monument of a compact and cultivated intellect.

# CHAPTER XII.

## HAMBURG.—'THE DRAMATURGIE.'

> *' Let me think*
> *Of forms less and the external.  Trust the spirit,*
> *As sovran nature does, to make the form,*
> *For otherwise we only imprison spirit*
> *And not embody.  Inward evermore*
> *To outward,—so in life, and so in art*
> *Which still is life.*
> *                    Exact*
> *The literal unities of time and place,*
> *When 'tis the essence of passion to ignore*
> *Both time and place?*
> *                    ' Tis that, honouring to its worth*
> *The drama, I would fear to keep it down*
> *To the level of the footlights.'*—MRS. BROWNING.

LESSING entered upon his Hamburg appointment full of joyful expectation, which found expression in the Prologue he issued on the opening of the theatre. After having accorded a sincere compliment to the town of Hamburg on the good service done in founding a national theatre, Lessing rapidly sketched the plan of the enterprise.   He candidly proclaimed that the German stage was still in its infancy, and that it was a question of educating public, actors, and authors at one and the same time.   He therefore begs patience and indulgence.

'For it is not possible to do all at once.  Still, what we do not see grow, is found to have grown

after a while. The slowest, who does not lose sight
of his goal, will always outstrip him who wanders
aimlessly. This 'Dramaturgie' is to be a critical index
of all the plays performed, and is to accompany every
step made by the art, both of the poet and the actor.
The choice of the plays is no trifle ; but choice pre-
supposes quantity, and if masterpieces cannot always
be performed, it will be seen where the fault lies.
At the same time it is well that the mediocre should
not pretend to be more than it is, so that the dissatisfied spectator may at least learn to judge from it.
To a person of good sense, whose taste we desire to
form, it is only needful to explain why such and such
a piece has failed to please him, if one desires to teach
him good taste. Besides, some mediocre pieces must
be retained, if only because they contain certain
excellent parts in which this or that actor can show
his whole power. A dramatic critic's most delicate
perception is evinced in distinguishing infallibly in
every case of pleasure or displeasure, what and how
much is to be charged to the poet and to the actor.
For to blame the one for the fault of the other, is to
injure both. The former is discouraged, the latter
made too confident. The actor especially may insist
on the observance of the utmost strictness and im-
partiality. The justification of the poet can always
be effected, his work remains and can always be
brought before our eyes. But the art of the actor is
transitory in its effects. His good and bad pass by
rapidly, and the liveliness of the impression too often
depends more on the passing mood of the spectator
than on the actor himself. Visible gifts of nature are
very needful to his profession, but by no means suffice.
The actor must everywhere think with the poet, and

must even think for him when the poet has proved himself mortal.'

His opening criticism, he adds, will not appear until some ten days later, in order that the first burst of public opinion may have blown over.

But before that date Lessing was already aware that there was 'something rotten' in the state of affairs. He writes to Karl:

'Dearest Brother,

'I hardly know myself what to relate about my circumstances. I must tell you in confidence, that a number of things are going on in our theatre that do not please me. There is discord among the *entrepreneurs.* No one knows who is to do what. Meanwhile I have made a beginning with my weekly paper, of which I here send you the first numbers. They are printed at my own press.'

These very first numbers gave offence both to the public and to the ever-wakeful vanity of the performers. The principal actress of the troupe had stipulated beforehand that she should not be mentioned in the 'Dramaturgie.' The second lady, whom Lessing had praised highly, while delicately hinting that her performance might be even better than it was, resented this hint from the paid critic of the theatre. She complained to one of the directors, her special protector; Lessing was forbidden to mention her name also. Others then became aggrieved, and the result was that a few weeks after the opening of the theatre Lessing abandoned all criticism of the actors, and confined himself to the pieces. The loss to histrionic science is serious, the scanty remarks on the dramatic art contained in the 'Dramaturgie' are masterly, full of keen insight and truth. Lessing was

certainly in a false position. He was known to the
public to be connected with the management, and consequently his criticisms were held to have an official
stamp, and misunderstandings with the actors were
inevitable.

And yet Lessing's demands on these had by no
means been excessive. His general canon for the
performance was : 'We must be satisfied with the
representation of a piece, if among four or five persons
some have acted excellently and the others well.' It
is truly graceful and modest when he adds : 'I only
know one way of flattering an artist, whether of my
own or the other sex, and this consists in presup-
posing that he is above all petty sensibility, that art
is everything in his eyes, and that he wishes to be
criticized, even preferring to be judged amiss than
not judged at all.'

But as there is no accounting for the vanity of
artists, so there is no combating it, and Lessing was
soon weary of the vain attempt. At the conclusion
of the 'Dramaturgie,' in a tone of bitter irony, he
appears to excuse this ultra-susceptibility of the
actors. 'We have histrionics but no histrionic art.
If such an art existed formerly it is lost to us. It
must be rediscovered.' There are no clear and precise
rules as to its conduct, hence 'all arguing on this
matter appears capricious and ambiguous, and it is
little wonder that the actor whose sole guide is
traditional routine feels himself offended at all points.
Praise will never appear to him sufficient, censure will
always appear excessive—nay, often he will not even
know whether praise or blame was intended.'

Lessing's former high opinion of Eckhof was confirmed. He regarded him as the soul of the new

theatre, and openly stated that he himself had to learn from him the true basis of the histrionic art.

'This man may perform any part he likes, even the most insignificant, he still proves himself the first-rate actor.' He further adds that the various rules laid down by him with regard to the utterance of moral maxims, the movements of the hands, gestures of warning, fear, &c., are merely an abstract of what he has observed in Eckhof. 'How easy, how pleasant it is to follow an artist who not only succeeds in the admirable, but creates it!'

Critics are not legislators, but judges and police.

Lessing did not pretend to make laws, but to interpret and enforce them, and therefore proceeded throughout on a system of critical induction. Taking Hamlet's instruction to the players as a text, he shows how it is possible for the actor to be too vehement in his enunciation, and points out the painful effect produced by an excessive strain on the voice. He warns against too much realism in pantomime, and against over reliance on the phantasy of the spectator. It is not always the actor of most feeling who produces the most effect, but sometimes the one who experiences none of the sensations he presents, and merely imitates a good model. For according to the law that the modifications of the soul which produce certain changes on the body may in their turn be brought about by these bodily changes, feeling may exist where we do not discern it, and we may fancy we discern it where it does not exist.

Lessing insists on the necessity for rapid acting, especially in the lighter kinds of comedy. In treating of the subject of a play, he remarks that even the weakest and most confused have had a kind of success, if only the author has been fortunate in his choice of subject. Indeed it often happens that just in such pieces good actors appear to the best advantage.

'It is very rarely that a masterpiece is represented in as masterly a manner as it is written. Mediocrity generally succeeds much better. Perhaps because the actors can put more of themselves into it ; perhaps because mediocrity leaves us more time and repose to regard their acting, or perhaps because everything depends on one or two prominent personages ; while in a superior play every person ought to be more or less a principal actor, and if he is not, by spoiling his own part he helps to spoil all the rest.'

The dramatic artist differs from other artists in that the man transforms his own body into art and impersonates before an audience what he has never seen. Lessing was therefore led to inquire into the precise relation held by this to the other arts. He had said in the 'Laokoon' that the drama is destined to be a living painting through the representation of the actor, and ought perhaps on that very account to adhere the closer to the laws of material painting. He was far from regarding dramatic art as mere mechanism or naturalism. The same idealism that breathed through the 'Laokoon' is enforced here.

'The art of the actor stands midway between poetry and painting. As a visible painting beauty must be its highest law, and yet as transient painting its posture need not always have that repose which renders antique works of art so impressive. It may and must allow itself the wildness of a Tempesta, the audacity of a Bernini. Such effects retain in this art

all the expression peculiar to them, without the offen-
siveness which they would have in pictorial art
through the permanence of the impression.  Only it
must not linger too long among these effects, it must
gradually prepare us for them by the preceding movements, and by the succeeding ones must resolve them
back again into the ruling tone of the seemly, and it
must never seek to give these effects all the intensity
that the poet's treatment is capable of attaining.'

In the 26th and 27th critiques Lessing discusses
the subject of orchestral accompaniment, or the relation of dramatic music to the various kinds of passion
represented.   In reference to the question whether
the *entr'acte* should form by means of two contrasted
moments a vehicle of transition from the sentiment
of the preceding to that of the succeeding act, he
points out the necessary difficulty.   Suppose that the
dominant passions in two successive acts were directly
contrasted, the two distinct musical movements must
necessarily be of the same contrasted character.  Now
arises the difficulty of passing from one to the other
in such a manner that the transition may not be too
startling.   The poet may effect the transition by a
gradual rise and fall of intensity, but the musician
cannot do this in two sharply divided passages ; and
the sudden leap from the restful to the stormy, from
the tender to the raging, must be too noticeable and
painful.   Suddenly we become melancholy, then
furious, without knowing how or why : we feel, without perceiving a direct sequence in our feelings.
Poetry, on the other hand, never allows us to lose the
thread of our emotions.   Here we know not only
what we are to feel, but why we are to feel it, and
this knowledge renders these sudden transitions not

only tolerable but even agreeable ; in fact, this power
of making sudden transitions intelligible is one of the
chief advantages derived by music from its union
with poetry.

This analysis of music was but another attempt
to elicit from the art itself the peculiar ends to which
it is fitted. Lessing's knowledge of musical form and
the intellectual penetration he displays in treating it
are remarkable; but it must be regarded somewhat
in the light of an individual utterance. Lessing's
objections to music are those of a critic who judges
by abstract reason, while music is so eminently an
emotional condition, that it is almost an axiom that
the predominance of the intellect subdues the emotional sensations, and that consequently the severely
intellectual mind is rarely highly musical. It may
enjoy music, but it does so in the manner of Lessing,
who required a distinct objective explanation for the
feeling aroused in him by this medium.

But long before Lessing had advanced so far in
his critiques, the theatre was showing signs of approaching dissolution. The larger mass of the public,
on whom the pecuniary success of an undertaking
is dependent, were extremely indifferent to all such
considerations of high art. Envious and ignorant
cabals injured the slender popularity of the undertaking. The financial committee had administered
badly, money ran short, and already in September
the inevitable end was foreseen. It advanced with
giant strides. In October the directors, deserted by
the better-class public, were compelled to resort to
harlequinades to fill the house. In November Lessing
had to behold acrobats perform their tricks after a
representation of his 'Minna von Barnhelm.' The

appeal to the patriotism of the Hamburgers was useless. 'Minna von Barnhelm' had even been forbidden by the magistrates. The Prussian consul
dared not accord permission without a direct authori-
zation from Berlin. What marvel that Lessing contrasted the attitude of his nation with that of the
French? Du Belloy's 'Siege of Calais' gave him
occasion to vent his indignation. The piece had been
received in France with patriotic acclamation, and
was therefore of course duly lauded in Germany.

'If this piece did not merit all the fuss that the
French made over it, this fuss in itself is honourable
to the French. It shows them as a people jealous of
their fame, on whom the great deeds of their ancestors
have not lost their impression. It shows them convinced of the value of the poet and the influence of
the stage on virtue and morals, and that it does not
number the former among its useless members, nor
reckon the latter among the matters that concern
only busy idlers. How far behind the French are
we Germans in this particular! To speak plainly,
as compared with them we are still true barbarians!
I may look about me in Germany where I will, the
town has yet to be built from which it might be expected that it would show to a German poet the
thousandth part of the regard and recognition which
Calais has shown to Du Belloy. It may be called
French vanity. How far removed are we as yet from
being capable of such vanity? And what marvel? Our
learned men themselves are mean enough to
strengthen the nation in their depreciation of all that
does not actually fill the purse. It is true, nothing
is lucrative among us which has the least connexion
with the fine arts.'

When towards the end of the year a troupe of
French comedians arrived at Hamburg, the national
theatre saw itself forced to close its doors. Early in
December the troupe repaired to Hanover with the
intention of returning to Hamburg in the spring. In
their farewell address they begged their compatriots
not to forget the German actors! Lessing remained
in Hamburg, tied by his connexion with Bode's
printing press. He continued writing at his 'Dramaturgie,' with which he was considerably in arrears.
His object now was to spin it out until the return of
the company, in the hope that by means of his journal
he might keep alive such interest as existed. His
own pecuniary condition was a sorry one. The
shattered finances of the theatre had deprived him of
his promised salary, and the printing press had not
only absorbed the slender capital obtained from the
sale of his library, but he had been further forced to
borrow money for it, while besides all this the family
at Camenz were clamorous for funds.

Hamburg : December 21, 1767.

'Honoured Father,

    'If it were possible to describe to you the com-
plications, troubles, and labours in which I have been
involved during the last years, how dissatisfied I have
almost always been, how exhausted in the powers of
body and mind, I am certain you would not only forgive my former silence, you would even regard it as
the only proof of my filial regard and love that I am
at present able to give you. When I do write it is
impossible for me to write otherwise than as I think
and feel at the moment. You would have had a
most unpleasant letter to read, and I should have
become even more dissatisfied with my circumstances,
if I had been imagining the sorrow I must be causing

my parents. Therefore it was best to let them know
nothing of it, but this could only be done by not
writing at all.'

Lessing does not speak plainly about the theatrical
undertaking, perhaps because even now he could look
for no approval from his old father.

'Certain proposals drew me hither to Hamburg,
but these have also not come to much, and I have at
length resolved to let my maintenance and my fortune
depend on myself alone.'

Referring to the printing press set up with Bode,
he says :

'When the work is once under weigh, I hope to be
able to live on my share as an honest man ; and this
prospect is the more flattering to me, that I look
forward to sharing my better circumstances with my
brothers and sisters.'

Yet this prospect was so far distant, that in the
following spring (1768) Lessing saw himself forced
to refuse a hundred thalers asked of him by his
father.

'I am almost crushed by work and cares, and it is
not the smallest of the latter that I know my parents
to be in such pressing need and am not able to help
them as quickly as I could wish. . . . I am more a
stranger here than at any place where I have ever
been, and can scarcely rely on one or two whose
assistance I have already abused and whose powers
are not extensive.'

His letters to the Berlin friends grew more and
more infrequent. He tells Nicolai that it is a sin and
a shame that he does not write to him, and promises
to write to Moses soon if he ever again finds a quiet
happy hour, and meanwhile he trusts Moses does not
interpret his silence amiss.

In May 1768 the German comedians returned to Hamburg, where they were greeted by hosts of creditors. They had brought back with them the able actor Schröder, and renewed hopes of success were entertained only to be yet more speedily dashed. To the indifference of the public was united a new element of discord. Hamburg's ecclesiastical welfare was at that time guarded by Pastor Melchior Goeze, a *bon vivant*, sufficiently learned, but of narrow and intolerant spirit. He and Lessing were on the best of terms. Lessing had a fancy for all types of his fellow creatures, and he visited him often, discoursing theology in which Goeze was well read, and turning over his valuable library of Bibles. This intercourse astonished his friends, and mocking tongues suggested that either Lessing was converting Goeze, or Goeze him. Goeze had a fanatical hatred of the stage, yet made an exception in favour of the plays of Lessing, Weisse, and Gellert. But he was scandalized beyond measure when he discovered that the Church itself harboured a playwriter. Another Hamburg pastor, Schlosser, in his youth had written a comedy which had actually been performed and printed. Goeze seized the occasion to denounce the theatre and its authors from the pulpit and in writing. His attacks provoked replies, to which he again responded. A perfect war of libels and epigrams resulted, until at last the Senate had to put an end to the matter by edict. But while its pastors fought for and against the theatre, their timid flocks deemed it wiser to hold aloof from the place denounced by the clergy as the school of Satan, though lauded by their opponents as a school of morals.

Contrary to the expectation of his friends, Lessing

did not engage in the quarrel. Probably his recent
experiences with regard to the theatre had been too
painful. But from the first, long before the dispute
broke out, he had protested against any overt or disguised attacks on the clergy as a class. The theatre
had been opened with a play of von Cronegk's in
which occurs a sentence :

> Heaven can pardon, but a priest never,

that had elicited a murmur of applause. Lessing
blamed this entirely. He calls such phrases coloured
glass instead of precious stones, witty antithesis
instead of common sense.

'If Ismenor is a cruel priest, does it follow that
all priests are Ismenors ? It is useless to reply that
the allusion refers to priests of a false religion. No
religion in the world was ever so false that its teachers
must necessarily be monsters. Priests have worked
mischief in false religions as well as in true ; but not
because they were priests, but because they were
villains who would have abused the privileges of any
other class in the service of their evil propensities.'

The better-class audience being again withdrawn,
the managers saw themselves forced to appeal once
more to the lower orders. The list of the *répertoire*
was found among Lessing's papers, no doubt as
material for a projected continuation of his 'Dramaturgie.' It still includes plays, but ballets, harlequinades and intermezzos take a larger share. By June it
was scarcely possible for an audience to reach the box
office, besieged as it was by noisy creditors. After this
the house was often kept closed for days, so poor were
the receipts. In September Lessing bids Nicolai come
to Hamburg at once, if he wishes to see the theatre.

'It will expire at Easter. So that has come to an end also,' he adds sorrowfully.

The end came already in November. The project begun with such high hopes had resulted in a miserable fiasco.

'*Transeat cum caeteris erroribus,*' is Lessing's short funeral comment in a letter to Ramler. To the nation at large he is more explicit.

'When the public asks, Well, what has been achieved? and answers itself with a sarcastic "Nothing," I ask in return, what has the public done in order that something might be achieved? Nothing again; nay, even worse than nothing. Not enough that it not only does not help the work, it has not even allowed it to take its natural course. Alas for the goodnatured notion of procuring a national theatre for the Germans, when we Germans are not even yet a nation. I do not speak of the political constitution, but only of the moral character. One might almost say its moral character was an unwillingness to possess individuality. We are still the pledged imitators of all that is foreign, especially the servile admirers of the never sufficiently admired French. Everything that comes to us from the other side of the Rhine is beautiful, charming, lovely, divine. We had rather contradict our eyes and ears than think it otherwise. We had rather be persuaded that uncouthness is unconstraint; boldness, grace; grimace, expression; a jingling of rhymes, poetry; howling, music; than doubt in the slightest degree the superiority which this amiable nation, this first nation in the world, as it is accustomed modestly to style itself, has received from just fate as its share of all that is good, and beautiful, and noble, and seemly. This pleasant dream of founding a national theatre here in Hamburg has vanished, and as far as I know the place, it is likely to be the one where such a dream could least of all be fulfilled.'

The sole enduring result of this 'sweet dream' is Lessing's ' Dramaturgie,' and this too is a fragment and anything rather than a systematic book. It accompanies the theatre no further than the first fifty-two performances, and the last portion, published as a volume instead of a paper, was not issued until Easter 1769, after the enterprise had been long dead. There were various reasons for this. From the beginning, Lessing was in arrears, first advisedly, then because, as he saw the failure of the scheme, other interests grew more absorbing. Added to this the piratical system of reprint permitted in Germany, had fastened on the work. Lessing appealed to the national honour, remarking that although he could not forbid the public to favour the cheaper reprint, he must give it to understand that by so doing it must lose the work itself. For if the number of copies needful to cover expenses could not be sold, it must remain un-published. The public notwithstanding continued to admire the work and save its pockets. Lessing an-nounces with bitter resignation that he by no means regrets his inability to elaborate the rest of his material.

'I withdraw my hand from this plough as willingly as I put it there. The world loses nothing because instead of five or six volumes of ' Dramaturgie,' only two will see the light. But it might lose if some day a more useful work, by a better writer, should be thus repressed.'

It is largely owing to this disgust that the

P

'Dramaturgie' is by no means a homogeneous work. Written at various times and in various moods, it even happens to Lessing to contradict on one page what he had said on the preceding. He acknowledges this. He had not written systematically, his ideas were to be set forth day by day, *apropos* of this or that performance, and he continually digresses from his path into polemical discussions or philosophical reflexions. The treatment is unequal, the language now colloquial, now erudite, passing from the one to the other, quite regardless of the taste of his readers. Questions propounded incidentally are resolved from the most immediate point of view, and the provisional solution does not oblige the author to solve all the collateral points. He did not care to do so.

'My thoughts may appear to be more and more disconnected or even contradictory. What matter so long as they are thoughts which give my readers material for thinking? I do not seek to do more than scatter *fermenta cognitionis.*'

His original plan of following the actors step by step had been frustrated. 'What these papers were to have been I explained in my preface, what they have really become my readers will discover. Not wholly what I promised to make them, something different, but yet I think nothing worse.'

'Truly I am sorry for those of my readers who have looked for a theatrical newspaper in this journal, as varied and coloured, as amusing and droll, as a theatrical paper may be. Instead of forming the contents of the current paper into little amusing or touching novelettes, instead of incidental biographies of ludicrous, peculiar, comical creatures, as those who occupy themselves with writing comedy must be, instead of diverting and slightly scandalous anecdotes about actors and especially actresses, instead of all such trifles as they expected, they receive long serious dry criticisms about old and well known plays, heavy disquisitions about what ought or ought not to be in a tragedy, sometimes even expositions of Aristotle. And they are to read this? As I have already said, I pity them; they have been shamefully deceived. But between ourselves, it is better you should be deceived than I. And I should be much deceived if I had to make your expectations my law. Not that your expectations would be very difficult to fulfil. Really not. I should rather find them very easy if only they would accord better with my intentions.'

The continuation was growing a burden to Lessing's restless activity. ' I must still finish my " Dramaturgie,"' he writes to Nicolai (September 1768), ' and I fancy the end will reveal that I have written it with my head full of antiquarian fancies.'

The want of symmetry and congruity in this work renders it a difficult task to seize its dominant idea. If any division can be made, it is twofold. As is usual with Lessing, he desires to overthrow and build. The object to be destroyed is the predilection of the Germans for the French theatre. This was the purport of the negative criticism, while to substitute other opinions in place of the commonly accredited was the purpose of the dogmatic portion. The first thing to do was to demonstrate the wretched poverty of the contemporary German drama. The theatre had been opened with a play by von Cronegk. Lessing does not hesitate to point out that the drama of this much

lauded poet is a miserable concern. This first specimen of his scathing criticism raised some discontent.

'I was much taken aback,' writes Lessing, 'at
being assured I had annoyed some of my readers by
my candid criticism. If modest frankness without
any hidden intentions, displeases them, I am in
danger of often thus incurring their displeasure.'

Cronegk's tragedy had been crowned a few years
previously by Lessing's friends, it was placed in the
same category with his own, Brawe's and Weisse's.
That does not deter him. 'If the lame run a race
the winner still remains lame,' he quietly remarks.

The German comedies had no genuine colour or
ring, and dealt with provincial trivialities or impossible
personages, while their tragedies were miserable imitations of the French, fettered by the false and arbitrary rules enjoined by Gallic tradition. Weisse's
Tragedy of 'Richard III.' gave him an opportunity of
exposing the emptiness and untruth to nature of this
much praised masterpiece of correct imitation, and so
effectually that though Lessing's opponents continued
to laud Weisse as a great tragedian, he himself had
the good sense to abandon playwriting and turn to
juvenile literature, in which he achieved a creditable
success.

This exposure of French theories and fallacies
occupies the greater part of the 'Dramaturgie,' and
small wonder, for of the fifty-two plays performed, all
but eighteen were translations from the French.
Lessing could theoretically point out the goal towards
which the German drama should strive, but how to
attain it, so long as German life was in a condition of
immaturity? Wanting all domestic models, having no
stimulus from the events of the age, the German

drama had been sunk into a state of torpor. Gottsched and his followers had converted it into a travesty of French levity, whence all French charm and *esprit* had evaporated, to be replaced by an infusion of German coarseness.

'Most of the performances of us Germans in *belles-lettres* have been the attempts of young men. The prejudice is almost universal among us that it is only befitting to young men to work in this department. Men should have more serious studies or more important business imposed on them by church or state. Verses and plays are toys, by no means useless preparations with which to occupy the years up to twenty-five at most, but as soon as we approach manhood, we should dedicate all our faculties to a useful profession, and if this profession should leave us time to write something, we must only write what is consistent with gravity and our civic dignity; a legal compendium; a good chronicle of our dear native town; an edifying sermon, and such like. Therefore our *belles-lettres* possess so few works that a man accustomed to think would take up with pleasure when he wishes to think for once outside the uniform tiresome circle of his daily routine, for the purpose of recreation and refreshment. What nourishment can such a man find in our trivial comedies?'

Is such an instance conceivable among the Germans as that of the French dramatist Du Belloy, who threw up the law for love of the stage, became an actor, composed plays, and was as happy and celebrated as ever the law could have made him? 'Woe to the young German genius who should try to follow in his footsteps. Contempt and beggary would be his certain lot.'

While thus remorselessly demonstrating to his countrymen that they possessed no dramatic literature, it is a satisfaction to Lessing to prove to them that the models till now venerated are as far removed from the ideal of perfection as their own imitations of them. Starting from the assumption which he held in common with Aristotle, that tragedy is the highest form of drama, he therefore required it to furnish the criterion of excellence, and, from this standpoint he is prepared to prove that the French have misapprehended the rules of ancient drama more than any nation. His reasons for this are far removed from contemptible national prejudice. His protests are those of an accurate scholar who sees that the French have misread and misapplied the laws laid down by Aristotle.

'Do I mean by this to say that no Frenchman is capable of composing a really touching tragic work? That the volatile spirit of the nation is incapable of such an undertaking? I should be ashamed if such an idea had occurred to me. I am quite convinced that no nation in the world has received any mental endowment beyond all other nations.'

He only wished to show that the French do not possess a real tragedy and that the reason is their belief that they possess it exclusively. The French under the outside mimicry of the antique concealed the deadliest hostility to its vital purpose, while the English virtually coincided with its supreme principle, the imitation of nature, though pursuing this common end under a different law of art. The Greek and English theatre differ as one species in nature differs from another, the Greek and French, as the natural differs from the monstrous. The hostility of the

French theatre to the English and Spanish is obvious, Lessing was the first to detect its virtual hostility to the Greek.

The ancients once more form the broad immovable basis on which Lessing rests in his 'Dramaturgie' as in his 'Laokoon.' But while in the 'Laokoon' the laws that guided the fine arts had to be discovered by inspection and meditation on the writings of Homer and the works of the ancients, here the code was extant in the 'Poetics' of Aristotle. And did not the French incessantly invoke the principles of the 'Poetics'? True, but Lessing is prepared to demonstrate to them, out of Aristotle himself, how utterly they have misread the Stagyrite, and that no nation has more misconstrued the precepts of ancient drama. Some casual remarks which they found in Aristotle, about the most fitting external arrangements, were accepted by them as the essential, while they enfeebled the essential so much by all manner of restrictions and glosses as to be of necessity disabled from approaching the sublime effect contemplated by the philosopher. Lessing's reverence for Aristotle is very great, but not on account of his traditional authority.

'I would soon set aside Aristotle's authority, if only I could set aside his reasons also. I have my own ideas about the origin and basis of this philosopher's "Poetics," which I could not give here without running to too great length, yet I do not hesitate to declare (even though I should incur the risk of being laughed at in these enlightened times) that I consider them as infallible as the Elements of Euclid. Their fundamental principles are just as true and certain, only not so definite, and therefore more exposed to misconstruction. I trust to prove incontrovertibly of tragedy in particular that it cannot depart a step from the rules of Aristotle without departing just as far from perfection.'

Lessing never doubts the genuineness or integrity of Aristotle's work, and wherever the text offers difficulties or contradictions he employs all his acumen to remove any appearance of incongruity. Aristotle must be throughout explained out of himself he says ; and whoever wants to learn his dramatic canons must not seek them only in the ' Poetics,' but in the ' Rhetoric ' and the ' Ethics.' The closest imitations of the ancient models was the watchword of the day, and hence arose the errors combated by Lessing. Imitation of the ancients, well and good, but intelligent not servile imitation. Was it adherence to rule that affected the audience of Sophocles ? By no means, it was because the plays riveted their attention, stirred their emotions and exalted their souls.

' It is not enough that the tragic poet's work has an effect on us, it must also have that effect that belongs to its species. To what end the tiresome labour of dramatic forms, why build a theatre, invite the whole town to one spot, if I wish to effect no more by my work and its representation than to rouse some of the emotions which may be produced by a good story that anyone may read at home by his own fireside ?

' The public will put up with what it gets. That is well and again not well, for we do not care greatly for the board where there is always something to put up with. It is well known how intent the Greek and Roman people were upon plays, especially the former upon tragedy, how indifferent, how cold are our people towards the theatre ! Whence this difference, if not from this cause ? While the Greeks felt themselves animated by the stage with such strong, such unusual sensations, that they could hardly await the moment when they should have them again and again, we on the other hand experience from our stage such feeble impressions that we seldom think it worth time or money to obtain them. Most of us go to the theatre from curiosity, fashion, *ennui*, for society, from a desire to stare and be stared at, and only a few, and these few but seldom, from any other motive.'

How far do masterpieces of Corneille, Racine and Voltaire approach the Greek standard ? *Les bienséances, le style noble, les beaux vers*, have never yet stirred up the deepest emotions of man's soul.

'Given twenty Addisons,' says Lessing, ' and this correctness will never be to the taste of the English.'

It is from Voltaire, the idol of the French public,· the *protégé* of Frederick and the model of good taste that Lessing first proposes to prove the essential falsehood of the French theories. Aristotle had said that tragedy purifies our passions by the ideal excitation of our feelings of fear and pity. While the first aim of dramatic art is to interest and amuse, its second and higher function is through amusement to elevate our souls and bring our higher faculties into play, by appealing to our sympathies. ' Tested by this standard what do Voltaire's tragedies effect ? They leave the audience cold and unmoved, and why ? because Voltaire has not descended into the depth of the human heart, and hence has not found the language that goes direct to the heart. His work is beneath himself.'

' I am always glad to quote from M. de Voltaire.

Something may be learned from his most trifling observations, though not always what he says in them, yet at least what he should have said. *Primus sapientiae gradus est falsa intelligere*, and I know no author in the world who aids us so successfully to find out whether we have reached this first step of wisdom, as M. de Voltaire, but I know none who helps us less to attain the second, *secundus vera cognoscere*. It seems to me that a critic cannot do better than proceed according to this maxim. Let him first seek some one from whom he can differ, then he will gradually approach the subject and the rest will follow. I openly avow that in this work I have especially chosen the French writers for this end, and particularly M. de Voltaire. If anyone should think this method to be more audacious than profound, I could tell him that even the profound Aristotle almost always employed it.'

Lessing opens his attack with 'Sémiramis.' Voltaire had written in its preface : 'From us French the Greeks might have learned a more skilful exposition and the great art of so arranging the scenes that the stage should never remain empty and there should neither be exits nor entrances without reason. From us they might have learned how rivals answer each other by witty antitheses, how the poet by a number of lofty brilliant thoughts should dazzle and astonish. From us they might have learnt—Oh! of course,' adds Lessing, 'what is not to be learnt from the French ! Now and then a foreigner who has also read the classics a little might humbly beg permission to hold a different opinion. He might object that all these advantages of the French have no great influence upon the essential of tragedy, that they are beauties

such as the simple greatness of the ancients despised.
But what avails it to cavil at M. de Voltaire? He
speaks and the world believes.'

In 'Sémiramis' English influences are distinctly
visible. Voltaire had not visited England in vain, he
had become acquainted with Shakespeare and deigned
to borrow some spectacular effects from him. The
ghost in ' Hamlet' was the prototype of that of Ninus.
Voltaire had congratulated himself particularly on his
boldness in daring to exhibit a ghost on the French
stage. Lessing did not think much of this object of self
laudation. Comparing the spectre of Ninus with that
in ' Hamlet' he shows that Voltaire has not understood
the laws of the wonderful so happily obeyed by
Shakespeare. Shakespeare's ghost only appears at
night, mysteriously ; Ninus shows himself in broad daylight, and before a numerous assembly. This is to lose
sight of the truly tragic and poetical effect psycholo-
gically produced on our emotion and to substitute a
clumsy mechanical incident that excites our ridicule.

' Where could Voltaire ever have heard that ghosts
are so bold ? What old woman could not have told
him that they shun the sunlight and have no love for
large assemblies ? The ghost that takes liberties that
are against all tradition and against all spectral *bien-
séance*, does not appear to me a right sort of ghost, and
everything here that does not help the illusion, hinders
it. Voltaire's ghost is nothing but a poetical machine,
it is only there to complicate the action, and it does
not interest us in the least for itself. Shakespeare's
on the contrary is a real personage, who acts, whose
fate interests us, who awakes fear but also pity.'

Voltaire had apologized for his ghost by an appeal
to the historic truth of a belief in apparitions, and in-

sisted on the moral lesson deducible from this prodigy, that the Highest Power will make exception from its eternal laws for the sake of bringing a hidden crime to light. This moral does not seem to Lessing the most edifying imaginable, since it would be a more becoming conception of the Highest Being not to deem him obliged to make exceptions to his laws in order to punish crime, but that this punishment should naturally result from the actions themselves. Thus Voltaire in the moral purpose of his work has proved himself too little of a philosopher, and for its poetical conception too much.

Treating of the historical truth of a drama, Lessing follows Aristotle in defining historical truth as not an end but a means. To expect historical accuracy from a dramatist is absurd. If tragedy usually seeks its subjects in history it is because the situation is ready given. We do not come to the theatre to learn what such or such a person did, but rather what any person of a given character would do under certain conditions. The purpose of tragedy is far more philosophical than the purpose of history, and it is degrading it from its true dignity to make it a mere panegyric of celebrated men, or to misuse it as an incentive to nourishing national pride. The characters must remain intact, the incidents may be varied as dramatic exigencies require.

In ' Zaire ' Voltaire has shown his incapability of rendering true feeling. ' Love itself,' said a French critic, ' had dictated "Zaire" to Voltaire.' ' Rather say, gallantry,' remarks Lessing, ' I only know one tragedy at which Love itself wrought, and that is Shakespeare's "Romeo and Juliet." Voltaire understands the official tone of love, but he does not know its secret wiles, its slightest living expression. How can anyone compare the cold man of letters to the poet full of passion and fire?' Voltaire is therefore shown to be no fit model for the Germanic spirit. It is Shakespeare who is far more in harmony with their mode of thought, as Lessing proclaimed years ago ; and he is glad to be able to add that a translation of this great genius exists, 'a work from whose beauties we may long learn before the defects of Wieland's rendering offend us so much as to make another translation needful.' With a significant glance at Voltaire he remarks : ' Shakespeare requires to be studied, not plundered.' For he holds Voltaire's ' Orosmane' to be only a mechanical copy of Shakespeare's ' Othello.'

And in like manner as ' Sémiramis ' and ' Zaire ' have served Lessing as a text to extol Shakespeare at the expense of Voltaire, so ' Merope ' gives him occasion to exalt Euripides at the expense of French tragedy. He shows how the conceited poet ranks not only below Euripides, whom he and his fellow tragedians think they have far surpassed, but even below the Italian Maffei, whose ' Merope ' was really the basis of Voltaire's, although he had tried by all manner of falsehoods to detract from Maffei's merits. Lessing demonstrates from Voltaire's own play how utterly he has misconceived the purport of the unities, how he has violated psychological truth for the sake of apparent conformity, and sacrificed truth to nature to love of rule. He further mockingly exposes his pretensions to classical scholarship, derides his childish vanity, his sophistic and unjust treatment of other dramatists, his perfidy, his inaccuracies. ' There are only two untruths in this passage,' he once writes, ' that is not much for M. de· Voltaire,' and he defends Thomas

Corneille, whom Voltaire had attacked as ignorant of chronology. Voltaire's own historical knowledge was not so very profound ; this moreover signifies little in a play, where moral accuracy is the one thing needed. As to the rules, no one is such an adept as Voltaire in evading them, however clumsily, when it suits his purpose. His dramas walk on high stilts, and are devoid of any spontaneous emotion, his characters express admirable sentiments but are as cold as stones, and meanwhile M. de Voltaire preaches the rules and talks of the passions. Yet throughout Lessing does not deny due recognition to Voltaire's poetical and critical faculties, but he desires to put an end once and for ever to his aesthetic dictatorship.

This leads Lessing to investigate the subject of the boasted regularity of the French, their observance of the three unities, their connexion of scenes, the motives alleged for entrances and exits, and the surprises practised on the audience. ' It is one thing to be at home with the rules, another really to observe them. The French understood the former, the latter only the ancients appear to have understood. Unity of action was their first dramatic law, unity of time and place were its natural consequences, which they would scarcely have observed more closely than was needful for the unity of action, had it not been for the union of the whole action with the chorus. Since the events had to be witnessed by a number of people, and this number remained always the same, and would neither go further from their dwellings nor remain longer from them than mere curiosity could generally prompt, it was hardly possible to do otherwise than confine the place to one and the same individual spot and the time to one and the same day.

As for the element of surprise Lessing considers this a poor pleasure. Why should the poet surprise us? Let him surprise his characters as much as he will, our interest can but be enhanced by having long foreseen what comes so unexpectedly to them. This again leads Lessing to pronounce on the merit of intrigues that consist in mysteries. He blames them in general as artifices far inferior to the development of a situation openly established. So convinced indeed is he of the inutility of these stratagems to a true tragedian, that he seizes the opportunity of justifying the prologues of Euripides. To hold the spectator breathless by riddles is a second hand merit, and such charms are destroyed by a repeated representation. Lessing asserts with regard to Euripides, that 'Alcestis' was not really a tragedy, as had hitherto been supposed, but a satyric drama. The correctness of this surmise was not proved till some time after his death, when the discovery of a notice by a Scholiast revealed that such was really the intention of the play.

It was however reserved to Corneille to bear the final attacks of Lessing's criticism. It was he who, at once the creator and pattern of French drama, had stood in the way of all amelioration because he had nominally built his theories on those of Aristotle, whom he had critically interpreted. He has enervated, mutilated and destroyed Aristotle's precepts. And why all this? To justify his own plays. He had construed the Greek φόβος (*phobos*) now as terror, now as fear, just as it suited his purpose. He loved the horrible, and pretended that it was a factor in Aristotle's scheme. He makes us shudder but not weep. He moves us, but with morbid disgust; and when he desires to be pathetic he is maudlin. Therefore he should not be called the Great Corneille but the Monstrous, 'for nothing is great that is not true,' and abstract vice is the untruest thing of all, and therefore the most untragical. Evil must be repulsive, but not unnatural, or it fails to produce any impression ; we cannot identify ourselves with monsters, so we are supremely indifferent to their fate. Macbeth, Richard III. remain men for all their perversions, Corneille's Cleopatra makes a bravado of her crimes. Shakespeare's villains excuse their crimes by constraint or necessity ; those of Corneille find an absolute delight in the commission of evil deeds. But Lessing does not pretend to the full honour of these discoveries. In the last century an honest man called Huron was imprisoned in the Bastille and finding time hang heavily on his hands, in spite of his being in Paris, from sheer *ennui* studied the French poets and found that he could not admire ' Rodogune.' Even Voltaire could not admire it, though out of goodness of heart he had protected the grand daughter of the poet. From one of these men the present Dramaturgist must have learnt his objections, for it must be a Frenchman who opens the eyes of a foreigner to the faults of the French. ' For that a German should think by himself, should of himself have the audacity to doubt the excellence of a Frenchman, is positively unimaginable.'

Racine is as little to his taste. His tragedies are the fruits of a superfine court routine, from which passion is banished, and stale maxims and oratorical fencing play the chief parts. For him the essence of poetry lay in diction and versification.

It must be borne in mind that the French had

themselves upheld their claim to classical perfection
and that it was therefore quite permissible to Lessing
to judge them from this standpoint. He was fully
aware that the faults of the French drama are those
of the French, and to be sought for in their nationality,
while the artificiality of tone as a standard of taste
argued *ad nauseam* between the English and French
writers was equally founded on national distinctions.
In England and Germany, the drama was a popular
amusement, in France it had originated at court. The
former appealed to the national taste at large, the latter
to a lettered audience familiar with the rules. The
former had been engrafted on the nation, the latter had
sprung from its life. The lively French form the
most patient and pedantic audience—' la nation la plus
sensée dans ses plaisirs, la plus folle dans ses affaires,'
says Gautier. Nature was therefore not only not
understood but avoided by them, for nature is not
compatible with rule ; genius is nature in its highest
expression, and genius is always simple. It may
have caprices, but it seldom closely follows rules ; they
may prune its exuberance, but must not impede its
growth. 'Nothing is more chaste and more seemly
than simple nature. Coarseness and vulgarity are as
far removed from it as bombast and verbosity from
the sublime.'

The perception of the inherent co-relation of fear
and pity as evinced by sympathy, is the distinctive
merit of Lessing's exposition of Aristotle. The explanation of this is his dominant idea under all his
digressions, and tested by this Aristotelian standard
Lessing justifies his preliminary remark that the
French tragedies are not true tragedies, because the

Q

effects they produce are other than those that belong
to the essence of tragedy.

Lessing also finally resolved the question of perfect
characters. They are removed from human sympathies by means of their chilly supernatural virtues,
and on this same ground he, without, it is to be feared,
remembering Calderon, rejects the Christian martyr
tragedies. They depict suffering without corresponding guilt, and are thus excluded from the range
of feelings called forth by retribution, while here the
relation between cause and effect is not obvious.
' For is not the character of a true Christian quite
untheatrical ? Are not the quiet suffering, the invari-
able meekness that are his essential characteristics,
at variance with the whole business of tragedy, which
strives to purify the passions ? Does not his expectation
of a compensatory happiness after this life contradict
the unselfishness with which on the stage we desire to
see all great and good actions undertaken and completed ? '

From an equally positive cause the element of the
terrible must be banished from the stage. The French
had bestowed the surname ' The Terrible ' on Cré-
billon as an honour, and had referred to Aristotle's
incontrovertible authority in its defence ; Lessing
proves to them that it was precisely Aristotle who
had rejected such themes as absolutely unsuitable for
tragedy. Terror is so far from the purpose of tragedy
that the ancients, if one of their characters had committed a great crime, would rather strive to excuse
it by attributing the fault to Fate, or to the decree of
an avenging Deity, than allow their audience to receive
the impression that a man could be capable of such
degradation. For this would prevent their expe-

riencing that real tragic emotion which is a kind of
pleasant torment. On the other hand, neither are the
sufferings of absolutely perfect characters permissible,
since the thought that innocent persons should be
made to suffer so much is horrible. We require the
element of undeserved calamity, and yet there must
be some justice, too, in the course of events, so that
while we feel sorrow for what occurs, we may also feel
that it was inevitable. While condemning the introduction of such unjust suffering, because it arouses
murmurs against Providence, Lessing says:

'Let no one say that history awakens them, that
these feelings are evoked by something that has really
occurred. That really occurred? Granted, then it
has some good reason in the eternal endless harmony
of all things, and that which in those few fragments
presented by the poet appears as blind fate and
cruelty is in reality wisdom and truth. Out of the
poet's few fragments he ought to be able to make a
symmetrical whole, where one thing is explained by
another, and where no difficulty occurs, whose solution
we cannot find in the poet's plan, but are forced to
search outside of it in the general harmony of things.
The work of the earthly creator ought to be a reflexion of the work of the eternal Creator, ought to accustom us to the thought how, as all is resolved in
Him for the best, so it will also be here. Does the
author forget this, his noblest end, so entirely that he
interweaves the incomprehensible ways of Providence
into his little circle, and purposely awakens our
horror? Oh, spare. us, ye who have our hearts in
your power! To what end these sad sensations? To
teach us resignation? It is only cold reason that can
teach us that, and if we are to retain trust and a

cheerful spirit in our resignation, it is most needful
that we should be reminded as little as possible of the
perplexing examples of such unmerited dreadful fate.
Away with them from the stage! Away with them,
if it could be, from all books.'

In this wise, while alive to the absurdity of trying
to establish an arbitrary standard, Lessing shows that
there are eternal principles of truth in art, and that the
French have throughout offended against them. They
have mistaken the horrible for the tragic, external for
internal unity. It is interesting to observe how full
light only dawns on Lessing while writing. At first
he treats the French plays respectfully, and accords
them serious analysis, then gradually as he sees through
their hollow pretensions he slily, then openly ridicules
them, and proves by play after play how their pretended obedience to Aristotle has resulted in watery
rhetoric. He does not get at his verification by the
facile literary method of assuming facts, his results
are scientifically proved and developed before our
eyes. Having at length demonstrated that the elevated sentiment of true tragedy is too far removed
from the comprehension of the volatile French,
Lessing justly grants them the palm in comedy, and
for the very reason that makes them fail in tragedy.
Since true comedy is the picture of society, where
could material be found more readily than among the
most sociable people of Europe, the people endowed
with most grace, pliancy, and lightness? Comedy is
as elevating as tragedy in its particular department.
It arouses our sense of the ludicrous, and laughter, if
it does not convert a confirmedly vicious man, may confirm the morally healthy in their health. And he draws
a fine contrast between laughter and derision (*Lachen*

*und Verlachen*). It is from a want of understanding of this difference, that Rousseau had vehemently attacked the use of comedy. Lessing speaks with due appreciation of Molière, whom he names together with Shakespeare ; he praises Destouches, Marivaux, Quinault, Regnard. He justifies the latter against his own countrymen, who had censured his character of the ' Distrait' as more suited to tragedy than comedy, because such a defect should awaken compassion, not ridicule. By no means, says Lessing ; absence of mind is not a moral defect. It is a bad habit, for are we not masters over our attention, and what else is absence of mind but a misplaced concentration of attention ? He deals more gently with mixed comedy than in his younger days. He finds that the transition from the comic to the pathetic is most natural, since human life is nothing but a chain of such transitions, and the drama is to be a mirror of life.

At the same time he has emancipated himself from his unbounded admiration for Diderot. While acknowledging the obligations he owes to him, he thinks Diderot is in danger of confounding nature with realism, and in his revolt against Racine's insipid *bienséances* he outrages dignity of style. Lessing knew the ancients better than Diderot. He had besides a more refined taste, and while rejecting the conventional as much as Diderot his revolts always retained a conservative colour, for he knew that art in its very nature must retain a touch of the unnatural, since it is an artificial product. Idealism in the limits of the natural was the watchword of Lessing. From this point he treats the Spanish drama, hitherto an unknown land to his countrymen, in which he had become well versed in the rich library of a Hamburg

merchant.   He drew attention to its mixed character,
its singular beauty, originality, and wealth, united to
grotesque, romanesque, adventurous absurdities.   To
them the Greek maxim that the half is greater than
the whole, was indeed applicable.   Lope de Vega had
referred to nature in explanation of these excesses.

'It is said that tragi-comedy of Gothic invention,
faithfully imitates nature.   This is true, and not true.
It only imitates one half faithfully, and entirely neglects the other.   It imitates the nature of appearances,
without in the least regarding the nature of our feelings and emotional faculties.   In nature all things are
connected together, all things intersect, interchange,
are modified one by another.   But in this infinite
variety it can only be a drama to an infinite intellect.
To give finite spirits a share of its enjoyment, they
must receive the power of setting it the limits which
it lacks, power of abstraction to guide their attention
at will.   The destination of Art is to lift us above this
abstraction into the domain of the beautiful, to facilitate
a concentration of our attention.   If in daily life we seek,
as far as possible, to avoid and evade distractions by
contrary sensations, it must necessarily disgust us to
find again in Art what we would gladly abolish from
nature.'

But Lessing's sagacious spirit at once perceived
that this proposition must be modified, or it might be
applied to the exclusion of Shakespeare from legiti-
mate drama.   'Only when one and the same event in
its course assumes all shades of interest, and one does
not merely follow the other, but necessarily springs from
it, when seriousness produces laughter, sadness joy, or
*vice versâ* so immediately that the abstraction of one
or the other is impossible, it is then only that we do

not demand it in Art, and Art knows how to draw advantage from the impossibility.'

This justification of Shakespeare and the romantic school, and its reconciliation with the classical conceptions of the beautiful, may be deemed the key-note of the 'Dramaturgie.' Yet the two natures always at war in Lessing, are observable throughout ; the one attaches itself to the text of Aristotle, establishes definitions, deduces rules ; the other willingly leaves genius free, and desires no other judge for the works of the poet than the spontaneous feelings of the auditor. Yet throughout a conciliation is observable, more readily felt than described.

This work designed for the end of emancipating the German spirit from a servile adherence to verbal rule, ends nevertheless in a bitter complaint of the liberties taken by young geniuses, who had chosen to construe Lessing's attacks on the French into a justification of lawless license. The German spirit, when it ceased to copy the French, fell into an opposite error and attained a state of chaos in which a ' Goetz von Berlichingen ' could be produced that held a natural succession of historic facts to be dramatic, without a logical chain of ideas. Lessing had sought for a medium course. He did not fight against rules, but against their irrational application, and before he broke off his ' Dramaturgie ' he found himself alone. The young writers of the day had far outstripped him in their wild war-cry for ' the liberty of genius unfettered by rules.' In the closing pages he gives them a significant warning. Idealistic in art, he was so in a thoroughly realistic spirit. His clear intellect revolted against the sentimental lawlessness that was rapidly springing up. The license taken by these

young writers was calculated to make them carelessly
fling away the achievements of all time. They
demanded from the poets that each one should discover the art afresh. It is impossible to repress
genius; 'not every critic is a genius, but every genius
is a born critic.' Having demonstrated to his nation
that they have no national drama, Lessing forestalls
any reflexion that might be made regarding his own
productions in that department. The closing remarks
in which he disclaims for himself all pretensions to
genius have been fruitful of endless discussion in
Germany. He knew that he was a calm thinker, that
criticism took the first rank in his intellect, that he
was wanting in that enthusiasm, that divine madness
he named ἀκμή, which is its crown and blossom. His
incisive perception was never more clearly shown than
in this self-estimate. Goethe justly remarks that
though Lessing denied to himself the name of genius,
his enduring works testify against him, yet for all
that his poetry is rather a monument of what may
be produced by a refined taste, than a spontaneous
utterance.

'I am neither actor nor poet,' so runs this remarkable confession. 'It is true I have sometimes had the
honour of being regarded as the latter, but only because I have been misunderstood. It is not right to
draw such liberal inferences from the few dramatic
attempts I have ventured. Not everyone who takes
up a brush and lays on colours is a painter: The
earliest of my attempts were made at that time of life
when we are but too apt to regard inclination and
facility as genius. What is tolerable in my later
attempts, is due, as I am well aware, solely and alone
to criticism. I have always felt ashamed or annoyed

when I have read or heard anything in disparagement
of criticism.   It is said to suppress genius, and I
flatter myself that I have gained from it something
very nearly approaching genius.   I am a lame man
who cannot possibly be edified by abuse of his crutch.'

*' Er war ein selbstdenkender Kopf, und selbstdenkenden Köpfen ist es nun einmal gegeben, dass sie das ganze Gefilde der Gelehrsamkeit übersehen, und jeden Pfad desselben zu finden wissen, so bald es der Mühe verlohnt, ihn zu betreten.'*—LESSING : *Anti-Goeze,* ix.

LESSING'S dejection was naturally great at finding that the interest of the public in the national theatre was hopelessly defunct, that his ' Dramaturgie ' had fallen into the hands of the reprinters, whom Luther had already called a more pernicious brood than highwaymen. This discouragement is visible at the close of the ' Dramaturgie,' which he finally employed for his own purpose as a preliminary study for, and a commentary to, the ' Poetics ' of Aristotle. His interest in classical studies had revived, and he was indifferent whether the public cared to follow him or no. He began to contemplate the completion of his ' Laokoon,' when chance gave his occupations a polemical instead of a didactic character. Publishing business had taken Lessing to Leipzig[1] for the Easter fair of 1768, and while there his

[1] This is the visit to which Goethe refers in ' Wahrheit und Dichtung,' book viii., when, in a wayward, capricious mood, he allowed Lessing to pass through Leipzig without making an attempt to see the man he so much admired—a circumstance he never ceased to regret.

attention was directed to attacks on his 'Laokoon,'
which had been appearing for some time past in the
journal of the Halle Professor, Klotz. This Klotz was
a young man of facile talent, insinuating character,
and unbounded ambition, who, repelled by the dry
tone of pedantry generally affected by German professors, had conceived the by no means despicable
aspiration of introducing a graceful treatment of
aesthetic subjects, so as to open to the general public
what had been till then confined to schoolmen.
Frederick the Great, who hated pedants, had given
Klotz an appointment at Halle, whereby he was placed,
like few scholars of his time, in a position of pecuniary
ease, so that, still young himself, he was able to protect other young authors, and this, united to a goodly
share of vanity and a love of publicity, had tempted
him to constitute himself the head of a literary coterie,
which content at first merely to popularise aesthetics
gradually began to cavil at the most erudite scholars.
Such an accusation against Lessing had been repro-
duced by the editor of an Altona newspaper. The word
'an unpardonable fault' exasperated Lessing beyond
measure. His mental state was unquestionably over-
strung, and it only needed some such impulse from
without to cause his suppressed indignation to
find vent. He forgot that he had in the 'Laokoon'
spoken of Klotz as a scholar of refined and correct
taste. He did not stop to consider that some of
Klotz's objections, made on philological and antiquarian grounds, were not without foundation, such as
his remarks on the highest pathos attained by
the Greeks, the contrast between the Roman and
Greek national character, and so forth. The man's
malice, his childish susceptibility to praise and blame

disgusted Lessing, who was a veritable Don Quixote
in the realms of the learned world.   Only true wisdom
and erudition were to be held of account, all shallow-
ness must be proscribed.   He could not admit as a
fact that occasionally such men contribute more to
the popularisation of a subject than the truly learned.
True, Lessing himself was not such a one ; he combined the thoroughness of the scholar with the attractions of the elegant writer, a combination so rare in
Germany that Klotz's popularity is thus alone sufficiently explained.   Lessing further despised his
spirit of cliqueism, but his anger exceeded bounds
when he found that Klotz carried this so far as to cir-
culate scurrilous reports against antagonists.   Antiquarian interests had been reawakening in Lessing
for some time ; the adversary he loved to combat in
his writings was once more to hand ; he had a measure
of wrath to vent, and the result was a second ' Vade
Mecum.'

' I must see if I can still make a literary letteret,'
he writes to Nicolai, announcing his intention to quell
this factious coterie and show no mercy.   ' The man
brags too much and would like to be held an oracle
in these matters.   All the same, I am convinced that
no more poor ignorant fellow has ever sought to possess himself of the critical tripod.   His thing about engraved gems is the most wretched and impertinent
compilation from Winckelmann and Lippert, whom
he has often misunderstood, and everything he has
added of his own is miserable.'

It was in this very essay, much praised by Klotz's
friends, that he had ventured his first direct attacks
against Lessing.   ' He has done me the honour of
mentioning me three times in this little book, in order

three times to correct me. But all three times he has either not understood me out of shortsightedness, or not cared to understand me out of spite.'

Lessing replied to the article in the Altona paper by one in the Hamburg journal. He described it to Nicolai as his declaration of the war against Klotz which he felt himself called upon to wage, since the only other man who could worthily have conducted it, Winckelmann, was dead. 'The second author within a short space,' writes Lessing, 'for whose life I would gladly have sacrificed a few years of my own.'[1] Later, when Lessing was censured for his conduct towards Klotz, he plainly expresses his opinion of the professional *esprit de corps*, upheld at all costs to learning. 'I have only waited to see whether anyone would attack the awkward Goliath of the learned Philistines. At last I could not put up with his stupid sneers any longer without casting a few stones out of my scrip at his head. I well know that he has been always despised by really learned men, but I do not know whether their silent contempt is sufficient to avenge the public whom he misleads. Some one ought at length to lift up his voice. And truly, if there are none, or at any rate so few, who testify openly to being on my side, I fear that by the help of his accomplices, scattered all over Germany, he will soon manage to outvoice me again.'

The war once opened, the attacks followed one another with amazing rapidity, considering the profoundly learned nature of their contents, and prove how completely at home Lessing was in the subject. His letters to Nicolai show that he had not even the most needful books of reference at hand. Within the

[1] The first was Sterne.

space of four weeks he had written twenty-five of his
'Antiquarian Letters.' Michaelmas that year (1768),
the first part appeared as a book. At the same time he
wrote an essay 'On the Ancestral Portraits of the Old
Romans' (*Ueber die Ahnenbilder der Alten Römer*),
also directed against Klotz. Nicolai declined its publication, and it remained a fragment to be published
among Lessing's remains, breaking off at the most interesting point. Its purpose was to refute a pretended discovery made by Klotz, really, as it afterwards appeared,
a plagiarism from Christ, that these portraits had been
works of encaustic painting, while Lessing contends
and demonstrates by proofs from authors and internal
evidence, that the ancestral portraits preserved in the
atrium were nothing but painted wax masks.

Mendelssohn disapproved of this controversy, he
held it unworthy of his friend. Lessing defends himself, it was needful once and for ever to demolish
these bunglers. He does not mean to bury himself in
antiquarian studies. Archaeology alone is a poor sort
of study ; he only values it so far as it is an additional
hobby-horse wherewith to shorten the journey of life.
Nicolai blamed the want of courtesy displayed in
his treatment of Klotz. Lessing replies that he
will justify himself on this account in his preface, that
such things must be said with some heat or not at all.

In the preface he quotes Cicero's answer to the
lukewarm Atticus, ' Vide quam sim antiquorum
hominum ! ' contending that the ancients did not
know the thing we call politeness, that their urbanity
was as far removed from it as our rudeness. Lessing's
polemics resemble those of a wise man who has
patiently looked on at a scene of confusion until he
can bear it no longer, and, suddenly roused to action,

overturns good and bad alike. The 'Antiquarian Letters,' like the 'Vade Mecum,' will be always read for their wonderfully caustic sallies, their drastic vigour, the astonishing vivacity with which purely erudite subjects are treated, carrying on the reader over heavy passages by dint of unlooked-for humorous turns. Digressions there are none. Never did Lessing keep more closely to the matter in hand. He follows his opponent step by step: if he attempts to digress he follows him into the domain of his digressions. He is secure of his vantage ground, and he evinces this security by a confidence of tone that is authoritative but never arrogant. The peculiar charm of his style, its dialectical character, is pre-eminent in these Letters, which seem an easy conversation naturally developing out of itself. No sign of effort or labour is apparent ; the reader assists at questions and replies as though they were enacted before him. What does he care for the shallow errors committed by a Halle Professor named Klotz who has been long dead and forgotten ? and yet the charming manner carries him along, and he reads with interest to the end.

Klotz had fastened upon a passage of the 'Laokoon,' wherein Lessing averred that the ancients did not attempt to paint subjects drawn from their poets, and pointed in reply to the Homeric subjects treated by the ancients in the pictures found at Herculaneum and elsewhere ; a correction based on a misinterpretation of the text of Lessing, who had censured Caylus' endeavour to paint an epic in pictures, but never denied that the ancients may have painted the subjects sung by their poets, only asserting that in so doing each artist kept within the limits of his art, and

did not attempt to follow the other line by line. The
first eight Letters that dealt with this subject created
a sensation ; the ninth, treating of ancient perspective,
met with the respectful approval of competent judges
as a veritable masterpiece on a little-known theme.
The remaining Letters were all occupied with the subject of gems, and here nothing is easier than to expose
Klotz's trite and flashy knowledge. He examines
the authorities quoted by Klotz ; they are either
second-rate, or he has misconstrued their meaning, or
he has copied their quotations inaccurately, or at
second-hand. As regards Klotz's own opinions on
this subject, they are worth nothing, and what wonder,
the Professor knows nothing.

Throughout these 'Antiquarian Letters' the aesthetic
interests placed foremost in the 'Laokoon' take second
rank. Here the purely archaeological comes first,
Lessing puts forward his most learned side ; technical,
optical, etymological, literary and scientific arguments,
various readings of classical authors, are the weapons
brought to bear on Klotz, whose weak side, a want of
thoroughness, they effectually exposed. Klotz had not
calculated on such an investigation of his work. He
tried to conciliate Lessing, then finding that in vain,
he refused to reply, pretending that the quarrels
of the learned did not interest the public at large.
Finally he had recourse to acting the part of the
generous enemy, but even this manœuvre Lessing
frustrated, exposing its deceitfulness. For while
affecting a modest demeanour towards Lessing himself, Klotz had caused his satellites to attack him in all
the journals, had endeavoured to exasperate Nicolai
against him, and, what enraged Lessing more than
aught else, some of these libels had reached the

pastoral home at Camenz, and had caused sorrow
to the beloved old father, then already bowed down
with anxieties and enfeebled health.

The second volume of 'Antiquarian Letters,' delayed for a year by the need of engraved examples
of intaglios, shows a more bitter tone on Lessing's
part, and also betrays disgust with the subject, whose
pettiness was not long to his taste. Nicolai, who
published the first volume with success, is obliged to
announce to him that the second hangs fire. With
the. fifty-first Letter Lessing breaks off these personal
controversies, but before doing so, he once more
justifies the sharpness of his invective against Klotz.
'The man is a mere dealer in antiquities (*Alter-
thumskrämer*), not an antiquarian (*Alterthumsforscher*).
The former has inherited the fragments, the latter the
spirit of antiquity. The one scarcely thinks with his
eyes, the other actually sees with his thoughts. Before the one can say : thus it was! the latter already
knows whether it could have been thus.'

This, he says, is the scale by which a critic should
measure his procedure. 'Indulgent and flattering towards the tyro, doubting amid admiration, admiring
amid doubt towards the master, discouraging and
incisive towards the bungler, contemptuous towards
the boaster, and as bitter as possible towards the mis-
chiefmaker.'

He is not angered. It is not anger that has
guided his pen, but calm deliberate reasoning, and
wherever a word is bitter, hard, sneering, satirical, it
is put there advisedly. Till now he has had to deal
with the author merely, but Klotz has forced him also
to deal with the man and the Professor; for the one has
attacked his personal character, the other has vaunted

his professorial dignity to the disparagement of the untitled Lessing. Klotz had spread the report that Lessing was the real though disguised chief of the party that was exercising a literary despotism at Berlin. Nicolai was at the head of the *Allgemeine Bibliothek*, not Lessing, who had still to write his first contribution to that paper. Klotz and his crew have discovered a faction where none exists, co-operation where there is only individual effort. It is nothing but a vision seen by Klotz and his friends.

' Good luck to their visions and to all the knightly deeds they may give rise to! But would that a kind fairy would open the eyes of these heroes, if only in so far as I am concerned. I am indeed only a windmill and not a giant. Here I stand on my place quite outside the village, alone on a sand-hill. I come to no one, I help no one, and am helped by none. When I have something to put on my grindstones, I grind it with whatever wind may blow. All thirty-two winds are my friends. I do not ask a finger's breadth more of the whole wide atmosphere than my sails require to revolve in; only I wish them to be left free sailing room. Gnats may swarm among them, but mischievous boys must not be constantly wanting to chase one another in and out between them, still less must any hand attempt to check them that is not stronger than the wind that turns me. If my sails fling anyone into the air he must regard it his own fault, nor can I set him down more gently than he happens to fall.'

' Klotz threw a pea at Lessing, and Lessing returned an avalanche of rocks upon him,' was said by a contemporary. All, not excepting Goethe, blamed the violence and acerbity of his attack on Klotz, who, no doubt, deserved a lesson, but was too trifling an adversary to merit such exhaustive notice. Klotz was certainly silenced, but he gave out everywhere that he was only collecting materials for his defence. Even in after years Lessing vindicated his character in this matter. 'If the scale goes down too far on the side where the wrong lies, one must throw oneself with all one's force on to the other, in order, if possible, to restore the equilibrium.' His irritation and discontent were on the increase. Already in September (1768) he was busy with plans for quitting Hamburg, intentions which, contrary to his wont, he communicated, perhaps to enforce a moral restraint upon himself. To his brother he writes:

'Next February I am going by the first ship from hence to Leghorn, and from there direct to Rome. I am selling all my books and belongings, the catalogue is already printed, and the auction fixed for January 16th.' And to Nicolai:

'Next February I am going to leave Hamburg; and where am I going? Direct to Rome. You laugh, but you may be quite certain that it will happen. . . . What I want at Rome I shall write to you from Rome. From here I can only tell you that I have at any rate as much to seek and expect in Rome as at any place in Germany. Here I cannot live on 800 thalers a-year, but in Rome I can live on 300. I shall be able to take about enough with me to live for a year; when that is gone, well, it would be gone here too, and I am quite sure it must be more amusing and entertaining to hunger and beg in Rome than in Germany. I have already dissolved my connexion with Bode, and nothing in the world can hold me here any longer. All circumstances seem to tend to make my history the history of Solomon's cat, who every day ventured a little further from its home, until at last it never returned.'

The dissolution of the connexion with Bode had been perfectly amicable, the undertaking simply did not pay. Not only that the piratical reprints detracted from their receipts, but both Bode and Lessing had all manner of expensive fancies regarding print and paper. The latter they imported direct from Italy, the former was varied in inks and forms, elegant vignettes and tail-pieces were employed, and so forth, refinements to which the public was indifferent, and which necessarily enhanced the price of their books. Nicolai had warned Lessing that publishing must be learnt like any other trade. Lessing turned a deaf ear to his remonstrances, he considered that what he might lack in practice would be more than supplied by his refined and thorough literary knowledge. Perhaps these qualities might have sufficed, had they been united to steady business faculties, punctuality, and promptitude. But these were totally absent. For instance, Lessing complained of the reprint of his 'Dramaturgie,' and that the public bought the pirated edition, but more than once Nicolai had to tell him that the public was not wholly to blame, since the market was better supplied with the spurious than the original paper. This failure made him ponder over a project that should not alienate authors and publishers, but should enable the former to make the offspring of their brains as profitable as other merchandise. His views were embodied in a pamphlet, 'Live and Let Live,' advocating a scheme already broached by Leibnitz, of publication by subscription, this to be raised by the publisher, who would receive commission on the sales, the net profit going to the author.

In November Lessing writes to Ramler: 'You have been ill, dearest friend. But how can one be well in Berlin? Everything one sees there must stir up one's gall. Come quickly to Hamburg, we will put to sea and roam into the world a few thousand miles. I give you my word, we shall come back healthier than we went, or perhaps we may not come back at all, which comes to the same thing. I do not suppose that Rome will please me for a longer time than any other place in the world has hitherto done. If, therefore, the 'Collegium de Propaganda Fide' wants to send some one to a place where not even a Jesuit will go, I will go. Then, when we meet again after twenty years, what shall I not have to tell you?'

The news of Lessing's intended journey to Rome spread and was reported in the papers with various conjectural addenda. One was enabled to state that he was about to turn Catholic; another, that he was going to Rome to play Protestant, as he had played Saxon in Prussia; another, that he was about to become Papal librarian; yet another, that he was going to teach archaeology. These rumours annoyed Lessing, especially as they were credited by some of his acquaintances. 'How can they be so spiteful towards me as to repeat all this?' he writes. 'For this is assuredly spite. I want to go to Italy to learn, and malicious fools proclaim me as one going to teach!' Winckelmann's friend, Muzell-Stosch, heard the rumours and offered Lessing an introduction to Cardinal Albani, hinting that he might fill the post rendered vacant by Winckelmann's murder. He gracefully declined the offer and wrote to Nicolai concerning it:

'I claim to make no acquaintances in Rome except chance acquaintances. Had Winckelmann not been such a particular friend and client of Albani's, I think his *Monumenti* would have turned out differently. A great deal of rubbish has been admitted into it just because it stands in the Villa Albani. From an artistic point of view these things are worthless; from an archaeological there is also not so much as Winckelmann has purposely seen in them. Whatever I may see, and however I may live, I can do it without Cardinals.'

The spring of 1769 however came, and found Lessing still in Hamburg. He was engaged upon the second volume of his 'Antiquarian Letters,' and contemplated a third part. The voyage to Leghorn was abandoned; he now meant to go overland in May and visit Cassel, Nuremberg, and Göttingen, in one of which towns he would stay a month to complete his 'Laokoon.' So many fools were busy chattering about it, he wanted to finish it and show them what was the positive goal he had aimed at in the essay; and he briefly sketched the outline to Nicolai. Meantime, offers of an appointment as dramaturgist at Vienna had reached him. He refused this, because he did not wish again to be connected with the theatre. But he continued to defer his departure week by week, and though want of funds had much to do with this, he did not entirely lose Vienna out of sight. The Emperor Joseph II. was holding out to literary men a magnificent project for the revival of arts and sciences that was to inaugurate a new age of gold. Klopstock corresponded with the young Emperor on the subject, and painted glorious visions of all that might be achieved. Lessing shared the illusions of Klopstock, and would not listen to the sagacious remonstrances of Nicolai, who warned him against Austrian despotism, and pointed proudly to the more real liberty he would find in Berlin. How could Lessing expect to find liberty of speech in a place where Mendelssohn's ' Phaedon ' was confiscated ? The whole thing was a financial project, started in the hope that the famous authors would publish their works in Austria and so bring money into the country. What high-flown ideas of literary revival could be expected from a plan approved by Kaunitz, hatched in a country that favoured reprints on the same mercantile principles that it forbade the importation of herrings, viz. to keep money at home ?

Lessing would not hear of this. ' Let Vienna be as it may, I promise better luck to German literature there than in your Frenchified Berlin. If the " Phaedon " was ever confiscated at Vienna, it can only have been because it was printed at Berlin, and it was not possible to imagine that anything could be written at Berlin in favour of the immortality of the soul. You don't tell me anything else about your Berlin freedom of thought and speech. It reduces itself wholly and solely to the freedom of bringing to market any number of *sottises* against religion. An honest man must soon blush to make use of this freedom. . . . Let some one at Berlin speak up for the rights of sub- jects and against extortion and despotism, as is done now even in France and Denmark, and you will soon discover which is the most slavish country in Europe.'

Nicolai was right, however, and Lessing was not long the dupe of the false liberalism of Joseph II. with whom this scheme had been the mere fantasy of a fickle spirit. The Italian plan again occupied his thoughts, but want of funds delayed its execution. Lessing writes to Karl :

'I must turn all I have left into money, and even
then I shall scarcely be able to pay my journey. My
heart bleeds when I think of our parents, but God is my
witness that I am not wanting in will to help them ;
but at this moment I am certainly poorer than any one
of the family. For the poorest is at any rate not in
debt, and I, while lacking the most needful, am up to
my ears in debt. May God help us ! '

He compares his condition to a bog into which
one sinks the deeper the more efforts one makes to
extricate oneself. He worked and worked, and yet he
seemed to get no better off ; he formed project after
project, but none would answer to his hopes ; and then
the heavy demands from Camenz. He was nearing
his fortieth year, he was less robust than formerly,
disappointments and anxieties had told on his iron
constitution, and he was still ' the old bird on the roof.'
' When the bad forties come,' he said, ' it is all over
with a man.' His impaired health, an unwonted sensation, depressed him. 'I must think it is all the fault
of those wretched forty years. If that is so, I decline
with thanks the forty yet remaining to me.'

In this state of indecision he took up his ' *Schlaf-
trunk* ' with the intention of completing it, but a
trifling interruption made him abandon the idea ; he
was, besides, weary of the theatre. Antiquarian
interests were the strongest just now, but he was
equally weary of attacking Klotz. He would write a
more abiding work, starting from the theme of his
disputes. The result is the charming little essay,
' *Wie die Alten den Tod gebildet*' (How the Ancients
represented Death). Its object was to confute the
notion that the ancients represented Death as a
skeleton. Lessing had already touched upon this in

his 'Laokoon,' and Klotz had endeavoured to refute
him by referring to figures of skeletons discovered on
antique gems and urns.

In this essay Lessing answers Klotz's objections,
but he prefaces it by saying: 'I should be sorry if
this disquisition were to be estimated according to the
circumstance that prompted it, for this is so contemptible, that only the manner in which I have used
it can excuse me for having been willing to use it
at all.' After quoting the passage in which Klotz
attacks him, Lessing says that he has no wish to deny
the existence of skeletons in ancient art, but that he
desires to show that they are not intended to sym-
bolise death. He divides his essay into two parts and
proceeds to prove :

Firstly. That the ancient artists really represented the God of Death under an entirely different
image from that of a skeleton.

Secondly. That the ancient artists when they
represented a skeleton, meant by this skeleton something entirely different from Death, as God of Death.

The form under which the ancients represented
Death was that of a boy, twin brother of Sleep.

This was the Homeric idea as attested by a passage from Pausanias, who describes a figure of Night
in the temple of Juno, in Elis, holding in her arms two
boys, exactly alike, except that one is white, the other
black, one sleeps, the other seems to sleep. These
are Sleep and Death. One reason why this fact had
been so little recognised was that all figures of winged
boys had been supposed to represent Cupids. Lessing
shows that many of these figures hitherto regarded as
Cupids were in reality figures of Death, who was
represented by the ancients as a winged boy holding

a reversed torch.  He quotes passages from ancient writers, and refers to many representations of Sleep together with his twin brother.  Undoubtedly his twin brother must be Death, as Homer tells us. Then if such was the representation of death, the skeleton must have some other meaning.  Why should the ancients, who regarded beauty before all things, choose so horrible a figure to represent any-thing so calm and beautiful as the state or abstract notion of death ?  There is no horror in the thought of being dead, nor in the act of dying, as the transition to this repose, but some forms of death are horrible, and there are some circumstances under which it is terrible to die.  This is the idea embodied in the Greek divinity Κήρ, who presided over violent deaths and dreadful fates, and was entirely distinct from Θάνατος.  Since then these two divinities were distinct, it might be suggested that the skeleton was to represent Κήρ ; yet this could not well be.  Why should the act of dying be represented by that which follows after death ?  Besides, Pausanias has left an account of the real form in which this divinity was represented.  What, then, are these skeletons ?  They are, says Lessing, *larvae*, the departed souls of evil men ; and since the word actually means a skeleton, there can be no doubt as to the correctness of this suggestion.  That we now represent Death under the form of a skeleton is no sufficient reason for supposing the ancients to have done so.  It had been said that their ideas of death must necessarily be horrible, since they had far sadder and drearier notions of it than ourselves.  But must not that religion that first taught that death was the natural fruit and wages of sin, have immeasurably increased the terrors of dissolution ?

It is then our religion that has banished the beautiful image of death and introduced in its stead the horrible skeleton.

'Yet since this religion has not revealed this terrible truth to us in order that we might despair, and since it also assures us that death cannot be otherwise than easy and beneficial for the righteous, I cannot see what should prevent our artists from banishing the terrible skeletons, and again taking possession of that other better image. Even Scripture speaks of an angel of death, and what artist would not rather form an angel than a skeleton? It is only misunderstood religion that can remove us from the beautiful, and it is a proof that religion is true, and rightly understood, if it everywhere leads us back to the beautiful.'

When the essay was completed and the library sold, Lessing found he had still not enough funds with which to live a year at Rome. At this crisis appeared a *Deus ex machinâ* in the person of J. A. Ebert, a Hamburger by birth, and one of the circle of literary men whom the Duke Charles of Brunswick, and his intelligent heir-apparent, Duke Ferdinand, the luckless general of Jena, had attracted to their court. Ebert had spoken of Lessing to the hereditary Prince, had read him some of the 'Antiquarian Letters' and extracts from Lessing's private letters, with all of which the Prince was delighted, his fine intelligence recognising the worth of the man. When Ebert further added that Lessing intended to go to Italy, probably not without an after-thought that he would thus frustrate the plan, the Prince expressed a wish to see him first, and begged Ebert to request Lessing to make it convenient to pass through Brunswick *en route.* Lessing wrote to Ebert saying he held it in every wise his duty to meet the Prince's desires, and enclosed a copy of his essay, ' How the Ancients represented Death,' requesting Ebert to show it to the Prince if he deemed it advisable, but adding that he could not allow it to be expressly handed to him in his name, as that was more than a polemic against Klotz deserved. Lessing further learnt that during a late visit at Berlin the Prince had sought out Moses Mendelssohn. Whereupon he wrote to Ebert :

' I know nothing in the world which would have better secured to the Prince my entire respect and admiration than his seeking the acquaintance, at Berlin, of my oldest and dearest friend. There could be no doubt that they would like each other, and what would I not give if it were possible for the Prince to draw him from that place which is, as I know, quite against his inclinations.'

Lessing's visit was deferred from a desire not to have to return to Hamburg if possible. He did not find it so easy as heretofore to tear himself away.

' Unfortunately I am so firmly rooted here that I must tear myself away gently, or a piece of flesh will remain hanging here and there.'

Early in December however he appeared at Brunswick, where he made a favourable impression on the court. It was his peculiarity not to do himself full justice before strangers, but Ebert had prepared the way. The post of Ducal Librarian at Wolfenbüttel, with a salary of 600 thalers, was offered him. Lessing accepted the post on the express condition that the appointment should not interfere with his Italian journey, and only be delayed the needful time for him to get into working order. Notwithstanding his resolve he returned to Hamburg, partly because he was immersed in debt and did not see his way to quit it with honour, partly because there were tenderer feelings involved.

As elsewhere, so also in Hamburg, Lessing had associated freely with the inhabitants. At Hamburg his acquaintances lay chiefly among a mixed circle, consisting of Jews, Christians, merchants, actors, and journalists; only the purse-proud Hamburg patricians had never been to his taste, though he left no side of Hamburg life unexplored. He used to declare that he had never known the full scope of his mother-tongue till he came to Hamburg, where he learnt to speak the peculiar broad (*Platt*) German of the people. Life in a republic was also singularly agreeable to his views of liberty and independence. Among the families whom he visited chiefly were the Reimarus, Dr. Johann, a physician of Lessing's age, and his clever sister Elise. This house was the common meeting-place of all the intellectual society of the town, but the father who first gave it that character, Hamburg's greatest contemporary celebrity Hermann Samuel Reimarus, whose theological writings Lessing afterwards edited in part as the ' Wolfenbüttel Fragments,' had died shortly before his arrival.

But the house to which he was most attracted was that of the silk manufacturer, König. The worthy man, his clever and original wife, as well as their large family of little children, of whom Lessing was passionately fond, all exerted great attractions over him. He speaks of König in a letter to Gleim as his especial friend, and that König returned the compliment is proved by the circumstance that, in 1769, when setting out for a journey to Italy, he entrusted his family to Lessing's care should anything occur to him. He did indeed die very suddenly at Venice, leaving his affairs in a most involved condition. Lessing loyally stood by his widow, aiding her to the best of his power, though the capable woman of large masculine intellect was quite competent to cope with business details. But the constant intercourse that König's injunction necessitated gave birth to a warmer feeling on both sides. Frau König would not listen to any solicitations on Lessing's part. Her first duty was to extricate her affairs out of the embroilment that threatened to engulf her children's all, but each mutually felt the other a dear and valued friend, and it is certain that Lessing's irresolution about leaving Hamburg, and his sudden wish to find an assured subsistence, were influenced by this feeling. He continued to linger, unable to tear himself away.

Ebert warns him that the Prince is getting impatient; Lessing puts forth pretext after pretext, and begs Ebert to keep his memory green at Brunswick. Still he does not come ; he announces his arrival for a certain day, but no sign of him when the day dawned. Ebert felt this was getting serious ; he knew the temper of princes, and that delays are not to their mind. In vain he urged ; Lessing is fertile in excuses, real and imaginary. Now the snow has blocked the roads, now he has not all the books he wants, now he wishes to stay and meet Herder, who is passing through Hamburg. The leave of absence accorded by the Duke had expired, and still Lessing did not come. Ebert ventured to hint that a post had duties.

' God knows that I am longing to be at rest,' he writes to him in March, ' since I am to be put at rest.

The sparrow's life on the roof is all very well when it is not necessary to look forward to an end. If it cannot last, every day it lasts is too long.'

Ebert jestingly remarks that Lessing's reluctance to leave and come to his affianced bride, the library, looks as though a more corporeal one detained him in Hamburg ; but adds, ' from that suspicion you are too well secured.' This time, however, he was not. It was his heart that held him to Hamburg, and right sore it was when he at last tore himself away, travelling direct to Brunswick, where he arrived in April 1770.

# CHAPTER XIV.

## WOLFENBÜTTEL.

### (1770-1772.  AGED 41-43.)

*' Unabhängig von dem Schmuck*
*Prunkender Erscheinung—*
*Unabhängig von dem Druck*
*Hergebrachter Meinung.'*

NEARLY everything that German literature has to
show of princely patronage during the last century
emanated from the little Duchy of Brunswick. Charles,
the reigning Duke in Lessing's time, had transferred
the seat of government from Wolfenbüttel to Brunswick, and, instigated by the Abbot Jerusalem, had
there founded the celebrated Collegium Carolinum.
To supply it with able professors the Duke had
invited men like Gärtner, Zachariä, Ebert, Eschenburg,
and Schmid to settle in his dominions, and literature
was encouraged and fostered.  His eldest son and
heir, Prince Ferdinand, had been carefully educated.
Jerusalem had been his early preceptor, in Rome he
had enjoyed daily intercourse with Winckelmann, and
he corresponded with the most eminent men of his
day, Voltaire, d'Alembert, Marmontel, and Mendelssohn.  Like his uncle Frederick the Great, he affected
to be a poet and musician.  His marriage with
Augusta, Princess of Wales, awoke at the court an

interest in the English language and literature. The Duchess Amalie, of Weimar, Goethe's friend and patron, was also a daughter of this house. It was therefore no empty compliment when the Hereditary Prince invited Lessing to his dominions, and let him know through Ebert that he had not only justified his expectations, but surpassed them. The old Duke, whose reign was now but nominal, gave his assent to his son's wish that Lessing should fill the post of ducal librarian.

Early in May 1770, Lessing was formally installed. He was to have 600 thalers salary, free lodging, and firing: a sum not mean according to contemporary German requirements, and on which Lessing might have subsisted, had he not arrived hampered with debts. The lodging assigned was in the large dilapidated palace, situated just opposite the library.

The post of librarian was really not vacant, the Prince had created a vacancy for Lessing. Lessing writes to his father that not only the reigning Duke, but the whole house had received him with condescension and kindness.

'However, I am not the man to force myself upon them, rather I seek to keep as distant as possible from anything connected with the court, and entirely to confine myself within the circle of my library. The post itself is just as though it had been made for me, and I need the less regret that I have hitherto refused all other offers. It is also sufficiently lucrative to enable me to live comfortably ; but the best part of it is the library, which must be known to you by fame, but which I have found far more excellent than I had ever imagined it. Now I may well forget my books that want forced me to sell. I wish I might yet have the pleasure in my life to take you about here, for I know what a lover and connoisseur you are of all manner of books.

'I have really no other official duties than those that I make for myself. I may boast that the Prince was more anxious that I should use the library than that it should use me. However, I shall try to combine both, or really the one follows from the other.'

In his letters to his friends there breathes a spirit rather of resignation than of content. To one who had been so long 'the old sparrow on the roof,' there was something oppressive in a settled post. He writes to Ebert, May 7, 1770 :

'I slipped away from you. But is it worth while to bid farewell when one dies—or travels from Brunswick to Wolfenbüttel! Do not suppose, because I place these two together, that I consider myself to be dead. It is not possible to live more quietly and contentedly than I have done these three days. Such a life must certainly seem death to you court revellers who banquet and feast every day. Well you may exclaim with the French lacquey, "Vive la vie!" I say, "Vive la mort," if only that I may have nothing in common with a Frenchman.'

Wolfenbüttel, then distant a five hours' drive from Brunswick, certainly looks a dead alive place even now that the railway to the Harz traverses it; how much more so then ! A whilom capital, with the wide streets and palatial buildings destined for the abode of a court, presents a more dreary and forsaken aspect than any other forgotten place. There was no society, the best people had followed the court. Lessing could not but soon miss the stirring life of Hamburg, with its world-wide commerce and maritime variety. He missed, too, the houses at which he had been an intimate and welcome guest ; he missed one above all. Indeed one of the first letters written from his hermitage at Wolfenbüttel was addressed to Eva König. He apologises for not writing sooner :

'You least of all, dear friend, will reproach me with that which I can only properly explain to you if you make a merit of it. I am unsettled all day long when I have written to Hamburg, and three days pass before everything here pleases me again as it should. Yet you must not suppose I am not content here. Only when one remembers that one has often been very happy elsewhere, it is difficult to persuade oneself that one is so still. How is Amalie ? how is my god-child ? Everything is so empty and large around me that I would often give a great deal if I could at least have one of my little companions in Hamburg about me. In thought I have been walking out with you all the evening. If only I were doing so in reality, what should I not have to ask you ! . . . . Shall you still travel this summer? I would go fifty miles after you if you were to pass through here, and I should be so unfortunate as to miss you.'

In her reply Eva König tells him she is going to take the waters at Pyrmont. Will he not come too ? That his tiresome old Wolfenbüttel and accursed castle should lie so out of the way !. If she had faith sufficient to move mountains she would soon place it elsewhere. Lessing did not accept the invitation to Pyrmont, but in June had the pleasure of entertaining Frau König and her brother on their way thither. Frau König thanks him in August for his hospitality, and announces that she will pass through Wolfenbüttel again shortly, as she must go to Vienna to look personally after her factory affairs, that grow more and more involved. This time she came alone ; but no definite engagement seems to have taken place, though no doubt there was an understanding. She writes him several letters *en route*, thanks him for all his kindness, and relates the adventures of her journey with much verve and humour : how the postilion was drunk, how the lights had gone out, and, stranded in a desolate place in the Thuringian forest, miles away from help, she had come to the rescue with lighted fircones. Lessing thanked her for her news, and begs her to continue to look at misadventures from the ludicrous side :

'The ludicrous is often the only pleasure that travelling affords. Take this with you everywhere, for laughter keeps the body in health.'

A brisk correspondence was now set on foot between the two. The letters have in great part been preserved, and are a most valuable contribution to our knowledge of Lessing's character, for he was singularly free from the subjective tendency of the period, and rarely spoke of himself and his feelings. These love-letters were not filled with the long-winded out-pourings of sentiment then so common. They write about politics, literature, the stage ; she tells him about the performances in Vienna and retails the latest news received from Hamburg friends. He tells her of his work and prospects, and she enters into all with ready comprehension and sympathy. At Brunswick Lessing had to abandon the charms of the faro-table, but his love for play and speculation made him buy lottery tickets. A great part of the letters are occupied with the choice of numbers, and so forth. She is ill, and he recommends her medicines, and sends her powders. He is merry, and she enters into his jokes.

Meanwhile conjectures were rife among Lessing's friends as to what form his next literary labours would take. Their guesses fell on every theme but the right one. If Lessing's post did not compel him to any official duties, he held it right nevertheless not to be a librarian in vain. His first proceeding was necessarily to make himself acquainted with the contents of the library. The Bibliotheca Augusta was, as Lessing said, one of the few libraries that had really been collected with intelligence, not accumulated by chance. Leibnitz had once been its librarian ; he too had commended its riches. These consisted more especially in over six thousand volumes of MSS., and to these Lessing naturally first devoted his attention. Chance came to his aid. It happened that within the first weeks of his appointment he discovered among these MSS. one of great theological importance. No less a treasure, he tells his father with genuine delight, secure for once of sympathy—no less a discovery than a work by Berengarius of Tours (Berengarius Turonensis), the existence of which was not only not established but was actually denied by Catholics. Berengarius was Archdeacon of Angers in the eleventh century, that era of general disruption of existent conditions, and the awakening of a new spiritual life in the Church. As Canon of Tours and director of the Cathedral school, Berengarius exerted a great influence, which he used for the spread of enlightened thought. It was a sort of middle term between speculative and positive belief. Berengarius denied the doctrine of the real presence. Lanfranc, afterwards Archbishop of Canterbury, at

that time head of the convent of St. Stephen at
Caen, accused him of heresy and contempt of authority. Berengarius had replied to these accusations.
Meanwhile he was denounced as a heretic, and cited
to a council at Vercelli, condemned, deprived of his
temporalities, and he and his adherents threatened with imprisonment and death if they did not
recant. Berengarius thrice renounced his alleged
error, and then again avowed it, retiring from all
worldly concerns, and spending the rest of his days in
the unostentatious practice of piety. A considerable
sect that followed him were reckoned by Catholics
among the most dangerous heretics, and all Berengarius' writings on which they could lay hands were
destroyed. And it was a copy of the treatise in which
Berengarius refuted Lanfranc of Canterbury that had
fallen into Lessing's hands. Here was an opportunity
for another rehabilitation, for how had not the memory
of this good man been perverted !

> Ye who, secure 'mid trophies not your own,
> Judge him who won them when he stood alone,
> And proudly talk of recreant Berengare—
> O first the age and then the man compare.[1]

Even Luther had commended the papal excommuni-
cation that had befallen him, while this treatise proved
beyond dispute that Berengarius had held essentially
the same doctrines with regard to the Eucharist as
Luther, and had moreover contended that this teaching
alone was the true doctrine of the Church. It was
an ecclesiastical treasure, and an important addition
to the Vindiciae Lutherianae of the German clergy.
Even Mosheim had purposely or inadvertently omitted

---

[1] Coleridge : 'Lines, suggested by the last words of Berengarius,
ob. Anno Dom. 1088.'

to render justice to Berengarius, who had been branded as a heretic by all parties.

'The thing we call heretic,' says Lessing, 'has one very good side. It means a person who has at least wished to see with his own eyes. The question is only whether the eyes were good. In certain centuries the name heretic was even the greatest recommendation a learned man could present to posterity, greater even than the names magus, magician, exorciser; for among these there was many an impostor. How had Berengarius merited this suspicion? Does it mean to imply that he was weak enough to deny recognised truths? Let that be far from us. I do not know whether it is a duty to sacrifice happiness and life to truth; at any rate the courage and determination it requires are not gifts which we can give to ourselves. But this I know to be a duty, that if we desire to teach truth we must teach it wholly or not at all; clear, round, without riddle, without reserve, without doubt as to its power and utility; and the gifts that this requires lie in our own control. Whoever will not attain these, or when he has attained them will not use them, serves human reason badly if he takes from us gross errors while reserving from us the whole truth, and trying to satisfy us with a middle course of truth and lies. For the more gross the error, the shorter and more direct the road to truth; while on the other hand subtle errors may keep us eternally removed from truth, seeing it is more difficult to recognise that they are errors.

'Because Berengarius was weak, must he of necessity have been purposely false? Because I am forced to pity him, must I therefore despise him? The man who amid threatening dangers is faithless to Truth

may yet love her dearly, and Truth will forgive his
infidelity for the sake of his love. But whosoever only
considers how he may bring her to men under the disguise of paint and masks, would like to be her pander,
but he can never have been her lover.'

A man like Berengarius who has consecrated his
life to the search after truth, and who in the maturity
of age has continued to sustain what he thought true
against all dangers, such a man does not submit to
authority like an infant or relapse into the early
superstitions of childhood. It is an idea as false as
the notion that he had not replied to his accusers, for
here is the reply.

'Whosoever would never be timid or weary in the
combating of prejudices, must first overcome this
prejudice, that the impressions of childhood are not
to be destroyed. The ideas of truth and falsehood
imparted to us in childhood are the most superficial
of all, are those that can the most easily be for ever
obliterated by self-acquired ideas, and those in whom
they reappear when advanced in years bear testimony
against themselves that the ideas under which they
tried to bury the others are even more superficial
and shallow, and still less their own than those of
their childhood. It is only of such men that we can
possibly believe the horrid tales of sudden relapses
into long abandoned errors on their deathbeds, which
would serve to bring every fainthearted friend of truth
to despair. Of these only can the stories be true, not
of a Berengarius. A Berengarius will certainly die
as he taught, and thus do all die who teach as
sincerely and seriously as he.'

Lessing tells Frau König that in the next catalogue of forbidden books in Vienna she will find his
' Berengarius.'

'You cannot imagine in what an odour of sanctity I have put myself with our Lutheran theologians. Prepare yourself to hear me proclaimed as nothing less than a pillar of our Church. But whether this will exactly suit me, and whether I shall not soon lose this good character, time will show.'

His father did not live to witness the publication of this essay. He was struck down with apoplexy in August. The blow was a great grief to Lessing. He at once constituted himself head of the family and promised his mother he would pay all debts, only requesting time.

In reply to Karl, who had spoken somewhat disparagingly of his 'Berengarius,' he says :

'God only knows, that I never more needed to write for money than now, and this necessity has actually influenced the materials about which I have written. Whatever requires a particular cheerfulness of spirit, an especial exertion, whatever I must extract out of myself rather than out of books, I can have nothing to do with at present. I tell you this that you may not be surprised if, in spite of your disapproval, I should write a second part to " Berengarius." I must bore the board where it is thinnest; when I am less troubled from without, I will take up the thick end again.'

In October, Mendelssohn paid him a visit. He congratulated him on his discovery, adding he did not envy it. Lessing took this remark in the sense that his friend despised such occupations. Indeed, Moses would often ask him when he took up some new branch : Will this serve to amend or augment the knowledge of mankind ? Will their powers of reflexion be strengthened ? the paths to happiness be smoothed ? for every work must serve some end.

Besides these theological labours, and various projects and money-producing exertions, that occupied the
whole summer of 1770, Lessing was employed in
preparing for the press a new edition of his writings.
This labour was undertaken sorely against the grain,
and entirely to please his friend and publisher, Voss,
who hoped thereby to check the hateful system of
piracy. Lessing excuses himself for this step in the
preface. He had long condemned the greater part of
these writings, and deemed them forgotten by the
public :

' The public grows daily in discernment of taste,
but many authors remain behind, and woe to him who
does not always feel that he has remained behind,
and is vain enough to continue to reckon upon the
applause he thinks he received twenty years ago.
Only the piratical reprint with which these writings
are threatened has extorted from the author the
wish to frustrate the malicious intention to bring
him forward again in all his feeble immaturity.'
He begs for indulgence, remarking ' it would be
folly to waste on the repairs of a tottering hut, materials that would suffice to construct an entirely new
edifice.'

Lessing found the labour greater than he had
anticipated ; he tells his brother that it costs him more
exertion than the whole rubbish is worth. Ramler
undertook to see the poems through the press, and to
revise and amend them. Lessing begs him to strike
out whatever is ' too mediocre.' It is a work of
charity that Ramler is doing for him.

He himself revised his epigrams and wrote some
new ones, a circumstance he regarded as a sign of
advancing age. He also prefixed an essay on this

form of writing. As was his custom, he began by combating former definitions. Scaliger had assumed every little poem to be an epigram ; Boileau called it 'un bon mot de deux rimes orné.' Batteux's definition was, 'an interesting thought, happily set forth in a few words.' Lessing declares them all to be wrong. If any of these suggestions were correct, we must suppose the name epigram to be given to these productions because they were short enough to find room on monuments : which is scarcely a sufficient explanation ; nor can it be the subject of an epigram to which it owes its name, since subjects are so widely varied that it is impossible to suppose them confined merely to such as would be suitable for a monument. The reason for the appellation must then lie in the form of the epigram. We cannot imagine an inscription separate from that on which it is inscribed. If we see in the distance an important monument, it naturally excites our curiosity, which remains aroused until we are near enough to read the inscription explaining the monument. This process is repeated in the epigram, which must therefore consist of two parts : the first exciting our curiosity, the second satisfying it. He then proceeds to criticise the principal epigrammatists at some length, and estimates Martial at the same high rate as he had done in his boyhood, only that his ripened analytic understanding can now give adequate reasons. Many Greek and Roman poets have made epigrams, but for him there has only been one true epigrammatist, Martial ; for he alone formed in his own mind a distinct conception of the essential nature of an epigram and adhered to it.

Lessing further continued his researches amid the

treasures of the ducal library. These consisted of archaeology, theology, and poetry, and gave full scope to his multifarious knowledge. He was also thus able to make the library useful to other scholars who applied to him for advice and aid. With a view to reveal the treasures possessed by German poetry, in rivalry with the Percy ' Reliques,' then exciting great attention, he published some remarkable pieces by a Silesian poet, Andreas Scultetus, a contemporary of Opitz, and some of the productions of the Minne-singers.

The dreary desolation of Wolfenbüttel weighed on his spirits. He felt impelled to make occasional excursions to Brunswick to come in contact with his fellows. Eva König twits him with these frequent visits and his Brunswick dissipations. Why, he re-plies, he lives almost as retired a life in Brunswick as in Wolfenbüttel, and his whole dissipation con-sists in drinking an occasional glass of punch with Zachariä. He had even given up drinking wine. Poverty would have kept him from leading a gay life, even if his will had not. She then rebukes him for taking life so dismally, tells him he is growing hypo-chondriacal, and urges him to visit Brunswick more frequently. She herself often feels melancholy, she tells him, for her affairs go badly and life seems hard. This rouses him to comfort her.

' I must tell you that I consider melancholy a most wilful disease, which is not shaken off because one does not want to shake it off.'

He then hears of Frau König's illness at Vienna : this puts him into a fever of anxiety. She tries to cheer him and keeps up her courage for his sake. He will not be behindhand with her, and assures her he will rather hope the best than torture himself in advance.

'And in this manner I will also write to you ; a healthy man to a healthy woman, a happy man to a happy woman. For truly, if one is the former one must needs be the latter also, and can be if one only will. Therefore do not be uneasy for me ; I have made it a rule always to be happy, however little occasion I may see for it, and as I live here there are more people surprised that I do not perish from *ennui* and disgust, than would be surprised if I really did perish. It certainly requires art to persuade oneself that one is happy, but then in what else does happiness consist than in such self persuasion ?'

In April 1771, Eva König had again passed through Brunswick on her return from Vienna, and from this time forward there is a change in their mode of address. 'Dearest Friend' takes the place of 'Dearest Madam,' 'Dear Sir.' It was on this occasion that Lessing half seriously, half in joke, begged Frau König to write him no more letters save the one in which she can announce to him that nothing further bars the way to their mutual happiness. She took the remark *au pied de la lettre* ; this led to a passing misunderstanding, which only served to strengthen their intimacy.

During the summer Lessing was taken ill. His work did not fill and satisfy his spirit, and the sedentary habits it involved told on his health. His letters of the period reflect his mental state.

'I am no longer ill,' he tells Karl in July 1771, 'but if I said I was as I should wish to be, I should not speak the truth. Among all unfortunates I think the most unfortunate is he who has to work with his brain, even if he is not conscious of having one. But what is the use of complaining!'

'The dust of books falls more and more upon my nerves,' he writes to Gleim (June 1771). 'Soon they will be entirely incapable of certain delicate emotions. But what I no longer feel I shall not forget having felt formerly. I shall never, because I have grown blunt, be unjust towards those who are not yet blunted. I shall never despise any sense because I am unfortunate enough to have lost it.' And, refer-ring to the nature of his literary occupations, he adds : 'But I will rather confess that I have, alas ! fallen so low as to find pleasure and nourishment in things that a healthy stomach regards as dry and indigest-ible.'

Mendelssohn had sent him Ferguson's 'Moral Philosophy.' He expresses his thanks for it, and says it is just such a book as he has needed for some time. 'Most of the books I have here are such as must at length kill reason and time. If we cease to think for a long while, we at last lose the power of thinking. And yet is it well to think the truth ? to occupy one-self seriously with truths in whose constant contra-dictions we live, and, for the sake of our peace, must go on living ? And of such truths I foresee I shall find several in this Englishman.'

'Since I wrote to you last,' he tells Karl, 'I have not even been able to occupy myself with theological nonsense, let alone attending to anything more sensible.'

He is writing this letter half in a dream, he cannot long fix his attention on anything, and mental exer-tion is out of the question. Sometimes he cannot write more than two or three lines a day, and that

only with the greatest exertion. His doctor has re-
commended taking the Pyrmont waters, and a change
of air, and he intends to go to Hamburg. This idea
alone sustains him, or he would lose all patience.

On August 30 he sent Karl the last sheets of his
first volume. 'To-morrow I go to Hamburg, and if
I there regain my good humour in other society, and
other air, a letter to Ramler shall be the first thing I
take in hand.' For up to this time he had never
thanked Ramler for the trouble of revision, because,
as he said afterwards in his letter of excuse, he had
been suffering from a veritable hydrophobia of all
that concerned writing.

Lessing lodged in the house of Frau König, and
during this visit their formal betrothal took place privately, in the presence of a few intimate friends.
There was, however, to be no question of marriage
until Frau König's affairs were in order. This she
held a stern duty she owed to her children, and Lessing acquiesced in her high-minded resolve to save for
them out of their patrimony whatever she could.
Their happy reunion was saddened by the death of
Frau König's mother. Lessing had gone to Berlin
for a few days, and writes from thence :

'My heart bleeds when I consider the sorrow you
feel, but ought not to feel, on account of your mother's
death. This blow was so expected, is so entirely in
the necessary course of things—yet I am not wise to
seek to comfort you with cold reflexions. Would to
Heaven that the assurance that there is one person in
the world who loves you above everything, might
prove some comfort to you. This person expects all
the happiness that is still destined him from you
alone, and implores you for the sake of this happiness

to cast off all sorrow for the past, and fix your eyes
only upon a future when it shall be my sole endeavour to procure you new repose, and new and daily
increasing pleasures.    I embrace you a thousand
times, my best and dearest friend.'

It was on the occasion of this visit that Lessing
endeavoured to publish a posthumous work by S. H.
Reimarus, 'An Apology for the Rational Worship-
pers of God.'  Reimarus had for many years filled the
post of Professor of Oriental Literature in Hamburg.
He was held a model of learning and piety ; Paley
was indebted to him for materials, and his 'Principal
Truths of Natural Religion' was held a text-book.
He had been the first in Germany to recommend
Franklin's lightning conductors, and to recognise the
value of inoculation.    And this same man had secretly written a heterodox work, in which he had
criticised every point of Church doctrine wherever it
departed from reason.   His daughter Elise had confided to Lessing an insight into this, the darling work
of her father's life, which he had entrusted to her care
with the desire that it should not be published until
the times were ripe.   Lessing begged the loan of it,
had already shown it to Mendelssohn at Wolfenbüttel,
and discussed the advisability of publication.   With
his almost romantic love of truth, and disbelief in the
expediency of esoteric doctrine, he was eager to make
the MS. the common property of the world.   Nicolai
and Mendelssohn both advised against his putting his
head into the hornet's nest of theology ; but Lessing
was not easily diverted from any purpose that had
taken firm root in his mind.   He never would believe
that truth in any shape could obstruct or hinder the
cause of truth ; the honest thoughts of any human

mind were an acquisition to the world, and as such should not be withheld from it. Voss announced his willingness to issue the work, provided the theological censor's consent were obtained. When this was refused, the project had to be abandoned, but Lessing did not lose sight of his resolve.

After his return from Hamburg he spent some more happy quiet weeks in the house of Frau König. During this time he became a freemason. He had long felt a curiosity regarding this secret society, and was pleased when invited to join the brotherhood. He rapidly passed the three degrees of St. John and became a master-mason. On the day of his reception, when asked by the Worshipful Master of his Lodge whether he had not told him the truth, and that there was nothing contrary to morality, law, or religion in their society, Lessing replied with some warmth, ' No. Would to Heaven I had found something of the kind, I should at least have found something.'

At the end of October he returned to Brunswick, refreshed and strengthened in body and mind. 'I shall remain here in Brunswick till to-morrow,' he writes to Frau König, 'and then welcome my little solitary Wolfenbüttel, where my third thought will always be, you know who. Be sure and let me know everything about you, important and unimportant, yet nothing that concerns you can be unimportant to me. Above all, never let me hear that you are ill or sad. If only I could share my health and my light-heartedness with you!' A few days later he writes to her again from Wolfenbüttel : 'I should certainly be infinitely happier if my solitude were enlivened by intercourse with the only person for whose constant society I have ever sighed. But the mere hope that this happiness is in store for me makes me happy. And ought we to be unhappy because we are not quite so happy as we could wish to be?'

In this cheerful frame of mind Lessing once more turned to composition, and to oblige his publisher resumed his Leipzig idea of writing a tragedy that should treat the story of 'Virginia' in a modern way. The brutal figure of Appius Claudius is converted into the youthful sentimental libertine, Hettore Gonzaga, whose miniature principality of Guastalla reflects the licentiousness of Louis XIV.'s Versailles. He is already furnished with a *maîtresse en titre*, the Countess Orsina, of whom however he is weary when the play opens, having been smitten by the charms of Emilia Galotti, the daughter of one of his officers. The Galottis, who lived quietly on their country estates, have always avoided court society, but latterly the mother has insisted, against the wishes of the father, that her daughter should benefit by a city training, and they have spent some time in the capital ; and here, at a Vegghia in the house of the Chancellor Grimaldi, the Prince has met Emilia and become enamoured of her beauty. The obstacles that stand in the way of his desires, obstacles with which he is unfamiliar, only serve to exasperate his passion. His feeble vacillating spirit is unhinged and stormtost. A petition laid before him is granted because the petitioner bears the name Emilia. A painter who accidentally shows him a portrait of Emilia Galotti is told he may ask the treasurer for 'as much as he likes' in payment. The court favourite and purveyor of the princely pleasures comes on the scene, and after informing the Prince that the Countess Orsina demands an interview, whic his refused, incidentally relates as

town gossip that one Count Appiani is that day going
to be married to Emilia Galotti, and to remove her
from the principality to his Piedmontese estates, to
live a life of rural quiet. This news cumulates the
Prince's despair, and he would abandon all hope, but
that unfortunately he has at his elbow one of those
friends, fatal to autocrats, who scruple at no infamous
actions that may secure royal favour. Marinelli
invents a stratagem by which Count Appiani is to be
charged with a mission of honour that will brook no
delay. Should he refuse this, a contingency Marinelli
holds barely possible, he has still a resource left. The
marriage is to be solemnised at the Galottis' estate of
Sabionetta, not in town ; the bride, bridegroom, and
mother drive out there this afternoon to join the
Count Galotti. The road passes the Prince's summer-house, Dosala ; how easily might an accident be
made to occur in this spot ! Only before he takes
any further steps, Marinelli desires the Prince to
give him *carte-blanche,* and to sanction anything he
may do.

'Everything, Marinelli,' cries the delighted Prince,
'everything that will avert this blow.'

The Prince is left full of restless longing, irresolute
what he should do, until at last the thought strikes
him, not to let all depend on Marinelli. Why not
also act himself ? He knows that at this hour it is
Emilia's custom to hear Mass at the Dominican
church : if he could speak to her there ! It is worth
the trial. At that moment a councillor presents
himself with business papers.

'Anything to be signed ?' asks the Prince, in his
impatience to be rid of this troublesome disturbance.

'A death warrant,' says the minister.

'With pleasure,' exclaims the absent Prince. ' Give
it me ; quick.'

Meanwhile Count Appiani has declined the honour
destined for him, and the bridal party start for
Sabionetta. But before the royal villa their carriage
is attacked, the Count is shot, and Emilia carried out
of the fray and into the house by servants, who appear
under the guise of rescuers. The Countess Galotti is
purposely retained behind ; but at last brought to the
villa and told by Marinelli that her daughter is cared
for ' as though in the realms of bliss,' she suddenly
wakes to suspicion ; she recalls the Prince's marked
attentions at the Vegghia, attentions that at the time
had merely flattered her maternal vanity. She
remembers that Emilia had told her of the infamous
whispers that had reached her ears this very morning,
while in the presence of the most Holy. Appiani had
resigned his breath cursing the name of Marinelli.
There is treachery here—treachery, and how is she, a
poor defenceless woman, to rescue her daughter out
of the wiles of these villains ? She forces her way at
last to Emilia, who, deaf to all the Prince's blandish-
ments, falls fainting into her arms. Meanwhile their
natural defender arrives. A servant has galloped to
Sabionetta and brought the terrible tidings of the
Count's death and the family danger to Colonel
Galotti. He enters Dosala hurriedly, and demands
his wife and daughter ; he knows only too well the reputation this summer-house enjoys. Chance makes him
arrive together with the Countess Orsina, whom a misunderstood arrangement with the Prince brings to the
villa. In her jealous anger, that is not unmingled with
noble motives of compassion, she confirms Galotti's
worst fears as to the Prince's designs, demonstrates to

him that this is no accident, but a deep-laid plot, an
abduction, and an assassination.   She animates him
to vengeance, and seeing he is without weapons, she
lends him the dagger with which she has herself
intended to stab the faithless Gonzaga.   Galotti hides
the weapon and conceals his emotion, firmly but
quietly claiming his daughter.   Marinelli tells him in
the name of the Prince that Emilia cannot join her
father : a crime has been committed, justice must be
vindicated, and pending judicial inquiry, the Galotti
family must be separated, not allowed to speak with
one another ; the form of the trial absolutely demands
this precaution.   Emilia, by the special favour of her
sovereign, shall be kept under the guard of the most
estimable of women, the wife of the Chancellor Grimaldi.   There can be no further doubt as to the
Prince's designs now, for Count Galotti knows Grimaldi's house to be the scene of the Prince's pleasures.
However, he pretends to submit, and only begs to be
allowed once more to see his daughter.   He wishes to
assure himself of the sentiments of the girl before he
resolves on any form of action ; perhaps she is the
accomplice of the Prince, and all this an everyday
farce.   But he finds her calm ; at once, as her mother
had described, the most timid and most determined
of her sex, unable to master her first emotions, but
after reflexion prepared to meet her fate.   When she
hears her father's purpose to plunge his dagger into
the hearts of the two miscreants, she pleads for them:
'No, for Heaven's sake, father! This life is all the
wicked have ;' she begs it for herself, for she fears lest
she should succumb to the seductions of the Grimaldi
house, where, in the one short hour she spent there,
she felt a tumult arise in her breast which it took the

sternest discipline of religion weeks to lull. She
pleads that in olden times there was a father who, to
save his daughter from dishonour, plunged the first
knife that came to hand into her heart, and thus gave
her life a second time. But such deeds are of the
past ; there are no such fathers now.

'There are—there are, my daughter,' cries Galotti,
plunging the dagger into her heart. Then, 'O God,
what have I done?' he exclaims.

'Broken a rose before the storm had blasted it,'
sighs Emilia, dying. 'Let me kiss this fatherly hand.'

The sounds have attracted the Prince.

'What is it? Is Emilia not well?'

'Very well, very well,' replies the father, throwing
the dagger at the feet of the Prince. 'You are perhaps waiting till I turn the dagger against myself, to
close my deed like a shallow tragedy. You are mistaken. I go to deliver myself up to justice. I go to
await you as my judge. But afterwards—there—I
shall await you before the great Judge of us all.'

'Marinelli,' moans the weak prostrate Prince,
'miserable wretch, go hide yourself for ever. Go,
I say. God, O God, is it not enough that Princes
should be men : must their friends be devils in disguise!'

This tragedy, with its concentrated action and
nervous laconic diction, is a model of artistic exposition of plot. Its singleness of purpose, lack of
episodes, and paucity of personages are antique in
their stern rigour, and stamp it a masterpiece for all
time. Yet, with these unquestionable merits, the play
leaves reader and spectator cold with an undefined
sense of something inharmonious. While reading or
seeing, the necessity for close attention to the con-

densed vigour of the play captivates the mind, it is
not until released from this tension that criticism steps
in. Criticism has fiercely contested the merits of
' Emilia Galotti.' Overlauded by some, it has been
underrated by others, but this sharp diversity of
opinion evinces that there is something to be censured
and excused. What is this something? Lessing himself in his 'Dramaturgie' has laid down the rules to
be applied to dramatic criticism, and following him we
at once turn to the pages of Livy, and seek for the
analogy between Emilia Galotti and her prototype.
Indeed, perhaps but for his own rules he would not
have been judged so severely. In Appius Claudius
we find a gross barbarian who claims the daughter of
Virginius as his slave, and consequently his victim if
he chooses, and since such deeds were of everyday
occurrence in Rome, it would hardly have roused
public attention but for the popularity of Virginia
and the deed that frustrated the Decemvir's design.
The limits of Rome are to Virginius the limits of the
world, and death the only escape. Virginia, young,
innocent, ignorant of the traps laid for her, is stabbed
without knowing wherefore. It is her inevitable fate,
and the story is tragically correct from the antique
standpoint of thought. Not so Emilia Galotti. There
arises a confusion between modern and ancient mode
of thought—the two do not and cannot blend. In
the Roman story we have the element of undeserved
calamity; our sympathies are fully roused; we feel
things could not have been otherwise and the proper
justice is dealt to the villains in the due course of events.
It is otherwise in ' Emilia Galotti.' She is not ignorant
of the Prince's design, she fears for her virtue, and her
murder is closely allied to suicide. A strong sense of

revolt at this sudden tragedy seizes us : was it inevitable, we ask ? Does not the action pass in civilised times ? Cannot Galotti legally claim his daughter from the Prince's hands ? Let the Prince of a tiny state be never so great an autocrat, his sway is limited by square miles, and he himself may lose severely by his tyranny. He is not above the law, else why are legal inquiries twice named in the play ? If Emilia loved the Prince then she did wrong, and there is poetic justice in the drama, though her punishment in that case would still be disproportionate to her guilt. But Lessing disclaimed this intention, and consequently Emilia's actions are devoid of adequate motive and singularly repellent to sympathy. In lieu of innocent Virginia, 'the sweetest girl in Rome,' we have a cold young woman who is perfectly aware what is meant by the Prince's advances, who never shows the smallest concern on hearing of the murder of a man who in a few hours was to be her husband, and for whom she is said to feel affection, and who begs her father to deprive her of life on a plea that shocks good taste.

 ' I have young warm blood, my father, like any other. My senses too are senses. I will answer for nothing. I will warrant nothing.' So well-informed a young lady repels our sympathy. Every actress who has undertaken this *rôle* instinctively felt this; they foisted in a nascent love for the Prince on Emilia's part, and this presupposed, the shocking element is at least eliminated.

 The play throughout is marked by close cool observation, and terse characterisation, rather than by eloquence. Rarely does one of the personages rise to an impassioned utterance ; we can see that Lessing felt himself as he sketched them, but he fails to have us under his control and to convey to us

the precise impression of what he feels. And nowhere is this defect more evident than in the person
of Emilia, the heroine to whom all our heart should
go out as it goes out to blithe Virginia; we see his
intention, but we do not feel satisfied. Were the play
less closely realistic and accurate, we should not
measure it by so accurate a standard. As it is
Schlegel's objection, which at first offends as puerile
and hypercritical, that the territory is too petty, and
hence extrication from it too easy, to justify the
necessity of the catastrophe, assumes on consideration
some show of justice.

Judged therefore as a tragedy proper, 'Emilia
Galotti' does not meet all requirements. Poetic justice
is grossly violated, for it is virtue that is punished and
vice goes free. Judged on the other hand as an intrigue
play of the eighteenth century the ground of objection
is shifted. Tragedy of intrigue is of its essence transient,
dependent on external social conditions, laws, and
customs, not on the eternally fixed immutable rules
of right and wrong : such a play may become worn out,
grow impossible and perverted, because no longer
adapted to the conditions of politics and society.
'Emilia Galotti' is such a play, and if it was Lessing's
design to expose the corruption of the petty courts,
the false and maudlin sentiments of the eighteenth
century, with its affectation of classic virtues grafted
on the romantic feelings, he has once again shown his
master power of grasping the current tendency of his
age. But its main idea was too subtle for dramatic
exhibition ; psychological analysis is not in place in
rapid presentation. Nevertheless, 'Emilia Galotti' is
remarkable, if only as the first open manifestation of
social and moral opposition to the current frivolity

and licentiousness of the courts, the first warning signal given by liberalism to the throne.

Gossip had spread abroad in Brunswick that Lessing was busy writing a drama that exposed the libertinism of his ducal master. Meanwhile, Döbbelin had begged the play from Lessing for performance on the birthday of the Dowager Duchess. To allay these rumours, which were baseless so far as the first conception of the play was concerned, and also because he did not consider a tragedy, and this tragedy in particular, well suited for a gala representation, Lessing submitted the first acts to the ducal approval. The Duke consented to the performance, but even so the play might not have been finished in time, Lessing's usual dilatoriness having intervened, but for Döbbelin's threatening to furnish it with a catastrophe out of his own head. The piece was therefore performed in March 1772, and was applauded on the whole, though the ducal mistresses objected to the Countess Orsina, and the courtiers to Marinelli. The Prince had attended the performance *incognito*, and had followed the whole attentively, but Lessing could not be induced to be present either at rehearsal or representation.

'For what should I have been at the performance?' he wrote to Karl, 'to hear shallow criticisms, or reap yet shallower praise?'

This marked absence, however, gave some show of countenance to the whispers that he had intended a satire on the court whose servant he was : a rumour whose untruth was palpable to anyone who at all knew Lessing's fearless rectitude, which would never have allowed him to withdraw in a cowardly fashion from the consequences of his deliberate acts. The real fact was that he was out of heart with the play, and that illness was again making itself felt. He was not in a fit mental condition to judge of it. He begs Karl to send him his opinion on his tragedy, for he had been unable to consult with any soul about it.

'Yet one must speak to some one about one's work if one does not want to go to sleep over it. The mere assurance that we are on the right road, that is given by our own criticism, however convincing it may be, is yet so cold and fruitless that it can exert no influence on our work.'

In answer to a rapturous letter from Ebert the day after the performance, Lessing replied : ' If I did not know how much too warm a friend you are, your letter might persuade me that I have done something extraordinary ; but to-day, when it is to be hoped you are cooler, you would write in a different tone ; and how much will you not retract when once you read the play in print.' Lessing encloses two printed copies, one for Ebert and one which he begs him give the Prince, and say that the slightest approval of his Highness would be agreeable to the author, but that his reason for not accompanying the work by a letter is the notion that he should have to apologise to the Prince for this piece of authorship out of his regular course of employment, 'and I so much dislike apologising. By and by you can perhaps tell the Prince that it is really a work the greater part of which was completed some years ago, and to which I have only given the finishing touch.'

He did not pay much attention to criticism, adverse or otherwise, only he was annoyed when his brother inquires whether it is true that he intends to alter the catastrophe.

'Whoever has told you that I have altered the

conclusion of my tragedy has told an untruth. What do they want me to alter in it? In short, do not believe anyone who tells you anything else about me and the new piece, except that I am taking all pains to forget it.'

# CHAPTER XV.

*' Nur wer die Sehnsucht kennt*
*Weiss was ich leide,*
*Allein und abgetrennt*
*Von jeder Freude.'*

PERHAPS Lessing had never attached so little value
to any of his works as to 'Emilia Galotti.' His head
was full of other matters. He had been more or less in-
disposed all the winter, his eyesight had been failing.
His mother, and especially his miserly sister, pestered
him for money, so that he had to draw a year's salary
in advance. He was anxious on account of Frau
König, whose affairs grew more instead of less involved; and he was himself unsettled by repeated
underhand inquiries whether he would accept a post
at Vienna. He replied, as he had replied before,
that if these invitations concerned the theatre, he
would have nothing to say to them. At the same
time he did not utterly repel all advances, for a reason
which he did not mention to his brother, but of which
he made no secret to Frau König, namely, the proba-
bility that she might have to settle in Vienna on
account of her factories, and that he would thus not
only be near her, but that such an appointment might
hasten their union. All Frau König's letters that

winter were full of details of unfortunate business
affairs, complicated by illiberal restrictions imposed by
the Austrian Government.

'I would gladly eat bread and water in the most
miserable corner of the world, if only I were out of
this labyrinth,' she writes.

He answers : 'Remember your own words, that
you are not to blame for all this misery. Only remain cheerful, that you may remain in health. Lose
whatever you must lose, keep as much for your
children as you can keep, and calmly leave all else to
Providence. If you have nothing further to seek in
Vienna, if nothing obliges you to live there rather than
at any other place, then Vienna is for me also a most
indifferent spot, for which I would not exchange my
present situation under the most advantageous terms
in the world. I shall then certainly refuse all advances from thence, and make no further use of them
except as a means to enforce some improvement
in my condition here. And then, my love, you
can have no further excuse not to keep your word
to me. If you would rather live in the most miserable corner on bread and water than continue in
your present confusion, Wolfenbüttel is enough of a
hole, and we shall not want for bread and water and
even something more.'

But as Frau König's prospects grew darker, so
that she was threatened by the total loss of her fortune, her high-minded generous soul made her re-
pent that she should ever have allowed Lessing
to be drawn into her troubles. 'I can look back
calmly upon the whole of my past life,' she writes,
'up to the moment when I was weak enough to
confess an affection that I had firmly resolved to

conceal, at least until my circumstances should take a favourable turn. I am convinced you would no less have taken a friendly interest in everything that befell me, but you would not have made my concerns your own, as you now do, although you ought not to do so. For my determination is not to be shaken. If I am unhappy I shall remain so alone, and your fate shall not be interwoven with mine. You know my reasons for this: nay more, your candour would not permit you to disapprove them. Do not therefore call them excuses. The word excuse wounded me. Ask your heart whether in a similar case it would not act in the same manner; and if it answer No, then believe that you do not love me half as much as I love you. The only thing I beg is that you will not allow your plans to be influenced by me, but will act just as you would have acted if you had not known me.'

Lessing replies that he would on no account counsel her to any actions contrary to rectitude, but he thinks she strains her obligations to her husband's creditors too far, and advises her to go again to Vienna and look after matters in person, instead of trusting to others: ' I think you will do more than any man.' Meanwhile he will keep his Viennese offers open, since he finds they do not concern the theatre, but the Academy of Sciences that had once before been mooted ; and when Frau König is on the spot, perhaps she will make personal inquiries as to the feasibility of the scheme. After all, his Wolfenbüttel post is a mere *pis-aller*, only he is haunted by a shrewd suspicion that the Viennese appointment would require him to make some personal advances, particularly at court, since his Protestant faith would weigh against him in the eyes of Maria Theresa. ' But

to offer myself is a very hard nut for me to crack, and
it would be difficult to move me thereto except for
the sake of a person whom I love more than myself.'

In March 1772 Frau König followed Lessing's
advice, and went in person to Vienna. While awaiting her reports from thence, Lessing wrote in answer
to a letter from Ramler regarding 'Emilia Galotti' :

'Dearest Friend,

'How much I am indebted to you for your
praise, and your friendly endeavours to procure a
good reception for my "Emilia," you can judge for
yourself. But now for a better kind of praise
that we can give among ourselves, your criticism.
You have promised it me, and I expect it confidently and soon. I will confide to you that criticism
is the only means to spur me on to more, and to
refresh me. For, since I am not in a position to
apply the criticism to the criticised piece, since I am
altogether spoilt for improving, and moreover hold it
to be almost impossible to improve a drama when it
has once been brought to a certain stage of completion—for improvement should concern more than
trifles—I should certainly use the criticism on something new. Therefore, dear friend, if you too wish
that I should do something new of this kind, you see
it is requisite, to provoke me by censure, not to make
this particular thing better, but in general to make
something better. And, since this better must necessarily have its faults, so this alone is the ring through
the nose whereby I can be kept incessantly dancing.'

'Emilia Galotti' completed, Lessing felt his
mental faculties unduly exhausted, and tells Karl he
purposes never to try them so again. The general

*malaise* and dejection felt before his Hamburg visit
attacked him with redoubled force. ' I have almost
got back to the point where I was a year ago, and if
I have to exert myself it may become worse. This
my condition of general discomfort (for I cannot call
it illness) is to blame for my not having yet seen my
new play acted, although it has been already represented three times.' He resolved to be once more a
true librarian in his sense of the term ; examining the
treasures of the library, and setting apart those which
might seem suitable for publication. He commenced
by a general rearrangement of the contents, in anticipation of his possible retirement from his post. In
consequence he laid aside the revision of his works
for Voss. ' The contributions from the library must
needs be made, for I will not be called librarian for
nothing ; and in the end it might be held to my discredit if I occupied myself only with extraneous
work.' He will not hear of any theatrical work. ' No
one,' he writes, ' likes to submit to labour from which
he receives no profit whatever, either in money,
honour, or pleasure. In the time that a piece of ten
sheets takes me I could easily and well write a hundred sheets of something else. It is true that I have
lately reckoned that I have at least twelve comedies
and tragedies by me, each of which I could complete
within six weeks. But why stretch myself upon the
rack for nothing at all ? They have lately, from
Vienna, offered me a hundred ducats for a play, but
I want a hundred louis d'or. You will say this is
very grasping on my part, assuming even that my
pieces are worth as much. I reply : Every artist tries
to live as comfortably as he can by his works, why
not also an author ? If my plays are not worth one

hundred louis d'or, then I would rather hear nothing more about them, for then they are worth nothing. For the honour of my dear Fatherland I will not put pen to paper, even if in this respect she depended solely and alone on my pen. For my own honour it is enough if the world sees that I could be capable of doing something in this line. Therefore money for my fish. . . . Money is just what I need, and I need it now more than ever. I wish in a year and a day to owe no man anything, and to that end I must use my time better than for the theatre.'

He had owned to his brother that only while at work could he forget the annoyances of his position. Karl therefore again urged him to dramatic work, remarking that it was surely indifferent at what he worked, so long as he worked.

'You are wrong,' he replies, 'if you believe that under present circumstances it is indifferent to me at what I work. Nothing less, either in regard to the work, or in regard to the prime object for which I work. I have often in my life been in very miserable circumstances, but never yet in such as compelled me in the strictest sense to write for bread. I have begun my contributions solely on that account because this work pays, since I need only send one scribble after the other into the printing-office, to receive from time to time a few louis d'or to live from one day to another.'

To Frau König Lessing does not so openly speak out his depression. He still tries to cheer her under her trials ; he tells how hard he is working at the re-arrangement of the library, as though he were going to live and die there. And who knows whether this may not be the case? Matters at Vienna seem in-

clined to spin themselves out. No matter; he will
live here, as we should always live, ready at any
moment to go away, and yet willing to stay on.
He then laughs at himself for falling into a moral-
ising tone, and says in his excuse that he possesses
a special gift of finding some good thing even in
the worst circumstances : a gift of which he is prouder
than of anything he knows or can do. He had had
some thoughts of continuing his ' Antiquarian Letters,'
when Klotz's sudden death put an end to this purpose. He had been afraid lest Klotz should stand
in the way of his Vienna appointment, ' but the man
has been wiser than I calculated,' he writes to Frau
König, to whom he imparts all his plans, literary and
otherwise. ' He has died. I should like to laugh at
this chance, but it makes me graver than I could have
believed.'

Rheumatic pains, toothache, vertigo, and failure of
sight, that prevented him from reading and writing,
embittered the spring (1772), so that Lessing let two
months elapse before writing to Frau König. Then,
under date June 27 (1772): ' Which of us both now
most needs cheering ? that is the great question. You
at least have nothing but cares whose end you can
foresee by one means or the other, while I am not
rarely disgusted with the whole of life. I dream away
rather than live away my days. A continuous labour
that exhausts me without giving me pleasure (this
refers to the rearrangement of the library); a residence that is unendurable to me, owing to the entire
absence of society (such society as I could have I do
not like), with no prospect but that of eternal monotony : all these things have so bad an influence on my
mind, and so react on my body, that I do not know

whether I am ill or well. Whoever sees me compliments me on my healthy looks ; while I should like to answer these compliments in each case by a box on the ears. For what is the use of my looking sufficiently well if I can do nothing proper to a man in health ? I can scarcely guide my pen, as you will see from this illegible letter, which I have had to break off four or five times. My comfort is that this state cannot possibly last.'

In this eternal monotony he was more and more consumed with longing for his beloved Eva, while the prospect of their union seemed to grow more and more indefinite. Her portrait, he says, is his only pleasure, the best and dearest companion of his Wolfenbüttel solitude. 'Ah when—but you know what I wish.' After this Lessing let a month pass without writing a letter ; he was ill, dejected, concerned on her account. Then he kept silent till October, when he roused himself to write, reproaching himself, and full of anxiety lest his friend should grow suspicious of this long silence. He apologized for not writing for so long, but he hopes he knows she will not doubt him. Now, however, he must open his heart to the only person in the world to whom he can really do so. And he lays bare to her his circumstances, and the vile mood that has hindered him even from writing to her.

'But you will ask what was then at fault ? Thousands and thousands of things, all so petty that they cannot be told, but which taken altogether had so extraordinary an effect upon me, that to put it briefly, during the whole time when I sent no news of myself, I might as well have not lived at all. Not that I have been ill, although I have not been well. I have been

worse than ill ; irritable, dissatisfied, furious with myself and the whole world, you alone excepted.   In
addition to this, I had involved myself in a task that
required far more time and exertion than I had foreseen.   During the last few days I have been obliged
to make a little pause in this work, and perhaps it is
this that makes me feel somewhat calmer at present.
I will make use of these moments that will doubtless
soon vanish again. . . . . You know, my love, what I
have often confessed to you, that I cannot possibly
endure this place for long.   In the solitude in which I
am forced to live I grow more stupid and angry from
day to day.   I must go again among human beings,
from whom I am almost entirely shut out here.   For
what does it avail me that I can call on this or on that
person here or in Brunswick ?   Visits are no social
intercourse, and I feel that I must of necessity have
intercourse, and that with people to whom I am not
indifferent, if only a spark of good is to remain in me.
Without society I go to sleep, and only wake now
and then to perpetrate some folly.   Therefore hear,
my love, the plan I have made for myself, for how it
will go with you I see clearly.   You will never get
away from Vienna, at any rate not yet awhile.   If
therefore I also stay here and lay my hands in my
lap, nothing will come of what in happier moments
I pictured as so possible and so easy.   This plan
can save me, or nothing.'

This plan was to remind the Duke of the promised Italian journey.   The way would lead him
through Vienna, and he was determined to see after
things there with his own eyes, so that he might, if
possible, stay with her for good.   In any case he will
thus see her again ; meanwhile he must work hard all

the winter, and afterwards nothing shall retain him from
hastening to her. It makes his heart ache to think
how little happiness she too is enjoying, engulphed in
vexatious business affairs, and separated from her
children. A letter of the same date to his brother
breathes a similar spirit :

'Wolfenbüttel : October 28, 1772.

'Dear Brother,—You know probably by experience how matters stand with me when for a long time
I send no news of myself ; I mean that I am then
extremely dissatisfied. Who would seek to widen the
sphere of his life by friendship and sympathy when
life altogether almost disgusts him ? Or who cares to
hunt afar off for pleasant sensations if he sees nothing
close at hand that can afford him a single one ? For
some time past I had been free from illness, and have
therefore not been idle. I have worked more than
I am generally accustomed to work ; but only at things
which, I may truly say, a greater bungler than I might
have done just as well. I shall shortly send you the
first volume of " Contributions to History and Literature, from the Treasures of the Ducal Library at
Wolfenbüttel," &c., with which I mean to go on con-
tinuously until I once more have inclination and
strength to work at something more sensible. But
that is scarcely likely to be soon. Indeed I do
not even know whether I wish it. This dry librarian
work can be so easily written off without any participation of mind, and without the slightest exertion.
Meantime I can always satisfy myself with this consolation, that I am doing my duty to my office, and learning something at the same time, even granting that
not the hundredth part of this something is worth
learning. Yet why do I write all this to you, and

distress you more than my total silence would have done? I wish that you, for your part, may really be as happy as from your letter you seem to be. I am sorry that you kept silence so long, thinking that I was away. I have not gone further the whole summer than from Brunswick to Wolfenbüttel, and from Wolfenbüttel to Brunswick. Even these changes I shall have to renounce for the future. Yet this shall be the least of my cares, and I will gladly withdraw still more from all society, and pinch and struggle here in solitude, if only I can thereby acquire peace in other matters.'

The latter remark refers to his urgent money needs, owing to the Camenz demands and debts. Thus passed the year, and with the commencement of the new one (1773) he seemed a trifle more cheerful. He writes to Frau König:

'January 8.

'I can no longer disguise from myself the fact that I am more hypochondriacal than I ever thought to become. The only thing that reassures me is this, that I see from experience that my hypochondria cannot have taken very deep root, for as soon as I leave this accursed castle and go among men I can manage for awhile. Then I ask myself, why remain longer in this accursed castle? If I were still the old sparrow on the roof, I should have been off again a hundred times. During the last eight days I have been obliged to go into society. I had to go to court for the new year, and did with the rest what is certainly no use when one does it, but may do harm if one neglects it, namely, I have scraped and bowed and used my mouthpiece; the only wish that I really felt all the while was . . . alas! you know only too well

what, my love. Can it be that there is no happy year
more in store for me?'

He repeats how he is devoured with longing to
be with her, how every letter he writes to her makes
him unsettled for a week and incapable of work. He
apologizes for having left her so long without a letter;
it is a habit of his—he does not know whether he can
call it a good or a bad one—that he cannot write to a
person whom he loves, with his head full of dark fancies
and his heart overflowing with gall.

In this same January (1773) Lessing issued the
first volume of his 'Contributions.' He had received
the ducal permission to print whatever he held fit,
independent of the censor, and the opportunity was
thus given into his hands to serve the cause of
enlightenment. For since the Wolfenbüttel library
was peculiarly rich in MSS. bearing on theology, and
since Lessing held that no words of a truth-seeking,
honest-minded man could ever be harmful, it was his
intention to introduce sundry papers of this nature.
His design was to substitute continuous progress in
the place of religious immobility, to oppose to the
radical and flippant negations of the Berlin school of
enlightened rationalism the gravity of historical criticism. Discussion, he held, must be salutary in as far
as it cleared the ground for truth ; discussion was
progress. The *Aufklärerei* sect of Nicolai was as
narrow as the most dogmatic adherents of authority,
and equally unable to conceive of anything beyond
the grasp of their own understandings. Lessing
desired free examination, but it was to be learned and
thorough. He desired tolerance ; but it was to be
inspired by charity. The tendency of the age was to
encyclopaedic knowledge ; but Lessing was the first

who resuscitated old books and documents, not as
mere curiosities, the monuments left by past periods,
but as additions to the history of the human mind.
He is therefore no mere collector, but for all his own
contempt of his labours as a librarian, he remains the
philosophical thinker through whose endeavours runs
a definite thread of purpose. He does not merely
impart his discoveries and the result of his investigations, but in each case shows the path or the
circumstance that led to the discovery, because, as he
explains : 'The manner in which one has come to a
matter is as valuable, even as instructive, as the matter
itself.' In such a department a certain sense for the
small, the seemingly trivial, is useful and necessary.
This loving examination of minutiae was a literary
quality that Lessing combined, strangely enough, with
a wide range of vision. He defends this treatment in
his notice of the ancient glass windows of the Hirschau
Monastery. The weary reader will exclaim with
disgust : 'What! broken glass ' ( *Vitrea fracta*). 'Yes,
by your leave! even in the learned world one must
live and let live. What does not serve us may serve
another ; what is not important or attractive to us is
so to another.'

In these words lies Lessing's apology for his
'Contributions,' of which two volumes were published
in 1773. Their contents were varied, and in their
isolation are of interest only to the erudite. The only
theological contribution of the year was rather in
support of orthodoxy than otherwise ; not only historically but dogmatically. It was neither more nor less
than two small writings of Leibnitz, which Lessing
had discovered in the ducal library, and which had
been overlooked by the editor of his collected works.

The one dealt with the question of eternal punishment,
the other was Leibnitz's defence of the Trinity. More
remarkable than Leibnitz's short preface is Lessing's
exposition and philosophical defence of eternal punishment as promulgated by Leibnitz. The paper on the
Trinity was written in reply to the Socinian Wisow-
atius, and the defence was scarcely intelligible without
the attack ; Lessing accordingly printed both. Curiously enough, in one obscure passage of the MS.
Mendelssohn helped him to find the true meaning.
' Is it not strange,' he wrote to Moses, ' that you should
restore the true reading of a treatise that must seem,
and is, complete nonsense to you from end to end ?
It is nonsense to me also, and no doubt was the same
to Leibnitz ; and yet I am convinced that here still
Leibnitz thought and acted as Leibnitz : for it is
unquestionably better to defend an unphilosophical
position philosophically, than to reject it unphilosophically.'

The theologians praised, the neologians condemned,
when they read these papers. Karl reproached his
brother with making advances to the orthodox party.
' What do I care for the orthodox party ? ' he replies.
' I despise them as much as you do, only I despise
our new-fangled parsons still more, who are too little
of theologians and not nearly enough of philosophers.
I am convinced that if once these shallow heads get
uppermost they will in time tyrannize more than the
orthodox have ever done. Nor do I despise certain
learned labours as much as you, even if at first sight
they seem more laborious than useful. What you
consider for instance as a vain labour of Kennicott's
has accidentally helped us to a part of the lost books
of Livy.

Lessing sent the first volume of his 'Contributions' to Heyne with the following note :

'Wolfenbüttel : January 13, 1773.

'You once prophesied that the discovery of Berengarius would cost me dear, inasmuch as I should acquire a taste for discoveries that would rob me of my time and would but rarely reward me. Herewith the fulfilment of your prophecy! If you are so good as to believe that I could have written something better, I pray you not to forget that a librarian ought to write nothing better. And a librarian I am, and I do not wish to be one merely in name.

'I am, with profound esteem, &c.,

'LESSING.'

In the meantime Lessing's resolve to go to Vienna and see Frau König or to take some desperate and decisive step was frustrated by the Hereditary Prince, who early in February desired him to attend on him in Brunswick. With this request Lessing complied, and the Prince of his own accord told him that he wished to give him a position more suited to his deserts. A Hofrath had lately died whom the Duke employed specially in such questions as concerned the history and law of the ducal household. The Prince thought it would be easy for Lessing to acquire the needful skill and knowledge to fill his place. The salary appertaining, combined with his income as librarian, would enable him to live respectably in Brunswick. The only condition annexed was, that Lessing should abandon his projects of quitting the service of the house of Brunswick or roaming about the world. If he acquiesced, the matter should be laid before the Duke for formal assent, on the Prince's return from a short journey to Potsdam. Lessing accepted the proposal with delight. Here he was at last at the goal of his desires. He returned to Wolfenbüttel confident that, at longest, in a fortnight he would see an end put to all his misery. Of course he at once informed Frau König. 'I do not know,' he says, 'whether the Prince had got wind of my plans. But you can easily imagine what I answered him. I accepted his offer for the present, not however concealing that without a better prospect I should not have endured to remain here any longer.'

The Prince went to Potsdam and returned; Lessing awaited a definite summons to Brunswick. None came. So the weeks passed and the matter remained at the same point. He could not write to Frau König. He felt his honour compromised and that he had been shamefully played with. Not till April did she again hear from him. His impatience and irritated mood found vent in this letter:

'I could go mad! What will you think of me? What must you think of me? I wrote to you more than eight weeks ago that something was pending here for me that should decide my future once for all, and which I hoped would decide it as I could wish. *How* I wish it no one knows better than you. I thought confidently that not a week, not a fortnight would elapse before I could write to you with certainty of the matter. And if I did not write to you sooner than when I could write as I wish, eight weeks might easily pass again, and who knows if in the end I should not have to write to you that I have been deceived. Now is not this enough to drive one mad! Without the slightest provocation on my part, they

expressly send for me, make ever such a fuss over me,
stuff me with fair words and promises, and afterwards
act as though nothing had been mentioned. Since
then I have been twice to Brunswick, have shown
myself, and desired to know how matters stood. But
no answer, or as good as none! Now I am here
again once more, and have sworn not to set foot in
Brunswick until the matter is as voluntarily brought
to an end as it was voluntarily set on foot. If they
once let me make an end with the library, and with
certain work that I can finish, and can only finish in
Wolfenbüttel, nothing in the world shall hold me here
any longer. I think I can anywhere find as much
as I give up here. And even if I did not find it?
Rather beg than submit to be treated thus.'

A few days later he writes to his brother, apolo-
gizing for his renewed silence, which has not arisen
from want of brotherly affection. He tells him also
of the advances made, and of the suspense in which
he has been kept. 'But in a year and a day at latest
I shall write to you from another place than Wolfenbüttel. No doubt it is a good thing to study for a
while in a large library, but to bury oneself therein is
madness. I notice as well as others, that the work I
am doing now is blunting me. But for this very
reason I want to complete it as soon as may be, and
to continue and issue my "Contributions" down to the
last paltry item that was to be inserted according to
my plan. Not to do this would be wilfully to lose the
three years I have spent here.'

For three months Lessing kept his resolve, and
spent all his time in his own rooms or in the library.
A young Frenchman, François Cacault, was at the
time studying there. He had read Lessing's ' Drama-

turgic,' and had been irritated by the attacks on his nation, contending that 'les règles du bon goût sont partout les mêmes.' At last he determined to go and see Lessing for himself, and was so charmed with him that he completely changed his mind about the 'Dramaturgie,' which he forthwith translated into French. Nicolai gleefully writes to Lessing : ' And so you have completely transformed M. Cacault, and have justified my remark that it is needful to know Lessing in personal intercourse to do him full justice.' As Lessing was seeing no one else, that visitor was not unwelcome, and he and Cacault spent most evenings together. Else he rather pretended to be busy than was really so. His condition of despondency and weariness was mastering him. He would have taken some desperate step, and spoken his mind to the Prince in a manner that would have endangered all his future prospects, had not Frau König urged him to be patient and moderate. He began twenty letters to her, but left them all unfinished. At last, in June, circumstances forced him to go to Brunswick. He stayed six days, and returned somewhat more cheerful ; but in the main no progress. Still he was able to rouse himself to write to Frau König. ' Can you believe it,' he says, 'that I still do not know where I am ? This behaviour is intolerable to me, and nothing short of your express injunction has availed to restrain me from taking a rash step, which nevertheless I am still constantly tempted to take. Shall I not at last be obliged to take it ? I vow I cannot bear it much longer. It must bend or break.'

Again the weeks passed on and no news. In August the all-powerful Minister von Schliefert died. He had till then managed affairs, and was notorious

for his procrastinations ; and, from some remarks let
fall by the Prince, Lessing was justified in supposing
that he was the cause of the delay. On the Minister's
death the Prince took the reins of government, and
endeavoured to repair by economy the shattered state
of the ducal finances. Now, therefore, Lessing might
expect that his affair would be brought to a conclusion. Nothing of the kind, and in September Lessing
tells Frau König 'he is in danger of succumbing to
bitterness of anger.' He cannot write to her ; he is
physically and mentally incapable, he tears up letter
after letter, and all the while he is tortured with the
thought of what she must think of his silence, and
lest she should doubt his love. And yet he only
defers writing out of mere idle hope that from day to
day he may be able to send good news. 'You alone,'
he repeats, 'have hitherto prevented me, and still
prevent me, from taking an over-hasty step, whose
evil consequences I foresee, but which all the same I
should certainly have taken if I should not at the
same time have forfeited thereby the only serious
hope that I ever cherished in all my life. You know
what hope, my love.'

Nevertheless he did send in two remonstrances,
but without avail. He confided to Karl that he should
venture a third, and then, if they forced him to ask
for dismissal, he would of course at first be in some
perplexity whither to turn, but he certainly hoped
only at first. But as this condition of uncertainty
grew protracted, Lessing's courage failed him, and his
obstinate resolve not to show himself in Brunswick,
or to go among men, only heightened his condition of
hypochondria. His failing eyesight made the long
winter evenings doubly painful to endure alone. In

this state of bitterness and wounded pride he kept up an obstinate silence even towards Frau König. In December he breaks it. It is the selfsame old story, he says : he is angry, depressed, morose.

'For the last four months I have as good as never left Wolfenbüttel and my accursed castle. I have only been twice to Brunswick for a few hours, for I have sworn never again, while my present condition lasts, to remain there a night, where they (you know who) behave to me in a fashion that is unendurable ; in a fashion that at any other time, under other circumstances, nothing in the world could have made me endure. I will therefore, however, not even run into the danger of coming in his way. If he wants to boast of having led me by the nose, let him. But all my life I shall not forget it. Next January it will be a year since he personally made me the first advance. I will wait till then to tell him my mind in as bitter a fashion as certainly never before was employed towards any prince.

' But what can I do meantime, except busy myself among my books, so as, if possible, to forget among them all visions of the future ? For a far longer time than to you, my love, I have not written to a soul: neither to my mother, nor my brothers, nor anyone else. Neither do I answer anyone who writes to me on other than library concerns. The best thing to do would be to issue a circular to all my acquaintances, from most of whom I do not even desire to see a letter, requesting them to regard me as dead. For in truth, my love, it is almost impossible to me to write. Even to you I have begun more than ten letters and torn them up again. I can send you this one piece of good news, that I am very well. I believe anger keeps me well.'

As Frau König was the only person to whom
Lessing opened his heart, so she was the only one
who could appease him. Her own affairs were anything but prosperous, and she was suffering as well.
But she endeavoured her uttermost to cheer him.

'I would gladly bear all my troubles, if only you
were happy and content. You cannot believe how
much I feel it, that I cannot think of you otherwise
than in so sad a condition of spirit that it almost
makes me doubt whether you can really be so well as
you imagine. It may be wrong of me to say this to
you, but the fear lest you should be neglecting yourself urges me. You cannot possibly be well, or you
would have power and desire to resist the angry mood
revealed in every line of your letter. It is true you
have been badly treated, or rather they have mistaken
the manner in which to deal with a man like you.
But so long as the post offered to you is not disposed
of, you have no reason to be as indignant as you are.
That the person in question intended to deceive you
in making the offer, I cannot believe, for I should have
to picture him the basest wretch. I would rather believe that other business has caused him to forget the
matter, and no one reminds him of it since you do
not. And if what a stranger told me is true who
lately passed through these parts, the house is in
such difficulties that matters may soon come to a
national bankruptcy, and it is therefore not astonishing if things of this kind are forgotten. Meanwhile it grieves me that it should be you who suffer
under it. A hundred times already I have wished
that the whole business had never been named. . . .
Spare me your circular, please ; I shall not accept it.
I would rather renounce everything in the world than

X

your letters. I suppose you were not serious in your intention of sending one to me, or I should have to consider you as a most cruel man, and that you are not.'

Frau König's clearsighted penetration had here hit the right mark. When the hereditary Prince assumed the conduct of affairs, as the goodnatured old Duke was fast falling into imbecility, at best engrossed by his mistresses, he found financial affairs in a lamentable condition. The calamity of a state bankruptcy could indeed only be averted by the most desperate measures, measures revolting to our modern ideas, for the Prince, who was willing to convert his jewels into money, saw himself at last forced to sell what was infinitely more precious—his subjects. England and Holland were the purchasers. Schiller, in '*Cabale und Liebe*,' has treated of such a transaction, common at the time with the minor German courts. In the midst of these affairs Lessing had been forgotten ; some excuse is therefore to be made for the Prince. He certainly acceded to Lessing's requests when he could, for next January (1774) Lessing saw himself obliged once more to apply for his salary in advance, his Hamburg creditors threatening him with distraint. At Frau König's solicitations he refrained from writing his threatened letter to the Prince, but his moroseness increased, and for four months he again kept an obstinate silence. She implored him to break it, at least to let her know whether pleasure or displeasure was the cause : in the former case she could forgive him, not in the latter.

'For you must not be unhappy, at any rate not for so long a time as you now have been, and then too, I consider that I have a well-founded claim upon

your confidence, and should feel aggrieved if you did
not write to me because you had nothing pleasant to
write.' She then informed him of a rumour that had
reached her concerning contemplated unsectarian
appointments at the University of Heidelberg, and
asked if he wished her to make further inquiries.

He assented to this, though he hated teaching.
'For here I cannot endure any longer. From day to
day things grow worse, and the salaries that have
been dwindling for a year and a half will doubtless
soon become yet smaller. From the Prince, as I now
know him, I may certainly anticipate that if to-day
or to-morrow he comes to the throne, he will rather
sell the whole library together with the librarian as
soon as he can find a purchaser. But how can they
[in Heidelberg] be induced to think of a man whose
name is only known to them by plays? . . . Offer
myself? I would go to death with more cheerfulness.
And as what should I offer myself? A man like me,
when he offers himself, seems everywhere most superfluous, or at any rate he is then only wanted as cheaply
as possible. Setting this aside, your idea is certainly
a very good one, and I did not laugh at it, my love.
I should be seriously pleased at it if I had not
sworn never again to rejoice over a hope. If, however,
you are able to do anything unofficially in the matter,
you have my full permission, and I beg of you at any
rate to write to me whatever more you may hear.'
Touching his silence, he gave her his word of honour
he had not known a single happy day since he wrote
last, and therefore what could he do better than bear
his anger in silence and not burden others with it?
He kept his resolve too firmly. This letter was the

only one Frau König received from him during that whole year.

February 2, 1774, he writes to Karl that he must not expect any apology for his long silence : it would only be the same old story. He asks indulgence for not having read some of Karl's plays sent to him for revision, and says : ' If this astonishes you I must tell you, that I only read ' Götz von Berlichingen ' a few days ago, and then only in part. Leave me your plays a little longer ; I will certainly read them still, but not until I can read that kind of thing with a calmer and more cheerful mind. From this you perceive I have at least not abandoned all hope of being yet again calm and cheerful.'

' Götz von Berlichingen ' by no means won his approval. It had appeared a year previously, and had been hailed as an illustration of Lessing's ' Dramaturgie.' Goethe was named the German Shakespeare, and the young fermenting minds of the day whose advent Lessing had predicted in the closing chapters of the ' Dramaturgie ' were extravagant in their overlaudations of the golden literary age that had dawned. Lessing from his Wolfenbüttel solitude judged more sedately and correctly. He did not underrate Goethe's genius, but he protested against the comparison of a drama which transgressed all the higher rules of composition, with the plays of the greatest artist in the world. ' Götz ' was a dramatized chronicle, not a drama ; and it did not seem to him so great a feat that a gifted poet, who allowed himself a dispensation from all rules, should be able to string together a series of interesting scenes. The representatives of the *Sturm und Drang* period were inclined to look down on Lessing, with his rigid

adherence to Aristotle, as antiquated. They raised a
war-cry for absolute unconstraint. But Goethe himself
saw the error he had committed in ' Götz,' and amply
acknowledged it in later life. As the first production
of the Romantic school with its mediaeval leanings, its
young blood and its unhealthy sentimentality, it properly made an epoch. But Lessing's mind was too
healthy and too antique in form, to throw him into
the spirit that had evoked it. Though it was he who
made ready the way for the Romantic school, he
never inclined to it. Had he been in a happier mood,
there is no doubt it would have drawn from him a
polemic of some kind. As it was he contented himself by saying to Karl that theatrical matters have
long ago ceased to interest him, and it is perhaps well,
or he should certainly be in danger of growing angry
over the current theatrical confusion, and to begin a
quarrel with Goethe, for all his genius, on which he
insists so much. ' But Heaven forefend! Rather would
I like to play a little comedy with the theologians, if
I need comedy.'

Ramler sent him a copy of his ' Anthology.'

' Many thanks for your beautiful " Anthology," ' he
writes ; ' I could almost envy you that you still collect
flowers, while I am condemned to gather nothing but
thorns. That is your own fault, you will say. I think
not ; I see nothing but thorns on my field, and it
happens to be my field. In vain do you remind me
of our mutual resolve to plant a more flowery one.
It was not to be. I am at an end, and every poetical
spark, of which in any case I had not many, is extinct.
But your fire still burns brightly. . . . How much I
wish to see you again! Would it were your firm
resolve to visit me! In any case you travel every

year. Why do you not come once to Brunswick, where you have never been, and where you have so many friends ?  I, who wanted to roam the world, shall in all likelihood moulder away in' this little Wolfenbüttel, and never even see Berlin again.  Think of this, and hold out to me the sweet hope of your visit, one of the few hopes by whose help I trust to endure the melancholy winter that lies before me.'

An application from Wieland for contributions to his paper, the ' *Merkur,*' he answered with ' What contributions do you expect from me ?  Works of genius ?  All genius is confiscated just now by certain people with whom I should not like to find myself a fellow traveller.  Literary contributions ?  Who will read them ? '

This somewhat bitter tone is attributable to ' Werther.'  The hero was generally reported to be Jerusalem, the son of the Abbot of Riddingshausen, a young man whom Lessing had learnt to know and love, and whose melancholy suicide in 1772 had made a deep impression on his mind.  Lessing saw how utterly distorted was this so-called portrait, and he inveighed with justice against such public caricatures. Added to this the lacrymose sensibility of ' Werther,' with its love-sick vapourings, was completely revolting to Lessing's manly character.  The man ' who desired immensely and willed feebly,' who perishes because he is too weak to live, whose diseased spirit has not a spark of self-respect or manly resistance to ill fortune, was doubly removed from the sphere of Lessing's comprehension at a time when he was himself suffering from the hope deferred that maketh the heart sick. Still as ever he is the just critic.

'My dear Herr Eschenburg,

'A thousand thanks for the pleasure you have procured me by sending me Goethe's romance. If so warm a production is not to cause more harm than good, do you not think it should have a short, cold epilogue ; a few hints how Werther came to have such a peculiar character, how another youth to whom nature has given similar leanings should defend himself? For else such youths might easily confound poetical with moral beauty, and believe that *he* must needs have been good who could so powerfully engross our sympathy : and that he certainly was not. Nay, if our Jerusalem's spirit had been wholly in this condition, I should almost have to despise him. Do you think that any Greek or Roman youth would thus and therefore have committed suicide? Certainly not. They knew better how to guard themselves from the vapourings (*Schwärmerei*) of love ; in Sokrates' time, such an ἐξ ἔρωτος κατοχὴ whom τολμᾶν τι παρὰ φύσιν impelled, would scarcely be forgiven a girl. To produce such little-great, contemptible, admirable originals was reserved to a Christian education, which so well understands how to convert a physical necessity into a spiritual virtue. Therefore, dear Goethe, another little chapter, and the more cynical the better.'

Nicolai's dry, pedantic spirit, free from any leaning to sentiment, was yet severer on ' Werther.' He agreed with Lessing's objections to its tendency and published a parody, 'The Joys of young Werther,' in which Werther shoots himself only with chicken's blood, marries Charlotte, and lives happy ever after.

Lessing preferred to confine his attention to severer

paths of literature. In this year he issued a third
volume of the ' Contributions from the Ducal Library.'
The most noteworthy article dealt with Adam Neuser,
an unfortunate Lutheran divine, who had to resign
his post at Heidelberg on account of his religious
views, went to Transylvania where he joined the
Socinians, and at last fled to Constantinople, where he
apostatized to Islam, and died in the year 1576. For
this latter step he had been branded by Christians of
all denominations. Lessing had found in the Wolfenbüttel library a letter from Neuser to a friend, wherein
was ample extenuation of his step, revealing the persecutions he had suffered from his Christian brethren,
and freeing him from the suspicion of having entered
into a treacherous agreement with the Turks. Here
was another good man's fame to resuscitate ! Lessing
points to the barbarous cruelty of his Christian perse-
cutors, the theologians, whose reply to the repentant
heretic's promises of reform always amounted to this :
Off with his head first ; reform can follow after if it
pleases God. . . . ' Bene est, quod saltem nil in
gratiam Neuseri scripserint,' a reformed theologian
had ironically remarked to some Lutherans, who laid
the charge of this apostasy on Calvinism. ' Bene !'
retorted Lessing, ' I say it is bad that it did not happen,
bad that after two hundred years I must be the first
to win the ear of posterity for an unhappy man—an
unhappy man who was persecuted out of Christianity.
Or if he was wrong in allowing himself to be persecuted out, is he therefore right in nothing ? If the
conclusion is to be the soul of history, if we are to
judge all that has gone before by this, then it would be
as well if we had no history at all.'

' The chief consideration to which Neuser's history

must lead a thoughtful reader, I need not indicate at
length ; but it is that which reminds me of fragments
of a very important work among the very newest
manuscripts of our library, and particularly of one of
them, so forcibly, that I cannot here refrain from saying a word about them in general, and transcribing
this one as a specimen.

'They are, I say, fragments of a work that was
once completed and destroyed, or of a work that was
never finished. For they bear no general title ; their
author is nowhere named ; neither have I been able
in any way to learn how and when they came into
our library. Nay, I do not even know for certain
that they are fragments of *one* work, but I only conclude that this is so, because they all have one aim,
all refer to revealed religion, and criticize Biblical
history in particular. They are written with the
greatest boldness, but at the same time with the
greatest earnestness. The investigator never forgets
his dignity ; flippancy does not seem to have been his
failing, and nowhere does he permit himself mockery
or jokes. He is a true steady German in his mode of
• writing, and in his views. He gives his opinion
straight out, and despises all small modes of surpris-
ing the reader's approval. As the handwriting and
general appearance of his papers show that they may
have been written about thirty years ago, and as
many passages bear testimony to a profound knowledge of Hebrew, and the author everywhere philoso-
phizes on Wolfian principles, these combined circumstances have reminded me of a man who lived about
that time at Wolfenbüttel, and who found, under the
protection of an enlightened and gracious prince, that
toleration which furious orthodoxy would rather he

had not found in all Europe ; of Schmid, the Wer-
theimer translator of the Bible.'

Lessing then inserted the first of the fragments
out of Reimarus' manuscripts, ' On the Toleration of
Deists.' It was the mildest of the papers that he thus
tentatively put forth. He expected that it would
make some stir, but it fell flatter than he had anticipated. Only from Karl had he to listen to objections
on account of the way in which he was frittering away
his time and energy. He replied :

' Frequent change in work is the only thing which
sustains me. True, in this way much is begun, and
little completed. But what of that ? Even if I never
finish anything more in my life,—nay, granting that
I never have finished anything,—what does it matter ?
Perhaps you will think this sentiment somewhat
misanthropical, and you accuse me of being so in
my views of religion. Now, without examining how
much or how little cause I have for being satisfied
with my fellow-men, I must tell you that in this
matter you have quite a false idea of me, and that
you thoroughly misunderstand my attitude towards
orthodoxy. Should *I* grudge the world further enlightenment ? Should *I* not wish with all my heart
that everyone should think sensibly about religion ?
I should despise myself if I had had any other object,
even in my scribblings, than to help forward these
great ends. But leave me my own way in which I
think to accomplish this. And what is more simple
than this way ? I do not want to have the dirty
water, which has long been useless, kept, but I do not
want it thrown away until I know whence to take
cleaner. I do not want to have it thoughtlessly
thrown away.

'Fortunately orthodoxy had been pretty well done with. A partition-wall had been set up between it and philosophy, behind which each could go its own way, without hindering the other. But what do people do now? They tear down the partition-wall, and under pretence of making us reasonable Christians, they turn us into most unreasonable philosophers. I beg of you, dear brother, to inquire more closely into this matter, and to look less to what our new theologians discard, than to what they wish to set up instead. We are agreed in this, that our old religious system is false. But I could not say with you that it is a patchwork of bunglers and half-philosophers. I know nothing in the world in which human understanding is more clearly shown or has been more exercised. The system of religion which people now want to put in place of the old *is* a patchwork of bunglers and half-philosophers; and it has far more influence on reason and philosophy than the old system ever assumed. And yet you blame me for defending the old? My neighbour's house threatens to fall in. If my neighbour wishes to pull it down, I will give him due help. But he does not wish to pull it down, he wishes to prop it up at the cost of total ruin to my house. Let him leave that alone, or I will treat his falling house as if it were mine.'

Pertaining to the library contributions, though issued independently, was a work 'On the Antiquity of Oil Painting,' assigned by Lessing to the ninth century, which proved that the brothers Van Eyck were not the first to use this medium. The treatise made some noise, and the notion was extensively combated. Waagen has however confirmed Lessing's view that oil painting was known in Italy before Van

Eyck's time, without at the same time diminishing the honour due to Van Eyck.

It is evident that Lessing's mind was at this time only open to severe and dry researches. The MS. of 'Halladat' which Gleim sent to him for perusal, was deferred several days, though it was sent by a messenger who had orders to wait for a reply. He was ill in body and mind, so that he neglected the most needful concerns. Hand and head refused their services. Things could not go on thus much longer. To Karl he said, in April 1774 :

' I will assuredly not remain another year in my present wretched position, happen what may. My friends must not on that account accuse me of restlessness. At a place like Wolfenbüttel, removed from all intercourse such as I need, it has never been my intention to spend my life in guarding books. To-morrow I shall have been doing so for four years ; and as I feel only too keenly how much drier and more blunted my intellect and senses have become during these four years, in spite of all my widened historical knowledge, I should not for anything in the world like to do so for four years more. But I must not even do so for *one* year more, if I am ever to do anything else. It is all up here. Here I can do nothing more. You will read nothing of mine this Fair ; for I have done nothing the whole winter, and am well satisfied that I have at least accomplished that great work of philosophy or cowardice, that I am still alive. May God help me on in this noble work, which is well worth while that we should daily eat and drink for its sake ! '

And again in November:

' Dearest Brother,

'It is very good of you not to be angry at my long obstinate silence. I begin this letter also without knowing whether I shall finish it. Of such beginnings of letters to you my writing-table contains more than one. I am glad that you are well, that the hypochondriacal mood in which you wrote one of your last letters was only transitory. Mine is more obstinate. The only means of deadening it is to throw myself out of one paltry literary investigation into another. It is on this account that my "Contributions" are the only. thing I still continue, and yet I fear that I shall not long be able to continue even these. I see that ruin awaits me here, and am at length resigned thereto.'

The new year dawned, and Lessing was resolved to break away and seek new scenes and people. He made no plan whither his steps should tend, save that somehow they must lead towards his dear Eva. He did not face any questions of prudence or otherwise. His patience was at an end. He would away, no matter where. He said he was resigned to stay and perish, but he could not do so without making one last desperate effort. He wrote to Frau König announcing this resolve:

'Yes, my love, I myself should not understand how it was possible for me not to write to you for so long, if I could not well recall from day to day how it came to be deferred. All last summer I was suffering from fever, but still the fever was not much at fault. Had I been able to send you a single little piece of news, not agreeable but at least not very disagreeable, I should really have had the best opportunity of doing so during the fever. But to worry you still more, my dearest, with things that I would gladly get rid of myself and which I am of necessity obliged to think of, when I think of you, even if I could have been capable of that in the greatest heat of the fever, I should despise myself. Even now, if I expressed myself somewhat more clearly about it, this letter would certainly never be completed. God be thanked that I know you to be gradually on the road to rest. These three past years have been a horrid dream for you.'

He expressed his delight at the prospect of reunion: 'If I still know what it means to be glad! You will find me in health; better than, alas! I may expect to find you. To my acquaintances I seem as happy as it is possible to be. God grant them that they may not say some day, we have been terribly deceived in him. I have got so far as to see that all my sorrow, all my endeavours to escape from these accursed circumstances, are in vain. Therefore, what will happen, must.'

He went to Brunswick to make a last attempt in his affair, and, this failing, he requested a half-year's salary in advance, and leave of absence for a journey to Berlin. 'For a fortnight I have been at Brunswick,' he tells Karl, 'and in a most unpleasant situation, so that I must break away by some violent step, if I do not want to be suffocated here in the mud. In a fortnight at latest I go to Leipzig; whether from that place I shall go first to Dresden or to Berlin, I cannot say yet.'

He himself called this journey a venture, but reassured Frau König he had not burnt his ships behind him. No one at Brunswick knew that his real goal was Vienna; and only from Dresden did he

apply for an extended leave to go there, promising to
return to Wolfenbüttel in two months at latest. At
Leipzig he spent a few days with his friend Weisse,
renewing their old friendly intercourse. Weisse
thought him softened down, and declared that he likes
him better than even before. He noticed that he had
something on his mind that he did not confide, and
felt convinced his restless spirit was about to break
away from the assured position of Wolfenbüttel : a
marvel to Weisse, who liked rest, while Lessing protested he had lived free for so many years and yet
not starved, and he hated both Wolfenbüttel and the
people of the court. Their conversation turned on
' Werther,' and Weisse quite expected Lessing would
some day attack the book. Lavater's ' Physiognomie '
was also touched upon. Lessing condemned it as
proving too much. If Lavater's theories were well
founded, it would be needful to see the whole naked
body, as an ugly face was often placed on a well-
formed figure. Lavater's character was one naturally
antipathetic to Lessing's. He had moreover offended
Lessing in his most vulnerable point, his affection for
Moses Mendelssohn, by public attempts, more distinguished by zeal than by good taste, to effect the
latter's conversion.

From Leipzig Lessing went to Berlin, where he
spent a fortnight with his brother and in the circle of
his friends. Here he met with offers to keep him in
Prussia. He did not pay much heed ; such offers
often came now ; he must go to Vienna first and see
after matters there. Frau König's affairs were at last
arranged ; indeed it was only ill-health that had retained her the last months. Lessing wrote from
Berlin, announcing his visit, and entreating her for his

sake to stay in Vienna till he could join her. His secret wish was that they should travel back together.

'If only I could fly!' he writes to her from Dresden. His impatient longing to see her again is expressed in every line he wrote, while waiting for the ducal permission. Prague, which he had never seen, could not detain him a day, so great was his longing. March 31 (1775) he arrived at Vienna, sooner than Frau König had dared expect him, and these two sorely tried mortals again enjoyed the bliss of meeting.

# CHAPTER XVI.

## ITALY.

### (1775-1776. Aged 46-47.)

*' Wenn etwas ist gewalt'ger als das Schicksal,*
*So ist's der Muth, der's unerschüttert trägt !'*—Geibel.

ALAS, that the bliss should have been so brief! The
irony that seems to run like a fatal thread through
Lessing's life was about to entwine him in a cruel web.
One ardent wish was to be accorded at a moment
when it had sunk to secondary importance beside a
more engrossing one.

Ten happy days of intercourse were granted to
Lessing and Frau König at Vienna. His public
reception far exceeded his expectations. He was a
fêted guest. ' Emilia Galotti ' was performed in his
honour, and his appearance in the house was greeted
with acclamation. With his release from the oppressive atmosphere of Wolfenbüttel his spirits had risen,
his starved intellect had been recruited in Berlin, so
that he was once more the old brave, cheerful Lessing.
His candid and noble bearing won him all hearts.
The influential Councillor von Gebler wrote to Nicolai,
calling him that rare combination, a truly great and
amiable scholar. ' This I know, that if our Academy
of Science is ever established, and I can do anything
towards securing it such a great ornament, I shall not

Y

neglect to do it.   No German scholar has ever been
received here with such distinction as our excellent
friend, and that from our sovereign down to the
general public.'

But ten days after Lessing, Prince Leopold of
Brunswick arrived at Vienna.   He was the youngest
son of the reigning Duke, an amiable, intelligent
youth of twenty-three, the same who afterwards
perished in the waters of the Oder while endeavouring
to save the lives of some poor persons, and whose
memory has been embalmed in verse by Goethe.   He
was an especial favourite of Maria Theresa, who
wished to retain him in her dominions, and offered
him a regiment.   This was against the traditions of
the House of Brunswick, who all served under Prussia.
The Prince had to ask for his father's permission and,
pending the answer, wished to take a short tour in
Italy.   The journey was not to carry him farther
south than Venice ; by that time he expected to have
a definite reply.   It was his wish that Lessing should
accompany him, and he promised to accommodate all
difficulties with his father respecting the extended
leave of absence.

This proposal placed Lessing in a painful perplexity.   His prospect of marriage now seemed
immediate.   On the other hand, his private affairs
were still in a sorry state.   Would it be wise, under
such circumstances, to refuse the request of a son of
the house he served ?   Nay, might not his readiness
to accede, even at personal inconvenience, operate in
his favour ?   Then there was the old wish to see Italy,
the tour was not to exceed eight weeks, the sacrifice
of time was not great.   He assented.   Maria Theresa,
delighted that her favourite should have so pleasant a

companion, accorded Lessing a second interview. She chatted with him about Vienna, its public institutions, its theatre, and learned men, and asked him how he was satisfied with what he had seen of her capital. Lessing, too truthful to condescend to flattery, replied evasively. Maria Theresa thought his cautious replies covered a reproach. 'I think I understand you,' she said ; 'I know well that good taste does not advance with us as it should. Will you not say where the fault lies ? I have done all that my power and insight allowed ; but I often think I am only a woman, and a woman cannot achieve much in such matters.' She expressed her satisfaction at his intended journey, and, hearing they would go to Milan, gave Lessing an autograph letter to the governor of Lombardy, Count Firmian.

On April 25 the Prince and Lessing started. Frau König felt the parting sorely. ' It was a sad day for me. I can say with truth that the few days I spent here with you were the only happy ones of my whole residence. May God forgive your Prince Leopold for robbing me of your company ! I shall never pardon him.' Baron von Gebler had told her to convey a hundred thousand respects to Lessing. ' He almost put me on the rack to find out whether you were well disposed towards him. Though I acquiesced sincerely, he repeated the question at least six times, and said each time, " I heartily wish him well, and only desire that we may retain him here." And I thought in my heart, I do not wish that, for my dear Lessing is far more in place in the Wolfenbüttel library than among court sycophants. At any rate the library will interest him longer than they would. Am I not right ? '

Lessing's great regret was that this journey had come so suddenly as to find him unprepared. He had not the books he needed, his interest had lately been diverted from aesthetics ; 'and what I had known and forgotten was no due preparation.' The travellers' road led them by way of Salzburg to Brescia, and thence to Milan, where they made their first considerable halt. Lessing's eyesight, which had been troubling him for some time past, suffered from the dust and sun of Lombardy. But his letter to Karl expressed his delight at this foretaste of Italy, that had renewed his old resolve to live and die there. Everything he saw and heard charmed him, but for writing he had no time, as he had to attend to the Prince. This circumstance indeed became the principal drawback to the journey. The Prince's time was spent in receiving or returning visits, in dining out or in gala receptions. To do Lessing honour, he was everywhere asked with the Prince, and might not refuse, so that he found himself forced to go through the shallow and tedious routine of court festivities in interesting places whose artistic treasures he craved to survey. He began to wish for the time of return, and indulged in visions of repeating his visit under more favourable conditions.

'Not an hour passes,' he wrote from Milan to Frau König, 'wherein I do not find reason to regret that I am not rather travelling with you. For I shall derive little advantage from this journey, as I am invited everywhere with the Prince, and so all my time is lost in visiting and dining. To-day we dined at the Archduke's. Only the advantages which I hope to derive from this journey in Wolfenbüttel can make such a mode of life endurable to me.'

Late in May the travellers reached Venice. The

air of the lagoons did not suit Lessing, and the daily
and hourly dissipations into which he was perforce
drawn aggravated his discomforts. He was taken ill.
But a yet more unpropitious event occurred. At
Venice the Prince found a reply from his father,
placing impediments in the way of his wishes, and he
consequently determined to extend his journey, in
hopes the Duke might yet yield.

'And now,' Lessing wrote to Frau König, 'let me
complain of the worst of all. We do not return at
once to Vienna, but go first to Florence. The Prince
cannot and will not return to Vienna before his concerns there are regulated. And this is what comes of
having to do with princes! You can never count
with them on any certainty, and if once they have
you in their clutches you must just fain endure,
whether you will or no. One of my first errands here
in Venice was to S. Cristoforo, to see where our
friend reposes, and to shed a sincere tear to his
memory. The same man in whose arms he had died
took me thither, and from him I received the assurance that his death was only due to natural causes. I
know that you were not free from suspicion, and
wished to be satisfied on this point. That you can
now be. About a little monument that you must
place on his grave, more by word of mouth.'

Lessing witnessed the marriage of the Doge with
the Adriatic, especially brilliant that year on account
of a concurrence of royal personages. At Bologna the
Cardinal Legate and the aristocracy did the travellers
all honour, but Lessing's own communications were
only resumed at Florence, whence he wrote to Frau
König early in June, that he believed they were now
on their way back. He was only afraid lest their

stay in Turin should be extended beyond his wish.
He longed to be back in Germany, and with Frau
König. Sightseeing in the heat tired him ; he felt ill,
and was full of regret that he had been persuaded to
separate from her on such uncertain prospects. Yet
what was he to do ? He had now made this sacrifice
to the Prince ; in any event he must endure to the
end. He admits that he is writing in a hypochondriacal mood. He is filled with yearning for
her, and only disappointed not to have found letters
from her.

It was really this which embittered Lessing's Italian
journey, and induced the sombre impatient mood which
unfitted him to enjoy such delights as he could have
secured, notwithstanding the serious drawbacks to
the true enjoyments of an Italian journey in the aristocratic mode of travelling forced on him. After the
first letter at Milan, Lessing had not received a line
from Eva König ; after this Florentine letter she
heard no more from him until January 1776, when
he announced his return to Vienna. While she was
waiting from week to week for news, and torturing
her mind with fears on his account, only relieved by
an occasional mention of his name and his whereabout in the newspapers, he, deprived of even this
slender and uncertain source of intelligence, feared
lest she was ill—worse, even dead. With these black
thoughts he dragged himself through the length and
breadth of Italy, and hence his Italian impressions
are lost to posterity. He did keep a note-book, but
its entries are scanty and laconic—the personal jot-
tings that aid memory, but not the copious out-
pourings that can interest or are comprehensible to
an outsider. They deal with matters of erudition,

discoveries he had made in the various libraries, architectural notes, social and political observations, and fragmentary memoranda of conversations with Italian scholars.

At Turin, as he had anticipated, their stay was prolonged ; and then the Prince, still not receiving the answer he desired, resolved yet further to extend the trip. They went to Rome by way of Pavia, Parma, Modena, and Loretto. Including three days devoted to Albany and Frascati, they only sojourned a fortnight in the Eternal City, and much of that time was wasted in audiences of the Pope and Cardinals. The intelligent Pius VI. conversed for a long time with Lessing, whose fame had reached him through Cardinal Albani. A nephew of the Pope presented him with a costly antique cameo. Lessing tried to see whatever he could, but the time was too short. It is said that once the princely servants sought him a whole day in vain, till he was at last discovered sitting wrapt and alone before the Laokoon group, endeavouring to derive new thoughts from its contemplation. From Rome they passed on to Naples, where Lessing visited Sir William Hamilton, and admired his splendid collections. Here a ducal courier reached the Prince, bearing an order that he should return home forthwith. To this there could be no demur, and the travellers at once set out to reach Germany as quickly as might be, after having run through the whole peninsula as far as Naples, including the Isle of Corsica, in less than eight months. At Bologna a letter from a Brunswick friend contained a passing reference to Frau König, and Lessing thus received the first assurance that she was living. He accompanied the Prince as far as Munich, and then hastened to Vienna. The first thing he found there was a large packet of letters from Frau König, which, thanks to the negligence of officious friends who had promised to expedite them, had accumulated there while he was breaking his heart for lack of only one. He saw from them how first she had borne patiently with his apparent neglect, but how at last, when no answer came, not the smallest word of love or remembrance, even her strong heart had broken down, and she penned a last despairing appeal. Had all the beautiful things her Lessing had seen made him quite forget her? Had he not promised to quiet her anxiety by frequent letters? Did he no longer know that all her trouble and grief would be stilled by but one word, one little word, from him? She tells him she is back again in Hamburg, and that the hour she arrived is one of the few happy ones she had again enjoyed for six years: it resembled the hour when the note announcing his arrival was brought her at Vienna. And now!

Lessing's reply made all right again. He begs her to retain for him that love which is all his happiness and all his possession. He assures her, by all that is holy, that since the letter received at Venice he has not had a line from her. What could he think but that she was dead, or so seriously ill that she could send no news? These black thoughts had poisoned all his enjoyment of Italy. As a desperate resource he had come to Vienna to make inquiries about her, and behold! the earnestly desired letters. He hears she is well, but he implores for direct assurance from herself. She replied at once. His letter had rescued her from the terrible anxiety which she had endured six months on his account, or rather on her own, for the newspapers occasionally informed her he was well, also that he had decided to settle in Rome, and then it grieved her to hear Lessing was well and happy, and had forgotten her. That her letters never reached him she had not dreamed. Next Easter her affairs would be quite in order, and she would have five hundred to six hundred thalers yearly income left. They would have been in order ere this, but she had had no heart to attend to them, devoured as she was with anxiety for him. One of her children, too, had been ill. Little Fritz, his godson and her pet, was flourishing, and quite the most alert and clever of her children, almost making her believe in the old notion that godfathers influence their godchildren. Now that Lessing was back, she trusted all would be well. It was a bad habit of hers to anticipate the worst; he must wean her of this. She urged him to abandon other projects and try to come to some satisfactory arrangement at Wolfenbüttel; she felt assured her dear Lessing was more in place there than elsewhere.

Lessing's reply was written from Dresden. He had left Vienna earlier than he had intended. He had not visited any of the great folks, and had departed sooner because Prince Kaunitz had asked him to dinner. From this Frau König will see he had abandoned all idea of Vienna. At Dresden the Kurfürst made advances to him, and assured him that if he desired again to settle in his fatherland he should not regret the step. Here he consulted with a friend concerning a new edition of Winckelmann's works and letters which he projected publishing. He also spent four days with his aged mother, whom he had not seen for eleven years. Thence he went to Berlin, where he intended to stay three days and remained

three weeks.  He was feeling the cold keenly, and
the suffering induced made him relapse into low spirits.
From Brunswick he received letters with the best
assurances but no certainty, and therefore, meanwhile,
he only gave ambiguous replies to various offers
now constantly made to him.  The cold weather
changed to wet, and he resolved to wait no longer.
He complained that he was made to go out so much
by his friends, when he would far rather have been
left at home in peace.  He was out of temper, unde-
cided, disgusted with all about him, or rather seriously
ill, for such a state must be illness.  ' Oh, God !' he
exclaims piteously to Frau König, ' when will this kind
of life end ? when shall I at length be able to live for
you and for myself in peace and solitude ?'   In order
to reach Wolfenbüttel he had to borrow largely from
his brother, as his funds had been exhausted at Camenz.
The nearer he approached Brunswick the more gloomy
his mood became.   What should he find there ?
Would his affairs at last have advanced a step ?  And
if not, had not his whole Italian journey been for nothing, since it had certainly been in vain as far as
mental profit was concerned ?

On February 23 Lessing returned to Brunswick, after a year's unanticipated absence.  He at
once hurried to pay his respects at court.  Everyone received him with cordiality, except the Hereditary Prince whom he missed.  But his affairs were
*in statu quo.*  This neglect exasperated him bitterly.
' I shall wait another week or fortnight,' he wrote to
Frau König, ' and shall then bluntly write to the
Duke that the total derangement of my affairs obliges
me to seek an improvement of my condition, and,
since I do not see this before me in Brunswick, I am

necessitated to ask for my dismissal. Then, if they want to do anything for me, they will do it on this declaration. If not—well, then indeed I shall receive my dismissal. Verily, my love, I cannot contemplate that future without throwing down my pen.' To Karl he told the same tale. If the court will not listen to his proposals, he can only comfort himself with the remembrance that all the various changes of abode to which he has been forced by necessity have proved more fortunate than otherwise.

All Frau König's womanly gentleness inspires her reply. It was not for nothing she had feared to receive Lessing's first letter from Brunswick. She entreats him to look more calmly at the matter. The mode in which he intends to place his affairs before the Duke seems to her most imprudent, more especially so as he holds the Prince to be no friend of his, and he is therefore putting a dangerous weapon into his hands. ' It seems to me I would not act thus even in the most involved circumstances, and that yours are not, or your debts must exceed what I know. Else I cannot think how for a miserable thousand thalers you could so compromise your honour as to announce your circumstances to be totally deranged. That would be, according to my mind, throwing yourself away. Not so if you write to the Duke and tell him you could not support yourself on your salary, and had been forced to eke it out from your private means, and were therefore obliged to beg for an addition. I am just as certain you would not be refused, as I am certain that the matter would end very badly if taken in hand as you propose.'

Meanwhile Lessing, who was remaining at Brunswick, met the Prince in the street by accident. The

Prince greeted him cordially, expressed his satisfaction at seeing him again, declared that Lessing's return had never been announced to him, that he wanted to speak with him and begged him to wait a few days at Brunswick : he would appoint an interview. Lessing replied that he would stay till Sunday. He waited till Monday morning, but heard nothing. Then, goaded to the uttermost, he could no more be restrained. He wrote the Hereditary Prince the threatened letter, and placed his whole conduct so graphically before him, that, as Lessing remarked, he could not fail to be piqued. Only in consideration of Frau König's advice, he worded it all as mildly as he could. The letter had due effect. Lessing's threat of demanding his dismissal from the Duke came as an unexpected blow to the Prince, who wished to keep him in Brunswick. The Prince was on the point of joining his regiment at Halberstadt, but he wrote a conciliatory letter, though Lessing thought it somewhat too haughty, and sent a councillor to him begging him to desist from his purpose, and offering him better conditions. Lessing replied that this was all very well, but the Prince himself must make him these offers. He would not put in the smallest petition, and he further stated that he should not hold this slight amelioration as binding him to remain if something better came in his way. The councillor reported the interview to the Prince, who on hearing of it very nearly lost all patience with Lessing. But he so well knew his value and was so anxious to retain him in his service, that he determined to speak to him in person on his return, feeling assured he could then remove all misunderstandings. On April 5 the Prince wrote that he had returned to Brunswick, and would be glad to see Lessing on the 6th. This letter did not reach Lessing till the 7th, when the Prince had again departed for Halber-stadt. Lessing was furious, and chose to think that the Prince had purposely misdated his letter. The old mood of sullen anger once more mastered him. He told Karl he could not chew through the cud of all his annoyances by letter; enough that he was in the dark as to the Prince's ultimate designs, and was living in the most unpleasant state of uncertainty, in which he was prepared to meet the worst, and could do no work beyond putting the affairs of the library in order, so that he might be able to leave any moment. To this annoyance was added that his sister was demanding money from him and Karl with the bitterest strictures on their parsimony, and Lessing had to protest again and again that they neither of them had the money to give.

It was in the month of April of this year (1776), that Lessing edited the literary remains of the young Jerusalem. This task was undertaken as another rehabilitation and a protest against Goethe. On his return from Italy he found the 'Werther' fever still raging with intensity, and suicide all the fashion. Everywhere the names Werther and Jerusalem were coupled; Lessing desired to show the world that this was a distortion of truth. Karl Wilhelm Jerusalem had been a youth of unusual promise, clear insight, a lover of truth, a calm thinker, warmhearted but strong, not a weakling like Werther, only capable of contemplation and sensibility. He had given Lessing his friendship during the short year he had lived in his neighbourhood, and Lessing admits that he would find it hard to name another mortal whom he had learned to love so warmly in a year and a day.

Jerusalem had let him see a side of his character that was perhaps unknown to his many friends. They rarely met except *tête-à-tête*, and then the theme for conversation was readily found. No matter whence they started ; they soon found themselves engrossed in speculations on the sensations, the domain of the beautiful, the purpose of life, and so forth. These conversations led Jerusalem to develop his ideas into essays, and it is these remains of his clear understanding that Lessing wished to present to a world that had not hitherto looked on Jerusalem as an author, which indeed Lessing now first made him. 'His course was brief, his pace rapid. Still, to live long is not to live much. And if only to think much is to live long, then his years were only too few for us.' Lessing says that their conversations by no means ended in agreement : Jerusalem inclined to Mendelssohn's empirical philosophy that Lessing was fast outstripping ; but what mattered that ? It was none the less the lively suggestive intercourse of mind with mind. 'The pleasure of a chase is ever worth more than the booty, and variance that merely ensues because each seizes truth from another point, is concord in the essential and the richest source of mutual regard upon which alone men can build a friendship.'

Early in July the Duke was struck down with apoplexy, and the Prince returned to Brunswick. He sent for Lessing and made him verbally the same offers as he had made him through the councillor : to increase his salary by two hundred thalers, to excuse him repayment of the money he had drawn in advance, to place from eight hundred to one thousand thalers immediately at his disposal, with a house near the library, to be vacant next Michaelmas. The

Prince further hinted that the serious illness of the reigning Duke might lead to other and yet more advantageous changes for Lessing. In the meantime the Duke bestowed on him the title of Hofrath.

'What will perhaps astound you most,' Lessing wrote to Frau König, 'is, that I could not avoid accepting the Hofrath title ; that I did not seek it you are surely convinced, as you know me, and also that I told the Prince pretty plainly how little I cared about it ; but I had to fear giving the old man offence.'

Frau König, during this time, had been putting her affairs in order. She had a weary mass of papers to go through, and wished her Lessing were there to aid her. Did he not once, to oblige her, entertain an old woman four mortal hours, and would he refuse this favour to his Eva ? Their correspondence throughout this year had been brisk. The letters were short and dealt chiefly with their own affairs, but now that union seemed really near and possible, verbal communication was desirable. Lessing therefore, in August, paid a flying visit to Hamburg. After his return he wrote yet more frequently. He complains of the house destined for him. It is small and old-fashioned : would Frau König like him to look out for a newer one in the town ? By no means, she replies ; she will soon make the house look nice and comfortable, and has no intention of living in the town, far from the library and without the possibility of looking in on Lessing at all hours. Then Lessing had to hire a cook ; they correspond about her wages ; about the carriage that was to carry Frau König, Lessing, and four children back from Hamburg ; how many horses they will need, and so forth. In the midst of these preparations came an offer from the Palatine,

Charles Theodore, of a yearly pension of a hundred
louis d'or, if Lessing would take part in labours
for the Academy of Sciences recently founded,
and of which the Palatine sent him a diploma of
membership. The obligations the post imposed
would, he was assured, be trifling. With the permission of the Duke and Prince, Lessing accepted
the offer. The Palatine then held forth yet more
tempting terms. Lessing deferred taking any further
steps just then ; his chief desire now was to hasten
his marriage. His debts, that had pressed on him like a
nightmare, were at length discharged, and he hoped
to be able not only to live at ease, but to help his mother
and sister more efficiently. He seemed suddenly
relieved from all material cares. If only life and
health were granted him, he saw no cause to feel
uneasy for the future. About his health he seems
to have felt anxiety ; for the first time in his experience
he ardently craved for longer life, or else, as he told
Frau König, he will have put her to inconvenience
and expense for nothing. He begged her to make all
arrangements that their wedding may be of the most
private character, for he must confess he had not even
bought a new coat for the occasion. He told Karl he
meant to marry, but not when, and requested to be
spared Epithalamiums : his brother need not harness
either his own or others' Pegasus. He had not even
gone through the formality of asking his mother's permission.

On October 8 the marriage was quietly celebrated near Hamburg, at the country house of one
of Frau König's friends. A few days after Lessing
took home his wife to Wolfenbüttel he wrote
announcing the event, to Karl : ' I have much to tell
you about my marriage, and ought to tell it. You

know my wife, although you may hardly remember her, as you only saw her once. If I assure you that I have ever held her to be the only woman with whom I should venture to live, you will then believe that she possesses all I seek in a wife. If I am therefore not happy with her, I should certainly have been more unhappy with every other. In brief, come to us next summer and see.'

# CHAPTER XVII.

## MARRIED LIFE.

### (1776–1778. AGED 47–49.)

*' Here was a man familiar with fair heights*
*That poets climb. Upon his peace the tears*
*And troubles of our race deep inroads made,*
*Yet life was sweet to him ; he kept his heart*
*At home. Who saw his wife might well have thought,*
*" God loves this man. He chose a wife for him—*
*The true one !"*—J. INGELOW.

FOR once Lessing's anticipations were not to be disappointed : he was most happy in his married life. But
even here the ill star that presided over his lot worked
sorrow only too soon. This, however, was still
hidden in the future, and all looked bright and smiling when he brought home his wife and her four
children to the old-fashioned little house that is still
occupied by the Wolfenbüttel librarians. A calm
happy time dawned. In the society of his beloved
wife, Lessing regained his old cheerfulness and
elasticity of spirit. Even his productive vein, that
had suffered under the past years of oppressive waiting, showed signs of revival. He was still busy with
the issue of his 'Contributions,' but he felt the power
for better things return. Once more, after his old
habit, he made plan upon plan, and spoke of this col-
lation as tiresome, thankless, time-frittering work.
He who till now had been a restless nomad settled

down to the most homely domesticity. ' People of our
sort,' he tells Karl, who married about the same time,
' can only become good house-fathers, orderly and
exact, when they become so to please others.' And in
quite fatherly fashion Lessing begs his brother to buy
him various articles of finery for his womenkind,
feathers, flowers, and silks. All his letters breathe a
spirit of content and peace that had been too long
absent. He urged his friends to visit him and witness
his happiness with their own eyes. Mendelssohn
accepted the invitation, and wrote :

' You seem to me now to be in a calmer, more contented mood, that harmonizes far better with my
mode of thought than that clever but almost bitter
humour that I have noticed in you for some years. I
did not feel strong enough to repress the sallies of
that humour, but I heartily wished that time and circumstances and your own reason might conquer it.
It seems to me that all I hear from you and see confirms me in the pleasant thought that my wish is now
fulfilled. In this better frame of mind I must needs
speak to you, if only to teach me what has most led
to this pacification : the wife or freemasonry ? Better
reason or riper years ?'

Unquestionably the wife, would have been
Lessing's reply, and with truth. The influence of
Frau König upon Lessing's unquiet fiery temperament was most beneficial and salutary. The pictures
preserved to us of his interior are charming, and present him in a most lovable light. In the spring of
1777, the historian Spittler spent three weeks studying in the Wolfenbüttel library. He ever after recalled them as three of the happiest and most instructive in his life, on account of the personal intercourse

he enjoyed with Lessing, who allowed him not only free admission to the library, but, what Spittler prized far more, free access to his house, so that he was in daily intercourse with him, and could listen to the treasures of wisdom and knowledge which Lessing ungrudgingly poured forth in private life. Lessing's conversation was pre-eminently suggestive and stimulating. He spoke fluently and well, in a penetrating, agreeable baritone voice. He never monopolized the conversation, but was always attentive to draw others into its flow ; and though he could not disguise his ample and versatile learning, his talk in the social circle was never pedantic or beyond the comprehension of all his hearers. He detested the schoolmen who wanted to draw him into a corner and discuss *au fond* pedantic trivialities. In writing he could be the minute scholar as well as any of them, but in the circle of his home or friends he was the genial host. His easy and graceful deportment nowise betrayed the sedentary bookworm. He was also distinguished from the typical German man of letters in his uniformly neat dress, always made with quiet elegance and attention to fashion. There was something exceedingly characteristic in all he said or did. His manner was decided and firm, but free from the slightest taint of arrogance. A winning benevolence shone out of his deep blue eyes, eyes that were his greatest beauty, whether they danced with merriment, flashed with anger, or looked boldly out into the world. It was a joke among his friends, that everything Lessing did was idiosyncratic and original, from his tread to his knock at the door. He several times tested this, trying to imitate that of Mendelssohn, of Nicolai, of his brother : it was no use. Even if he

was not expected his friends would exclaim, There
comes Lessing ! His house was appointed with the
same unostentatious elegance that appeared in his
dress. Disorder and dirt were his enemies ; and, profoundly learned man as he was, his study did not
show the outward untidy signs, so often held *de
rigueur*. It was his habit to rise about six and work
in his study for some hours, and only when writing
did he allow himself to sit crookedly or to wear a
loose coat. In due time he would go and wake the
children. If he had no duties at the library he would
write till dinner ; if he had, he would dress carefully
after breakfast and repair to his post. The dinner
hour was half-past twelve, and it rarely happened but
Lessing brought in some unexpected guests who had
been visiting the library or the librarian, for he had
become a celebrity, and people travelled far and wide
to speak to him or see him. ' Never mind if there is
not enough to eat,' he would say to his wife when
such invasions exceeded bounds, ' make up with bacon
and eggs.' And his wife, who was as hospitable as he,
invariably gave the visitors a hearty welcome, and
placed such fare before them as lay in her power ;
while the guests knew only too well that the best
food of all was that mental one which Lessing
liberally supplied. At table he was especially talk-
ative and agreeable. It was a rule with him that the
food partaken of should not be criticized, nor passing
annoyances form the theme of discourse. Cheerful
talk he held the best condiment to a meal, and his
jokes and heartiest laughter were reserved for home.
The afternoon he commonly devoted to recreation
and a short walk. At nine a frugal supper was served,
at which again visitors were often present. These

were usually more intimate friends, with whom
Lessing would afterwards play a game of his favourite
chess, sucking an empty pipe if smokers were present,
to appear sociable. He never smoked himself, and
had only done so once, when at school in Meissen,
and then only because it was forbidden. Between ten
and eleven he went to bed, enjoying a deep sleep that
never forsook him, and which, according to his account,
was always dreamless. Though naturally of a passionate disposition, he controlled himself strictly, and
it was rarely that his passion obtained the mastery,
but when it did his outbreaks were furious. To his
servants he was the most considerate of masters, always
fearing lest they should be doing too much. To his
children he was the most devoted of stepfathers. He
watched with tender care over their moral and intellectual training, striving ever to impress upon them
that they could never learn too much or too thoroughly,
' for one does not learn for this world alone.' Courage
and uncompromising truth were the virtues he chiefly
sought to impress upon the boys, and he never re-
sorted to corporal punishments except twice, when
they had lied and been cowardly. He would join as
warmly in their play as in their lessons, even the most
fatiguing games found him unwearied.

Unlimited generosity was a fundamental trait of
Lessing's character. He never walked without stray
coins for beggars in his pockets. It is said that at
Breslau these coins were often not only silver but
gold. At the time a friend warned him against such
reckless expenditure, and bade him think of his old
age. 'I hope,' he replied, 'I shall never lack money
so long as I have these three fingers, and it does not
lack here,' pointing to his forehead. When it was re-

presented to him that not all beggars deserved support, he answered, 'Ah God, if we also only received what we deserve, how much should we get?' To be in need was a passport to his interest; to be assailed, a challenge to his chivalry. He would carry the defence of the persecuted to the extent of sophistry; his greatest enemy was safe from him if in grief or under oppression. 'Whom all attack I leave in peace,' he would say. It cut him to the heart when he could not fulfil to the uttermost all the demands from Camenz. It was especially from his sister that he had to hear unjust reproaches on this theme, and his gentle replies to these unfair accusations reveal the warmth and goodness of his heart. He often had poor scholars staying with him for months, and several of his *protégés* did not merit the sacrifices he made for them. He was no respecter of persons; he spoke as candidly with the Hereditary Prince as with the beggar; and it was this independent, assured tone, so far removed from the cringing flattery usual at the petty courts of the period, that puzzled the Prince and slightly alienated him. And according to all testimony, if there was one person in Lessing's house who exceeded him in charity, activity, and serene amiability, it was Lessing's wife.

Not long after their marriage Lessing saw himself obliged to make an excursion to Mannheim, in accordance with the terms of his pension, and in order to examine various attractive offers that reached him from that place. Frau Lessing accompanied him. She was decidedly inimical to his rashly exchanging the quiet learned solitude of Wolfenbüttel for any turbulent court life, but agreed with him that it was right he should be alive to his material interests.

From the first Lessing had suspected that the real object of the Palatine's anxiety to attract him concerned the theatre, for which it was desired to have the prestige of his name, and with the theatre Lessing was determined to have no more dealings. He keenly recalled his Hamburg experiences, and quailed at the thought. It was a craze at that epoch among the little courts of Germany, to be the centres of an intellectual regeneration, and, conformably to the ideas propagated by Lessing, the foundation of a national theatre was deemed the great work reserved for the century. Mannheim also wished to be the home of this national theatre, and the Palatine desired that Lessing should organize it. But he dared not ask him directly, as Lessing had too openly expressed his aversion to such undertakings. He was therefore summoned to attend on affairs of the Academy, and when there more distinct propositions were made to him. He declined the office of dramaturgist, but consented to assist with advice in the engagement of actors, also to assist in the project of founding a school for the histrionic art. He had not much confidence in the whole scheme ; he estimated it correctly as a manoeuvre on the part of the Prime Minister to please his master, and that he wished for a famous man like Lessing as his tool. He was therefore puzzled on his return what to write to Karl about Mannheim.

‘ Certain things cannot be spoken of. Yes, spoken of they may be, but not written. One either writes too much or too little, if one has not oneself arrived at a conclusion. In speaking, one can correct oneself every moment ; this cannot be in writing. But so much I may tell you in confidence. Thus far the

Mannheim journey strengthens my experience that the German theatre is always vexatious to me ; that I cannot meddle with it, no matter how little, without annoyance and expense.

' And yet you take it amiss that I prefer throwing myself into theology ? Certainly, if theology rewards one at last as theology has done ! Well, so be it : I should complain of that much less, because it is certainly true that in my theological teazing or evil savouring, whichever you like to call it, I am more concerned about sound reason than about theology : and I only prefer the old orthodox theology, which is tolerant at bottom, because the former is at open warfare with sound reason, and the latter would prefer to bribe it. I make peace with my avowed enemies, so that I may be better on my guard against my secret ones.'

Lessing had just issued another ' Contribution,' in which he had inserted five more extracts from the MS. of Reimarus, under the title of ' Wolfenbüttel Fragments,' and he waited, not without a certain grave amusement, to see how the clergy would receive these more outspoken attacks. They kept so quiet at first, that two months after the publication, he was able to write :

' The silence of the theologians concerning the " Fragments" of my Anonymous writer strengthens the good opinion I have always entertained of them. With due care one can write what one likes as far as they are concerned. Not that which you take away from them, but that which you wish to give, angers them ; and with reason. For if the world is to be kept going with falsehoods, then the old ones, already current, are just as good as the new.'

During this time a faction had been forming
against Lessing in Mannheim, and the Minister von
Hompesch, having extracted some valuable advice
and help from him, cast about to avoid acquitting
his obligations. He pretended that in renouncing
the post of dramaturgist Lessing had renounced his
pension as well, and he wrote to him to this effect.
Lessing replied to von Hompesch with one of his
candid unvarnished epistles, in which he put his base
deception pretty plainly before him, and begged him
to rest assured that the moment his master or he circulated any erroneous statements concerning him, he
should publicly refute them out of their own mouths.
The Palatine and his minister found themselves constrained to pocket this letter, whose tenor can have
been little familiar to them. They paid Lessing the
costs of his journey, presented him with thirty copper
medallions of all the Palatines, and kept silence
about a matter so little to their credit. Consequently
Lessing did the same. Only in his private letters is
seen what he thought of the affair.

'The idea of a German national theatre is all
vanity. At least in Mannheim they never connected
any other idea with it than that a German national
theatre should be a theatre in which none but natives
should act. How thankful I am that I have quite a
different kind of comedy which I can have acted for
me as often as I please!

'With regard to the national theatre, you should
have remembered what Christ said of the false pro-
phets who would personate Him towards the end of
time : "Then if any man shall say unto you, Lo, here
is He, or there, believe it not." If they shall say unto
you, Lo, he is in Vienna, believe it not. Lo, he is in

the Palatinate, go not thither. If only I had recalled that text in time, I should still have had to go to Mannheim. This is all I can or care to tell you about the affair, with which I would rather have had nothing to do.'

Yet neither this temporary annoyance, nor the loss of his aged mother, which he felt deeply, could long weigh upon Lessing, who was now so happy and content within his own four walls. Late in the year Mendelssohn paid his promised visit. It is recorded that so strong was the prevailing feeling against Jews, that even the sage Moses ever felt himself as belonging to a proscribed class, and on his first introduction to Frau Lessing he timidly presented her with a bouquet of flowers as a peace-offering, to soften the bad impression of his beard and gaberdine. He soon saw that such precautions were not needed towards a woman as large-minded as Lessing himself. Mendelssohn was a cherished guest, and he on his part was delighted to witness his friend's well-being. When he departed he took back Lessing's eldest stepson, who wished to enter the Prussian military service. On Christmas Eve, not long after their departure, Frau Lessing gave birth to a son, who died within a few hours.

To Eschenburg, who had expressed his sympathy, Lessing wrote :

‘ January 3, 1778.

‘ I seize the moment when my wife lies unconscious, to thank you for your kind sympathy. My joy was only short. And I was so unwilling to lose him, this son, for he had so much sense, so much sense. Do not think that the few hours of my fatherhood have already turned me into such an ape of a father.

I know what I say. Was it not sense that he had himself drawn into the world with iron forceps? That he soon scented evil? Was it not sense that he seized the first opportunity to get away again? True, the little headstrong boy is dragging away his mother also. For yet there is little hope that I shall keep her  I wanted for once to be as well off as other people. It has ill agreed with me.'

Two days after, Frau Lessing's condition was still critical.

'Wolfenbüttel: January 5, 1778.

'My dear Brother,

'Pity me that this time I have such a valid reason for not having written to you during the time you were so kind to my stepson. I have just lived through the saddest fortnight I ever had. I was in danger of losing my wife, a loss which would have much embittered the remainder of my days. She was confined, and made me the father of a pretty boy, who was healthy and sound. But he only remained so four-and-twenty hours, and afterwards succumbed to the cruel way in which he was drawn into the world. Or perhaps he thought little of the meal to which he had been so forcibly invited, and crept away again of his own accord. In short, I hardly know that I have been a father: the joy was so short, and the sorrow was so overborne by the greatest anxiety. For the mother lay unconscious for fully nine or ten days, and every day and every night they had to send me away a few times from her bed, telling me I was making the last moments harder for her, for she knew me for all her unconsciousness. At last the illness has suddenly taken a turn, and since three days I have the surest hope that I shall this time keep her whose society

becomes more and more indispensable to me, even in
her present state.'

Eschenburg calls his letter tragical, and sincerely
trusts he can send better news.

' I cannot remember what that tragical letter can
have been that I am supposed to have written you.
I am very much ashamed if it betrayed signs of
despair ; also my fault is not despair, but rather
thoughtlessness, which only at times expresses itself
somewhat bitterly and misanthropically. My friends
must just continue to bear with me as I am. The
hopes for the recovery of my wife have sunk again
since the last few days, and really now I have only
the hope of soon being able to hope again.'

But three days after he has to announce the worst.
He does so with a laconicism that betrays his desolation:

' My wife is dead ! and I have now gone through
this experience also. I am glad that many more such
experiences cannot be in store for me, and feel quite
relieved.'

'What a sad messenger to my stepson I must
make you,' he writes to Karl. ' His good mother, my
wife, is dead. Unquestionably I had not deserved
such happiness. If you had known her ! But it is
said to be only self-praise to laud one's wife. Well,
then, I will say nothing about her ; but if only you
had known her ! You will, I fear, never see me as our
friend Moses found me ; so content, so peaceful within
my four walls.'

On the day Lessing wrote this his wife had been
borne to the grave, and a vicious attack on his ' Fragments,' written by Pastor Goeze, had been put into
his hands.

'Yesterday morning,' he writes to Eschenburg (January 14), 'the last of my wife was completely taken from me. If I could buy with one half of the days yet remaining to me the happiness of spending the other half in the company of this woman, how gladly would I do it! But that may not be, and I must begin anew to loiter along my path alone. A good store of literary laudanum and theological diver-. sions will help me to survive passably from one day to another.'

And he kept his word. He threw himself with the whole weight of his bereavement into the theological arena. He was ready to play at that comedy he had congratulated himself upon being able always to have performed for his own benefit whenever he felt so disposed. Indifferent to life, regardless of any storm he might raise, so long as it deadened the intensity of his grief while advancing the cause of humanity, Lessing girded himself for a struggle, whose results made him to be named, not inaptly, the Luther of his time, and verified Cardan's prophecy that a great change in religion would take place in the eighteenth century. He was able to say with his favourite Bayle, whom in some mental characteristics he so much resembled : 'J'aurais cru qu'une querelle avec les théologiens me chagrinerait, mais j'éprouve par expérience qu'elle me sert d'amusement dans la solitude à quoi je me suis réduit.'

# CHAPTER XVIII.

## THE 'WOLFENBÜTTEL FRAGMENTS.'

### (1778.)

*'Die Wahrheit, die man fühlt, nicht die der Priester, sehn
Und für uns sehen will, freimüthig nachzugehn.'*—S. HENZI.

*'Unser Zeitalter ist das Zeitalter der Kritik, der sich alles unterwerfen
muss. Religion durch ihre Heiligkeit, und Gesetzgebung durch ihre Ma-
jestät, wollen sich gemeiniglich derselben entziehen. Aber alsdann erregen
sie gerechten Verdacht wider sich, und können auf unverstellte Achtung
nicht Anspruch machen, die die Vernunft nur demjenigen bewilligt, was
ihre freie und öffentliche Prüfung hat aushalten können.'*—KANT.

FOUR years had elapsed since the publication of the
first 'Wolfenbüttel Fragment,' claiming the benefit of
toleration for Freethinkers equally with Jews, Turks,
and Heathens. The thesis thus propounded had
attracted no notice. The orthodox did not hold themselves attacked, and the Berlin rationalists, with Nicolai
at their head, comprehended no larger and more
enlightened form of toleration than the toleration of
indifference. But it was this very indifference that
was hateful to Lessing. He did not believe in stagnation; he saw how in the Nicolai coterie it had
engendered a conceit and spiritual arrogance, rivalling
those of the theologians. The two current tendencies
of theologic thought, the intellectual and the pietistic,
were rapidly ossifying, and what avenue was left for
truth? To rouse both parties, Lessing put forward

yet bolder extracts from the MSS. of Reimarus, not, as he explained, because they expressed his own views, but because he felt assured that they must excite a salutary discussion. In publishing them he did no more than what Leibnitz, whom he so much resembled, approved in the evening of his life, when he urged the publication of Bodin's '*Heptaplomeres*,' which, like the MSS. of Reimarus, had been long familiar to a select circle. That truth should be a common possession, was another principle which Lessing held with Leibnitz, as he himself explains:

'In his search for truth Leibnitz was never influenced by received opinions. Firmly convinced that no opinion could possibly have been received which was not true from some point of view, and in a certain sense, he was well content to turn and twist this opinion about till he succeeded in rendering this point of view visible, this certain sense comprehensible. He struck fire from flint, but he did not hide his fire in flint.'

'The Anonymous writer,' says Lessing, 'was so cautious, that he did not wish to vex anyone with truth, and I—I do not believe in the least in such vexation, firmly convinced that it is not the abstract truth brought forward for examination, but only truth proposed to be reduced to immediate practice, which is capable of exciting vehement religious passion in the multitude. The Anonymous was so discreet a man that he did not wish to make either himself or others unhappy by premature utterances, and I—I hazard my own safety like a madman, because I am of opinion that utterances, if they only have foundation, never come too early for the human race. My Anonymous, who wrote I know not when, believed that the times must become more enlightened before he could openly preach what he held truth ; while I believe that the times are enlightened enough at least to examine whether that which he held truth is really so.'

' I drew the Anonymous into the world, not against his wishes, I presume, but certainly without his wish.'

The five 'Fragments' which Lessing inserted in his 'Contributions' (1777) had the following titles : 'The pulpit denunciations of rationalism ; ' 'The impossibility of a revelation to which all men could accord solid faith ; ' 'The passage of the Israelites through the Red Sea ; ' 'That the books of the Old Testament were not written to reveal a religion ; ' and ' Concerning the accounts of the Resurrection.' The mere headings evince that these papers are negative, and regard all positive creeds as human devices. The Anonymous writer defended reason, man's noblest possession, against the divines who decry it as a weak, fallacious guide, and show their sophistry in disparaging the very weapon which they themselves are compelled to employ in their own arguments. He further demonstrated the untenability of the Revelation theory, criticized the Old Testament as bearing no stamp of divine authorship, exposed its discrepancies and the legendary character of the Mosaic miracles.

The ' Wolfenbüttel Fragments ' are no longer read. Modern theological criticism has far outstripped their crude speculations, belonging to the mechanical school of Deism, that held miracles as sheer impostures. Exegetical examination was unknown ; a narrative was either false or true, wilfully perverted or dictated by Heaven. Written before the growth of myth was

A A

understood or had been scientifically investigated, they were imbued with that early spirit of rationalism, which in its earnest wish to be useful, ceased to be reasonable, and grew fanatically intolerant, indiscriminately condemning the past as worthless and rotten. The rationalist could see in the adherents of orthodoxy only the blind followers of a cunning imposture ; while these based their beliefs upon a rigid theory of inspiration. 'The child-dream of a dead universe, governed by an absent God,' was then in its heyday. On the other hand the historical value of the 'Fragments' is unquestionable. Enlightenment owes them vast obligations, since their publication gave birth to a controversy whose like had not agitated Protestantism since the Reformation.

Reimarus was a forerunner of David Strauss ; he wrought in the spirit of Wolff's philosophy, as Strauss in that of Hegel. The relative nature of truth was as yet unrecognized, as well as the gradual adaptation of truth to the requirement of every age. The spirit of inquiry that begot the Reformation was a breath of it ; Bodin preached it in his '*République ;*' but the minds of men were unprepared for it. In Lessing's day it was floating in the air ; he seized it and gave it written shape. He had the honesty that places a man above the factions of creeds, and a good portion of the personal indifference to odium needed by the innovator. In the notes—'Hints,' he names them—with which he accompanied his 'Fragments,' he seeks to establish the legitimacy of free discussion on controversial themes. Until our time, he contends, religion had been as ill attacked as defended : the author of the 'Fragments' seemed to him to approach the ideal of a worthy adversary. But in the same sentence he expresses a wish that a man may arise who will no less approach the ideal of a defender of religion.

Lessing has been reproached for hiding his opinions. The classifiers of human minds have been unable to force him into any of their categories, and it was their utter misunderstanding of his purpose that furnished for Lessing the amusing element in the discussions excited by the publication of the 'Fragments.' He was not afraid of the issue. Religion was to him apart from theology, it consisted in feeling. This was his fundamental axiom. He carefully distinguishes between Christians and theologians, saying : ' How do this man's hypotheses and explanations and proofs concern the Christian ? The Christianity which is so true, in which he feels himself so happy, cannot be a fiction, for it is here. When the paralyzed man feels the beneficial shocks of the electric spark, what does it concern him whether Nollet or Franklin is right, or whether both are wrong ?' He turned against the conservatives, whose belief in the letter closed their minds against the theory which Lessing, with advanced insight, called to his aid : he turned against the innovators whose reform meant destruction. 'Dirty water,' says Reimarus, ' ought not to be poured out before you have clean.' ' But,' retorts Lessing, ' he who does not pour out the dirty water can never have clean.' For the author of the 'Fragments' Christianity as a positive religion fell with its props of miracle, revelation, and fulfilment of prophecy. Not so for Lessing. He only inferred that the props were vain. Such arguments might confound the theologian, but they did not touch the simple Christian. The weight of Lessing's intellect leaned to untrammelled individual thought, and he regarded those who followed Reimarus, and the orthodox, as the two extremes ; the neologians holding the central place. He could sympathize with all three parties and with none. This was extremely puzzling to his contemporaries. His own thoughts are reflected in some MS. notes published post-humously. Preparing to study the manner in which the Christian religion had been founded and spread, he wrote : ' Undertake this investigation as an honest man,' I say to myself: ' look everywhere with your own eyes, distort nothing, embellish nothing. As the conclusions follow, so let them follow : do not check their course, do not influence it.'

For some little time the theologians were silent. Then a storm of abuse burst upon the editor, or, as some asserted, the disguised author of the ' Fragments.' Controversial attacks poured from the press, and Lessing was plunged into a vortex of dispute. These tracts are now happily consigned to the oblivion that awaits polemics, their tenor can only be inferred from Lessing's answers. The kernel of all his arguments is the relation between the Bible and Christianity. But his adversaries did not place themselves on his platform. They admitted or ignored the point in question—the validity of the historical foundations—and only occupied themselves with the danger to faith involved in the investigation. Thus they laid themselves open to the vigorous dialectics of Lessing, who, insensibly substituting himself in the place of his author, ended by entering the lists in person. In replying to his earliest opponents, he still entrenched himself behind his editorial capacity. Schumann, of Hanover, had controverted him, but with politeness, and Lessing replied without a trace of irritation or ill-will. Schumann had laid down that only those who had read everything ever written on the Bible, and who knew the history and language of all nations, and possessed keen insight and logical faculty, could judge of the Bible. Since that was possible to very few, Schumann refers to the fulfilled prophecies of the Old Testament, and the miracles of the New, as proof of the Spirit and Power spoken of by Paul and Origen.

'Sir,' says Lessing, in an introductory note to his tract, 'Concerning the Proof of Spirit and Power,' 'Sir, who could desire more to read your new work than I ? I hunger after conviction so much, that, like Erisichthon, I swallow all that only looks like nourishment. If you do the same with this sheet, we are the right sort of men for each other. I am, with the regard that one inquirer after truth never ceases to hold for another, yours, etc.'

Then follows a closely argued reply to Schumann's strictures, whose purport is this : Miracles of which I am an eye-witness are to be distinguished from those transmitted on historical testimony. If I had been a contemporary of Christ and an eye-witness of His miracles, I might have yielded my reason captive ; but I hear of these by tradition, and though no one doubts that the accounts of these prophecies and miracles are as trustworthy as historical facts can be, yet these are always regarded as not demonstrable after long lapses of time. If historical truth cannot be demonstrated, it follows that nothing can be demonstrated through historical truth. Why, therefore, should undemonstrated truths claim to be believed as demonstrated, and why should long use give them a right to be unconditionally credited ? If even the miracles could be proved incontestably from history, such proof must still partake of the shifting nature of historical data, and we should not be justified in deducing a conclusion that lies out of the domain of history. Historical truths have no bearing beyond the domain of established fact. We all believe that Alexander lived, and conquered half Asia ; but who upon this would build up a belief of great and far-spreading import, in consequence of which he would deny every other fact that in the least clashes with this ? For might not the whole history of Alexander prove as fabulous, and be based on a mere poem, as was the ten years' siege of Troy ? Thus, if the resurrection of Christ were proved, does it follow thence that we are obliged to believe Him to be the Son of God, if this idea is contrary to all the fundamental ideas we hold on the Divine essence ? Would not this be passing from historical to metaphysical proof, a vitiating of the whole process, a sort of paralogism as foreseen by Aristotle, ($\mu\epsilon\tau\acute{a}\beta a\sigma\iota s$ $\epsilon\acute{\iota}s$ $\acute{a}\lambda\lambda o$ $\gamma\acute{\epsilon}\nu os$)? If the further reply be attempted, that these matters must be more than historically certain, because attested by inspired historians who cannot err, I answer that it is unfortunately only historically certain that these historians were inspired. 'And this is the ugly wide ditch I cannot jump as often and as earnestly as I have tried. If some one can help me over let him do it, I beg him, I implore him.'

Lessing thus went further than his Anonymous author ; for not content with shaking the historical proof, he contended that, this proof established, there followed no reason for believing what was contrary to reason.

This pamphlet was followed by a lively dialogue

'The Testament of John,' quite in the spirit of Lucian. Lessing had ended the preceding pamphlet with a wish that all who were separated intellectually by the Gospel of St. John might be united by his Testament, apocryphal it is true, but none the less divine. He refers to the touching legend preserved by Jerome, how the aged John, spent by years, could repeat only the simple words, 'Children, love one another;' and when charged with monotony, insisted that 'Such was the precept of the Lord, and he who followed this did enough.' In the dialogue his adversary says he has never heard of a Testament of John, and can find it in no learned catalogue. 'Must everything then be a book? The last will of John, the last remarkable, often repeated words of the dying John, they can also be called a Testament, can they not? These words should be written in golden letters in every church; they contain the germ of all Christianity.' His opponent objects.

'Then Christian love is not Christian religion?' asks Lessing.

Yes and no, says his adversary: yes, if combined with the Christian dogmas; no, a useless and absurd incumbrance on the road to hell, if practised without this faith.

He: Why should they take the yoke of Christian love upon themselves, if the dogmas do not render it easy and meritorious?

I: Very true, we must let them run this risk. I only ask, however, is it wise of certain other people, on account of the risk these people run because of their Christian unchristian love, to deny them the name of Christian?

He: *Cui non competit definitio, non competit definitum.* Did I invent that?

I : But if we extended the definition a little? And
that in accordance with the saying of a certain good
man : 'Whoever is not against us is for us.' You
know him I suppose, this good man ?

He : Very well. It is the same who in another
place says : 'Whosoever is not with me, he is against
me.'

I : Ah so, yes certainly, that silences me. Oh, you
alone are the true Christian, and as well read in Scripture as the devil.'

This bitter conclusion reveals Lessing's rising
anger. Here, according to him, was the sum and substance of religion. But this was what the theologians
could not and would not allow.

An archdeacon of Wolfenbüttel had defended the
narratives of the resurrection against the Anonymous
writer. He neither mentioned Lessing by name nor
did he name himself, but he knew whom he was
attacking as well as Lessing knew who was attacking
him. To this apologist Lessing replied with a refutation called a *Duplik*. The main part consists of a
strictly critical discussion of all the discrepancies in
the Gospel narrative brought forward by the Anonymous writer. Lessing easily proved that his 'Neighbour,' as he calls him, had not advanced a single sound
argument. In the commencement Lessing's tone is
cool, but in the course of exposition it becomes more
and more excited. It angers him when his Anonymous writer is treated with lofty contempt, as an
ignoramus unfitted to take part in controversy : a taunt
which he knew well could be refuted by merely giving
his real name. The charge that the Anonymous
writer had wilfully blinded himself against truth
aroused Lessing's indignation. It is not possible, he

protests, that a man should wilfully, consciously deceive himself.

And he then speaks the famous words that have almost become identified with his name :

'Not the truth in whose possession a man is or believes himself to be, but the earnest efforts which he has made to attain truth, make the worth of the man. For it is not through the possession but through the search for truth that his powers are strengthened, in which alone his ever-growing perfection exists. Possession makes him calm, indolent, proud—

'If God held all truth in His right hand, and in His left the ever-living desire for truth, although with the condition that I should remain in error for ever, and if He said to me "Choose," I should humbly incline towards His left, and say, " Father, give ; pure truth is for Thee alone."'

He again insists that after a lapse of years we should not always investigate anew the foundations of our building. This lesson is conveyed under the guise of a parable about the temple of the Ephesian Diana. 'I praise what stands above the earth, not what lies hidden under the earth. Forgive me, dear architect, that I do not want to know any more about that than that it must be good and firm. For it bears and has borne so long. . . . Strange that men are so little content with that which they have before them. . . . When will people cease wishing to hang nothing less than eternity on a spider's web ! No scholastic dogmatism has inflicted wounds so deep on religion as historical exegetics are inflicting now.'

To the reproach that he might have employed his leisure better than by throwing this brand into the theological camp, Lessing replies :

'If I have not used my leisure to the best advantage, what matter? Who knows if I should not have
used it still worse with something else? It was at
least my intention to use it well. It was at least my
conviction that I could thus use it well. I leave it to
time to show what my openly expressed opinion shall
and can achieve. Perhaps, according to the laws of a
Higher Dispensation, the fire is to continue to
smoulder for a long while yet ; to irritate healthy
eyes by its smoke for some while still, before we can
enjoy both warmth and light together. If it is so, then
do Thou Eternal Fount of all Truth, who alone knowest
when and where it should pour forth its waters, forgive
a useless and officious servant. He desired to clear the
mud from Thy paths. If he has thrown away grains
of gold with it, yet Thy grains of gold cannot perish.
. . . And now one word about myself, and I conclude. I am well aware that my blood flows differently now that I end this *Duplik* than it did when
I began. . . . Shall I excuse myself? . . .
Promise to be more careful another time ?

'Can I do that? Can I promise? Yes, yes, I
promise never even to resolve to remain calm and
indifferent concerning certain things. If a man may
not grow warm and interested in matters he clearly
recognizes as distortions of reason and Scripture,
when and where may he grow so ? '

The interchange of polemics with Schumann and
the ' Neighbour' proved mere forerunners to the ultimate turmoil. Lessing's old Hamburg friend Goeze
became his chief adversary. Lessing's replies to him
have obtained not merely a fame equal to Pascal's
' Provincial Letters,' but a larger amount of popularity,
in virtue of the highly comic and dramatic character

that distinguishes Lessing's polemics, and renders them palatable to many to whom theological subtleties and patristic lore are wholly indifferent. They exceed in critical sagacity, forcible reasoning, and lucid pointed style, anything ever written even by Lessing; and authors would do well to follow the example of Coleridge, who wrote in the fly-leaf of his copy, 'Year after year I make a point of reperusing the *Kleine Schriften* as master-pieces of style and argument.'

After Lessing's removal to Wolfenbüttel, he had continued on friendly terms with Goeze, who highly lauded his work on Berengarius. They had also interchanged visits. But it unfortunately happened that Goeze had asked Lessing for an official favour—a mere trifle—at the time when he was devoured with anxiety about his wife. The matter escaped his attention. Goeze complained of this discourtesy in a newspaper, not naming Lessing except as the famous librarian of a famous library, who grudged to others what he used himself. On hearing this, Lessing intended to write an immediate letter of excuse, but neglected that also. Thereupon Goeze began furiously to attack the editor of the 'Fragments.' The first of these attacks reached Lessing as he sat beside the corpse of his wife, and it is to this that he refers in his letter to Eschenburg. It was almost a relief to the undaunted gladiator that a new adversary should have entered the arena, in wrestling against whom he could forget his own overwhelming sorrow.

Goeze at once put the matter on a personal footing; he denounced the 'Fragments' themselves as no modest scruples, but the rankest calumnies, and said he should tremble for his dying hour if he were responsible for bringing such essays to light, concluding with a wish that their editor would in future give the world better matter than poison from the library treasures which he was appointed to guard. Goeze was destined to feel the full weight of Lessing's zeal for truth. In him Lessing found the typical self-satisfied, dogmatic theologian, narrow, shallow, unscrupulous, bibliolatrous, addicted to the flesh-pots of Egypt under the hypocritical guise of philanthropy ; in short, the pastor as he ought not to be. Goeze was by no means the worst of Lessing's opponents, but he was the most outspoken ; moreover, in his way, complete and consistent, and as such attractive to Lessing, who loved a whole nature of whatever kind. In every respect a man who answered to Heine's cynical definition : ' *Es sind in Deutschland die Theologen die dem lieben Gott ein Ende machen—on n'est jamais trahi que par les siens.*' Never did Lessing write so brilliantly, argue so closely, sally so humorously, as during his brief but rapid interchange of tracts with Goeze.

The prologue to 'the comedy' consists of a ' Parable,' in which religion is compared to the palace which a wise king had built of a peculiar architecture that fitted it for a variety of requirements. About this structure a foolish strife was carried on, chiefly by so-called connoisseurs, as to the original ground plans, various old drafts existed though their meaning was lost, and which were therefore explained according to the pleasure of each of these self-constituted critics. Once upon a time the watchmen of the palace cried Fire ! and what did these critics do ? Help to extinguish it ? Oh no, each ran and seized his own plan to decide which part of the palace

was the most essential, and which they should therefore save. They squabbled and wrangled over this, so
that the whole palace would have been consumed, but
happily its safety did not depend on them, for it was
no fire at all. The watchmen had been frightened by
the Northern Lights.

The interpretation is easy. The parable shows
the distinction between the essence and the historical
form of Christianity; that religion exists independent of critical questions, and that it was not endangered by any publication save in the eyes of those
theologians who, instead of defending it, only thought
of defending their own cherished ideas. This parable
was accompanied by 'A Request,' addressed to
Goeze, an ironical but perfectly good-humoured letter.
Lessing engages the pastor to render justice to his
intentions as editor of the 'Fragments.' It begins
with a lively distinction between a pastor and a
librarian. The one is a shepherd who only values the
herbs that agree with his sheep, the other a botanist
who gathers with care all the plants hitherto un-
named by Linnaeus, regardless whether they be
poisonous or no. Thus with him, if he found aught
among his entrusted treasures that he believes unknown, he publishes it, indifferent whether one person
pronounces it important, another unimportant,
whether it edify or scandalize. Useful and hurtful are
as much relative terms as great and small. If Goeze
held it his duty to withhold what might offend the
least of his congregation, Lessing equally held it his
duty to bring all that had ever been written into the
great foundling hospital of print. Each acted according to his light, and neither had a right to upbraid
the other. His request on which he thinks he has a

right to insist, is that Goeze should make a declaration ' as good as voluntary,' in his next ' Voluntary
Contributions,' to the effect that he had explained a
passage of Lessing's in a way wholly at variance with
the context. The remark that even if sceptical objections against the Bible could not be removed, Religion would remain undisturbed, had been construed
by Goeze as an acknowledgment on Lessing's part
that the objections were unanswerable, and he is now
publicly to declare that he has since been undeceived
by Lessing.

While Lessing was engaged on these ' pacific
sheets,' as he names them, he received the last numbers of the ' Voluntary Contributions,' wherein Goeze
attacked him with a passionate acrimony which made
it manifest that no peaceful understanding could be
established between them. Lessing therefore wrote
his ' Farewell Letter,' wherein he abandoned the conciliatory tone and replied to Goeze's sledge hammer
comments with warmth. His mettle was aroused, his
soul on fire. What especially kindled his anger was
not so much Goeze's personal attack on himself, with
its venom, its merriment, and affected commiseration,
as the self-satisfied spiritual pride with which he
treated Lessing's Anonymous writer as a schoolboy
and a poltroon. He assures Goeze that if it were a
question of balancing man against man, this Anonymous personage was of such weight that in every
branch of learning seven Goezes would not counter-
balance that man's seventh part.

' You may believe this, Herr Pastor, on my word ;
and now my knightly farewell shall be brief. Write,
Herr Pastor, and let write as much as you can compass;
I shall write too. If I allow you to be right when

you are not right in the least matter concerning myself and my Anonymous, it will be because I can no longer hold a pen.'

He will not be decried as a man less favourably disposed than Goeze to the Lutheran Church ; in fact, he insists that he is better disposed, that he has imbibed more of Luther's spirit, that revolted against torpor and stagnation, than one who would fain pass off a tender regard for a lucrative office as holy zeal. Oh that he could have Luther to judge between them !

'Thou Luther, great man, ill understood, and by none so ill-understood as by the short-sighted and stiff-necked, who, with thy slippers in their hand, shuffle along the way thou hast prepared, vociferating or indifferent. Thou hast freed us from the yoke of tradition ; who will free us from the more intolerable yoke of the letter ? Who will bring us a Christianity at last such as thou wouldst teach now, such as Christ Himself would teach ? '

Lessing was pretty sure that the matter would not end here, that Goeze would never allow an opponent to have the last word, though he always took care to have the first, and that he would regard as an attack what Lessing had meant as a defence. He was not mistaken. Goeze's assaults followed fast and furious. He accused Lessing of having put forward his positions ' as mere axioms.' ' How can this be ? ' asks Lessing, ' since everyone knows that axioms are positions which must be accepted by all who can understand them.' He then defends his remarks under the heading ' Axiomata, if such there be in these matters.'

The letter, he says, is not the spirit, and the Bible is not religion. It follows that objections against the

letter and against the Bible are not also objections
against the spirit and against religion ; for the Bible
clearly contains more than belongs to religion, and it
is a mere hypothesis that this more must be equally
infallible. Besides, religion existed before there was
a Bible. Christianity existed before the Evangelists
and Apostles had written. Some time elapsed before
the first of them wrote, and a very considerable time
before the whole canon was completed. Therefore,
let what will depend on these writings, it is clearly
impossible that the whole truth of religion can rest
upon them. If there was a time when religion was
already widely spread, in which it had already capti-
vated many souls, and yet in which not one letter had
been written that has come down to us, then it must
be possible that everything which the Evangelists and
Apostles have written should be lost again, and the
religion which they taught might yet endure. Religion
is not true because the Evangelists and Apostles
taught it, but they taught it because it is true. The
written traditions must be explained out of their
innate truth, and no written traditions can give it
innate truth if it has none. To each of these propositions he appends elucidatory comments, pithy,
logical, and pointed.

He explains his standpoint, Goeze having accused
him of not expressing himself in accordance with the
language of the Theological Schools. ' I am an
amateur in theology and no theologian ; I have not
been forced to swear to any system. Nothing binds
me to speak other language than my own. I pity all
honest men who are not so fortunate as to be able to
say this of themselves. But these honest men must
not try to cast the rope that fastens them to the

manger about the horns of other honest men ; else my pity ceases, and I can only despise them.'

Lessing warns Goeze no longer to affect to believe that he who doubts a particular proof of a thing doubts the thing itself. Goeze attempts to prove not so much by syllogisms as by tests. But are these tests indisputable? and do we not move in an everlasting circle, if we attempt to prove the infallibility of a book by a passage from the same book, and the infallibility of the passage from the infallibility of the book?

Goeze had propounded the question, Would a trace of Christ's teaching have reached us, had the New Testament remained unwritten? 'God forbid that I should ever think so meanly of Christ's teaching,' exclaims Lessing, 'that I should venture to answer this question with No. No, I would not repeat this No, if an angel from heaven had prompted it ; much less when a Lutheran pastor would put it into my mouth. All that happens in the world leaves traces in the world, even if men cannot point them out at once ; and should Thy teaching only, Divine Friend of man, although Thou didst command that it should not be written, but preached, have effected nothing, nothing whatever, even had it been only preached, whence its origin might be recognized? Should Thy words not have become words of life, until transformed into dead letters? Are books the only way to enlighten and improve mankind? Is oral tradition nothing? And if oral tradition be subject to a thousand intentional and unintentional perversions, are not books subject to the same? Might not God, by the same display of His immediate power, have equally guarded oral traditions from perversion as we say He has guarded the books? Out on the man, Almighty God,

who would be a preacher of Thy word, and yet boldly
asserts that to attain Thy end, Thou hadst but the one
way which Thou wast pleased to make known to him !
Out upon the theologian who, except this one way
that he can see, flatly denies all other ways that he
does not see. Defend me, good God, from ever
becoming thus orthodox, that I may never become
thus presumptuous ! '

It is not in a spirit of parody, but in heartfelt
earnestness, that Lessing often sees himself obliged to
turn Goeze's words against himself. With all esteem
due to his merits, he must observe that his positions
are often most dangerous heterodoxy, or most malicious slander. ' He may choose which. Indeed, both
are at his service.' Goeze ' wonders ' Lessing can hold
this or that view. ' I do not even wonder that he
wonders. May Heaven long preserve us in the same
relations, he wondering and I not !' The answer to
Goeze's tenth and last refutation, Lessing frames in
the form of a dialogue, which he names ' Pulpit
dialogue, or a dialogue and no dialogue,' and which
is highly amusing to read. He feigns that Goeze is
preaching, and after the common homiletic fashion
putting questions, and that he, Lessing, is interrupt-
ing the speaker, who however does not consider himself interrupted, but talks on regardless whether their
words chime in or no. He is wound up and must run
down, so Lessing at last grows tired of talking any
longer to a deaf man.

Lessing promises a copy of this pamphlet to his
brother Karl.

' I am very glad my *Duplik* has pleased you. I
am delighted that you are beginning to enjoy the
*haut-comique* of polemics which make all other thea-

trical work shallow and watery to me. In a few days
you shall receive a pamphlet against Goeze, towards
whom I have placed myself in such a position that he
treats me as unchristian. But these are nothing but
the skirmishes of the light troops of my army; the
main forces are slowly marching on, and the first
serious encounter is my " New hypotheses concerning
the Evangelists, considered as merely human historians." I believe that I have written nothing more
thorough of its kind, and I may add, nothing more
suggestive. I sometimes wonder myself how naturally
everything follows from a single remark which I found
I had made without exactly knowing how.'

Lessing, so chary of self-praise, so rarely satisfied
with himself, was for once content, and justly so.
The essay to which he refers is a most remarkable
production, almost prophetic in its foreshadowing of
the results of modern research. The first authorities
in Germany recognize it as the germ whence sprung
the modern explanation of the origin of the synoptical
gospels. It was intended to have been an extensive
work, but was never finished. Only its outline of
sixty-eight paragraphs saw the light, but here again
Lessing's 'Fragments' became more suggestive than
the finished work of many another writer. He flung
forth truths irregularly. Everything about him looks
fragmentary, and yet withal he electrified his contemporaries and bridged the chasm between two ages.
His touch was regenerative, even if he only skimmed
a subject, and he had a faculty of shooting light into
unexpected regions till then held to be dull and
barren. He persisted that he did not care for theology, that he had been dragged into it by the hair of
his head ; but the result justifies the remark of Nicolai,

that he had always noticed in him an itch to come
to close quarters with the theologians. Among his
posthumous papers are drafts of half-finished theological essays, in part answers to his adversaries, in
part suggested by their assaults. If he seemed
rather an advocate for orthodoxy than for the
rationalism of the period, it was because he contended that the grosser the error the shorter the way
to truth. Of Rational Christianity he pertinently remarked that he never knew where Christianity left
off and reason began. The theologians deemed him a
Freethinker ; the Freethinkers held him a theologian.
While still a boy he had begun to doubt; not scof-
fingly, as was the fashion, but earnestly, religiously,
in the Tennysonian conviction that 'there lives more
faith in honest doubt than in half the creeds.' He
acknowledges that as a lad he grew the more sceptical the more decisively anyone wished to prove
Christianity ; while the more triumphantly and wantonly anyone essayed to tread it down, the more he
felt impelled to uphold it in his heart. Where was
the way out of this labyrinth ? His fragmentary
poem ' *Die Religion,*' dating from 1753, breathes the
same spirit of reverent doubt. With regard to a
future life, he ever maintained his inability to comprehend why a future life might not be awaited as calmly
as a future day. He was inimical to all futile and
unverifiable speculations, and this too was in accordance with his whole being. He has been aptly desig-
nated as the ' supreme reason of an age of reason.'

His prime effort was to simplify religion, to mark
the divergence between essential and eternal truths,
and dogmatic and historical externals, for whose
poetical symbolism he had full comprehension, but

which were too commonly confounded by the mass as equally essential and necessary. In a fragment entitled 'Bibliolatry,' and directed against Goeze, Lessing has modestly but firmly characterized his attitude towards the church and religion in an extract from the 'Ion' of Euripides, by significantly substituting the word Christ for Phœbus[1]:

$$\kappa\alpha\lambda\acute{o}\nu \ \gamma\epsilon \ \tau\grave{o}\nu \ \pi\acute{o}\nu o\nu, \ \mathring{\omega}$$
$$X\rho\iota\sigma\tau\grave{\epsilon}, \ \sigma o\grave{\iota} \ \pi\rho\grave{o} \ \delta\acute{o}\mu o\nu \ \lambda\alpha\tau\rho\epsilon\acute{u}\omega$$
$$T\acute{\iota}\mu\omega\nu \ \mu\alpha\nu\tau\epsilon\hat{\iota}o\nu \ \mathring{\epsilon}\delta\rho\alpha\nu.[1]$$

'These lines,' says Lessing, 'Euripides puts into the mouth of Ion, sweeping the steps before the temple of Apollo. I too am not busied in the temple, but about it. I too only sweep the steps up to the shrine which the holy priests of the inner temple are content to clear of dust. I too am proud of this mean labour, for I know best to whose honour I labour.'

He held it no inglorious task to sweep the threshold before the divine seat of pure religion, and neither Goeze nor his ilk should find him slacken in his ardour.

Lessing had not been mistaken in his estimate of Goeze's tactics. Every number of the latter's paper contained abusive articles, pretended replies to the 'Axiomata,' but quite beside the point. They were headed, 'Lessing's weakness exposed.' Lessing answered by eleven tracts, entitled 'Anti-Goeze, or compulsory contributions to the "Voluntary Contributions" of the Rev. Mr. Goeze,' each headed by a pithy motto taken from the Fathers, the first paper being accompanied by the wish that it might, D. V., be the

---

[1] 'In a worthy toil indeed, O Phœbus, I serve thee before thine house, honouring thy seat of oracles.'—Buckley's Translation.

last. Lessing speaks of these tracts as drolleries (*Schnurren*).

'And such drolleries Goeze shall certainly receive as often as he writes any nonsense against me or my Anonymous, in his " Voluntary Contributions." I am firmly resolved on this point, even if my "Anti-Goeze" becomes a regular weekly paper, as dull and useless as any that was ever written or read in Hamburg.'

*Katzbalgereien* he calls them in another place, and admits that all he has written in this matter as a combatant he would not have written as a teacher.

'Jerome said that the accusation of heresy (and how much more of irreligion!) was of that nature *in qua tolerantem esse, impietatis sit, non virtutis,* and yet I would rather be guilty of this impiety, than abstain from making light of a virtue which is none at all. Decorum, good taste, *savoir-vivre,* miserable virtues of our effeminate age! Varnish are ye and nothing more; but just as often the varnish of vice as the varnish of virtue. What do I care whether my representations have this varnish or not? It cannot increase their effect, and I do not wish that people should have to search long for the right light wherein to see my picture.'

The first 'Anti-Goeze' was by no means the last. These philippics followed rapidly one upon another, and well reflect the genius of the German nation, a learned nation for which religious enlightenment and liberty of thought take the rank occupied in other countries by political aspirations. To contest its rights to march freely in the paths of criticism, was to command it to renounce its genius. And it was a Lutheran pastor who ventured to interdict the free examination of tradition, and to cite Luther as his justification! The mere mention of Luther's name rouses Lessing.

'The true Lutheran does not wish to be defended by Luther's writings, but by Luther's spirit; and Luther's spirit absolutely demands that *no* man be hindered from advancing after his own manner towards the knowledge of truth. But *all* are hindered if *one* be forbidden from imparting his progress to others. Reverend Sir, if you cause our Lutheran pastors to become our Popes, to prescribe to us where we must stop in our investigation of Scripture; to place limits to our investigation, and to the publication of our results: then I am the first to exchange these popelets for the Pope. And it is to be hoped many think as resolutely, even if they do not speak as openly. Now, Revd. Sir, pound on, and goad as many Protestants as possible back into the bosom of the Catholic Church. Such a Lutheran zealot can but please the Catholics. You are as admirable a politician as a theologian!'

Those on the other hand whom it does not scare into Catholicism, the clerical system of inspiration drives into Naturalism, as with the Anonymous. Lessing begs Goeze not to go blustering thus thoughtlessly. God knows he has no objections that he and all the school rectors of Lower Saxony should take the field against the Anonymous writer. He rather rejoices: it was to this very end he published him, that many might test and refute him. But he will not have it trumpeted forth on that account that he, Lessing, is an enemy to the Christian Religion, any more than the man who notifies to the medical officer that poison lurks in dark places, should be held the propagator of the pestilence.

'Shout me down you can every eighth day, you know *where*. Write me down, you certainly shall not.'

Goeze, defeated in his main assaults, attempts oblique sallies ; he taunts Lessing with his style, and says that his logic smacks of the theatre.

'Every man,' replies Lessing ('Anti-Goeze' II.) 'has a style peculiar to himself, just as he has his own nose; and it is neither polite nor Christian to laugh at an honest man's nose, however odd it may be. How can I help it, that I have no other style? That I do not affect it, I am well assured. I am also conscious that it is inclined to play the most extraordinary pranks with just the very matters that I have pondered most maturely. It plays with the subject the more wantonly, the more I have striven to master it by cool reflexion. It matters little how we write, but much how we think. And surely you would not contend that under tropes and metaphors, ambiguity and insincerity, sense must necessarily be hidden, that no one can think correctly and definitely who does not employ the tritest and flattest expressions? . . . How absurd to ascribe the depth of a wound not to the sharpness, but to the polish of the sword ! How equally absurd to ascribe the advantage which truth gives our adversary to his dazzling style ! I know of no dazzling style that does not borrow its lustre more or less from truth. Truth alone gives true lustre, and must serve as foil even to buffoonery and banter. Therefore let us speak of this, of truth, and not of style. I willingly resign mine to the criticism of the world, and I admit it is possible that the theatre may have somewhat spoiled it.'

Then follows a detailed patient analysis of his own style, than which nothing could be more acute. He

sees its faults and he also sees its good points, and
having expounded these to Goeze, whom they really
did not concern, and probably did not interest, his
accusation having been merely a random stroke of
malice, Lessing concludes :

'This, Revd. Sir, is my style, but my style is not
my logic. But yes, according to you my logic is the
same as my style, a theatrical logic. So you say.
But you may say what you like : good logic is always
the same, apply it to what one will. Even the manner of application is the same. Whoever shows logic
in a comedy would not lack it in a sermon, just as he
who lacks it in a sermon would never achieve a decent
comedy. . . . . When you, Revd. Senior Pastor,
persecuted the good Schlosser in so edifying a manner
on account of his comedies, a double question arose.
The one, May a clergyman write comedies ? To
this I replied, Why not, *if he can* ? The second,
May a comedian write a sermon ? And to this I replied, Why not, if he will ?

'But wherefore all this chatter ? What matter now
the paltry questions of theatre and style, when so terrible an accusation hangs over me ? I must, I must
take fire—or my coolness, my calmness will subject
me to reproach. How, Revd. Senior Pastor, have you
the effrontery to accuse me of direct and indirect hostile attacks upon the Christian Religion ?'

Lessing reminds him that he has already once
defended himself on this point, and that Goeze has
nevertheless repeated the indictment. He exposes
his libels and miserable criticisms, and promises again
not to rest in this feud, but his paper is full, and he
does not mean to let Goeze have more than one sheet
at a time. He shall receive his punishment by the

slow torture of drop by drop, poured on a bald
head.

The third 'Anti-Goeze' opens with the announcement of his willingness to investigate the reality of
these 'direct and indirect attacks upon the Christian
religion' charged against him. But stop: this shows
him that there must be at least *one* passage in the
New Testament that Goeze regards as uninspired,
'Judge not, that ye be not judged.' With what delicate and insinuating gentleness has not he (Geeze) set
about this ticklish work! Quite in the tone and in
the manner of a certain M. Loyal in a certain comedy
that one does not willingly name before certain
people. He is so anxious about my fame—what matters that bubble?—so anxious about my salvation. He
trembles so compassionately for my dying hour. He
makes me here and there such pretty speeches, that I
may not feel it all too painful that he casts me out of
my Father's house (John xiv. 2).

> Ce monsieur Loyal porte un air bien déloyal.

But what is all this to the purpose? Let us take up
the charges themselves. Enough that my heart does
not condemn me.'

These charges are the printing of the 'Fragments'
and the defence of the author. The first is notorious,
and as little admits of contradiction as requires it.
The second he absolutely denies in the sense which
Goeze attaches to it. He published these 'Fragments'
to promote free discussion, as he had already declared. If it were still to do, he would print them,
should all the Goezes in the world condemn him.
He does not follow his scholastic distinction, that it
may be true that religion gains objectively but loses
subjectively by every assault; and even if it be

granted, the gain stretches over all time, the loss is limited to the moment.

'The gain is for all good men who love conviction and enlightenment ; the loss affects but few who do not deserve consideration either for their intellect or their morals. The loss affects only the *paleas leves fidei* : the light Christian chaff which every puff of doubt separates and wafts from the heavy grains. Of these Tertullian says, Let them fly as much as they please, *Avolent quantum volent* ! But not so our Church teachers of to-day. Not a single husk of this Christian chaff is to be lost ! Rather would they leave the grains themselves unsifted and unwinnowed.'

What would Tertullian have said to the Revd. Gentleman who raises such a noise about the paper foundations of a possible heresy ?

'Would he not have said, " Shortsighted man, *nihil valebunt, si illa tantum valere, non mireris* " ? Your noise is to blame if these "Fragments " occasion more harm than they were meant to do. The Anonymous wished to acquire no name by writing, or he would have named himself. He wished to found no congregation, or he would have done so in his lifetime. In a word, he who printed these "Fragments " has far less responsibility than you who raise a frantic outcry about them. He only made it possible for many to read them. You bring about that many have read and must read them ! '

Perhaps, concludes Lessing, the Pastor prefers hearing this rebuke out of the mouth of a Church Father rather than from me. But his wrath against the 'unco' gude ' has been visibly rising in this paper, and he quits his tone of broad comedy to pen a passage truly sublime.

'Oh ye fools, who would like to banish the whirlwind out of Nature because it has there buried a ship
in the sandbank, and here dashed one to pieces on
the rocky coasts! Oh ye hypocrites! for we know
you. You do not care for these unhappy vessels, or
you would have insured them; you care solely for
your own little garden, your own little comforts, little
pleasures, little indulgences. The wicked whirlwind
has torn off the roof of one of your greenhouses, has
shaken your laden fruit-trees too roughly, overthrown
your own cosy orangery contained in seven earthen-
ware pots. What care you how much good the whirlwind may have effected in Nature? Could it not
have effected it without hurting your garden? Why
does it not blow past your hedge? or at least fill its
cheeks less full when it nears your landmarks?'

Goeze had started the ridiculous theory that to
obviate subjective injury and to extract objective advantage, all polemics should be written in Latin.
Here is fine scope for Lessing's ridicule, and he does
not spare him; he asserts that he will test argumen-
tatively a proposition which others would have sum-
marily pronounced absurd, but he admits it is probable that the one will lead to the other. Granted
the practicability of Goeze's proposition, is it fair?

'Can a law be fair that would admit as many
incompetent as it would exclude competent persons?
And who does not see that this would happen here?
Is it mere knowledge of Latin that confers compe-
tence to entertain and put forth doubts on religion?
Is mere ignorance of Latin to render all men without
exception incompetent to deal with such things? Is
no conscientious thoughtful man possible without
Latin? Are there no fools, no blockheads, with

Latin? I will not insist on De Roxas' conceit, that " Latin makes the true fool," but neither does it make the true philosopher.'

The next question is, would this unjust law be expedient : would it not rather render the plain man suspicious of the worth of a subject that no one dared treat openly?

'Would it not also be ill-judged, because it would increase the mischief which it is meant to repair? Objections against religion are to be written in Latin, that they may injure as few as possible. Injure as few as possible? Yes, as few as possible in those countries where Latin is only common to a certain class ; but in all Europe, in the whole world ? Scarcely. For if the number of those people in all Europe who know Latin, and yet are not capable of resisting every noxious impression of possible doubt, be not greater than that of those weak ones who, in each country, do not know Latin, what then ? To the devil a soul is a soul ; or if he makes a distinction in souls, he would even be the gainer. For instance, in lieu of a sleepy German soul, perverted by German writings, he would obtain a learned French or English soul. He would obtain a larded roast instead of a dry one. His vote therefore, the vote of the devil, this imprudent law would certainly secure, even were it not over and above *unchristian*, as must already be assumed, seeing it is unfair. For I understand by unchristian anything that is at variance with the spirit and purpose of Christianity. Now, as far as I understand this matter, the purpose of Christianity is not our salvation, anyhow, but our *salvation by means of our enlightenment*, which enlightenment is not a condition of our salvation, but our salvation itself. How utterly opposed, then, to the spirit of Christianity is the temper which would rather contribute nothing to the enlightenment of many than *possibly* offend a *few*. Must these *few* who never were, never will be Christians, who merely dream away their unthinking lives under the name of Christian, must this despicable portion of Christians be for ever pushed before the aperture through which the better part would see the light? What! This despicable portion is not the smallest? It must be spared on account of its multitude? Then what sort of Christianity has been preached hitherto, that the mass does not adhere to *true* Christianity as it should? What! If these nominal Christians be offended, and some of them, by reason of Freethinking works written in their language, declare that they will no longer be what they never were, what of that? Tertullian asks, and I with him: " *Nonne ab ipso Domino quidam discentium scandalizati diverterunt?*" Whosoever, before he begins to act or to write, thinks it needful to inquire whether his actions or writings may scandalize here a weak believer, there harden an unbeliever, or there play into the hands of a knave who seeks fig-leaves, let him at once renounce all action, all writing. I would not deliberately tread on a worm, but if it is to be reckoned sin to me if I tread on one by accident, I know no other resource but not to remove my limbs from the position wherein they find themselves, in fact, cease to live. Every movement in Nature develops and destroys, brings life or death; brings death to this creature in bringing life to that. Were it better to have no death and no motion, or death with motion?'

Goeze, who loved to affect liberality, replies that

this was not precisely his meaning ; only he wishes that the assailants should not be allowed to unsettle such questions as had been consecrated by the authority of ages.

'Oh, happy times, when the clergy were still all in all—thought for us, ate for us,' cries Lessing. 'How gladly would the Senior Pastor lead you back in triumph. . . . I affirm that his permission to make objections against Religion and the Bible, against what *he* calls Religion and the Bible, amounts to nothing. He gives and withholds, for he hedges it sternly and pettily with so many clauses that it is dangerous to use it.'

Lessing proves that it is Goeze who has made the Anonymous writer assert that the Apostles were wilful deceivers.

'Mr. Goeze knows right well that my Anonymous really maintained that the Apostles did precisely what all legislators, all founders of new religions and states find it expedient to do.'

But the mob for whom Goeze preaches do not perceive this, and, like all religious zealots, he rests his support on the mob. Wherefore, Lessing ends his fifth 'Anti-Goeze' with the significant warning :

'Even the vilest multitude, if only guided well by their rulers, become enlightened in due time, higher minded, better ; instead of remaining stationary at the same point of religion and morality where their fore-fathers stood many hundred years ago, as they ought to do according to a fundamental axiom with certain preachers. These do not break away from the mob, but the mob at last breaks away from them.'

Lessing now considers that he has disposed of Goeze's objections, and proved conclusively that a

Church which understands its true interests would not entertain the idea of limiting in any way liberty of speech and writing, and that least of all should an exception of points be allowed to be made, because this would arouse suspicions more injurious to religion than any attack upon the excepted points. For his part he, Lessing, has quite a superstitious regard for every book, especially one only extant in MS. He would have them all printed.

‘ But the Pastor will grow angry at my pursuing him thus step by step, till I force him at last into a corner whence he cannot escape me. He will already, before I have quite hedged him in, try to slip away from me and say : “ Yes, but who speaks of mere printing ? That might certainly be thus excused. The real crime consists therein that the Editor of the ‘ Fragments ’ has also undertaken the advocacy of the author of the ‘ Fragments.’ ” . . . I have nowhere said that I hold the whole cause of my Anonymous for good and true exactly as it stands. I have never said that, rather I have said just the contrary. I have said and proved that if the Anonymous is right in many separate points, it yet does not follow thence that he is right in his general conclusions. I boldly venture to add what looks like a boast. . . . I have not only expressly stated that I am not pledged to the opinions of my Anonymous ; I have, up to the time when I published the “ Fragments, ” never written or publicly maintained the slightest thing that could expose me to the suspicion of being a secret enemy to the Christian religion. On the other hand, I have written more than one trifle in which I have not only shown the teachers and doctrines of the Christian religion in their best light, but have defended in particular the Christian orthodox Lutheran religion against Catholics, Socinians, and Neologians. With these trifles the rev. gentleman is for the most part personally acquainted, and he has before now, verbally and in print, expressed his approval. How is it he only now recognizes in me the devil, who has disguised himself, if not in the garb of an angel of light, at least in that of a man of not the vilest type ? Am I really transformed, since I no longer breathe the same air as he ?'

He then prints at length the preface of Reimarus, in which is stated that he did not wish his writings to be brought to light before the time was ripe. 'Luther and all Saints, Revd. Sir, what have you read there ? Confess, you did not think me so wicked. The Anonymous, with all his freethinking, was at least so honourable that he did not wish to mislead the world by *his* views, while I do not hesitate to mislead it by the views of *another*. . . That is all true, Revd. Senior Pastor, that is all true. If only all the laudable modesty and caution of the Anonymous did not cover too much confidence in his own arguments, too much contempt of the common herd, too much distrust of his age ! If only in consequence of these views he had rather destroyed his MS. than left it for the use of intelligent friends ! Then you think also, Revd. Sir, that it recks not what the intelligent believe in secret, if only the mob, the sweet mob, be left quietly in the groove wherein alone the clergy know how to guide it. Is this indeed your opinion ?'

Goeze then complains of Lessing's mode of disputing, to which Lessing replies that he might retort the complaint. The imputation of having immoderately panegyrized his Anonymous is a more

C C

serious charge, and merits a more serious answer.
True he had called the work profound and argumen-
tative, had spoken of its author as an honourable, irreproachable man, had said that in all kinds of learning
seven Goezes weighed less than the seventh part of
him.   But did it therefore follow that he knew the
author intimately and personally ?   Quintilian says
that it is not possible for the same breast to harbour
honest and deceitful thoughts, nor can one mind
dwell upon the best and worst things, any more than
it is possible for one man to be good and bad at the
same time.   In this sense Lessing had felt himself
justified in calling his Anonymous irreproachable, and
as for his religion, he knew not where else to find such
true comprehensive conceptions of rational religion,
and, though he openly rejects all revelation, yet he is
not on that account a man without religion.   He,
Lessing, had not threatened, as Goeze says, to name
the author of the ' Fragments ; ' he had merely warned
him that it would be better not to treat the Anonymous too contemptuously, lest the discovery of his
name should bring him to confusion.                    .

    ' If the Revd. Senior Pastor has not here wilfully
written a falsehood, it is at least a proof how he reads
me.   He does not read that which I have written, but
only that which he would wish me to have written.
. . . It is true that I once thought that I recognized
my Anonymous in the person of the Wertheim Bible
translator.  . .  As soon as I found that I had been
too hasty in my conjecture about Schmid, I resolved
never again to indulge in such guesses.   Yes, I further
resolved that even if I assuredly learned the true name,
I would not now or ever make it known to the world.
By this resolve I abide, so help me God, supposing

even I had really learned the name since then. What miserable curiosity, the curiosity after a name! after a few letters combined thus or thus! I let it pass if together with and through the name we learn how far we may trust the testimony of a sneak. But here, where there is no question of testimony or of matters that rest solely on testimony, where reason is to prove conclusions, of what avail the name of him who is a mere vehicle of these conclusions? Not only is it useless, it is even injurious at times, since it gives room for a prejudice that lamentably detracts from all reasonable investigations. For either the Anonymous is known as a man not wanting in power or will to recognize the truth, and at once the mass who find thinking so difficult are carried away blindly ; or it is found that the Anonymous is a man who is under a cloud, and at once the mass will have nothing further to do with him, in the fixed and admirable belief that he who wants one sense must of necessity want all five. Even men of letters judge thus, who do not ordinarily count it a small matter to hunt down anonymous and pseudonymous authors ; and I should act and judge more unphilosophically than those men who, so to speak, have a right to make useless and unphilosophical discoveries? *Prudentis est*, says Heumann, *ita quosvis dogmaticos libros legere, quasi auctor plane sit ignotus.* Here the *quasi* exists. The reader need not forget what he has never known.'

As all advocates of weak causes harp on one string, Lessing has again to defend himself from the charge of being the apologist of the anonymous writer through thick and thin. It is not so ; he only speaks as an upright man who will not allow any person to be so

tumultuously condemned, and he is the more bound
to do so because he has of his own motive published
fragments of a work detached from their connecting
whole. But why have these fragments been thought
worthy of more attention than fragments deserve ?

'Here I must add what I am not ashamed to
repeat, since it has once been confessed. I have
thrust the Anonymous into the world because I could
no longer live under one roof with him. He was for
ever in my ears, and I confess again that I could not
always oppose as much to his whispers as I should
have wished. So I thought a third party must either
bring us nearer together or further apart, and this
third party can be none else but the public.'

And the public up till now had not given Lessing
one single satisfactory reply. As for Goeze, he does
not even count him among the opponents of the
Anonymous ; he has not refuted him in a single
point, but has only abused his editor.

Meanwhile Dr. J. Reimarus had grown uneasy at
these disputes. His father's name had several times
been connected with the 'Fragments,' and he feared
lest the authorship should be divulged. He had indeed from the first opposed this publication, which
had only the sanction of his sister Elise. Lessing
wrote to reassure him :

'Wolfenbüttel : April 6, 1778.

'I should like to see the man whom I have told
that your late father is the author of the "Fragments."
. . . . But I will take an early opportunity not only
to say a word in general about useless curiosity concerning the author, but to declare myself also in
particular concerning your father, so that people shall
desist in future from calling me to account on that

point. This opportunity will soon occur, since I am just now going to print a "Fragment," and that the last one, not in the "Contributions," but separately.'

In the middle of the Goeze controversy, Lessing issued the most daring of the 'Fragments,' 'Concerning the intentions of Jesus and His disciples.' He published it separately, unaccompanied by comments. In a short explanatory preface, he states that he would have preferred to have withheld it for a time, but it has been wrung from him. It was his intention that it should slip into the world in the sequestered corner of his librarian 'Contributions,' but what could he oppose to force? In this essay the character of Jesus, revered even by Deists, was for the first time debased to the level of a politico-religious fanatic and conspirator, just as the brotherhood of His disciples was held to be a pre-arranged plot for the deception of the world.

Lessing thought it needful to publish this, in order that opponents might understand whither the Anonymous tended, and attack him on that ground and no longer wrangle over side issues.

This 'Fragment' excited a storm of abuse, and according to Elise Reimarus, Goeze, transported beyond all bounds, applied to the Imperial Ambassador to prohibit Lessing from writing further. Whether in consequence of this or not, Lessing received (in July 1778) an order depriving him of his privilege of exemption from the censorship, while the last 'Fragment,' its preface, and the 'Anti-Goezes' were confiscated, the reason assigned being that this exemption had been accorded on condition that Lessing should publish nothing contrary to religion and morals. He justified himself on the plea that he had under-

stood this clause to mean that he should print nothing in his own name or of his own composition dogmatically adverse to religion, which condition, as he
understood it, he had strictly observed. To publish the
objections of others, he had held another matter, his
object being to afford an opportunity of confuting
them, and that our faith should not be reproached with
suppressing everything said against it. He would rather
abandon the publication of his ' Contributions ' altogether, than submit to an unchristian restriction which
he could not be brought to believe was in accordance
with the wishes of the reigning Duke. He himself
had accompanied the ' Fragments ' with a refutation
which had been more praised by worthy Lutheran
theologians than modesty allowed him to repeat. Notwithstanding he would obey, and have no more of the
' Fragments ' printed till they had been examined by
a ducal commission, but he hoped to be allowed to
continue his ' Anti-Goezes,' as he was the attacked
in this instance, and the bitterest things he had
brought forward against Goeze were only compliments compared with what the Senior Pastor had bestowed on him, and the whole quarrel had no bearing
on the Christian religion.

No notice was taken of this justification, and
Lessing was further commanded to deposit the MS.
of the ' Fragments.' He obeyed, saying it was unfortunately not complete, as the Hereditary Prince had
some sheets in hand, and significantly adding that this
copy was only one of many extant. He was quite
right in his surmise that this step was not taken at the
desire of the Duke, though the command bore his
lithographed signature. The Duke was now in the
last stage of senility, the Prince was absent with the

army, and one of the Ministers, Von Praun, who bore
Lessing a grudge, had gladly seized this opportunity
to avenge himself. It seems, however, that the
method of revenge which he chose proved the greatest
favour he could have shown to Lessing.

To Ebert, who was entirely on Lessing's side,
Lessing wrote :

' The confiscation amuses me excessively. It shall
not be my fault if this stupid step is not completed, whoever may be the real promoters. I do not
see why I should exempt from suspicion those you
name to me.[1] Individually, not one of them will
answer to it, but I know full well that half a dozen
sensible men are often collectively no more than one,
old woman.'

The Berlin and Hamburg friends were uneasy at
this news. Mendelssohn saw in the hubbub a realization of his worst fears of the consequences of Lessing's
meddling with the clergy. Lessing pacifies his friends :

' Wolfenbüttel : July 23, 1778.

' It is certainly true that the Ministry, at the desire
of the Consistory, have forbidden my new " Fragment " and my Anti-Goeze writings. They have
further forbidden me to print anything more from the
MS. of the " Fragments." I have my reasons for willingly submitting to the confiscation of the new " Fragments." Ought they not to confiscate my writings
also ? About that I tussle finely, firmly resolved to
drive matters to the uttermost, and rather solicit my
dismissal than submit to designed humiliation. Nothing has come from the *Corporus Evangelicum*, still less
from the Aulic Councillors, nor do I think I have

---

[1] Jerusalem and Von Praun.

much to fear from either.   For (you will laugh) I can
as surely divide the Aulic Council among themselves
as Paul divided the Sanhedrim.   As most of the
members are Catholics, I need only represent my
cause in such a way that the condemnation which the
Lutheran theologians will pronounce upon me shall
involve also the condemnation of all Papists, who as
little regard Scripture as being the foundation of religion as I do.   With this intention I have already
written the enclosed sheet.   You will see that I have
veered in such a manner as must finish off the Rev.
Senior Pastor.   For I suppose you have read his
last about " Lessing's weakness," and seen what
explanation he demands from me.'

To Elise Reimarus he wrote in the same tone :

'Wolfenbüttel : Aug. 2, 1778.

' Your anxiety, my dear friend, is very flattering
to me, and yet I must beg you to put it from you.
The matter is not really as bad as you fear.   True
they have confiscated the new " Fragment," and want
to forbid my further writing of such things.   But on
the last point I stand out firmly, and hope Goeze will
not have the pleasure to see me change my batteries.
They have made use of the absence of the Hereditary
Prince, and of the weakness of the old Duke, who is
incapable of attending to or signing anything.   But
the assurance that both have little or nothing to do
with the whole matter gives me a freer field for
troubling the Ministry as much as I like.   It is
possible that I might feel myself forced to demand
my dismissal, and for this the gentleman who might
give it me would have to answer in good time.   But
what would it be more than that ?   Goeze and Co. shall

gain so little by it, that one and all who have tried to draw off the water this way will regret their undertaking. For taking the matter as a whole, I in my person am as safe as I can be, and I hope to experience the amusement of seeing most of the theologians come over to my side, in order that, with a loss of a feather, they may save the main body for a while. In short, dear friend, do not be in the least anxious on my account. I will certainly not take any foolish step, were it only not to absent myself from a library which might be necessary to the prosecution of my quarrel. The remembrance that it is not indifferent to you what turn my fate might take, will comfort and cheer me in many a moment, when vexation at having involved myself with such miserable rogues threatens to gain the upper hand.

'Farewell, your cordial friend,

'LESSING.'

The step to which Lessing refers was one that he foresaw might lead to serious consequences, though he treated it lightly. The confiscation had had the usual result of causing the 'Fragments' and Lessing's writings to be reprinted, and extensively read by persons who would otherwise not have troubled themselves about theology. In Saxony, Lessing's fatherland, it was forbidden under penalty to read or sell the 'Anti-Goezes,' and Lessing was again interdicted by the Brunswick Ministry from printing anything concerning religion. He nevertheless issued a sheet under the title, 'G. E. Lessing's necessary answer to a very unnecessary question of the Revd. Senior Pastor Goeze, in Hamburg,' printing it in Berlin, but placing Wolfenbüttel on the title page, a fact which he

notified to the Ministry. It was Lessing's intention
to open herewith a new series of 'Anti-Goezes,' if Goeze
could not be silenced.

'It depends on Goeze whether my future answers
will be long or short,' he tells Karl, who has attended
to the publication. 'I have material enough for
folios, and folios can be condensed into sheets.'

Lessing's concise and pregnant answer proved as
subversive of the formal principle of the Protestant
Church, as Luther's Theses of the Roman. He
pierced what Strauss names 'the Achilles heel' of the
Protestant system, and indicated the possibility of
a reunion with the Catholic Church. The assertions
of Goeze and his school that the Bible was the only
foundation of the Christian religion, without which it
could not be proved, propagated, or subsist, was openly
directed against the Catholics. It was no mere
stratagem that Lessing united his cause with that of
'this large portion of Christians.'

Goeze's question had been, What did Lessing
understand by the Christian religion, adding that not
until he knew this, should he enter upon the point in
dispute, i.e. whether Christianity could remain if the
Bible had never existed or were lost. With this question
Goeze thought he had driven Lessing into a corner, for
he said sneeringly, that no doubt Lessing would never
have opened out this dispute if he could have seen
whither it would tend, and how he would be forced to
expose the real thoughts of his heart. The gods had
certainly smitten Goeze with blindness not to recognize
the superiority of his adversary. Lessing placed himself entirely on the historical ground, and replied that
he understood under religion the beliefs contained in
the creeds of the first four centuries of the Church.

In nineteen condensed theses he defines the substance of the *regula fidei* of the early Church, proving that this was extant before a single book of the New Testament existed, and that therefore the *regula fidei* and not the New Testament was the rock whereon the Church was built ; that the New Testament, as contained in our canon, was unknown to the early Christians, and such portions as they knew were not held by them in superstitious veneration, but were employed as commentaries and homilies ; that the whole value of the Apostolic writings consisted in their agreement with the *regula fidei*; but that they were not the source of the latter. The Scriptures were mere records, whose writers never intended that their words should be held in slavish and superstitious regard.

It was in this wise that Lessing approached the Catholic position, that the Church authenticates the Scriptures and not Scripture the Church. His study of the Fathers while at Breslau enabled him to meet the most learned patristic theologian on his own ground. In conclusion he does not doubt but that Goeze will give him an opportunity of carrying this controversy farther, and the rather to induce him, he has carefully refrained from any of those metaphors, tropes, or allusions to which the Pastor objects, and promises to avoid them in future if he will also employ the same precision and simplicity in his replies.

How greatly this Goeze controversy had helped to divert him in his sorrow, is shown by a letter to Elise Reimarus :

'Wolfenbüttel : Aug. 9, 1778.

'I am quite left to myself here. I have not one friend in whom I can entirely confide. I am daily troubled by a hundred vexations. I have to pay dearly for a single year spent with a sensible woman. How often do I feel inclined to regret that I wanted to be as happy as others. How often I wish that I could return at once to my old isolated condition, and be nothing, wish nothing, do nothing but what each moment brings with it ! You see, my good friend, this is my real condition. Under these circumstances, are you right to advise me to remain in a post that has long been burdensome to me, only to avoid gratifying a miserable enemy ? How much more unhappy I am if I stay here to vex him. But I am too proud to think myself unhappy. I gnash my teeth, and let the boat go as the winds and waves list. Enough that I will not upset it myself. I am glad that you understand the tactics of my last sheet so well. I will make evolutions he has not foreseen ; for since he has entangled himself in his own words, and asks not what I believe of the Christian religion, but what I understand it to be, my cause is gained, and one half the Christians must always protect me against the other. Thus Paul divided the Sanhedrim, while I need only seek to hinder what would not happen in any case, namely, seek to hinder the Papists from becoming Lutherans, and the Lutherans Papists. Thank you for your good wishes for the continuation of my controversies, but I hardly need them. This controversy has already become my hobby-horse, which can never throw me so as to break my neck. They wont refuse stabling to my hobby-horse here, unless I give notice myself. Farewell, my good friend : and as soon as the High Priest ventures a syllable against my necessary answer, be so kind as to send it me.

'Yours sincerely,

'LESSING.'

The Brunswick Ministry censured his step, and once again forbade him to print without their permission, either in or out of the Duchy. Of this interdict Lessing took no notice. Elise Reimarus had sent him Goeze's latest, which he admits is getting rather strong, and he is determined to answer it ! He tells Elise that his reply is ready, and he would send her the MS., but that he prefers to bring it himself, as business affairs for his stepchildren will oblige him shortly to visit Hamburg. If the business that brings him there is not of the pleasantest, yet he knows one house where he shall at least pass pleasant hours, though he fears he shall have to arrange his visits with more regard to prudence than to inclination.

About the middle of September he went to Hamburg , for which excursion the old Duke had given ' his dear Lessing leave of absence for a fortnight,' that extended to six weeks, owing to the serious illness of his stepdaughter Amalie, who had accompanied him. Elise Reimarus had been nervous as to his reception, for since the publication of the last ' Fragment ' people spoke of him as the arch-fiend. To her surprise and relief, Lessing's charming personality overcame all preconceived dislikes. He met with a warm reception everywhere, and not the least warm in the Reimarus circle, or ' congregation ' as they called themselves : a reception which, as Elise Reimarus remarks, could not fail to annoy Goeze. Here in Hamburg he printed his second necessary reply to Goeze, numbering it ' one,' as he anticipated a whole new series of ' Anti-Goezes.' To the amazement of friend and foe, this reply silenced Goeze effectually. Not a line, not a word came in answer, the real fact being that Goeze could not follow Lessing now that he had transferred his ground from humorous and piquant sallies to severely learned criticism.

Goeze had said that Lessing's idea that the Bible was not the only foundation of Christianity was too absurd to merit disproof, and merely quoted a saying of Irenæus to overthrow him. It was at his peril that he had misquoted the passage, and torn it unduly from its context, and his assertion that it was not needful to establish his position about the Bible was very naturally construed by Lessing and the public as a confession that he could not. Meanwhile Lessing carefully confuted Goeze's assertion that all Christian teachers, without distinction of party, rely upon the Bible as the sole foundation of the Christian religion. He expected an answer; and worded his tract in such a manner as to provoke one. But Goeze was absolutely dumb. Neither did the Brunswick Ministry notice Lessing's disobedience ; they perhaps saw they had gone a little further than the absent Prince would approve. Though the latter disliked these polemics, and had expressed a wish that Lessing had at least issued his last ' Fragment ' in Latin, so that it might not spread among the multitude, he was still too sincere a friend to enlightenment and freethought to see it persecuted in his dominions. Even the confiscated ' Contributions ' were again permitted to be sold.

But Lessing could not comprehend this sudden collapse ; he quite missed the lively interchange of tracts that had diverted his sadness. He was told Goeze was ill, and ordered to ride daily for two hours, precisely the two hours he had commonly employed in refuting Lessing. ' If this is so,' says Lessing, ' I will at once begin to pray for his recovery.' But whether it was that the prayer of such a heretic could not obtain an answer, or from whatever cause, Goeze never moved again, and the fierce quarrel of a year was finished for all time.

# CHAPTER XIX.

## 'NATHAN THE WISE.'

*' The Jews say, " The Christians lean on nought." " On nought lean the Jews," say the Christians. Yet both read the same Scriptures. Until thou fo low their religion, neither Jews nor Christians will be satisfied with thee. Say to them, " The direction of God is the true direction. . . . Will ye dispute with us about God ? He is our Lord and your Lord. We have our works and you have your works ; and unto Him we are sincerely devoted.'*
AL KORAN. THE COW.

LESSING had once before asserted that annoyance kept him in health, and truly his contention with the theologians seemed to have renewed his vital energy. For since his wife's death a very marked physical change had taken place in him. He withdrew more and more from society, went more rarely to Brunswick ; an inertness foreign to his nature, and an uncontrollable somnolency fastened upon him ; he would go to sleep amid noise and laughter, and suddenly start up with the question, ' What is the matter ? ' though when roused he resumed conversation with unimpaired mental vigour. He busied himself conscientiously with the care of his stepchildren, and incurred heavy sacrifices that it might not be thought that he lived upon their income. Of himself and his feelings, he spoke less than ever. Whenever he could be absent from the library he retired to write in the room where his wife expired, his only companion a favourite cat.

The friend to whom he felt most drawn was Elise Reimarus. She noticed his impaired health when he came to Hamburg, but the intercourse with congenial spirits enlivened him, and he returned to Wolfen-büttel resolved to fall upon his enemies in the flank, since he was no longer permitted to meet them in open combat.

'I must try if they will at least let me preach un-hindered from my old pulpit, the stage,' he told Elise, with whom he had discussed the project of a drama wherein he proposed to play the theologians a worse trick than with ten more 'Fragments.' The idea was not new. Indeed its first conception dates from Wittenberg, when his studies of Cardan caused him to balance the respective claims of various creeds ; but the draft had been laid aside unfinished, like too many others. His last reply to Goeze, contrary to express command, made him fear lest dismissal might ensue, and bring him into urgent need for ready money. He wished to be prepared for any contin-gency. One night what he calls an absurd fancy had overcome him. This was to take in hand the dis-carded sketch and work it out to completion. He imparted this notion to Karl, telling him that the main idea of the drama had a sort of analogy with his pre-sent quarrels, an analogy of which he had not dreamed when conceiving it. If he and Moses ap-proved the play shall be printed by subscription. He would not like its nature to be known too early ; but if they care to learn it they may refer to the story of the Jew Melchisedek, in the 'Decameron' of Boc-caccio.

Karl warmly applauded the project, in which he and all Lessing's friends expected to find a humorous

D D

satire on current theology. Lessing tells his brother
that he has quite misconceived his play; it will be
anything rather than satirical, but as touching a
drama as he ever wrote. It has nothing to do with
the 'black coats,' and he had no intention himself to
block the way to the stage against his piece, though
it might be a hundred years before it ever got there.
Happy the state where it can and may! The theologians will rage at it inwardly, but they will take
good care not to declare themselves publicly. He by
no means intends to let drop his skirmishes with
Goeze and Co., this is only a dramatic interlude to
gain time and strength. To write it the more rapidly
it should be in verse, as his prose had at all times
cost him more labour than his poetry. But one
obstacle remained, the lack of ready money for his
subsistence. He needed at least three hundred
thalers to enable him to devote close attention to an
all-absorbing task.

Karl's proposal of payment in advance from the
subscribers was not approved.

'For suppose I were to die suddenly? I should
then owe a thousand persons each a gulden, every
one of whom would abuse me to the amount of ten
thalers.' If Karl can find some one who will advance
the amount, he will give him an acknowledgment; if
he were then to die suddenly, *surely* he would leave
enough behind to meet the bill.

A worthy Jew of Hamburg, Moses Wessely, offered to advance the same on condition that Lessing,
whom he greatly admired, would write him an autograph letter.

'And if he does not write that letter?' asked
Karl, who knew the uncertainty of his brother.

'I shall send it him all the same,' was the reply, 'for he must acknowledge the receipt.'

Even this sum barely helped Lessing over his pressing needs ; and he feared lest his work should bear some impress of his pecuniary anxieties. He sent a touching reply to one of his sister's repeated demands, accompanied by a sum he could ill spare. ' If you knew what cares I have had since the death of my wife, and how miserably I have had to live, you would surely have compassion on me, and not load me with reproaches.'

In May 1779, ' Nathan der Weise ' appeared : 'the son of his advancing age whom polemics have helped to life,' was Lessing's curt self-criticism. He foresaw that the play might produce little effect on the stage, if ever it got there ; enough for him if it be read with interest, and among a thousand readers, one learns to doubt the exclusive sanctity of his own particular creed. Lessing called his work a dramatic poem, not a drama, and his reason for this was that, contrary to the laws of Aristotle, an idea, and not an action, is the nucleus of ' Nathan.' Still it was meant for a poetical drama, and Lessing's healthy critical faculty rejected as an anomaly the bare notion that a drama could be designed otherwise than for scenic representation. Closet plays were not admitted into his aesthetic domain, and though he despaired of his play reaching the boards, yet he wrote it with all due regard to dramatic exigencies. He always bore in mind that a play is amenable only to the laws of stage representation. Hence, if a play of his had failed, or left the audience unmoved, Lessing would have been the first to condemn it, and would have regarded as a sorry compliment the apology often put forward by enthu-

siastic critics, that excellency of workmanship is a
positive hindrance to the success of masterpieces on
the stage.

'Nathan the Wise' is the outcome of the Goeze
disputes. Since 'a verse may find him who a sermon
flies,' Lessing, in 'Nathan,' gave embodiment to his
attitude towards positive creeds, and he distinctly remarks that the sentiments expressed by Nathan are,
and always have been, his own. Nathan is Lessing
himself, not Moses Mendelssohn as has been incor-
rectly averred. For even Mendelssohn, with all his
eclectic liberality, had not reached that rare height
whence pure spirits look *sub specie aeterni*, with us,
of us, and yet raised above us, not by preternatural
but by essentially human means, that are to hand for
each of us: self-conquest, self-renunciation, and love.
Like Shelley, Lessing held the ideal aim of theatrical
art to lie in 'teaching the human heart, through its
sympathies and antipathies, the knowledge of itself,
in proportion to the possession of which knowledge
every human being is wise, just, sincere, tolerant, and
kind.' The germinal motive of 'Nathan' is but another
exposition of Lessing's views on the essence of
religion. 'The best positive religions are such as
contain the fewest conventional additions to natural
religion, that least hamper the good operations of
natural religion.' The purpose of the work is to develop a cardinal truth and teach religious toleration.
It is therefore as new as when first written, and it
would be indeed a happy day for the history of mankind when the interest of 'Nathan' should become
purely historical, through the extinction of fanaticism and bigotry. Every friend of enlightenment
prays with Burns that 'come it may.' Meanwhile,

' Nathan ' has helped, and will help, to reveal to those who are often intolerant from mere thoughtlessness, that truly all mankind are of one religion that takes visible shape in outer forms, mere liveries to the inner soul. The ' Bhagavad-Gita ' says : ' When thy mind shall have struggled through the snares of delusion, then thou wilt attain to indifference to doctrines.' Better still are the words of the Church Father Augustine, when he lays down that ' what is now called the Christian religion has existed among the ancients, and was not absent from the beginning of the human race until Christ came in the flesh ; from which time the true religion, which existed already, began to be called Christian.' This is the keynote to ' Nathan,' and it was a subtle trait of Lessing's that he chose for the representative of his toleration dogma a Jew, a descendant of the most exclusive nation, who deemed itself God's chosen people, a people that does not condescend to proselytize, since one cannot become, one must be born a Jew. Spurned and despised, thanks to the political supremacy of the Christians, the proudest people is also the most oppressed. It is easy to be tolerant when our religion is predominant, less easy when toleration must result from the victory of duty over inclination, the struggle whereon, according to Kant, rests the foundation of ethics. The natural inclination of the oppressed is to vengeance ; it finds its vent in Shylock, and these two stage Jews, Nathan and Shylock, may be regarded as the opposite poles. In Shylock, the Jew almost absorbs the man, he is deaf to the voice of mercy ; while in Nathan, disinterested love of his neighbour obliterates to absolute forgetfulness all distinctions of race.

Nathan is an embodiment of goodness, self-developed and matured, a perfection reached through spiritual knowledge and acquired in the school of sorrow. The Christians had not merely wronged him as a Jew ; they had in their fanaticism murdered his wife and seven children ; so that even Nathan felt his spirit broken, and for three days and nights lay in the dust, and raged and cursed himself and all the world, and swore unrelenting hatred to Christianity. But reason returned. It bade him exercise what he had long imagined, what surely is not more difficult to exercise than to imagine, resignation to God's will. All the evils that fate can pour on him do not in the end lead him astray. 'For yet God is,' whispers an inner voice. He will arouse himself, he will, he will, so God but aid his will.

'Nathan, Nathan, you are a Christian,' cries the friar, moved by this recital of self-conquest, when bigot hate threatened to get the upper hand. The simple-minded brother can find no higher expression of his admiration than to repeat his phrase, ''Fore God you are a Christian, a better Christian never was.' Then fearing he has been too complimentary to what he should spurn, he qualifies and excuses his own words with : 'Is not Christianity all built on Judaism?' He admits it has often vexed him, cost him tears, that Christians will forget so often that their Saviour was himself a Jew.

'Well for us both that you think so,' says Nathan, 'for what makes me to you a Christian, makes you to me a Jew.'

'Nathan the Wise' may be judged by the religious or the aesthetic standard. From the latter point of view it has many weak points, and deserves all Schiller's

strictures. Its involved story and the preponderance
of philosophical thoughts that never sententiously
offend, but yet hamper rapidity of action, render it
somewhat too chilly and abstract as a play. Still,
thanks to Schiller, and with the hearty approval of
Goethe, it was brought on the stage and obtained great
and merited success. Lessing possessed in no common
degree what Matthew Arnold calls the 'imaginative
reason' as opposed to the imagination engendered by
feeling. Perhaps this is the cause why he just missed
being a poet. In his verse reason predominated too
much. Poetry was with him an exercise of the intellect. The material of his nature was prose, which, in
inspired moments, under the white heat of intense
feeling, glowed into verse. And here, in 'Nathan,'
Lessing produced a work eternally great, a very
gospel of toleration, a protest against the thraldom of
bigotry, the slavery of 'the letter that killeth,' a poem
with all propriety entitled 'the Wise,' an epitome of
pure wisdom, high morality, and true religion ; such a
work as can only be written in the maturity of life by
a spirit that has struggled and overcome, and has
anchored secure, free from doubt, at peace with itself,
safe from the assault of enemies, internal or external.

> Introite, nam et hic Dii sunt,
> (Enter ! for Deity is also here)

was the motto chosen by Lessing for his poem.

The story is intricate, its main threads lead back
far before the opening of the play. The scene, laid in
Jerusalem during the Crusades, opens with Nathan's
return from a successful business journey. The first
news that greets him is that his house has been burned
during his absence, and that Recha, his daughter—as
she believes herself to be—has been rescued from the

flames by a young captive Templar, who has marvel-
lously escaped the death that awaits all Templars who
fall into Saladin's hands.  Recha persists in thinking
an angel has saved her.  'Is it not miracle enough
that Saladin has spared a Templar's life ?  And why ?
Because he so much resembled a brother whom he
adored, and who vanished some twenty years ago.
Is not this miraculous, incredible enough, that Saladin,
the just, the stern, should have been so moved by a
trait, a feature, as to allow a Templar to walk at large
in Jerusalem ?'  Thus Nathan gently reproves Recha
and her companion Daja for their childish belief in
miracles.  Is not all this wonderful enough for lovers
of the marvellous?  It is sheer pride and vanity that
requires a special messenger from Heaven for itself.
Are there not miracles about us every day, if only we
would look at them, and not let their everyday disguise and habitude strip them of novelty ?  But where
is this Frank, this so-thought angel ?  he must thank
him for his service of mercy.

Nathan finds him walking under the palms that
shade the holy sepulchre.  The Templar receives his
advances with all the haughty disdain of the Christian
towards the Jew.  His bearing is rude and uncourteous,
and yet Nathan, the wise, the shrewd observer of
mankind, sees that this hard and bitter rind conceals
a sweet kernel.  The Templar will not listen to thanks.
He has but done his duty ; his vows bid him succour
the distressed ; he should thus stake his life again, even
though the life he saved was but a Jew's.  Nathan
asks how he can serve him, he is rich.  The Templar
replies, he does not want to buy, nor has the wealthiest
Jew ever seemed to him better than the poor.  He
has been told that his people honour Nathan and call

him the Wise rather than the wealthy ; but he supposes
that rich and wise mean much the same to them. At
last Nathan, who sees that he is inexorable, begs he
will at least send his cloak to Recha, the cloak that
shielded her, that she may press on it a kiss of gratitude. Nathan weighs his words so well, his language
is so good, his sentiments so lofty, that the Templar is
attracted despite himself. He had not thought to find
Jews thus ; he falters, and feels constrained to tell
him why he scorns them. It is because they first
called themselves the chosen people, first imagined
differences among men, prided themselves that the
true God was revealed to them alone : a pride which
they have handed down as an heirloom and a curse to
Mussulman and Christian, whence has sprung the
pious madness that would force this better God, which
each nation thinks it owns, upon the whole wide world.
These words only serve to interest Nathan yet more
strongly in the young Frank, for has he not spoken
out of his very soul ? ' We must be friends,' he exclaims. ' Despise my nation as much as you like. We
neither of us chose our kindred ; but are we our
people ? And what is people ? Are Christian and Jew,
Christian and Jew ere they are men ? Ah ! if I had
indeed found in you one more soul to whom it is
enough to be a man.' Their budding friendship is
interrupted by a summons from Saladin to Nathan.
He is surprised. What can the Sultan want with him ?
Before they part the Templar tells Nathan his name,
a name whereat he starts ; it raises old trains of thought
and memory, and they then separate with a promise
soon to meet again.                           .

Al Hafi, Nathan's friend, a dervish and beggar,
whom Saladin had chosen as his treasurer, in the

belief that the poor best know how to assist the poor,
now comes to warn Nathan not to obey the Sultan's
summons. Saladin's reckless liberality has emptied
his coffers, the rich Jew is to come to the rescue. Al
Hafi invites him to join his flight to the Brahmins
by the Ganges, where begging or borrowing is unknown. He will but be stripped to the skin if he
stays here. ' That resource remains,' says Nathan,
and obeys the royal command.

Saladin is not easy at the prospect of this interview. He has heard Nathan well spoken of, and feels
ashamed to extort his gold from him. He greets
him, saying, he has long wished to see the man the
people call ' the Wise.'

The people, says Nathan ; what if they meant
the name more in reproach than honour, if wisdom in
their eyes were merely cunning to our own advantage ?
But a truce to word-fencing, and to business. Nathan
promises he will serve the Sultan cheaply with his
wares.

That was not the object of his sending, says
Saladin ; he wishes instruction from so wise a man.
He desires to know which faith, which law one who
has pondered these matters esteems as the best. He is
assured that Nathan is not a man to remain fixed
just where the chance of birth has placed him.

' ' Sultan, I am a Jew,' says Nathan, taken aback.

' And I a Mussulman. The Christian stands between us. Of these three faiths but one can be the
true.' Saladin leaves him to reflect on his answer.
Nathan is much perplexed. What would the Sultan ?
he foresees a trap in this. If he plays the stiff-necked
Jew, that will not serve ; if he accords the palm to the
Mussulman, Saladin will say rightly, then why not

turn Mussulman? He has come prepared for a demand
for money, and the Sultan asks: Truth. Truth pure
and unalloyed, as if it too were gold tied up in bags
that can be transferred from one pocket to another.
He must be cautious here—soft, he has it; it is not
only children whom we put off with tales. With
Saladin's permission, he will first relate to him an
ancient story.

In days of yore there lived an Oriental, who
owned a ring of priceless value, that had the hidden
virtue to make its owner beloved of God and men.
It never left his hand, and on his death he made
a disposition that should secure it an heirloom
in his house for ever to the best loved son. Thus it
passed from hand to hand for generations, until it
came to a father with three sons, all equally dear to
his heart. His end is near. In turn, he promises each
son the ring, as each one seems to him in turn the
dearest. At last, in dire perplexity, he summons a
jeweller, and orders two more such rings made exactly
after this pattern. When made, he himself cannot
distinguish the true one. Overjoyed he calls his sons,
gives each a ring and his blessing, and dies content.
What follows can be guessed. Each son claims to
be lord on the strength of his ring, disputes, discussions follow, the true ring cannot be distinguished, as
little as among ourselves the true religion.

'Is it thus you answer me?' says Saladin.

'I but seek to excuse myself from hazarding a distinction between three rings made purposely so much
alike.'

'True, true, the rings—you trifle with me—but not
the creeds. Their differences are distinctly marked
even to meat, drink, and dress.'

'But only not as to their ground of proof. Are they not all built alike on history, written or traditional, that must be received on trust; and whose trust do we naturally question least, but that of our family and our forefathers from whom we sprang? Can I ask of you to convict your forefathers of falsehood, in order to render credit to mine? Surely the same holds good for Christians?'

'By the Almighty the man is right, and I am answered,' thinks Saladin; but he is anxious to hear the sequel of the tale.

The end is that the sons could come to no agreement and went to law. Each swore in turn that his father had loved him best and given him his ring, and each asserted that his dear good father could never have been false. He would rather suspect his brothers of foul play. The judge said that he must dismiss the suit, since they cannot produce the father, who alone could decide. But stay, he remembers the true ring has the power to make its owner beloved by God and men; the counterfeit can have no such virtue. 'Say then, which of you do two brothers love the best? You are silent. Each loves himself the best. The rings act inwardly alone, not outwardly. Go, go; you are all three deceived deceivers, the real ring perchance was lost, and to conceal the loss your father ordered three for one. And now, if you desire my counsel instead of my judgment, I say to you, rest with the matter as it stands. Each of you has received a ring; let each one deem his true, and make it true by vying who can display most gentleness, forbearance, charity, united to heartfelt resignation to God's will. It may be that your father no longer desired to tolerate the exclusive tyranny of the one ring, and loving you all,

would not favour one son to the prejudice of the
others. Be that as it may, do you each strive as I
have said. If after a thousand, thousand years, the
virtues of the ring continue to show themselves in your
children's children, perchance one wiser than I will
sit on this judgment seat, who can decide.'

' Saladin,' asks Nathan, ' do you feel yourself to be
that man ?' ' I !' exclaims Saladin, touched to humi-
lity ; ' I ! poor dust that I am. Never, never ; his judgment seat is not mine. Go, go ; but love me,' he says,
seizing Nathan's hand.

The Jew then asks as a boon, to be permitted to
advance to the Sultan the money needed for his war
supplies, and, of which his generosities have deprived
him. He stipulates a reserve in favour of a Knight
Templar who has saved his daughter's life. Saladin
accepts this free-will loan reluctantly ; he esteems the
Jew now too much to rob him. The mention of the
Templar recalls the forgotten incident of his unwonted
clemency. He desires to see him again.

Meanwhile the Templar has seen Recha, become
inflamed with love for her, and asks her hand of
Nathan, who puts him off with excuses, influenced by
a suspicion confirmed in the end. This caution, which
the hot-headed youth deems to proceed from Hebrew
arrogance, angers him. He listens to Daja's story
how Recha is no Jewess but a Christian child rescued
by Nathan. In his pious zeal and pique he hastens
to impart this news to the fanatical Patriarch of Jerusalem, thinking thus to force Recha out of Nathan's
power. He did not expect that the intolerant
pharisaical prelate would give no quarter, and insist
that the Jew who could withhold from a Christian
child the privileges of her birth must be burned

for this frightful deed, this unexampled enormity. Nathan's virtues, his humanity, the fact that but for his pity the child would have perished miserably, avail him nothing. ' The Jew must be burnt,' reiterates the vindictive zealot.

Happily matters do not go so far. Nathan is now under Saladin's especial protection. While the Patriarch seeks to compass his bloodthirsty designs, a meeting between the Knight, Nathan, and Recha in the palace has revealed that the Frank is indeed the son of Assad, Saladin's brother, by a Christian wife, and that Recha is his sister, as is proved by a breviary just confided to Nathan by the lay brother who brought him the newborn motherless child to save it from certain destruction, during the siege of Gaza. And thus Christian, Mussulman, and Jew are united into one family, knit together by common affection and ties of blood.

This was the task Lessing had set himself in the play. The parable of the rings is no episode but its gist, and what is placed in the story as at the end of time is here accomplished in very truth : choice representatives of the three inimical religions join hands in brotherhood. In Boccaccio's story one ring is indeed the true one, but it is impossible to decide which. Lessing improves on this ; there *is* a true ring, but it cannot be recognized at sight. It acts upon its owner, and only manifests itself from within to without. But where is it, this true ring ? this true religion ? Alas ! as long as the quarrel about its possession endures, so long hatred, arrogance, and egotism will bear sway, and nothing can be decided ; and as soon as the power has manifested itself, the quarrel will end, and nothing further will be left to decide. The judge's decision is that of Lessing. He does not intend to extol one faith above the others. External creeds are accidents of birth ; true religion is no magic gift from above ; it manifests itself in character and action, and this prize must for ever be sought for, struggled for, by each individual for himself. Religion is a power that demands action from men, and discloses itself in our relations to God and to our neighbour.

Thus 'Nathan the Wise,' like every great poetical work, is founded on one of those beautiful fables deep-rooted in humanity : fables whose number is small, but which ever combine anew and reappear afresh in changed condition or in wondrous disguise. Lessing intended that his drama should prove its effect by means of its theme, and therein he succeeded. As a play it does not approach 'Minna,' nor is its exposition as masterly as 'Emilia.' On the other hand, its form is freer than 'Emilia,' and the rhymeless iambics in place of the cumbersome Alexandrine, are a happy innovation. Moreover, the versification gives it Oriental colour, while the whole play is picturesque. As regards time and place, though Lessing did not strictly observe chronological accuracy, a needless shackle as he had demonstrated, he yet happily employed historical facts to serve as framework to his characters. These also are ·chosen with care. If Lessing made the rancorous persecuting Patriarch, who really believes himself to be the chosen exponent of God's will, a Christian, it was because he deemed the fanaticism of intolerance especially despicable in a member of the creed whose gentle Teacher had bid men love one another. He also desired to show that Christianity did not necessarily imply superior excellence. If the world *would* point to Goeze as the

Patriarch's prototype, was it Lessing's fault? Recha and the Knight Templar, each in their way, are exponents of pure Theism : Recha from careful nurture, the Knight from conviction. This trait in the Templar is moreover historically correct. Many became thus enlightened during the Crusades beyond the exclusiveness of creeds, for these wars showed to them the misery which religions, regarded by their adherents as revealed, brought upon the world, and that goodness and true piety were not the special possession of one people. Daja is the silly, easy-natured soul who treats creeds as a garment that one puts off and on. Her own dress is the best in her eyes, and therefore she wants Recha to wear it. She loves Recha and would see her a Christian, but her letter-worship and consequent mischievous garrulity nearly bring about the persecution of her kind protector, Nathan. The catastrophe is unsatisfactory ; it does not appear why Lessing should have raised the element of love in the pair whom he intended to prove brother and sister at the last. When the Templar is made to say that Nathan, in his sister, gives him vastly more than he withheld, we are forced to smile. And such a play should leave us with something nobler on our lips than a smile of this nature.

The fierce discussions that have been waged about ' Nathan,' the panegyric, the execration bestowed on it, have created a literature of itself, the catalogue of which alone fills a good-sized volume. Its immediate effect was nevertheless, as Lessing had anticipated, an ominous silence. Only here and there a favourable word was spoken with bated breath. The high tone taken by the ' Nathan ' removed it above the comprehension of any but the finest spirits. The world could

not understand a man so far in advance as to preach,
in an age of scepticism and indifference, an ideal belief
that should subvert conventions and bestow individual
freedom of thought. Never before had Lessing so
hungered for any little word of praise. He had always
needed contact with his fellows, and now even some
of his oldest friends had withdrawn from him on
account of the publication of the 'Fragments.' He
felt daily more isolated and lonely.

'What do you say to my " Nathan " ?' he asks Elise
Reimarus on sending her some copies. 'Do not leave
me long without your opinion. I understand in your
opinion that of the whole congregation. I have need
truly that you should judge it a little well, to make me
contented again with myself; for I am this so little
now, that I can hardly picture to myself the possibility
of being so again.'

He does not hesitate to confess that he absolutely
needs praise and approval in order to jog along the
road of life. During this summer of 1779 he was far
from well. While still writing ' Nathan ' his peace of
mind had been poisoned, and the completion of the
play endangered, by an onslaught that was the more
stinging because the less expected. It came from
Semler, the first theological professor who had openly
taught the need of historical criticism and the temporary character of dogmas, and from whom Lessing
looked for support rather than obstruction. But
Semler, scared at the growth of a movement which he
had initiated, and whose progress he could not stem,
suddenly veered, and impugned the naturalism of
Reimarus and the good faith of his editor with an
insolence that was repaid to him in later years. For
as his strictures served to embitter Lessing's last

days, so his own were poisoned by similar calumnies. The plea by which Lessing had vindicated his publication, the desire to call forth a worthy champion into the Christian arena, was clumsily satirized by Semler under the form of a trial before the Lord Mayor, of an incendiary who had set fire to a house in order to prove if it were inflammable, and to give the firemen a chance of evincing their efficiency. The Lord Mayor will not condemn the man. ' He is no malefactor, he is a madman ; take him to Bedlam : ' and he was taken to Bedlam, and as everyone knows, there he remains to this day.

This public accusation of insanity angered Lessing. He resolved to answer Semler ; but deferred his reply in order to settle with his minor opponents. So weighty an adversary should receive a weighty reply. Every spare hour that illness permitted during the next few months, he devoted to projecting answers to his theological assailants, and thus the contemplated reply was never written. Nor did the others advance beyond projects. All power for sustained work was gone. Failing strength kept him indoors, and often in bed. If only he could take as many steps as he wrote words, he once said, he should soon be a healthy man. A little change of scene and cheerful society might be beneficial, but it grew more and not less lonely about him.

He was spared no annoyance which human malice could invent. A report was circulated that the Jewish Synagogue of Amsterdam had bribed him with a thousand ducats to publish the ' Fragments,' and thus blacken the Christian religion. He was denounced as Judas Iscariot the Second. Another mischievous calumniator threw out sinister hints respecting Amalie

König's continued residence in her stepfather's house. Lessing takes notice of this in a pathetic letter to Elise Reimarus. The girl is dear to him as his own daughter, indeed he had always regarded her as such ; still, rather than hurt her in the eyes of the world, he will let her go. She is the one, the only comfort of his life ; without her he would fall back into the terrible loneliness of his former existence, but which he will scarcely find so tolerable now he has known better things. Indeed, if she must go, he could easily be forced to throw himself once more adrift and end life as he began it, a vagabond, and a far worse one than formerly, since love of study and general curiosity and acquisitiveness would no longer rivet him as long in one place as it had done before in his youth.

Happily this last sorrow was spared him : Amalie König remained with the stepfather, whose fond affection she returned, until his end. Nor was that end far distant. Unstricken in years as he was, it was too surely evident to all who loved him that the keepers of the house had begun to tremble and the strong man to bow himself.

# CHAPTER XX.

## THE 'EDUCATION OF THE HUMAN RACE.'— 'ERNST AND FALK.'

*'Damit das Gute wirke, wachse, fromme,*
*Damit der Tag des Edeln endlich komme.'*—GOETHE.

THE inclination to excessive sleep, which had been somewhat lessened during Lessing's occupation upon 'Nathan,' returned on the cessation of sustained effort. He was also troubled with asthma and feverish attacks, all tending to confirm his impression that he was nearing death, and his answer to Karl's cheering assurances that there are no signs of failing power in 'Nathan' breathes the resigned tone of old age. He felt his intellect growing inert, and losing its versatility. He could not turn so rapidly and easily from one subject to another. He had now worked himself into the theological vein, and could not cast it off until he had exhausted his adversaries, and their stock of venom seemed inexhaustible. His life aim had been an arduous effort after knowledge and truth ; truth unalloyed, unwarped, uncoloured by prejudice or passion, the pure calm truth to which Bacon gives the name *Siccum lumen.* This search for truth, pursued in every form, landed him on religion, the most profound theme of humanity, the motor that underlies all existence, without which man's life lacks purpose or reality. The theses he had enumerated in his 'Necessary Answer' were the most positive propositions that had come from his pen ; but the notion of binding all ages by the rule of one was far from his mind. Fully impressed with the progressive and necessarily shifting nature of truth, he never expected any utterances of his to be regarded as final. To guard against petrifaction, to fling forth fermenting leaven into the world, was the underlying purpose of all he wrote. Hence his works must never be judged independently and separately, but in relation to his mental bent, and the occasion whence they sprang. He knew full well that in speculation nothing can be absolutely final, but he ever strove to make the ideal real by bringing it into connexion with humanity. When issuing the fourth 'Fragment' he had appended fifty-three paragraphs, headed 'The Education of the Human Race,' or a refutation of the dictum of Reimarus that the Old Testament could not be regarded as a divine revelation, since it took no account of the doctrine of Immortality. In these paragraphs Lessing admitted the fact, but denied the inference. In answer to a query from Dr. J. Reimarus as to their author, he replied :

'The "Education of the Human Race" is by a good friend who loves to frame for himself all manner of hypotheses and systems in order to have the pleasure of pulling them down again. These hypotheses will certainly displace the goal whither my Anonymous tended. But what matters that ? Let everyone speak what he deems truth, and truth itself be commended to God.'

The winter of 1779–1780 was a sad one for Lessing. He fell from one indisposition into another.

None were serious, but all hindered the full use of his intellectual faculties. It then occurred to him (since he must do something) to expand his education idea into a pamphlet. Early in February he sent the MS. to Voss, purporting to be only its editor.

Lessing did not live to see the effects produced by this little work of just one hundred paragraphs, wherein pregnant truths are embodied with masterly terseness and almost mathematical precision. The most various spirits, Christians and Jews, speculative philosophers, and socialistic politicians, have occupied themselves with this Essay, that unrolls dim vistas of endless progress. To Lessing may be attributed the honour of first preaching the gospel of humanity and the natural evolution of the relatively imperfect, as opposed to rigid perfection fixed and immutable. He even anticipated with a prophetic spirit the modern principle of a study of Nature in her universality, as controlled by laws of infinite continuity and harmony. In his fragment the 'Christianity of Reason' he foretells that one day a fortunate discoverer will extend the realm of natural science into a corroboration of a chain of all-pervading and endless development, though it may not be till after centuries have passed, not till all the phenomena of, Nature shall have been fathomed, so that nothing is left but to refer these to their true origin. The value of his ' Education of the Human Race' lies in its suggestiveness. It is a sketch that gives large glimpses into God's world and the life of man. It does not pretend to the dignity of a picture, filled up and shaded in, and hence it leaves every thinker's individuality free play. Reimarus had been purely destructive; not so Lessing, assured as he was that every matter that had ever occupied mankind, however distorted it might have grown with time, concealed a germ of truth that had rendered it subservient to the great purpose of fertilizing the world. The human mind must pass through phases of ignorance, doubt, and error, before it can become capable of receiving pure truth. This applies to so-called revelation, as to all else. Hence Lessing did not put himself upon the standpoint of the philosopher who endeavours to pierce to the ultimate ground of our knowledge. Throughout this little treatise he starts from the assumptions of established convictions, using them as mere vehicles to convey his ideas. In the preface he explains that the writer stands on an eminence, from which he believes that he sees somewhat more than the prescribed road of his time.

'But he does not call any hasty traveller who only seeks to gain his night quarters, from off his path. He does not demand that the prospect that so entrances him should entrance every other eye. And so, I think, he might be permitted to stand still and admire where he stands still and admires. If from out the immeasurable distance that a mellow evening light neither quite hides nor quite reveals to his gaze, he brought back a hint for need of which I have often been perplexed? I mean this hint: Why should we not rather see in all positive religions the paths whereby alone human reason could develop itself, and is still to develop, instead of smiling at them or growing angry? Nothing in the best of worlds merits this disdain, or indignation, and religions only should deserve it? God should have His hand in all things, and only not in our errors?'

Lessing then expounds his theory how God, as Preceptor of humanity, has dealt with the world.

Revelation is not a gift bestowed once for all. That
which education is to the individual, revelation is to
the race. And since education gives to man nothing
which he would not educe out of himself, only that it
gives it him more easily, so revelation gives nothing
to the human species which human reason left to
itself would not attain, only it gives it these things
earlier. As an experienced controversialist, Lessing
knew that errors are dispelled not by anathemas, but
by gradual enlightenment. Under the image of a
training school whose work is ever going on, he takes
a survey of the history of human thought, and indi-
cates its essentially progressive character. For the
sake of illustration he makes this fanciful contraction
from the general to the particular. In education
everything cannot be imparted at once ; the powers of
assimilation are not sufficiently developed, a certain
order must be maintained. In the school of humanity
there are three stages : The Hebrew people is the
first stage, and the Old Testament its class-book.
The Hebrews were rude and unruly people, who had
everything to learn. Only gradually could they rise
from the conception of a patriarchal national Deity to
the knowledge of the one God. So too could their
moral education only be conducted on the plan of
rewards and punishments addressed to the senses.
Their regards went no further than this earth, they
yearned for no life to come. To have revealed this
to them, before their reason was ripe to grasp it, would
have been the fault of the schoolmaster who urges on
his pupil too rapidly. When the child has at length
come to years of understanding, the Father sends it
into foreign countries that it may see the world outside. In the Babylonian captivity the stripling en-
larges his experience by intercourse with a people of

wider culture. He learns the doctrine of immortality, and asks why he was not taught this before? Then he seeks out his discarded Primer, in order to throw the blame on it; but lo! the blame does not rest on the book, but on the scholar who failed to apprehend the hints it contained. Thus enlightened in respect of their treasures, the Hebrews returned a better people than they left. But now a new danger arose. They attempted to extract more out of their text-book than it could yield, to insert what it did not contain, to allegorize over much, lay undue stress upon words, begetting a petty crooked understanding, a sure sign that they had outgrown their Primer. A better teacher was needed, and Christ came as the Instructor of the youth of mankind. He taught them the doctrine of immortality. The lesson of immediate retribution was superseded by the more elevated one of eternal sanction, which enforced purity of heart, not mere abstinence from actions that were injurious to civil society. If the disciples of Christ, who faithfully propagated His doctrine, combined with it other doctrines less enlightened and exalted, let us not blame them, but rather examine whether these chequered doctrines have not become a new impulse of direction for human reason. The New Testament has afforded and still affords the second best text-book for the race. It is necessary that each scholar should for a period hold his Primer as the first of books, that his impatience to finish it may not hurry him on to things for which he has not yet laid the foundation.

Then follows an exposition how revealed truths must be transformed into truths of reason before the ripe manhood of humanity can be reached, the third stage.

' Or is the human race never to arrive at this highest step of illumination and purity? Never? Never? Let me not conceive such blasphemy, All Merciful! Education has its goal in the race no less than in the individual. That which is educated is educated for something. No; it will come, it will certainly come, the time of perfection when man, his reason convinced of a better future, will nevertheless not need to borrow from the future the motives for his actions ; when he will do good because it is good, not for the sake of arbitrary rewards, that were intended simply to fix and encourage his unsteady gaze in recognizing the inner better rewards of well-doing.'

It will assuredly come, the time of this new and eternal gospel, proclaimed by all enthusiasts, whose only error is that they go on too fast, and believe their contemporaries, who have scarcely outgrown their childhood, can grasp maturity. The enthusiast often casts true glimpses into the future, but he cannot wait. He expects that for which Nature takes thousands of years to mature itself in the moment of his own existence.

' Yet beware, thou scholar of more forward capacity, who frettest and fumest over the last page of thy Primer : beware lest thy weaker fellow-scholars mark what thou dost divine or discern. . . . Go thine inscrutable ways, Eternal Providence! Only let me not despair of Thee because of Thy inscrutableness. Let me not despair of Thee, even if Thy steps appear to me to be going back. It is not true that the straightest line is always the shortest. Thou hast so much to carry on together on Thine eternal ways, so many side steps to make. And how, if it were as good as proved that the great slow wheel that brings the race nearer its perfection can be only put in motion by smaller swifter wheels, of which each contributes its unit force? It is so. Just the same path whereby the race reaches perfection must be traversed by every individual man, by one sooner, by another later.'

And until the day dawn for this new eternal gospel, the second Covenant, that has not yet been exhausted, must maintain its value and importance, even for those who have outstripped the stage of wonder and read it with their reason. Hence Lessing bids the more advanced scholars have patience.

'Until they come up to you, these weaker school-fellows, rather do you return once more to your Primer and examine whether that which you held mere turns of phrase, mere didactic stop-gaps, do not perhaps contain something more.'

But how to account for some being clearly from their birth so much further along their road than others? Lessing ventures the speculation of pre-existence. He names it an hypothesis, only insisting on it as such ; but it is one of the oldest, and must it be ludicrous merely on account of its age? since human reason lighted on it at once before the sophistries of schools had dissipated and weakened it?

'Why should I not come back as often as I am capable of attaining fresh knowledge, fresh skill? Do I bring away so much at once that it does not repay the trouble of coming back? Not on that account. Then because I forget that I have been here already? The recollection of my former state would permit me to make only a bad use of the present. And what I must forget now, have I of necessity forgotten it for ever? Or because too much time would be lost for me?

Lost? And what have I then to miss? Is not a whole eternity mine?'

Thus, with questions thrown forth unanswered, Lessing ends his 'Education of the Human Race.' And just this very incompleteness has rendered it so stimulative of thought. Crude and imperfect in its suggestiveness, its bold profound fancies haunt the brain, and tempt further efforts to solve the enigma of life : they teem, with fertilizing seeds of wisdom. Truly 'the King's chaff is as good as other people's corn.' Merely to indicate the commentaries bestowed on the treatise from Lessing's days to ours would be to write the history of freethought.

Five dialogues, in part written before this time, complete his 'swan-song' in the great question of humanity. Three numbers of 'Ernst and Falk, or dialogues for Freemasons,' had been published in 1778, with a dedication to the Hereditary Prince, Grand Master of the German lodges.

'Most gracious Duke,' so ran the preface, 'I also have slaked my thirst at the fountain of truth. How deeply I have imbibed, only he can judge from whom I expect permission to drink yet more deeply. It is long that the people languish and perish of thirst.'

But the Duke thought that Lessing had drunk deep enough, and signified that he had better publish no more. Two more dialogues, notwithstanding (in 1780), saw the light, as the author alleged, from copies taken without his authority. He even announced a sixth, but this was never written. These five dialogues are masterly in their *naïveté*, depth, and gentle blending of grave and gay. Their aim too is idealistic. Lessing stood aloof from political affairs ; his letters contain few allusions to contemporary events. Even

while actively interested in the Seven Years' War, his
correspondence turns on vaster themes. He hated
'the wretched thing called war.' At this time, when
advanced thinkers hailed the American struggle for
independence, Lessing only remarked that whatever
cost blood could scarcely be worth blood. He had
no confidence in sweeping reforms, and for him the
essence of Freemasonry consisted in a recognition of
the infirmities inevitable to the best of governments,
while acting as a wholesome counterpoise to the aggra-
vation of such infirmities.

It was a time of unrest in Europe; the spirit of
revolution was abroad. Authority received shocks
from all quarters, and the younger spirits unconsciously
felt the pervading ferment. Such a state of feeling
vents itself in Germany in a perfect epidemic of secret
societies, no matter how paltry their object. It was
the case now. All manner of Orders sprang up, and
Freemasonry, the oldest and worthiest of such cor-
porations, provoked renewed interest. Herein Lessing
recognized a hopeful sign. A counterpoise was needful
to rulers absolute in Church and State. A state is an
evil, but a necessary one; and would not be an
evil at all if order could exist without government.
But when Ernst asks, 'Will it ever come so far that
every individual will know how to rule himself?'
Falk, who represents Lessing, replies, 'Hardly.' Freemasonry, he explains, is no arbitrary institution, but a
necessary thing, founded in the nature of man and the
constitution of society; ascertainable, therefore, by
unassisted human thought. There is no secret except
such as is the most shrouded of all, because the intellect is not ripe to grasp it. Hence it is that Freemasons
take their apprentices through so many preliminary

stages, and why so few penetrate to the core of its
pretended mystery. The fault is in them, not in the
order. And if this be not the true ontology of Freemasonry, says Lessing, he should be curious to know
what is. He is confident that Freemasonry has existed
from all time, like Christianity; it is anterior to all
lodges, and exists outside of them, as religion is anterior
to all churches, and existed before all forms.

In these dialogues the question is rather of the
ideal of Freemasonry than of its actual condition. It
should annihilate all distinctions of caste, fortune,
nationality, religion. Freemasons should constitute
an universal brotherhood, that applies itself to heal the
inevitable ills of society, without subverting society
itself; for to abandon the social bond would be to
return to a state of nature. Order and freedom are
the high goals to which humanity should strive, and
these can only be attained in union. Though Rousseau
is not named, it is manifest that Lessing is here oppos-
ing his gospel of the peculiar sanctity incident to a
state of nature. The natural state Lessing shows is
imperfect, because it is not intellectual. His ideal
State, like Plato's ideal city, must not be founded by
the private passions of men, but in reason. With his
favourite, Aristotle, he lays down that the happiness
of the State and the individual are identical. Neither
can true humanity be evoked except by human intercourse. All things must work together towards progress, and how can progress proceed from a solitary
savage? Ernst's question, why there should not be one
State, living in amity, instead of many often inimical
ones, is answered by an appeal to variety of race and
climate, necessitating variety of governments and
creeds. It is the task of the Freemason to approach

each community, and break down the barriers of
nationality and creed. He must everywhere act as
mediator.

' He must quietly await the rising of the sun and
leave the candles to burn as long as they will and can.
To put out the lights, and when they are extinguished
to perceive that it is needful to rekindle the stumps,
or to put up new candles, that is not the office of the
Freemason.'

How far Lessing's doctrines are Utopian, how far
they exceed in spirituality, or approach in reality to
the secret of Freemasonry, only Freemasons can decide
This much is certain, that with few exceptions his
contemporary brother Masons deemed him a visionary.
But does not that in some sort corroborate the justice
and sagacity of Lessing's estimate ?

# CHAPTER XXI.

## JACOBI AND SPINOZA.—THE END.

### (1780-81.)

'———— *Vater—gieb! Das reine Licht*
*Der Wahrheit ist ja doch für dich allein.'*
  *So sprach Er. Wahrlich weise; denn er sah,*
*Wie gross sein Gott, wie klein er selber war.*
*Die ewige Weisheit aber sprach: ' Du irrst:*
*Die reine Wahrheit ist für mich ; doch die,*
*Die so wie Du sie suchen, finden sie*
*Bey mir ; und, Dich zu überführen, komm.'*

'YOU do not know what sympathy I begin to feel now with all sick people, even when they do not concern me,' Lessing writes to Elise Reimarus in the summer of 1780. ' I am myself not exactly ill, but not exactly well. I have had influenza—and indeed I have it still, for it has just come back.' Goeze himself had got into theological trouble by preaching an outrageous sermon against the Catholics, and had been censured by the very Aulic Council which he had sought to rouse against Lessing. Small wonder that he met with ridicule on all sides. 'Is it true,' Lessing asks his friend, 'that the Senior Pastor has recanted ? If he has done that, he is a complete knave and fool. For nothing could preserve the little honour he has to lose but that he should persist in defending all the nonsense he has ever preached or written, cost what it may.'

Early in July F. H. Jacobi paid Lessing the

memorable visit which was destined to excite such controversy concerning Lessing's philosophical opinions
as to cost Moses Mendelssohn his life, in his exceeding
zeal for his friend's memory. The two men had not
been personally acquainted. Lessing had read and
admired Jacobi's philosophical romance, ‘Allwill,’ and
had sent him a presentation copy of ‘Nathan.’ Here-
upon Jacobi expressed a desire to make Lessing's
acquaintance; proposed a visit and a joint trip to
Berlin. Lessing cordially invited him to stay at his
house. As to the journey to Berlin, ‘It would certainly be my wish. But it is my habit to wish what
I wish with so much keen anticipation of enjoyment,
that fortune generally thinks herself quit of the
trouble of fulfilling my wishes.’ The pedantic Jacobi
desired to lay out the subject of their conversations
beforehand: a proposal that amused Lessing, who
thought the subjects would find themselves.

During this five days' visit Jacobi incessantly
importuned Lessing for his views on Pantheism,
Theism, Spinozism, Freewill, and all cognate topics.
The joint visit to Berlin was not undertaken. It is
probable that by this time Lessing had had quite
enough of the importunate Jacobi, who tried his
best to force him into a regular exposition of his
philosophical creed. Jacobi was at that time deep in
the study of Spinoza, and scented Spinozism in every
utterance. He was too narrow-minded, and too much
possessed with a fixed idea, to follow Lessing's larger
views. He came to Wolfenbüttel with the purpose
of sounding Lessing, and he afterwards published an
abstract of their conversation. His veracity is un-
impeachable, and though he quotes Lessing's words
from memory, they are too characteristic not to be

F F

genuine. Still, due allowance must be made for the inevitable fallacies of memory, for Lessing's love of paradox, and for the amusement that he could not fail to feel in thus 'trotting out' the man of one idea, whom, according to Goethe, 'God had punished with metaphysics like a thorn in the flesh.' The incident recalls the dialogue between Lessing's Lay-brother and Templar.

'I am to sound the gentleman to see if he be such a man.'

'Proceed then, sound me.    (I am curious to see how this man sounds.)'

Lessing is a follower of Spinoza ; such was the startling announcement Jacobi made to the world soon afterwards.    He proved it by quoting Lessing's criticism on the monologue in Goethe's grand fragment of 'Prometheus.'    Jacobi had shown Lessing the poem in MS., and subsequently published it without the permission of Goethe, and much to his annoyance.    Herein also Jacobi scented Spinozism, the fact being that Spinozism was to him a generic term, into which every form of 'ism' fitted.    It was his monomania that all logical thinkers must end as followers of Spinoza, and that only faith could save them from this abyss.    He spoke with disrespect of the great Hebrew thinker.    Lessing, with his more just and balanced intellect, reproved the current execration of Spinoza.    His catholic sympathies and his propensity to seek the implicit truths contained in every doctrine, led him to resort to Horace's plan : '*Condo et compono, quae mox depromere possim.*'    His remark, ' If I were to call myself after any master, I know no other than Spinoza whom I would name,' was tortured by Jacobi into a distinct avowal of Spinozism.

Now Lessing's mind was too spontaneously energetic
for discipleship. He did not pretend to follow or to
found any philosophical system. He had no love for
metaphysics, and as opposed to Moses Mendelssohn,
in one of his letters he called himself a *bel-esprit*. He
was a thinker who thought on from day to day, im-
bibing and imparting ideas from all sources. Lessing
had said to Jacobi that there was nothing to object to
in Spinoza's 'Ethica.' But is the fact that one has no
objection to the ethics of a philosophy a confession of
adherence to it ?

Much ingenuity has been expended in determin-
ing Lessing's philosophical creed. One party claim
him for Leibnitz, another for Wolff, a third for
Spinoza ; one for idealism, another for eclecticism, a
third for pantheism. All seem unable to perceive
that he had no system ; that in philosophy, as in
religion, he did not believe that truth was the exclusive property of a sect. His mind, like every
thinking mind, had a speculative bias, but it revolted
against formalism. The direction which his speculations had taken in his latter years had made him feel
isolated from his friends. Mendelssohn was all understanding, Nicolai all utility, and now he was brought
into contact with Jacobi, who was all emotion. With
the exception of this one conversation, to which he
had been urged in an evil hour, Lessing had not of
late communicated his philosophical ideas to any one
but the younger Jerusalem. Nothing came to light in
this dialogue that was not already to be found in his
writings. Two essays from the Breslau period were
evidently suggested by Spinoza, as well as a letter to
Mendelssohn of that date. He had only been a little
more definite in conversation. The notes that accom-

panied Jerusalem's works, and especially the essay
on the freedom of the will, showed that in some respects he inclined to Spinoza's views on this point.
He does not distinctly say so, but he refers to a system decried for its conclusions, and which certainly
would be far more popular if people could be induced to consider these conclusions in a more rational
light. Spinoza had declared religious prejudices to
be the source of human vassalage, and that freedom
consisted in the intelligent love of God. This Lessing
also taught in 'Ernst and Falk,' and in his 'Education of the Human Race.' Spinoza says it is all ourselves, inward and outward, all expressions of one
mighty unity. Lessing says: Know thyself. Act, and do
not reason. Look within ; in your own nature lie the
unfathomed depths and mysteries of life. Do not
look above, that is not for us, we cannot grasp it.
Spinoza's was a dead God, Lessing's was a living one :
not an anthropomorphic creation, but a conscious existence, distinct from the universe, though pervading
it. Spinoza's God was to be recognized by intuition,
Lessing's by the world and his works. Spinoza's abstract nature tried to fathom the absolute. Lessing's
restless activity turned to real life, and there found
free play for his faculties. He laughed at those who
made heaven the subject of conjectures, and were lost
in labyrinths of mystery, filling the head and leaving
the heart empty. He smiled gently at Leibnitz's
theory of monads. His clear practical mind triumphed
over the theoretical day-dreaming of the Germans,
the accredited owners of cloud-land. He showed
the unfruitfulness of these self-complacent musings in
dream-land, and endeavoured by word and example
to rouse his countrymen, mentally and morally. His

unresting, scrutinizing intellect ever pushed onwards
to gain 'more light.' Hence he felt attached to Leibnitz, whose conceptions of truth he had declared to
be of such a nature that they could not be com-
pressed in narrow limits. And as with Leibnitz, so
with Lessing : it is difficult, nay, impossible even for
the most acute to detect his exact meaning. It is
more than probable that Lessing could not have accu-
rately defined it himself.

No doubt, however, as to Lessing's exact meaning
disturbed the mind of Jacobi, who set off for Berlin,
quite happily convinced that he bore all Lessing in
his note-book. On his return he again stayed with
Lessing, who accompanied him to Halberstadt, where
they visited their common friend, Gleim. Here Jacobi
received yet further confirmation of Lessing's pan-
theistic leanings. For when requested to write a
motto on the walls of Gleim's summer-house, what
did he write, but : "Ἐν καὶ πᾶν. Could anything be
more convincing ?

Fortunately for Lessing, the storm concerning his
Spinozism did not break loose during his lifetime.
After this visit to Halberstadt he refused Jacobi's invitation to Düsseldorf, where the latter owned a charming country house, and where he promised Lessing
complete rest and freedom from all aggressions.
Lessing gave the preference to Hamburg. He arrived there early in October, feeling ill and dejected,
but soon intercourse with sympathetic friends told on
him favourably, and he was once more the old Lessing,
'and what that means you best know,' Elise
Reimarus said in a letter to Nicolai. His charming
personality, animated conversation, and humour delighted all who met him. They could hardly credit

that this was the redoubtable Lessing.  A spark of
reviving youth seemed aflame in him, and when he left,
his friends were hopeful of complete recovery.  He
was sufficiently confident of this himself to enter upon
a contract for new plays with the Hamburg theatre.

But this appearance of strength was the last flicker
of the candle.  Hardly had he returned to his Wolfenbüttel solitude, than all signs of permanent recovery
vanished.  His first letter to Elise Reimarus, written
in disjointed sentences, reveals his broken courage and
hopes.

'In proportion to my haste to get home, was the
unwillingness with which I reached it.  For the first
thing I found was myself.

'And with this revulsion against myself, am I to
begin to work and be well?

' " Certainly," I hear my friends call after me, "for a
man like you can do all he wills."

' But, dear friends, what if this be only another way
of saying, Can all that he can ?  And whether I shall
ever feel this power of *can* again, that is the question?

' What is the good of a thing untried ?  Well then,
my dear friend, since you advise, be it so.

' I will send you news of my health regularly,
every week.'

He desires to be remembered to all her circle.  Ah!
if only he could have stayed among them!  If he
only had one of these friends to bear him company!

In the next letter he expresses his fears that a
change had occurred in his malady, and that the
*materia peccans* had fallen from his body to his soul.
In the following he announces that no particular crisis
had taken place, ' but what is not, may be, and I suppose death is also a crisis of illness.'

In November his patron Prince Ferdinand, who had on the previous March become the reigning Duke of Brunswick, apprised Lessing that he had received private information that the Corpus Evangelicum intended to reprimand the 'Fragment' publications. The Duke assured him that he would have his protection in event of an evil issue. To this gracious advance Lessing replied with a curt indifference that repelled the Duke. He afterwards regretted his peevishness, and confessed that no offer of service merited such a rebuff. 'I do not know myself why for some little time I have felt annoyed with our Duke. Notwithstanding all, he is a noble-minded man.' To atone for his error he consented to do some theological work for the Duke, though he hoped to have written plays, and thought he had done with the priests who were embittering his days.

Neither resolve was realized, for every day his sufferings increased. His eyesight nearly failed, he could only see to write on bright days and by help of strong glasses. Day by day his strength dwindled, it took him hours to pen the shortest note 'I am a rotten gnarled trunk,' he wrote to Mendelssohn in December. 'Alas! dear friend, the play is over.' The new year found him worse, overcome by numbness of limbs, difficulty of speech, and utter incapacity to write or spell correctly. Meanwhile his intellect was as fresh as ever, so that many of his friends thought his illness imaginary. He himself however was convinced of its gravity.

'I shall be the next,' he said, after attending a friend's funeral.

In January he made a little excursion to Brunswick, where, since his wife's death, he often spent

some time in a modest lodging which he had hired
on the market place. His friends remarked a change.
The fire of his eyes was dimmed, he dragged his
feet lifelessly, his difficulty of breathing was painful,
and every little exertion seemed too much for him.
Yet he persisted in dining twice at court and in joining an evening party. On his return from this latter
he was speechless. Still he imperatively forbade his
servant to send for a doctor, and expressed a wish to
be left alone. He passed a bad night, but next
morning the servant found he had risen, determined
to return to Wolfenbüttel. He was dissuaded with
difficulty. A doctor arrived who prescribed for him,
while news of his illness was sent to Amalie König,
who immediately came over. During his illness,
which lasted twelve days, he was composed and passive, at times quite bright. He spent many hours out
of bed, and received visitors with his wonted geniality.
He liked to be read to and hear all that was stirring.
At times he fancied his end very near, at others distant ; but he did not count on complete recovery, and
declared he was prepared to meet life or death. He
refused at first to admit the Abbot Jerusalem, but
when assured he came only as a friend, he saw him.
He wished to be spared all ecclesiastical importunity.
It is recorded, that on hearing that the dying Voltaire
had been molested by the Curate of St. Sulpice,
Lessing said to a friend, half in joke, half in earnest :
' When you see me dying, call a lawyer that I may
testify that I do not die in any of the reigning
faiths.'

His friends were alternately buoyed with hopes and
depressed by fears. On the morning of February
15th, he felt particularly well, and was able to receive

visitors, and talk and joke with them. He was up
and dressed, and when towards evening he was told
that other anxious friends were in the ante-room, he
rose to see them. When he opened the door, his face
too clearly bore the stamp of death, and scarcely had
he raised his cap in greeting, than his feet refused
their service, and he had to be borne back to bed.
With a look inexpressibly serene and transfigured, he
pressed his weeping daughter's hand. A stroke had
smitten him, speech was difficult. Still he rallied, and
seemed able to attend to a book that his *protégé*
Daveson was reading aloud, when, looking up, Daveson perceived he was at his last gasp, and in the arms
of his faithful Jewish friend, Lessing passed away
quite suddenly. When asked how he had died,
Daveson replied, 'As he had lived, like a sage, calm,
resolute, conscious to the last moment.'

'Lessing is dead,' wrote Goethe, whom the news
found just on the point of starting for Wolfenbüttel
to visit the great man whom he admired increasingly
as his intelligence ripened. 'We lose much, very
much in him, more than we think.'

It was long indeed before Germany awoke to the
consciousness of all that she had lost in Lessing.
The detraction of his adversaries had much to answer
for in this indifference ; the circumstances of his time,
perhaps, even more. It was a strange period of
transition in which his lot was cast, and it needed a
vision as comprehensive as his own to follow him in
all his various relations to its manifold aspects. It is
easy for us, though more distant, to see further.

Lessing was a man in whom two ages, two
opposed tendencies of thought were combined in

unique harmony. He exhibited in his person all the good elements of the eighteenth century, while he became the pioneer of the new. It was his peculiar characteristic to be at the same time the representative of his own and of a succeeding generation. For while the eighteenth century was negative and destructive, the nineteenth is affirmative and constructive: Lessing was both. He anticipated the nineteenth century in its tendency to return to the past, and its endeavours to disengage primitive truth from the disfiguring accretions of later ages. In this respect alone he presents a remarkable contrast to Voltaire : a contrast wholly to his advantage. In art, in religion, he helped towards the liberation of mankind from the shackles of mere tradition and authority as such. But while he destroyed, he built ; he did not use the thin weapons of sarcasm and *persiflage* to undermine both good and bad together, and leave his fellows shelterless. Hence it is that Lessing may lay claim to be the intellectual pioneer of our present culture. There are few departments of thought into which he did not penetrate, and none into which he penetrated without leaving the impress of his genius behind him. So varied and catholic were his interests, that to many he is only known as a theologian, to others as an aesthetician, to others again as a dramatist, poet, critic, or philologist. In one point only he did not free himself from a characteristic defect of his age ; and this was his indifference to the beauty and significance of Nature. In this respect alone he cannot be ranked as a precursor of Goethe, whom he anticipated in his attachment to the Greeks, Shakespeare, and Spinoza.

Born at the most depressed period of his native

literature, he lived to see the first fruits of Goethe's
genius, while the year of his death was marked by the
publication of the book which may be said to close
the eighteenth century mode of thought, the ' Critique
of Pure Reason.'

The sculptor Rauch exhibited correct and delicate perception, when among the crowd of famous
men that surround the monument of Frederick
the Great at Berlin, he placed Lessing with his
face turned towards Kant, as though exchanging
ideas with him. Both were great emancipators
of the human mind. Both strove to establish individual liberty of thought and action. Both tried
to awaken in their countrymen a just conception of
the nature of freedom. It is small wonder that interest in Lessing has revived latterly in Germany, for
the overgoverned and bureaucratic German still has
need of him. At the same time Lessing never confounded liberty and licence. He did not live to see
the French Revolution ; but he would have been the
first to proclaim that despotism was equally degrading
whether it wore an imperial diadem or a red cap. He
desired that each human being should be a man,
thinking for himself. He recognized this as the secret
of freedom, when he said, ' Think wrongly if you
please, but think for yourself.'

Looking at his literary activity in detail, we may
often regret that it is so fragmentary, that so much of
his energy should have been spent in ephemeral
themes and in personal altercations. But regarded
collectively, the same large-hearted purpose of knowledge and truth is seen to pervade it all. Lessing felt
himself summoned to act as the champion of truth,
and therefore bound to repress everything antagonistic

to the truth. Though the occasion was sometimes petty, the results were often grand. If he seemed the advocate now of this idea, now of that, it was because his intellect was not only powerful, but versatile, and could recognize the multiform aspects of truth. Immutability in mutability was the keynote to his life, as it is to the proper understanding of the world.

Such was the writer Lessing.

But beside the writer there stands the man, and rarely do the two harmonize as they do here. Lessing was not only a very great man, he was a good and strong man. The story of his life, which it is impossible to read without a feeling of deep compassion, is one of the saddest told. Yet he bore it with a fortitude so noble, he so rarely uttered a complaint against fortune, that while we admire, we hardly venture to intrude with pity on a nobility so far above our power. From early manhood one struggle and disappointment followed another, yet we cannot say that they came by any fault of his own. Endowed with a nature that needed tender affection and sympathy more than most, he had to do without it, and did without it, with a power of endurance quite marvellous. When in middle life he seemed to touch peace and find a responding heart; he was again condemned to disappointment; and when, after years of patient and heroic love, he was at last united to the woman of his choice, his happiness on earth was cut short by the overwhelming blow of death, within the brief span of a little year. But not even this cruel stab of fortune could quell the staunch champion of truth and humanity. He fought on his fight undaunted, against ignorance, bigotry, and tradition. He never relaxed in fervour for his cause until he was himself brought low by the unconquerable adversary.   He was young when he was taken, but he was spent with labour.

When Lessing laid himself down wearily to sleep, the foundations of his work had been strongly laid, fixed immutably, and their results are with us.   For his influence has been steadily on the increase, and the renewed interest taken in his writings, both here and in Germany, is not without its deep significance to those who read aright the signs of their times. Lessing's labours were not for Germany alone, they were for Europe.   It will be long before we have out-grown them, though we may occasionally and for a while entrust ourselves to less judicious guidance.

Few who have visited the quaint mediaeval city of Brunswick will forget the fine statue of Lessing, Riet-schel's masterpiece, that stands near the church of St. Aegidius.   Houses of the last century, with red gabled roofs, surround it, while close to it are some green trees. Raised above these, on a granite pedestal, stands the figure of Lessing.   Its material is fine bronze, more sombre than marble, but more fitted to a grim northern climate and to a man of the north.   He is represented in the dress of his time ; his head is slightly upraised, his eye looks forth firmly, un-dauntedly, leaving an impression on the beholder of attention, combined with self-restraint and dignity. The conventional cloak is wanting.   This was an innovation of the sculptor.   'I will make him with-out a cloak,' he said.   'Lessing throughout his life never cloaked anything, and just in him the cloak would have seemed to me a lie.'   Simple, dignified, bold, watchful as he was in life, so he stands there in brazen death : an effigy that seems to live and breathe, raised above our petty stature as the Colossus that he was, and yet humanly deigning to influence and help us by his genuine tenderness for the failings and frailty of our race.

Whoever sees him as he stands there, or reads the story of his life, cannot fail to repeat with his own Nathan :

'The man answers to his fame, his fame is but his shadow.'

LONDON : PRINTED BY
SPOTTISWOODE AND CO., NEW-STREET SQUARE
AND PARLIAMENT STREET